Les Écossais

ALSO BY LUCILLE H. CAMPEY

"A Very Fine Class of Immigrants"
Prince Edward Island's Scottish Pioneers, 1770–1850

"Fast Sailing and Copper-Bottomed"
Aberdeen Sailing Ships and the Emigrant Scots
They Carried to Canada, 1774–1855

The Silver Chief
Lord Selkirk and the Scottish Pioneers of
Belfast, Baldoon and Red River

After the Hector
The Scottish Pioneers of Nova Scotia and Cape Breton, 1773–1855

The Scottish Pioneers of Upper Canada, 1784–1855
Glengarry and Beyond

All published by Natural Heritage Books, Toronto

Les Écossais

The Pioneer Scots of Lower Canada,
1763–1855

LUCILLE H. CAMPEY

NATURAL HERITAGE BOOKS
TORONTO

Published by Natural Heritage / Natural History Inc.
PO Box 95, Station O, Toronto, Ontario M4A 2M8
www.naturalheritagebooks.com

Cover illustration: Hatton, W.S. after James Duncan, *Curling Match at Montreal, Canada East (Quebec).* This watercolour is a copy of the woodcut "Curling Match, Montreal" after James Duncan reproduced in the *Illustrated London News,* February 17, 1855, 145. *Courtesy of Library and Archives Canada C-040148, W.H. Coverdale Collection of Canadiana. Back Cover:* William Daniell, *Voyage Round Great Britain* Volume III (1818) *Loch Ranza, Isle of Arran.* Inhabitants of the Isle of Arran first emigrated to Lower Canada in 1829. *Courtesy of Birmingham Central Library, United Kingdom.*

Cover design by Neil Thorne
Book design by Norton Hamill Design
Edited by Jane Gibson

Printed and bound in Canada by Hignell Book Printing

Library and Archives Canada Cataloguing in Publication

Campey, Lucille H.
Les Écossais : the pioneer Scots of Lower Canada, 1763–1855 / Lucille H. Campey.

Includes bibliographical references and index.
ISBN 1-897045-14-X

1. Scots—Québec (Province)—History. 2. Québec (Province)—Emigration and immigration—History. 3. Scotland—Emigration and immigration—History. 4. Ships—Scotland—Passenger lists. 5. Ships—Canada—Passenger lists. 6. Passenger ships—Scotland—Registers. 7. Passenger ships—Canada—Registers. 8. Québec (Province)—Genealogy. I. Title.

FC2950.S3C35 2006   971.4'0049163   C2006-901175-3

 Canada Council
for the Arts
Conseil des Arts
du Canada
Canada ONTARIO ARTS COUNCIL
CONSEIL DES ARTS DE L'ONTARIO

Natural Heritage / Natural History Inc. acknowledges the financial support of the Canada Council for the Arts and the Ontario Arts Council for our publishing program. We acknowledge the support of the Government of Ontario through the Ontario Media Development Corporation's Ontario Book Initiative. We also acknowledge the financial support of the Government of Canada through the Book Publishing Industry Development Program (BPIDP) and the Association for the Export of Canadian Books.

*This book is dedicated to the memory of my mother
Cécile Morency, born in Ste-Marie-de-Beauce,
who was always proud of her French-Canadian heritage.*

Contents

Tables & Figures

TABLES

FIGURES

Acknowledgements

I am indebted to many people. In particular, I wish to thank Mary Williamson of Toronto for her generous permission to use her great-grandfather's splendid account of the *Berbice* of Aberdeen's crossing in 1853. I greatly appreciated the help given to me by Sophie Morel, Archivist at the Eastern Townships Research Centre, at Bishop's University, during my very enjoyable visit to Lennoxville. I am grateful to Patricia Kennedy of Library and Archives, Canada for her help in resolving the complexities surrounding Mrs. John McNider's diary of 1822. I thank Evelyn Scullion of Ottawa who provided me with biographical details for Malcolm Fraser and Roderick Mackenzie, two Highlanders who feature prominently in the book. Ken Hamilton of Halifax pointed me in the right direction when it came to studying the Chateauguay Valley Scots and I am grateful for his help and support. I also appreciated the help and advice which I received from David Johnson of Toronto, who provided material relating to the Rigaud seigneury and the Drummondville military settlement. I owe a special thank you to Sarah Katherine Gibson, Ph.D. student at the History Department of McGill University, for her help in locating source data and to Professor Brian Young of McGill University for opening my eyes to the treasures to be found at the McCord Museum. I am grateful to François Cartier for assisting me during my visit to the museum.

I also wish to thank the staff at the National Library of Scotland, the National Archives of Scotland, the Library and Archives Canada, the Toronto Reference Library and the Aberdeen University Library for their help. I am grateful to the many people who have assisted me in obtaining illustrations. In particular I thank Robert Hill of Montréal for his help in locating a photograph of Robert Sellar, and am grateful to Martin Lavoie at the Bibliothèque et Archives nationales du Québec for his help in locating illustrations and maps. I also thank Heather McNabb of the McCord Museum, Phyllis Smith of the Musée national des beaux-arts du Québec, Pam Williams of the Central Library, Birmingham, England, and Kellie Leydon at the British Museum.

As ever I am indebted to Jane Gibson of Natural Heritage, my publisher, for her help and guidance in the final editing stages. I thank Shannon MacMillan of Natural Heritage for her valuable assistance and Norton Hamill Design for their attention to detail in designing the book. I also thank my dear friend Jean Lucas for casting her eye over the original manuscript and providing me with such helpful comments. Most of all, I thank my husband Geoff for his unfailing help and guidance. He produced all of the tables, figures and appendices and worked alongside me in the various libraries and archives which we visited. Geoff has an endless ability to listen and to inspire and I could not have written this book without his support.

Preface

Modern-day visitors to Québec might be surprised to learn that people of Scottish extraction once predominated in several parts of the province. Having been Scottish strongholds, places like Thurso in the Ottawa Valley and Stornoway in the Eastern Townships are now entirely French-speaking. All that remains from this period is a handful of Scottish place names. In some cases Scottish place names have since been replaced by French names and it seems hard to imagine that Scottish colonizers had ever come to the province. However, in spite of the fact that their presence was relatively short-lived and is now hardly visible, Scots had a huge impact on the province's early development. Their role as early colonizers and entrepreneurs is one of the central themes of this book.

Although many studies of individual settlements have been written, no-one has thus far considered the overall Scottish influx to Lower Canada (Québec). Using wide-ranging primary and secondary sources, the book traces the direction of the emigrants flows from Scotland to different parts of the province and considers the various factors which drove and directed them. Why did Lower Canada attract so many Scots? Where did they settle? What happened to the customs and traditions which they brought with them? How did emigrant Scots and French Canadians regard each other? These are some of the questions which I have attempted to answer. The last question is, in many ways, the most interesting and most important.

Lower Canada was different from the other British colonies in having a large, long-settled French population, with its own traditions and laws.

When emigrant Scots began arriving in the late eighteenth century they adapted readily to Québec's way of life. France and Scotland share a long tradition of mutual co-operation and when Scots emigrated to Lower Canada their natural affinity for the French came with them. The Scots and the French were very comfortable with one another. Many Scots settled in the French seigneuries even though they had to comply with a near-feudal land system which made them tenants rather than freeholders. They were devout Presbyterians and yet many of them married into French society and produced sons and daughters who became Roman Catholics. These are some of the book's more unexpected findings.

One of the lasting legacies of the Scots was the considerable contribution they made to the province's economic development. They were prominent as fur traders, merchants, industrialists and bankers and were a major economic force in the province. They played a dominant role in the province's expanding timber trade with Britain and in doing so helped to stimulate emigration from Scotland. The timber trade acted like an enormous magnet, drawing Scots to the major timber-producing areas in the Ottawa and Chateauguay valleys and in the Gaspé Peninsula. Being among the earliest British settlers to arrive, they established themselves in the most favourable locations close to timber-collecting bays and along the rivers which flowed into them. Developed with Scottish capital and business acumen, the timber trade provided the ships which took emigrant Scots to the province and it underpinned the region's economy. In this way, the progress of Scottish settlements and the timber trade were closely linked.

Initially, Scots paid their own emigration costs and generally arrived in small groups. However, with the collapse of the Highland economy in the mid-1820s this pattern changed. Within a decade the Eastern Townships became a major refuge for the many hundreds of destitute people from the Hebridean Islands, first from Arran and later from Lewis, who were being cleared from their lands. The emergence of the British American Land Company and the financial assistance provided by Scottish landlords, who wanted rid of their surplus tenants, stimulated a growing influx of Scots who formed distinctive communities across large stretches of the Eastern Townships.

This study traces the progress of the many Highlanders and Lowlanders who sought the better opportunities which the province could offer. While Lowlanders usually located themselves in mixed British and American communities, Gaelic-speaking Highlanders formed their own settlements in remote locations, where they could continue to practise their customs and traditions. The survival of the Gaelic language helped Highlanders to retain their identity but, when its usage ceased, much of their culture was lost. Because Gaelic was primarily a spoken language, little of it was ever recorded. Religion played a vital role in helping Scots to keep alive the memory of the Scotland they had left behind. The clergymen, sent out by the Church of Scotland to preside over their congregations, were a valuable lifeline. Their reports, which contain detailed accounts of early Scottish settlements and the daunting challenges of pioneer life, provided me with some of my most fascinating documentary material.

Scots had an enduring and major impact on the province. They felt very much at home in Québec, but a number of their descendents left for greener pastures in Upper Canada and the United States when they saw better opportunities. This book tells the story of the original pioneer Scots.

Abbreviations

ACA	Aberdeen City Archives
AH	*Aberdeen Herald*
AJ	*Aberdeen Journal*
AU	Aberdeen University
BAnQ	Bibliothèque et Archives nationales du Québec
DC	*Dundee Courier*
DCA	Dundee City Archives
DGC	*Dumfries and Galloway Courier*
DWJ	*Dumfries Weekly Journal*
DCB	*Dictionary of Canadian Biography*
DPC	*Dundee, Perth and Cupar Advertiser*
DT	*Dumfries Times*
EA	*Edinburgh Advertiser*
EC	*Elgin Courant*
ETRC	Eastern Townships Resource Centre
GA	*Greenock Advertiser*
GC	*Glasgow Chronicle*
GH	*Glasgow Herald*
Grnk	Greenock
IA	*Inverness Advertiser*
IC	*Inverness Courier*
IJ	*Inverness Journal*

JJ	*John O'Groat Journal*
KM	*Kelso Mail*
LAC	Library and Archives Canada
LSR	*Lloyd's Shipping Register*
MG	*Montreal Gazette*
MM	McCord Museum
MT	*Montréal Telegraph*
NAS	National Archives of Scotland
NLS	National Library of Scotland
OLA	Orkney Library and Archives
PC	*Perthshire Courier*
PRO	Public Record Office
PP	*Parliamentary Papers*
QG	*Québec Gazette*
QM	*Québec Mercury*
SM	*Scots Magazine*
SRA	Strathclyde Regional Archives

Les Écossais

One

THE PROBLEMS OF CONQUEST

*They write from Guernsey that since the establishment of the Roman
Catholic Bishop in Canada, many French families of substance were
preparing to re-embark from thence for Quebec, which they had quitted
at the conclusion of the last war.*[1]

RITAIN'S VICTORY OVER FRANCE IN the Seven Years War, which
ended in 1763, gave her a new colony—the Province of Québec.
Its population of some 120,000 people, who were mainly French-
speaking Roman Catholics, was concentrated in the fertile lands along
the St. Lawrence River Valley.[2] They were the inhabitants of long-established communities, with their own distinctive language, culture and
religion.[3] Such people could not be expected to surrender their way of
life willingly.[4] Faced with this political reality, the Scottish-born James
Murray, the colony's first governor, allowed the French regime to continue largely unchanged although he was strongly opposed by British
commercial interests for so doing. The French population was given
the right to follow their traditional practices and laws, and Québec
became the only place in the entire British Empire where Catholics and
Protestants had equal status. The French families, who had fled to
Guernsey at the end of the war, clearly felt that it was safe to return to
Québec. In spite of the British Conquest, a leader sympathetic to their
interests was now in control of the province.

Murray was the first of many Scots to have a profound impact on the
province's future development. Having fought as soldiers in the Seven

Years War, many Scots had remained behind when their regiments were disbanded, and thus they were some of the province's earliest immigrants. Although Scots were very prominent as early settlers and would eventually play a major role in business, the professions and public life, their presence in the province was short-lived. They left in increasing numbers, from the mid-nineteenth century, to take up the better farming and job opportunities to be had further west and in the United States. As they left, a fast-growing Francophone population moved in to take their place. The Scots who remained were gradually assimilated into Québec's Francophone society and, as they did, became "les Écossais." Nevertheless, they never completely lost their sense of Scottishness and continued to uphold many of their customs and traditions. These much-cherished reminders of the old country left behind by their forefathers were an important part of the support system of the early pioneers.

This "Quebec taken" medal, designed by James "Athenian" Stuart, was produced in Britain by Thomas Pingo in 1759 to celebrate the capture of Québec. © Copyright the Trustees of The British Museum.

Although many Highland regiments came together to fight in the Seven Years War, the Fraser's Highlanders Regiment (78th) stand out as having been the most colourful of all the regiments in General Wolfe's army. When Wolfe first set eyes on them he thought they had "the most manly corps of officers"

Fraser's Highlanders (78th Regiment). Their uniforms and overall appearance attracted great interest when they first landed in 1757. Many of them joined the Royal Highland Emigrants Regiment (84th), when it was formed in 1775 at the start of the American War of Independence, and were instrumental in defending Québec when it came under attack in 1776. This painting by John H. MacNaughton shows the uniform in 1759. *Courtesy of Musée National des beaux-arts du Québec.*

that he had ever seen.[5] Little wonder they were so impressive during the siege of Québec in 1759. Having demonstrated their fighting skills on the Plains of Abraham, many of them remained in the province when the war ended. Men like Simon McTavish, the son of a lieutenant in the Fraser's Highlanders, would quickly establish themselves in the fur trade and rise to the top of the North West Company. And many other descendents of the Fraser's Highlanders would take their place as partners of the North West Company and in Montréal's commercial life.

General James Murray (1712–1794). Born in Scotland, he became a lieutenant-colonel of the 15th Foot Regiment in 1751. He commanded the 3rd Brigade at the Plains of Abraham and after James Wolfe's death on the battlefield took overall command of the British forces. He was appointed governor of Québec in 1759, remaining in that post until 1766. Portrait, c. 1770, by artist unknown. *Courtesy of Library and Archives Canada C-002834.*

General James Murray readily adapted to life in Québec. He was after all a product of "the auld alliance."[6] Sharing a common hostility towards England—their auld enemy, Scotland and France had a long tradition of mutual cooperation in their military and political endeavours. Sons of the Scottish aristocracy often undertook part of their education in France. General Murray's tolerant attitude towards the newly conquered French Canadians reflected his own partisan feelings for France and its customs. In fact, some former officers in the Fraser's Highlanders were themselves Roman Catholic and many were fluent in French. Consequently, these were men who saw no problem in being both Scottish and French. Even so, Murray's attitudes greatly enraged the British-dominated business community who wanted rid of French customs and institutions, believing them to be harmful to the spirit of commercial enterprise.[7]

Sir Guy Carleton, Murray's successor, continued with the same approach and introduced legislation guaranteeing French Canadians the right to practise their various traditions and laws.[8] The Quebec Act of 1774, which enshrined these principles, seems an odd piece of legislation for a conquering nation to enact. However, the growing threat of American hostilities had added a further dimension to the political equation. French-Canadian cooperation was more important than ever and this could only be won through assurances that Québec's traditional way of life was not under threat.[9] Most French Canadians remained neutral during the American Revolution and were staunch supporters of the British side during the War of 1812. Carleton's policy would therefore bring long-term rewards. In the meantime he and his officials were happy to leave well alone. Alexander Wedderburn, Britain's solicitor general, did not wish the colony to acquire "any considerable number of [British] inhabitants" and he certainly did not want "any temptation" to be held out to British subjects "to increase the colonies."[10] The Conquest of 1763 left Britain with a colony which needed to be placated. Colonization by British settlers would not begin in earnest for another twenty years.

Wedderburn's discouraging stance on emigration reflected the widespread alarm being felt at the time over the growing exodus from the Highlands of Scotland to New York, North Carolina, Philadelphia and the other southern colonies.[11] People were succumbing to "a spirit of emigration," which, according to one commentator, threatened to carry the entire inhabitants of the Highlands and Islands of Scotland to North America.[12] Deploring the "rapid strides" being made by emigration, the *Edinburgh Advertiser* called for "the speediest interposition of government to stop and impede its progress" or else "the nation will be drained of many labouring people, as well as artificers and manufacturers."[13]

The so-called "spirit of emigration" was taking hold in a major way on the Isle of Lewis. It lost 840 people to North America in 1773 and far more were expected to follow.[14] Lord Seaforth,[15] their landlord, rushed to Lewis from his London home "to treat with the remainder of his tenants" that summer, but to no avail.[16] He was desperate to keep his tenantry in Lewis since they produced the kelp which earned him such huge profits, although his tenants got only a pittance for their backbreaking work.[17] Having learned that some Lewis people had got as far as Dorset in May of the following year, he consulted his advisers about "stopping the emigrations at London."[18] The plan was to prevent people with outstanding debts from leaving the country. Later that summer

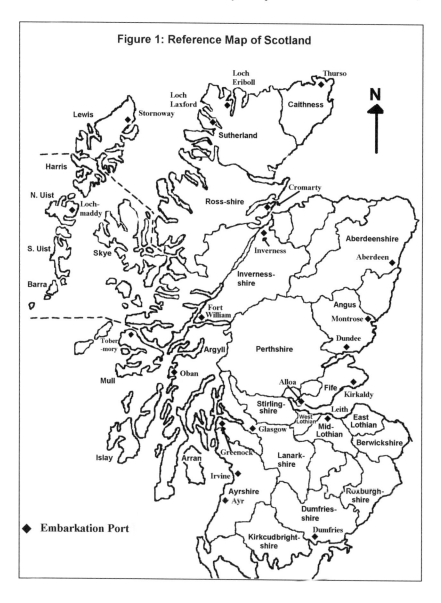

Figure 1: Reference Map of Scotland

his managers were hoping that "the proper letter will be wrote to the Collector and Controller [of Customs] at Stornoway about the emigrants."[19] However, Lord Seaforth's factor also advised that "fair words and mild usage is much recommended to be used to those who are thought to be at the point of emigration" and this seems to have stopped him from being overly coercive.[20]

In spite of determined efforts on the part of the Scottish establishment
to halt it, emigration had become an unstoppable force. It was being
fuelled by high rents, oppressive landlords and the positive accounts being
sent from North America extolling the better life to be had there. This
combination of push and pull factors brought thousands of Scots to North
America. Ironically, Lewis would later emerge as one of the principal
centres in Scotland to lose people to Lower Canada, although this would
not happen until the late 1830s, and then the circumstances would be
very different. Lewis people were now the reluctant ones. Positions had
reversed and it was the landlord who advocated emigration. Kelp markets had long since collapsed and widespread destitution gripped the
island. Stewart MacKenzie of Seaforth, wanting rid of his poverty-
stricken tenants, paid their removal costs. Hundreds of Lewis families
would come to Lower Canada over many decades and they would col-
onize large swathes of the Eastern Townships.

Meanwhile, the Quebec Act of 1774 had left the province with two
separate cultures and two systems of land tenure.[21] There were the long-
established French seigneuries and the new townships which were
created after the Conquest.[22] The seigneuries stretched along the St.
Lawrence River as far as the Gaspé, and along the Ottawa, Chaudière
and Richelieu rivers, while the townships mainly skirted their outer
edges.[23] The indigenous French population, who were confined mainly
to the seigneuries, paid rents as tenants to a proprietor while British
immigrants, who eventually settled in the townships, were able to
acquire their land as freeholds. Surprisingly the seigneuries also acquired
a good many of the early emigrant Scots who were attracted by the
prospect of living under the stewardship of a proprietor with capital
who could build houses, barns, roads, mills and public buildings.
Although they could not purchase their own land (becoming landowners was one of the prime goals of a new settler), they at least had a secure
base and better living conditions than would be available in an isolated
clearing in some wilderness.

Thus, despite its restrictions, the seigneurial system acted as a spur
to settlement. Roderick Mackenzie's Terrebonne seigneury to the north
of Montréal, Edward Ellice's Beauharnois seigneury to the south of Montréal and John McNider's Métis seigneury in the Gaspé Peninsula each
attracted Scottish settlers, who in turn founded their own distinctive

communities within areas that were almost entirely inhabited by French Canadians. These proprietors had actively recruited fellow Scots to farm their land. Also Sir John Johnson's adjoining Chambly and Monnoir seigneuries, to the east of Montréal, and his Argenteuil seigneury north of the Ottawa River had particular appeal to Scots. The Highlanders, who eventually founded the Glengarry communities, had been led by Johnson during the American Revolution War and, later, their followers would make a beeline for his seigneuries.

However, while a good many of the seigneuries were owned by Scots, few had any interest in acquiring British settlers.[24] Most of them used their seigneuries as bases for country pursuits and their various business interests. Having obtained seigneuries at La Malbaie, to the northeast of Québec City, John Nairne and Malcolm Fraser, both ex-officers in the Fraser's Highlanders, established diverse farming and commercial enterprises, but the thriving communities that they founded included very few Scots. Alexander Fraser, who had also served in the Fraser's Highlanders, purchased the seigneury of Vitré, near Montréal, and La Martinière and St. Giles near Québec City, although he failed to attract any British settlers.[25] The Inverness-shire-born James Cuthbert would become one of the wealthiest of the British seigneury owners. Serving as an officer of the 15th Foot Regiment, he had fought on the Plains of Abraham. The Berthier seigneury, opposite Sorel on the north side of the St. Lawrence, was his first purchase. Together with his later acquisitions his land holdings would eventually extend for some 50 miles along the St. Lawrence River.[26]

Having married Catherine Cairns, a Scot, and being a staunch Presbyterian, Cuthbert[27] brought a minister from Scotland to act as tutor for his children, and he also built his own Presbyterian Chapel. Having sent his three sons to France to be educated so that they would learn French, they returned as Roman Catholics, "much to the wrath of their staunch Protestant father."[28] Despite this Cuthbert mellowed and would later become a patron of the Catholic churches in and near Berthier. The fact was that James Cuthbert, and most of the other Scots who owned seigneuries, were content to live among French Canadians. They assimilated themselves readily into French society and became accepted. During the War of 1812–14 Cuthbert's son, James Junior—the new seigneur—commanded one of the local militia. Having received an order to recruit

The Old Manor House at Berthier, built by James Cuthbert in c. 1778.
The building was constructed in the old French-Canadian style, having a wide sloping roof with dormer windows. It replaces an earlier
building which had been burned by American troops on their retreat
from Québec in 1766 during the American War of Independence.
Watercolour by Walter Baker, c. 1900. *Courtesy of Toronto Public
Library (TRL) J. Ross Robertson Collection: MTL 3027.*

more troops, he went to Berthier and within a few days arrived in Montréal with one thousand men who were willing to fight on the British side.

Hence, Scottish integration into Francophone communities became
the norm in the years following the Conquest, but this situation changed
after 1783 when Britain was defeated in the American War of Independence. This defeat led the government to relocate around 6,000 people
of British stock from the United States to the province in order to bolster its population. Arriving as Loyalist farmers, they had no intention
of becoming assimilated into French society, but instead founded their
own distinctive communities. While some Loyalists came to live in Montréal and Sorel, and in the Gaspé Peninsula, the majority ended up in
Upper Canada after the old Province of Québec was divided into Upper
and Lower Canada in 1791. One of the most significant developments
at this time was the emergence of the remarkable Glengarry communities, founded by Loyalists from west Inverness-shire (Figure 1).

Located just to the west of the French seigneuries on the eastern
extremity of Upper Canada, the Glengarry settlements became an enormous magnet for subsequent waves of Highlanders.[29] "Discontented

Highlanders" from Appin (in Argyll) sent "a Mr Campbell," a former army officer, to search for land in 1791.[30] Having "explored the country all the way to Montréal and thence to the upper settlements," he no doubt reported favourably on the Glengarry settlements.[31] Highlanders were on the move. However, emigration was temporarily halted when Britain and France went to war in 1793, although it surged ahead with a vengeance from 1802.[32] By this time land scarcity had become a major problem in Glengarry.[33] New arrivals were being forced to move northwards across the border into Lower Canada in their search for land. Spearheading the advance was Archibald McMillan, a prominent Lochaber Highlander, who led a group of followers to Papineau and Argenteuil counties on the north side of the Ottawa River. As some of the earliest arrivals, these Highlanders were able to grab the prime river and coastline locations for their new settlements and thus benefit greatly from the region's burgeoning timber trade.

A third North American battle brought another, much larger, influx of Scots to the region. Fearing further attacks from the United States after the War of 1812–14, the British government relocated large numbers of Scots at public expense to the Rideau Valley in Upper Canada[34] and a smaller number of British settlers to Drummondville, further to the east in Lower Canada. The offer of subsidized emigration had a tremendous response from the Highlands and in the cotton districts near Glasgow and Paisley where redundant hand-loom weavers were living in a state

St. Andrew's Chapel in Berthier built 1786–87. It was the first Presbyterian Church to be built in Lower Canada. Its walls were two feet thick, being constructed of fieldstones with a covering of plaster. The small bell, which hung in the belfry, now resides in the McCord Museum, Montréal. Watercolour by H.R.S. Bennett, c. 1887. *Courtesy of Toronto Public Library (TRL) J. Ross Robertson Collection: MTL 3026.*

of grinding poverty. Given that the Rideau Valley settlements were situated just west of Glengarry, their presence produced an enormous Scottish nucleus on the south side of the Ottawa River. Attracting many followers, the region's best locations soon became fully occupied and once again the search for land took emigrant Scots across the border into Lower Canada. They would head east this time into the Chateauguay Valley, having been attracted by its fertile land and timber trade potential.

Emigration to Lower Canada only reached sizeable proportions after 1815 when, with the ending of the Napoleonic Wars, Scotland became mired in a severe economic depression.[35] Although many new townships[36] had been created by this time, most of them were acquired by land speculators who had no intention of establishing immigrants on their land and, as a result, huge tracts of land were put out of the reach of ordinary settlers. Faced with this state of affairs, most settlers took the only practical option open to them. They squatted on the land of their choosing and hoped for the best, although occasionally they met with opposition. The Scots who squatted on land in Godmanchester Township (Huntingdon County), discovered afterwards that most of the township was the property of Edward Ellice and, being unable to afford his charges, they had to leave. It was not an easy time for settlers. They had to cope with a bureaucratic muddle and a land-granting system which favoured elite individuals over their needs.

With its fertile land and proximity to good markets, the farming regions near Montréal had a particular appeal to emigrant Scots. Daniel Drummond, who originated from Comrie in Perthshire, came with his wife and brother in 1833 and established a farm at Petite Côte, now the Rosemount district of Montréal. Having been employed as a flour miller in Glasgow, he also purchased a gristmill at nearby New Glasgow (Terrebonne seigneury) and it remained in the Drummond family for a couple of generations. Thomas Irving arrived from Locherbie in Dumfriesshire in 1848 and found employment as a farm manager at James Logan's "Rocklands" farm. The farm included an area now known as Lafountaine Park, just below Mount Royal Avenue in downtown Montréal. Having occupied the farm for 45 years, Irving returned briefly to Scotland in 1857 to set up a business for importing Ayrshire cattle to Lower Canada.[37] Needless to say, he became widely known as one of the region's most knowledgeable and respected pioneer farmers.

However, the principal driving force behind the British influx to Lower Canada was its timber trade. The sudden large increase in tariffs on Baltic timber, first introduced during the Napoleonic Wars, gave Canadian timber a considerable cost advantage over traditional supplies from the Baltic.[38] The volume of shipping between Scotland and Canada increased dramatically, bringing affordable and regular transport to emigrants. As trading links developed, emigrants could simply purchase places in one of the many timber ships which regularly crossed the Atlantic. Although wheat and potash exports[39] remained substantial elements of Lower Canada's economy, timber rose in importance.[40] Floated down the Ottawa, Richelieu and St. Lawrence rivers to Québec on rafts, in readiness for exportation to Britain, timber provided much needed employment in winter months and gave settlers a product to sell in the early phase of land clearance.

When Lord Selkirk visited Montréal in 1803, he noticed that a majority of its "mercantile people" were "Scotch."[41] The dominant trio were Simon McTavish, James McGill and James Dunlop, who had moved to Montréal from the United States as Loyalists during the 1770s. They dominated the business and political life of the region and made themselves vast fortunes. And their early success helped to stimulate a continuing influx of Scottish merchants who sought the rich pickings which the province had to offer. Thomas Torrance, who had established himself as a spirit dealer in Québec City by 1804, told his brother in Glasgow that "every tradesman has good encouragement in this place…and merchants here have it in their power to make money if they have funds to trade with."[42] There were many others like Torrance. And when the timber trade rose in importance it would be mainly Scots who would become the principal financiers and merchants of the trade. In the forefront was Alan Gilmour who rose to become one of North America's greatest timber barons.

With this background, it is hardly surprising that the timber trade would have such widespread appeal to emigrant Scots. Amongst the earliest to arrive in Lower Canada, they could select favourable locations close to timber-collecting bays and along the rivers flowing into them. Felled timber would "find a ready sale…provided it is on the borders of a stream" and a settler could expect "a better price for his pot and pearl ash than in the upper country."[43] The clannish favouritism shown by close-knit Scottish business communities for Scottish settlers ensured that they would always be prime beneficiaries of the trade. In the early days most lumbering operations were carried out by small family ventures. Timber was sold as a preliminary step to creating settlements and the felling and transport activities were bankrolled by a cartel of merchants and storekeepers. The sudden intake of Scots in the Gaspé Peninsula during the late 1820s and early 1830s was entirely due to the Scottish domination of timber-felling operations on both sides of Baie des Chaleurs. Undoubtedly, the timber trade and the growth of new settlements were inextricably linked.

As governor, Lord Dalhousie met some of the Gaspé's pioneer Scots during his tour of the Maritimes and Lower Canada in 1826. As a Scot himself, he developed a great rapport with people like Mrs. Sherar, who lived in New Carlisle. "A tall, handsome old woman from the Highlands," she had a "very comely happy appearance, the very reverse of the old laird," her husband, who was "deaf, crabbed and ill-natured." After enjoying a "great deal of laughing and fun" Dalhousie promised to send Mrs. Sherar "a barrel of oatmeal for her winter porridge."[44] This was a side of the Earl which few Canadians saw. He had been a controversial figure, having been forced out of office in 1828 when he took on the radical reformer, Louis-Joseph Papineau, and lost.[45] However, Dalhousie left behind fascinating accounts of his visits and an intriguing set of petitions, which record the names of the many members of the public who were offering him their support.[46] The petitions sent to him by the inhabitants of New Glasgow, in the Terrebonne seigneury, and of the Hinchinbrook, Godmanchester and St. Regis Indian Reserve lands in Huntingdon County, reveal many Scottish names, demonstrating the large extent of Scottish colonization by this time.[47]

The eastward progression of British colonizers into the more remote stretches of the Eastern Townships required the organizational structure which only a land company could provide. The region had acquired some settlers, including a group from the Isle of Arran who settled in Megantic County from 1829, although the major influx did not begin until the British American Land Company arrived on the scene in 1834.[48] Being modelled on the Canada Company,[49] it secured 850,000 acres of Crown land south of the St. Lawrence River, bordering on Vermont and New Hampshire, and actively sought British immigrants to settle on these lands. Working closely with Stewart MacKenzie of Seaforth,

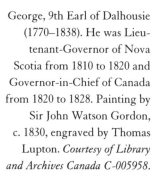

George, 9th Earl of Dalhousie (1770–1838). He was Lieutenant-Governor of Nova Scotia from 1810 to 1820 and Governor-in-Chief of Canada from 1820 to 1828. Painting by Sir John Watson Gordon, c. 1830, engraved by Thomas Lupton. *Courtesy of Library and Archives Canada C-005958.*

the proprietor of Lewis, the company attracted large numbers of his impoverished Gaelic-speaking tenants from the late 1830s. They arrived over several decades, establishing numerous communities which stretched across six townships in two counties.

By the middle of the nineteenth century Scottish concentrations were to be found principally along the north side of the Ottawa River, in the Chateauguay region to the south and west of Montréal, in the Eastern Townships and in the Gaspé Peninsula. The Scottish communities which developed along the Ottawa River in Bristol, Clarendon and Litchfield townships (Pontiac County) were a much later development, and probably resulted from the internal migration of Scots, who had previously settled in the Rideau Valley communities on the opposite side of the river.[50] In this way Scots were spread very widely and concentrated in relatively few areas. But their relative dominance was short-lived. By

1861 people of British ancestry accounted for just 20% of the overall
Lower Canada population, while the proportion of Presbyterian Scots,
in any one county, rarely exceeded 25% (Figure 2).[51] First generation
Scots accounted for a mere six per cent of the population by this time.[52]

This pattern of earlier Scottish domination and decline would keep
repeating itself over and over again.[53] Having dominated large areas of
the Eastern Townships by 1881, people of Scottish ancestry became a
mere minority group just sixty years later.[54] Many of their descendents
had left and when they did French Canadians took their place. Upper
Canada's better land and climate, the declining importance of the timber trade and the rising dominance of French culture made Lower
Canada progressively less attractive to later waves of British settlers.
Thus, the cycle intensified.

Following the outbreak of the rebellions in Upper and Lower Canada
in 1837–38, the number of new immigrants from Britain declined sharply,
although the dissent was quickly suppressed and emigration levels quickly
recovered.[55] However, by this time almost all of the British influx was being
directed at Upper Canada. The growing popularity of the United States
was another factor. As Thomas Brown, a soldier stationed at the Québec
Citadel in 1850, told his brother William in Leith, most Scottish emigrants
by this time "generally goes to the States in preference to the Canadas."[56]

The Insurgents at Beauharnois,
November, 1838. Watercolour
painted by Katherine Jane Balfour,
whose husband, Edward Ellice,
owned the seigneury. She and her
husband were both Scottish and
their seigneury had attracted a large
Scottish population. She painted her
captors from the window of the
room in which she was being held
hostage. The rebels are shown carrying pikes and clubs. Few had
arms or military training. *Courtesy
of Library and Archives Canada
C-013392.*

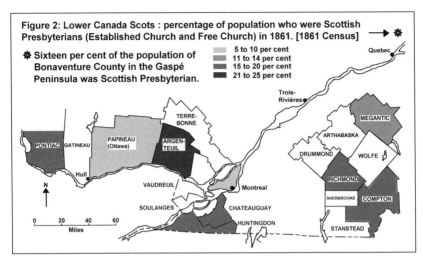

Figure 2: Lower Canada Scots : percentage of population who were Scottish Presbyterians (Established Church and Free Church) in 1861. [1861 Census]

❋ Sixteen per cent of the population of Bonaventure County in the Gaspé Peninsula was Scottish Presbyterian.

5 to 10 per cent
11 to 14 per cent
15 to 20 per cent
21 to 25 per cent

Robert Sellar, the outspoken Scottish radical, was convinced that Protestant farmers had been deliberately squeezed out of the Eastern Townships by the Catholic Church.[57] As far as he was concerned[58] a change in legislation in 1850, which allowed the Catholic Church to extend its parish system beyond the seigneuries into the townships, was proof of such a plot, but frustrations worked both ways. French Canadians, who were experiencing severe land shortages in their seigneuries, had greatly resented being kept out of the Eastern Townships. The simple truth was that British settlers were leaving the province for a whole host of reasons. Once their numbers had declined to the point where they could no longer support their Protestant schools and churches, they left in droves, and this pattern was repeated throughout the entire province.

Taking their religious beliefs very seriously, the early pioneers acquired their Presbyterian ministers and churches at the earliest opportunity. Moreover, the Presbyterian missionaries who were sent across by the Church of Scotland to manage their congregations, were in a class of their own when in came to dogged determination and diligence. Reverend William Mair served his combined congregations of Chatham and Grenville (Argenteuil County) for some 27 years while Reverend Archibald Henderson remained minister at the Presbyterian church in St. Andrews in the Argenteuil seigneury for some 49 years. Reverend Walter Roach presided over a church in the Beauharnois seigneury, which had been built entirely at the proprietor's expense. This was clearly a factor in the seigneury's amazing appeal to Scots. By the early 1830s

Robert Sellar. Born in Glasgow, he founded *The Canadian Gleaner* (later renamed *The Huntingdon Gleaner*) in 1863 and was its editor for nearly 57 years. He used the newspaper to express the liberal and anti-establishment views of the day. Although he is remembered most for his anti-Catholic rhetoric, his greatest legacy is his *History of the County of Huntingdon,* which contains vivid and comprehensive accounts of early pioneer life. Photo from *The Gleaner* archives, Huntingdon, Québec. *Courtesy of* The Gleaner *archives.*

the seigneury could support two ministers and two churches, making it one of the major Presbyterian strongholds of its time. By bringing Presbyterianism to these scattered communities, ministers played a valuable role in helping to reinforce Scottish values and traditions.

Reverend Duncan Moody had the vital skill of being able to speak Gaelic, but, having been a city dweller, he had enormous difficulties in coping with his straggling congregation of Highlanders who were spread out over large distances in Dundee Township (Huntingdon County). For long distance travel and tenacity the prize must surely go to the Reverend John Clugston, who was based in Québec City. He thought nothing of popping off to the Gaspé region to check on the progress of the Scottish Métis settlers or dashing off to the Eastern Townships to assess Presbyterian needs there. After the disruption of 1843, when the Free Church was formed, it won widespread support amongst the Hebridean settlers in the Eastern Townships.[59] By then Scots were quite happy to break free from the controls being exercised by the established church.

Our journey now begins at La Malbaie. Although this remote region retained few of its pioneer Scots, it has a special place in Canada's history, being the earliest of its Scottish settlements. The two Scottish ex-officers, who presided over the Malbaie settlements, adopted French ways when it came to their local community, but they also endowed the region with liberal doses of Scottish entrepreneurialism. As was the case in so much of British North America, Scots had a particular talent for enterprise and La Malbaie would be no exception.

Two

EARLY ARRIVALS, 1763–1803

I came here first in 1761 with five soldiers and procured some servants. One small house contained us all for several years and [we] were separated from every other people for about eighteen miles without any road.[1]

LIEUTENANT JOHN NAIRNE OF THE Fraser's Highlanders (78th) had good reason to visit the seigneury of La Malbaie (Charlevoix County), which was located some ninety miles northeast of Québec City. Arriving there in 1761 with a small number of men, including his friend Lieutenant Malcolm Fraser, he observed a picturesque countryside reminiscent of Scotland.[2] The Seven Years War had not yet ended, but by 1759 a decisive victory had been won over France on the Plains of Abraham.[3] Nairne and Fraser's regiment had played a key role in the capture of Québec and thoughts were already turning to the spoils of war.[4] The Treaty of Paris of 1763 would proclaim the close of the war, but even two years before this, General James Murray had been installed as the military governor of Québec. One of his key tasks was to plan how best to secure and maintain Britain's control over her newly captured province in North America.

After Montréal, the final French stronghold, fell to the British in 1760, General Murray had been able to purchase five large seigneuries which had become vacant following the departure of their owners to France. La Malbaie would have stood out as having particularly good defensive capabilities. Its position on the northern bank of the St. Lawrence River made it an ideal site from which to defend the province on its seaward approach.

The arrival of Captain John Nairne at Murray Bay (La Malbaie) in 1761. Watercolour by C.W. Jeffreys in 1929. *Courtesy of Library and Archives Canada C-040583, W.H. Coverdale Collection of Canadiana.*

Murray probably hoped that by granting land there to Nairne and Fraser they would attract settlers and encourage population growth. Dividing the 5,000-acre seigneury of La Malbaie into two parts, he gave Nairne three thousand acres at what became Murray Bay, apparently named after the General "at the special request of the said Captain John Nairne."[5] The adjoining two-thousand-acre grant, which went to Fraser, became known as Mount Murray (Figure 3). Although Nairne and Fraser went on to establish thriving settlements few of their inhabitants were Scots.

Men from the Fraser's Highlanders were not the only ex-soldiers to receive encouragement to settle on free land. But, with the exception of this one regiment, the government's policy of seeking loyal settlers for the conquered French province had attracted little response.[6] While it was originally thought that some three hundred of Fraser's Highlanders had accepted the government's offer of free land, which was determined by rank and length of active service, surviving army discharge lists indicate that only one hundred and fifty-eight men actually took this option. They were a cross-section of the clans that had fought in the Battle of Culloden in 1745–46, the officers being the cream of the Jacobite gentry.[7] And yet, few of them became farmers or made any attempt to recruit settlers from Scotland. Thus, although a large nucleus of Highlanders settled in the Province of Québec at the close of the Seven Years War, especially near Québec City and Montréal, they did not seek to build Scottish communities.[8] This was the case in spite of the growing zeal for emigration which gripped Scotland from the mid-eighteenth century.

North Carolina and New York had become the favoured destination of most emigrant Scots by the 1770s, especially those from the Highlands and Islands.[9] The Island of Saint John (later Prince Edward Island) also began attracting Scots after it was opened up to British settlers from 1767 but on a much smaller scale. Included among those who acquired land on the Island were eleven "of Colonel [Simon] Fraser's late battalion of Highlanders," who between them obtained four entire townships amounting to 39,000 acres.[10] A group of them sailed for the Island in 1768 with the apparent intention of using their holdings to foster Scottish colonization.[11] Given that three of the four townships, which had fallen under their control, became major Scottish strongholds, it would seem that they played some role in encouraging fellow Highlanders to settle on their lands.[12] However, while these former Fraser's Highlanders had probably promoted colonization on the Island of Saint John, they did not play a similar role in the colony of Québec. Most of them took French-Canadian women as wives and assimilated themselves into Francophone communities. Nonetheless, they did form

Uniforms of the Fraser's Highlanders Their cunning and ferocity were legendary. They fought in the Seven Years War (1758–63) under General James Wolfe at Louisbourg (Cape Breton), the Plains of Abraham and Ste Foye. Watercolour by Frederick M. Milner, appearing in "British Army in Canada"; Bathurst and Milner Collection. *Courtesy of Library and Archives Canada C-005731.*

an important and powerful nucleus of Scots whose descendents would rise to prominence as businessmen and entrepreneurs. Their sons would become major players in the fur trade, becoming the future partners of the North West Company, which from 1799 would be managed from Montréal by Scots.[13]

When John Nairne retired from the army on half pay and moved to Murray Bay, he was single as no doubt were the soldiers he brought with him. They married French-Canadian women, but Nairne was determined to share his life with a compatriot, choosing Christiana Emery, whom he married in 1769. When he first came to the area in the 1760s it was predominately French and Catholic. Over the years despite Nairne's several visits to Scotland to recruit settlers, this situation underwent little change. He entertained fanciful hopes that, with the help of a Protestant missionary, he could convert local Roman Catholics to the Presbyterian faith, but he failed even to get his clergy-man.[14] There were only five Protestant families at Murray Bay in 1791 and ten years later there were only three: Nairne and Fraser's families and an Englishman whose attendance at services was said to be "doubt-ful."[15] Nairne was greatly saddened by his inability to introduce Scottish culture and the Protestant faith to Murray Bay.[16] Even his children disappointed him by speaking only French when young. Nairne sent them

Portrait of John Nairne (1731–1802) by Henry Raeburn, c.1795. *Courtesy of Archives nationales du Québec P600-6/N277-445.*

This later Manor House at Murray Bay, which was built by John
Nairne's grandson, remained standing until 1960. It was built of stone
and some of its internal walls were decorated with pine panelling.
Courtesy of Archives nationales du Québec P600-6/N874-327.

to schools in Scotland for several years in the vain hope that they would
become Anglophones, but he was fighting a losing battle.

By 1798 Nairne could take comfort in the knowledge that his
seigneury had five hundred inhabitants, including one hundred men
who were able to bear arms. He had built a sumptuous manor house,
owned three 100-acre farms and was exporting furs, timber and whale
oil.[17] There were houses and barns, mills, fertile fields and a resident
priest with whom Nairne was on excellent terms despite his religious
differences.[18] With the outbreak of the American War of Independence
in 1775, he left Murray Bay to become a captain in the 1st battalion of
the Royal Highland Emigrants Regiment (84th) whose members originated mainly from the former Fraser's Highlanders.[19] Settling
permanently at Murray Bay after the war ended in 1783, Nairne resumed
his business and country pursuits. When he fell ill in 1802, he was taken
to Québec City where he died in the same year, leaving his wife to preside over the seigneury until her death in 1828. Her death was "lamented
by all, Catholic and Protestant, equally. Her greatest pride was in being
a Scotch woman and a Jacobite avowed."[20] Nairne too was mourned,
being remembered as the "founder, friend and patriarch" of a "flourishing colony."[21] This was a laudatory tribute to a sad but good man
who dreamt of establishing a Scottish La Malbaie. That was not to be.

Meanwhile, Malcolm Fraser (1733–1815) had been establishing diverse
farming and commercial enterprises at his adjoining seigneury of Mount
Murray. Like Nairne he retired on a lieutenant's half pay when the Fraser's

Highlanders was disbanded in 1763. Yet, the two men could not have been more different. Fraser had little time for the life of a country squire and concentrated his energy on his many business pursuits.[22] He readily adapted himself to French society and, unlike John Nairne, had no qualms about marrying a French Canadian. In 1760 he married Marie-Louise Allaire, a French Canadian, by whom he had five children (born 1761–70). After a brief second marriage to Margery McCord, daughter of the Québec merchant John McCord, by whom he had one child (born 1772), he later married Marie-Josephte Ducros, another French Canadian, by whom he had four children (born 1792–1800).[23] Spending a substantial part of his life in Québec City, he became a major property owner in the Upper Town and was appointed to a number of public offices, including justice of the peace.[24] However, his extensive land holdings in the country were even more impressive.

Having acquired Mount Murray in 1762, Fraser immediately began renting part of General Murray's seigneury at Île-d'Orléans. Four years later he also purchased from Murray a 3,000-acre holding, which lay behind Murray's Rivière-du-Loup seigneury on the opporiste side of the St. Lawrence. By 1768 Fraser had founded the Madouaska (or Madawaska) Company to manage his substantial fur trade business in which both Scots and French Canadians were employed.[25] Fraser then consolidated his land interests in the region even further by purchasing the Islet-du-Portage seigneury from Gabriel Christie in 1777. Five years later he took over part of a long-term lease for the Rivière-du-Loup and Madawaska seigneuries, which had previously been granted to Colonel Henry Caldwell (Figure 3).[26] A prime asset of the Rivière-du-Loup seigneury was its "fishery at Rakouna," which was earning a yearly rent of £32.[27]

Fraser also received an ex-officer's grant of 3,000 acres in Chatham Township (Argenteuil County) at the end of the American Revolutionary War. Like Nairne he had fought as a captain in the 1st battalion of the Royal Highland Emigrants Regiment from 1775 and returned to his previous life when the war ended in 1784. Later on, at the advanced age of 79, Malcolm Fraser would lead militiamen from Baie-Saint-Paul to Québec during the War of 1812.[28] When Joseph Bouchette visited Mount Murray in 1815, he observed Fraser's "well-situated" manor house on the east side of the entrance to the bay, which was "surrounded by a large tract of well-cultivated land."[29] Fraser died that same year.

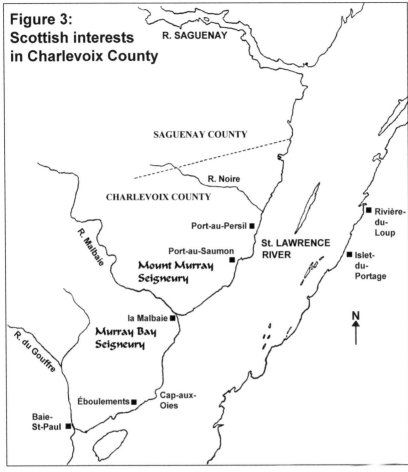

**Figure 3:
Scottish interests
in Charlevoix County**

R. SAGUENAY

SAGUENAY COUNTY

R. Noire

CHARLEVOIX COUNTY

Port-au-Persil ■

Port-au-Saumon
*Mount Murray
Seigneury* ■

St. LAWRENCE
RIVER

■ Rivière-
du-
Loup

■ Islet-
du-
Portage

R. Malbaie

la Malbaie ■
*Murray Bay
Seigneury*

N

R. du Gouffre

Éboulements ■

Cap-aux-
Oies

Baie-
St-Paul ■

In addition to furs, Fraser's property empire had yielded timber, potash and fish. His estates produced some wheat and livestock, but, because only a small amount of his land had been cultivated, his agricultural output had been relatively small.[30] Although most of his labour force was French, he had employed some Scottish labourers and craftsmen. William Campbell built canoes and "cut wood for the potash scheme," while Richard Murray supervised timber felling and also worked at the sawmill.[31] William Fraser managed his sawmill, while Ensign John Fraser rented "the farm of Mount Murray" for £20 per year.[32] Various payments were made to a Simon Fraser who was clearly acting as one of Malcolm Fraser's agents, whereas Lieutenant Neil MacLean was one of his moneylenders. John McLoughlin, his son-in-law, rented the "domaine at Rivière-du-Loup"[33] and with Fraser's help, Hugh Black-burn became the local liquor merchant.[34] Having come to Murray Bay from Scotland with his brother Christopher, Hugh married Geneviève Gagnon by whom he had twelve children.[35]

By the end of the eighteenth century, the mainly French population in La Malbaie was growing rapidly. There were few British immigrants and those who did come were like Hugh Blackburn and married into French communities.[36] However this was not the pattern throughout the entire province. Britain's defeat in the American War of Independence in 1783 resulted in a large influx of people of British stock to the southwest side of the province. These were Loyalists who were moved from the United States, at government expense, to strengthen and enlarge the province's defensive capabilities. Many men with fighting experience came with their families and reported for military service. Ever fearful of an invasion from the United States, the government stationed most of them along the Richelieu River. They began arriving soon after the outbreak of war in 1775 and, by the end of the war in 1783, the influx had grown to over 6,000 Loyalists.[37]

In the Maritimes, which had received nearly six times as many Loyalists, the process of relocation had required the forcible removal of the indigenous populations, although such a policy was unthinkable in French Canada.[38] Québec had a large and long-established French-Catholic population with its own distinctive culture and language, which was concentrated in the fertile lands along the St. Lawrence River Valley. From the early days of the Conquest, General Murray had adopted a conciliatory approach in spite of strenuous criticism from the newly arrived and powerful Anglophone merchants, who wished to have British institutions and customs imposed on the French population. Murray and his successor, Sir Guy Carleton, understood the political and demographic realities which faced them. Québec was vulnerable to attack from the United States and its population growth depended solely on "the Canadian race."[39] From this Carleton concluded that "the best policy to pursue is the preservation of the customs of this province."[40]

Carleton also realized the importance which the French placed on their cultural heritage. By satisfying them that this would not be in jeopardy under British rule, he hoped to win their co-operation. While this assurance probably dispelled any anti-British feelings they may have had, it certainly did not mean that the French would take up arms in the defence of British interests. John Nairne had discovered this in 1775, at the beginning of the American Rebellion, when he attempted to recruit a regiment from La Malbaie, Les Éboulements and Baie-Saint-Paul. While Murray Bay could claim thirty-two men of fighting age (between 16 and 55) few came forward.[41] But as the United States would soon discover, Carleton's policy had at least dissuaded the French Canadians from supporting the American Rebellion. A key turning point was the passing of the Quebec Act of 1774, which recognized the right of the French to uphold their language, religion and land tenure system.[42] General Frederick Haldimand, Carleton's replacement, went a step further and recommended that they should have territorial advantages as well. In his view the territory to the east of the St. Lawrence, what is now called the Eastern Townships, should be occupied exclusively by French Canadians. He could see defensive advantages in having "the frontier settled with people professing a different religion, speaking a different language and accustomed to different laws from those or our enterprising neighbours of New England."[43]

Most of the 6,000 Loyalists who came to the province could be found initially in the towns and villages along the Richelieu River and in Montréal and Québec (Figure 4). Because of its military importance, the river had attracted the majority of the Loyalists. American soldiers had used it in 1775 to launch an attack on Montréal and they had also travelled down the Chaudière River to lay siege to Québec.[44] Although the assault ended in a humiliating defeat for the United States, it was an object lesson in the need to protect vulnerable river routes. Loyalists were placed in the French seigneuries, which were situated along the Richelieu River, with the highest concentrations developing at Sorel, Yamaska, Chambly, Noyan, Foucault and St-Armand.[45] As a later development, the seigneury of Sorel was purchased by the government in order to strengthen and expand the military garrison there.[46] Becoming the principal Loyalist settlement, Sorel's population grew rapidly. By 1820 it was reported to be the only town between Montréal and Québec "wherein English is the dominant language."[47] Included among these Anglophones, some years later, were people who were said to be in need of "the services of a Scottish clergymen."[48] Clearly Sorel had acquired a substantial number of Scots as did nearby Chambly. By 1832 Chambly

Figure 4: Loyalists along the Richelieu River, 1775-85

had developed into a major Scottish stronghold, having three hundred and thirty six Scottish families.[49]

It had always been Haldimand's intention to move many of the Loyalists from the Richelieu River area to the upper St. Lawrence and Lake Ontario regions, and he achieved this objective to a large extent in 1784. As a result of the division of the old Province of Québec into Upper and Lower Canada in 1791, they would soon find that they had become residents of Upper Canada.[50] However, although they were only a relatively small number, others were dispatched to the Gaspé Peninsula.[51] Having received favourable reports about the farming and fishing opportunities which the region offered, Haldimand arranged for some three hundred and fifty Loyalists to be sent there in 1784. Sailing from

Trois Rivières and Sorel, they took up their designated holdings along the north side of Baie des Chaleurs.[52] Included in their number were thirty-one men from the Royal Highland Emigrants Regiment (84th), who had come to the area "for the purpose of establishing a fishery settlement."[53] A few more Loyalists followed that same year bringing the total to just over four hundred. Most of the Loyalists settled in the area between Pointe au Maquereau (Point Mackerel) and Restigouche with the largest concentrations developing initially in and around Paspébiac (near New Carlisle).[54] Some Loyalists joined small already established communities at New Richmond and Restigouche while the Paspébiac colonists went on to found another community on the east side of the Gaspé, which they called Douglastown (Figure 5).

Other Loyalists defied Haldimand's policy and sought to remain in areas of Québec that had not been designated for Loyalists.[55] Realizing that there was the rich farmland to be had to the east of the Richelieu River, in the region between Baie Missisquoi and Lac Memphrémagog, they petitioned for permission to settle there (Figure 4). Haldimand objected, strongly believing it unwise to locate Loyalists so close to the American border, but they persisted and many acquired tenancies in the seigneuries of Foucault,[56] Noyan and Saint-Armand in what later became Missisquoi County.[57] Coming under increasing pressure to open up the wilderness to the east of the St. Lawrence to colonizers, the gov-

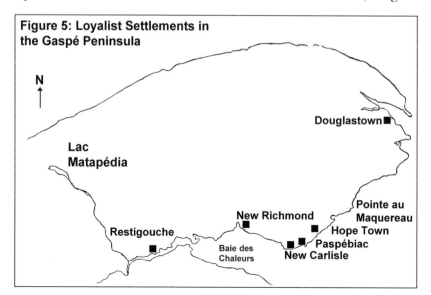

Figure 5: Loyalist Settlements in the Gaspé Peninsula

N

Lac Matapédia

Douglastown■

Pointe au Maquereau

New Richmond■

Hope Town

Restigouche■

Baie des Chaleurs

■■ Paspébiac

New Carlisle

ernment relaxed its opposition to population growth near the American border in 1791 and actively encouraged immigrants from New England. Predictably, the newly created Eastern Townships attracted some of the Loyalists who already had settled in the region between Baie Missisquoi and Lac Memphrémagog. Being scattered over a wide area, they were eventually to be found in the present-day counties of Missisquoi, Brome, Shefford, Stanstead and Sherbrooke. Some of them also dispersed to Huntingdon County, lying to the west of the Richelieu River, with most settling in Hemingford Township.[58]

In spite of being Québec's first military settlement, La Malbaie was totally unaffected by the Loyalist influx of the late eighteenth century. John Nairne and Malcolm Fraser had achieved what was expected of them in building up thriving communities although this had been done, not with Scots, as Nairne had hoped, but with French Canadians. La Malbaie's population had risen to 2,830 by 1790 and reached 10,000 by 1851.[59] The Frasers, McNicols and MacLeans had become assimilated into Francophone communities and little trace of their culture remained.[60] But the economic impact of some of these early Scots was immense. Nairne and Fraser had each established major estates and Fraser's business activities brought substantial employment to areas in and around La Malbaie and Rivière-du-Loup. One of Malcolm Fraser's sons, Colonel Alexander Fraser, was said by 1823 to have erected corn and sawmills at his manor at Rivière-du-Loup, "that are of great moment to the inhabitants" of the people living on the borders of Lac Témiscouata.[61] The entrepreneurial tradition clearly lived on in the Fraser family and it would take root in another Scottish family. Peter McLeod, the son of a North West Company worker, would soon rise from humble beginnings to found a major timber business in the Chicoutimi region.

McLeod was the child of an Ayrshire-born father and Marie-Magdeleine, who was a Montagnais.[62] His father, who worked for the North West Company until its merger with the Hudson's Bay Company in 1821 and later for the Post Office, opened his eyes to the lumbering opportunities in northern Lower Canada.[63] Being a Métis, he was able to take advantage of his mother's Aboriginal rights in the upper Saguenay region, a vast area which the Hudson's Bay Company had been leasing from the Crown. Together with his father, Peter McLeod launched his timber export business in the 1830s when he was in his late 20s.

The McLeod business was initially centred in Charlevoix County at Port-au-Persil, Port-au-Saumon and the Rivière-Noire (Figure 3). By staking his claim to the vast forested area stretching westward from the Rivière Ha! Ha! to the Rivière Péribonka on the north side of Lac Saint-Jean, McLeod was able to move the focus of his business to the upper Saguenay. Convincing twenty-three of his Charlevoix men to move to the much larger mills, which he and his father had built at the mouth of Riviére du Moulin, McLeod provided himself with a ready-made workforce. His friend, the Ross-shire-born Simon Ross, furnished McLeod's forestry workers with wheat and other food supplies grown on Ross's Glenfield Farm.[64] McLeod's obvious entrepreneurial skills ensured his

Peter McLeod (1808–1852), the founder of Chicoutimi. *Courtesy of Archives nationales du Québec P1000-S4-D83 Collection de la Societé historique de Saguenay.*

rapid success as did some of his other God-given attributes. A large and robust man, with "black eyes which resembled those of an eagle," his handsomeness was said to be "spellbinding."[65]

By 1842 McLeod had joined forces with William Price, the English-born timber baron who was rapidly acquiring vast timber interests in the province, and between them they controlled all timber operations in the upper Saguenay and St-Jean region.[66] With the help of Alexis Tremblay, one of his men, Price had been able to encourage a group of men, to move from La Malbaie and Baie-Saint-Paul, to the bottom of Baie Ha! Ha! Known as "la société vingt-et-un," they settled along the Saguenay as squatters and built nine sawmills at the mouths of the principal tributaries along the Saguenay. They were soon joined by large numbers of other settlers, and as Price had foreseen, the government had to yield to pressure to open up the region and the lands were offered for auction.

Peter McLeod's flourishing timber business created the town of Chicoutimi. By 1851 he and William Price were sending twenty ships a year laden with timber, having a sales value of £45,000, from Chicoutimi to Britain.[67] Timber ships were able to sail up the Saguenay to Grande-Baie, where the majority of the sawmills were located

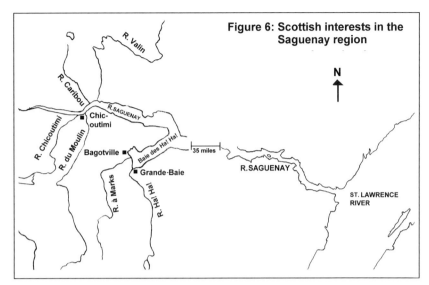

Figure 6: Scottish interests in the Saguenay region

(Figure 6). As the town's largest employer, McLeod had three hundred men working year-round at his sawmills and by 1856 the population of Chicoutimi had reached two thousand two hundred. Peter McLeod died in mysterious circumstances in 1852, when aged 44. His children, being illegitimate, were unable to claim their father's inheritance and his timber business fell into the hands of William Price.

The fur trade and two North American battles had brought many Scots to Lower Canada. The Scots who remained behind after the Seven Years War and the fur trade workers generally married into Francophone communities. However, the American Revolutionary War broke this pattern. This war brought Loyalists, who came with farming backgrounds and a desire to re-establish themselves in their own distinctive communities. Loyalist Scots were quick to spot the economic potential of the region's timber trade with Britain and, being among the earliest arrivals, they grabbed some of the best coastline and river locations. Appreciating the scale of the exodus, which was gathering pace as news spread in Scotland of the good opportunities to be had, Archibald McMillan, acquired extensive land holdings on the north side of the Ottawa River in Lower Canada. A Highlander himself, he planned the foundation of a number of Highland settlements along this river.

Three

NORTH OF THE OTTAWA RIVER

I have this year had letters from some of my family in Lochaber saying that many of them…will undoubtedly make their way to Lochaber in America.¹

FACING WHAT HE THOUGHT WAS a bleak future in Scotland, Archibald McMillan of Murlaggan, a prominent Inverness-shire tacksman,² led a group of Highlanders to Québec in 1802. They included tenants from the Lochiel estate on which he lived, as well as from the Glen Garry estate immediately to the north, together with people from a variety of locations around the Great Glen. Joined by his wife, Isabella Gray, and children, he settled initially in Montréal where he established himself as a general merchant.³ While McMillan remained behind in Montréal, most of the emigrants in his group headed upriver to the Glengarry settlements at the eastern extremity of Upper Canada. However, McMillan soon acquired extensive landholdings of his own, just to the north of Glengarry in Lower Canada. He established Highland settlements on these lands and, to commemorate the Highland region from which he and so many of his followers originated, he gave the name Lochaber to his principal township.

The Glengarry communities, whose name reflects the Inverness-shire origins of the first settlers, had been established in Upper Canada some 18 years earlier. The initial group came as Loyalists following the British defeat in the American War of Independence. Having been relocated from their previous homes in New York State, they came to the area in 1784 when the war ended. Establishing distinctive Highland communities, they attracted a steady stream of followers. By the early 1790s a total of 1,300 emigrants had arrived from various Inverness-shire locations—especially Glen Garry, Lochiel, Glenelg, Glen Moriston, Knoydart and Morar.[4] As it gathered pace, the exodus was seen as a fearsome development by most high-ranking Scots. Because it enticed good people away to foreign countries, they looked upon emigration as an evil which had to be stopped.

The emigration fever, which so concerned the Scottish elite, was drawing people in particularly large numbers from the northwest Highlands.[5] Having risen to new peaks in the early 1790s, emigration declined sharply in 1793 with the onset of the war between Britain and France.[6] But it resumed its upward trend, following the temporary peace of 1801, and, as it did, the ruling classes in Scotland did everything in their power to stop it. By this time Knoydart had lost a third of its population while Glenelg was also contributing large numbers of people to the emigration movement. "To such an extent has this prevailed that America too rejoices in a Glenelg with a population at least equal to that which the parent parish still possesses."[7] According to a contemporary commentator, the number of people who left the Highlands in the period from 1801 to 1803 "may be moderately calculated at 4,000 and 20,000 more...are capable of doing so."[8] While Nova Scotia and Cape Breton were attracting emigrants from many parts of the mainland as well as the Western Isles,[9] Glengarry's intake of Scots came principally from regions to the west of the Great Glen.

The Highland Society of Edinburgh feared the worst when they first learned of the impending departure of Archibald McMillan's Highlanders for Glengarry. Colin Campbell, a Greenock Customs official, warned them in June 1802 that a number of ships were being "fitted out" at Greenock, Port Glasgow and Saltcoats "for the purpose of taking out emigrants." Although the Society's propaganda campaign to thwart the exodus was in full swing, they were powerless to stop it.[10] Yet they did succeed in convincing the government that it should provide new passenger regulations. The 1803 Passenger Act, which stipulated more food and larger space requirements for emigrants, was duly passed, causing fares nearly to double and so greatly reduce the numbers of people who could afford to emigrate.

Archibald McMillan's group of 552 people escaped the fare increases, having travelled in the previous year. McMillan advanced £1,861 for the chartering of three ships: the *Helen* of Irvine, *Jean* of Irvine and *Friends of John Saltcoats*. He charged fares of £5.5s., leaving himself with a modest profit of £118,[11] and it seems that he provided his people with a good standard of accommodation.[12] The *Helen* and *Jean* had top quality A1 ratings from Lloyds of London while the "six feet by six feet" berths provided in the *Friends* were far roomier than average.[13] Realizing that he needed help in managing such a large group, McMillan placed John Corbet, Alexander Cameron, Angus McPhee, John Cameron, Alexander McPhee, Dougald McDonell, Lauchlin McDonell and Donald McMillan in charge of the passengers. Representing the main family groups in the various districts, they were found to be "useful in forwarding his views and impressing good order among the people."[14] A second contingent of 600 Highlanders, who were unconnected with McMillan's group, also left at the same time, sailing in a fourth ship, the *Neptune*.[15] They had originated mainly from the west coast districts of North Morar, Knoydart, Glenelg, Kintail and Lochalsh.

The *Neptune* passengers travelled in far less comfort then McMillan's group. They had no prosperous benefactor to bankroll them, although they did have a kind captain, who provided "his care during a passage of nine weeks."[16] Arriving in a destitute state, they needed financial assistance to proceed from Québec to Glengarry.[17] Some sixty local people raised just over £103 for them, with substantial donations being made by the owners of the *Neptune* and General Peter Hunter, the Lieutenant-Governor of Upper Canada.[18] By way of contrast, the McMillan group arrived in a healthy state with surplus rations. Their ships' captains had attempted to seize their rations, but, with McMillan's help, the group's grievance was brought before justices of the peace in Montréal who ruled in their favour.[19]

When the two 1802 groups reached Glengarry County, they experienced great difficulty in acquiring land. Because most of the available land was already occupied, they were unable to settle in large compact groups in the way their predecessors had done. Highland communities were already spreading westward into Stormont County (Upper Canada) and eastward into Soulanges County in Lower Canada (Figure 7).[20] This influx to Soulanges created long-lived and substantial Scottish settlements. By 1828 the "Presbyterian population" of Coteau-du-Lac was reported to have "exceeded four hundred souls" and ten years later the combined congregation of Côte St. George and Roebuck Mills in Lancaster Township (Glengarry County) was said to be "some 800 strong."[21]

Although land was available in other more distant districts on easy terms, it was rejected principally because the emigrants refused to be separated from their friends in and around Glengarry. Thus, as Lord Selkirk had noticed when he visited Glengarry, most of the 1802 arrivals "were received into houses of the old settlers" and "got pieces of land from the old settlers to crop," while "some of the poorer [people] have taken leases of the Clergy Reserves."[22] When the problem of land scarcity came to the notice of Archibald McMillan, he immediately saw the potential for creating satellite settlements north of Glengarry in Lower Canada.

Having taken up residence in Montréal, McMillan was barred from acquiring land in Upper Canada, but Lower Canada's land was readily accessible. In August 1804, he petitioned the government for land along the north shore of the Ottawa River, claiming that he had recruited 209 heads of households.[23] He then forwarded a further list of 75 names two years later.[24] McMillan's petition was successful and by 1807 he had acquired the entire Township of Suffolk, much of Grenville and a quarter part of Templeton.[25] Although they were close together, the townships did not constitute a single block of land. Suffolk and Templeton, in Papineau County,[26] were separated by Buckingham Township, while Grenville, in Argenteuil County, was separated from Suffolk by the seigneury of Petite Nation (Figure 7). One of McMillan's first actions was to turn Suffolk into Lochaber. He clearly agreed with his agent, John Munro, who advised that the Lochaber name "will be an inducement to those from that part of the old country to settle in it, who are every year arriving."[27] Settlers did certainly come, although not in the numbers that McMillan had anticipated (Table 1).

While the 1802 arrivals had complained to him about their difficulties in finding land in and around Glengarry, many of them rejected his offer of land grants in Lower Canada. Even if it meant staying with relatives and renting land, they still favoured Glengarry because it enabled them to remain close to their relatives and friends. Consequently, even though Highlanders "were pouring down every day in most astonishing numbers," few of them were heading for McMillan's settlements:

TABLE 1

Distribution List, provided by Archibald MacMillan, of lands in Templeton, Suffolk (Lochaber) and Grenville townships, 1804–07
[LAC RG1 L3 ff. 66558-61]

The Township of Templeton

Name	1st Range* No. of Lots	2nd Range No. of Lots	3rd Range No. of Lots	4th Range No. of Lots	5th Range No. of Lots	Quantum acres
Archibald McMillan		4, 6, 7				729
Isabella McMillan		9, 10, 11	12, N. ½ of 13	14	N. ½ of 14 1	200
Allan Cameron		¾ of 2				189
Donald Cameron (Dungallon)			2			200
John Cameron (Auchnasants)				1, 2		400
William Corbet					9	200
Lauchlan Cameron					4	200
John Forbes					10	200
Peggy Fraser					7	200
Alexander Goudie					11	200
Thomina Gray	7, 11, 12	3		12		1217
Hugh McBean					13	200
Duncan McDonell					3	200
Donald McMillan					6, ?	400
Mary McDonell				11		200
Rory McDougal				9		200
James McDouell				8		200
Peter McDougal				7		200
Daniel McArthur				5		200
Roderick McDonell			1			200
Ewen McMillan			5			200
Ronald McDonald			8			200
Donald McDonald			9			200
John McArthur			10			200
Alexander McDonell (Lagan)		½ of 13	½ of 13			200
John McDonell		½ of 14	½ 13			200
John McDonell	N. ⅓ of 14		½ of 14			190
Donald Morrison	50 ac sw of 10 ⅔ of 4					220
Duncan McDougal	200 ac S of 10					200
Alexander McDonell (Kilinean)	8					214

Name	1st Range* No. of Lots	2nd Range No. of Lots	3rd Range No. of Lots	4th Range No. of Lots	5th Range No. of Lots	Quantum acres
Alexander McDonell (Drover)	5	¼ of 2				205
Donald McGilles			3			200
James Waddal			6			200
James Wright				4		200

The Distribution of Suffolk (Lochaber)

Name	1st Range No. of Lots	2nd Range No. of Lots	3rd Range No. of Lots	4th Range No. of Lots	5th Range No. of Lots	6th Range	Quantum acres
Dougald Cameron			6, 7 & ½ of 9				198
Alexander Cameron					25		200
John Corbat	26		17, 18				627
Ewen Cameron		23, N. ½ of 24					193
Alexander Dewar		19, N. ⅓ of 20					211
Donald Dewar				20			200
Duncan Dewar				6			200
Duncan Dewar				5			200
Peter Dewar					19		200
Angus Fletcher				23			200
Angus Kennedy					12		200
John Kennedy		S. ⅔ of 20, 22					243
Peter McCouaig					2		200
Malcolm McCouaig			½ 9, 10, 11 & ½ 13				205
Malcolm McCouaig			27				200
Malcolm McCouaig					22		200
Malcolm McCrummin						28	200
Robert McCormick			28				200
John McDonell				27			200
Rachel McConaig				22			200
John McDonell				1			200
John McDonell					1		200
John McDonell					14		200
John McDonell						20	200
Donald McDonell						17	200
Duncan McDonell				19			200
Alexander McDonell		26					200
Donald McDonell			½ 13, 14				228

Name	1st Range No. of Lots	2nd Range No. of Lots	3rd Range No. of Lots	4th Range No. of Lots	5th Range No. of Lot s		Quantum acres
Donald McDonell			21				200
Christy McDonell						18	200
Norman McDonell						21	200
Donald McDonell					26		200
Donald McDonell						25	200
Roderick McDonell					15		200
Angus McDougal						27	200
Donald McIntosh						16	200
John McDougal				2			200
John McGillis				17			200
John McGillis				16			200
Donald McGillis				24			200
William McKinnon						23	200
Mary McLellan		28					200
Alexander McLeod			25				200
Donald McKinnon			23				200
Catherine McLauchlin				3		200	
Dougald McLauchlin					4		200
Duncan McLean					8		200
Roderick McLennan					16		200
Angus McLauchlin					18		200
Alexander McMillan			16				200
John McMillan	27	½ of 24					188
Ewen McMillan			24				200
Jane McMillan				8, 9, 10, 12 13 & 15			1200
Duncan McMillan					5		200
John McMillan					21		200
Ewen McMillan					28		200
						6th Range	
Duncan McMillan						14	200
Rodorick Morrison					7		200
Rodorick Morrison					11		200
Neil Morrison				26			200
Robert McNabb			20				200
Donald McPhee						13	200
Angus McDonell			2, 3, 4				206
Angus McDonell						24	200
John McCormick					23		200
John McMillan					9		200
							7394

The Distribution of Grenville (Ranges 1–3)

Name	1st Range No. of Lots	2nd Range No. of Lots	3rd Range No. of Lots	Quantum acres
Archibald McMillan Leader	6,7	9, 10		500
Peter Cameron		6		200
Mary Grant		8		200
Duncan McMillan			7	200
Duncan McKinnon			8	200
Rory McDonell			9	200
Neil McDonell			11	200

* Range number is the concession number.

TABLE 2
List of emigrants presented by Archibald McMillan, 1806
[LAC RG1 L3 ff. 66605-10, 66691-2.]

O = Old List, N = New List

Names	Religious Denomination	Males above 14yrs	Males under 14yrs	Females above 14yrs	Females under 14yrs	Place from whence they came
O 1 Alexander McDonell	Catholic					Scotland
O 2 Alexander McDonald, Drover	"		1	2		"
N 3 Neil Morison	Protestant		3	2		"
N 4 Alexander Smith	"					"
N 5 M Hopsack	"					"
N 6 John Barrie	"					"
N 7 Robert McNab	"					"
N 8 Hugh Brodie	"					"
O 9 Duncan McMillan	"					"
O 10 James Waddel	"	1	1	2		"
O 11 Alexander Cameron	"		2			"
O 12 John Cameron	"					"
N 13 Donald Morrison	"					"
O 14 Peter McDougall	"					"
O 15 Ewen McMillan	"					"

Names	Religious Denomination	No. of persons in their families				Place from whence they came
		Males above 14yrs	Males under 14yrs	Females above 14yrs	Females under 14yrs	
N 16 John Forbes	"	1				"
O 17 Ewen McMillan jr.	"					"
O 18 Archibald McMillan	"	3	2			"
O 19 Archibald McDonell	Catholic	2		1		"
O 20 Berry McDougall	"					"
O 21 Angus McDougall	"					"
O 22 Malcolm McCuaig	"					"
N 23 Donald McGillis	"					"
O 24 John McDonald	"					"
O 25 Angus Kennedy	"					"
O 26 Alexander McCulloch	"					"
N 27 Archibald McDonald	"					"
N 28 Duncan McDonald	"					Montréal
O 29 Angus McDonell	"					"
O 30 James McGillivray	Protestant					"
N 31 James McGrath	"					"
N 32 Ewen Cameron	"					"
N 33 Cornelius Jackson	"					"
N 34 William Jackson	"					New York
N 35 William Balston	"					Montréal
O 36 James Wright	"	3				"
O 37 Alexander McDonald	Catholic	3		3		"
O 38 Alexander Brodie	Protestant	1		1		"
O 39 John McArthur	"					"
N 40 John McCochim	"					"
N 41 Neil McIntosh	"					Montréal
N 42 Alexander Logan	"					"
O 44 Isabella McMillan	"					"
O 45 Thomina Gray	"					"
O 46 Jean McMillan	"					"
N 47 John Saller	"					"
N 48 P Cameron	"					"
O 49 John McDonald	Catholic					Côte St George
O 50 Alexander McDonell	"					Cornwall
N 51 Duncan McIntosh	"					"
O 52 John McDonald	"					Lancaster
O 53 John McGillis	"					"
O 54 Duncan McDonald	"					Kings T. S. *
N 55 William McKinnon	"					Lancaster

Names	Religious Denomination	No. of persons in their families				Place from whence they came
		Males above 14yrs	Males under 14yrs	Females above 14yrs	Females under 14yrs	
O 56 Archibald McDonell	"					Cornwall
O 57 W. McDonald	"		1			"
O 58 W. McGillis	"					Lancaster
N 59 Hugh McDonald	"					Kings. T.S. *
O 60 John McDonald	"					"
O 61 Duncan McDonald	"					Cornwall
O 62 Donald McDonell	"					Glengarry
O 63 Alexander McDonell	"					"
N 64 Allan McDonell	"					"
O 65 Dougald McDonell	"					"
O 66 Angus McDonell	"					"
67						
O 68 Donald McDonell	"					Cornwall
O 69 John McCorrie	"					Glengarry
N 70 Francis McDonell	"					"
O 71 Archibald McIsaac	"		3		1	Cornwall
O 72 Archibald McDonald	"					Glengarry
O 73 Donald McDonald"						"
N 74 Archibald McDonald	"					"
O 75 Donald McDonald	"					"
O 76 Hugh McDonald	"					"
O 77 Alexander McDonell	"					"
O 78 Duncan McDonell	"					Cornwall
O 79 Hugh McDonell	"					St. George
O 80 John McMillan	"					Glengarry
N 81 Donald McGillis	"					"
O 82 Alexander McDonell	"					Cornwall
O 83 Duncan McDonell	"					"
N 84 John McGillis	"		3		4	"
O 85 Duncan McDonell	"					Glengarry
O 86 John McDonald	"					"
O 87 Hugh Kennedy	"					"
N 88 Hugh McDonell	"					Cornwall
O 89 John McDonell	Catholic					Cornwall
O 90 Donald McLennan	Protestant					Lancaster
N 91 Rachel McGillivray	"					"
O 92 Duncan McLean	"	1				"
N 93 Kenneth McLennan	"		1		1	Longeuil
N 94 Henry McCuag	"		3		1	Lancaster

| Names | Religious Denomination | No. of persons in their families | | | | Place from whence they came |
| | | Males | | Females | | |
		above 14yrs	under 14yrs	above 14yrs	under 14yrs	
N 95 John McLennan	"	2	2	1		Glengarry
N 96 Alexander McPherson	"	1	3		2	Lancaster
O 97 John Grant	"					"
N 98 John McLean	"		3			"
N 99 Alexander McNaughton	"					N. Longeuil
N 100 Finlay McCuag	"					"
N 101 Donald McGilvray	"					Glengarry
N 102 Alexander McDonald	Catholic					"
N 103 Angus Kennedy	"					"
O 104 John McDonald	"					"
N 105 Archibald McDonell	"					Lancaster
O 106 Duncan McMillan	"	3		1		"
O 107 John Kennedy	"					"
O 108 John Cameron	"					"
O 109 Hugh McDougall	"					Glengarry
O 110 Alexander McDonell	"					"
O 111 John McDonell	"	1	1			"
O 112 Hugh McMillan	"			2		"
N 113 John McConnan	Protestant	1	1			Scotland Glengarry
O 114 Peter McCuaig	"	2	3		2	"
O 115 John Robertson	"				1	"
O 116 John Cameron	"					"
O 117 Lodon: Morrison	"					Scotland
O 118 William McGillivray	"					"
O 119 Malcolm McGrimmin	"	1		1		"
120 Mary McAllan	"		1		2	"
O 121 Malcolm McCouaig	"	1	2			"
O 122 Angus Fletcher	"					"
O 122 John McIntosh	"		1		1	"
O 123 Lodu' Harrison	"				1	"
O 124 Malcolm McCaskell	"	1		2		"
O 125 Finlay McMaster	"		1	3		"
O 126 John McGillivray	"					"
O 127 Peggy Fraser	"					"
O 128 Norman McConell	Catholic	1		1		"
O 129 Duncan McMillan	"	3		1		"
O 130 Donald McLachlan	"					"
O 140 Dougald McDonell	"	1		1	2	"

Names	Religious Denomination	No. of persons in their families				Place from whence they came
		Males above 14yrs	Males under 14yrs	Females above 14yrs	Females under 14yrs	
O 141 John McDougald	"					"
O 142 Mary McDonel	"		4		1	"
N 143 Alexander McMillan	"					"
O 144 Hugh McMillan	Catholic	2		1		Scotland
O 144 John McMillan	"				4	"
O 145 John McMillan	"	2		3		"
O 146 John McDougall	"					"
O 147 Ronald McDonell	"	3		2	1	"
O 148 John McDonell	"		2			"
O 149 Neil McDonell	"					"
O 150 Donald McMillan	"					"
O 151 Donald Grant	"					"
O 152 Fergus Beaton	"	2		4		"
O 153 John McDonell	"				3	"
O 154 Neil McDonell	"					"
O 155 Alexander McDonell	"			3		"
O 156 Hugh McMillan	"					"
N 157 Dugald Cameron	"	2	1	2		"
O 158 Robert McCormic	"					"
O 159 Dugald McDonell		3	2			"
O 160 Ronald McDonell	"	2		1		"
O 161 Mary McDonell	"					"
O 162 Donald McIntosh	Protestant	3		1		"
O 163 Hugh McMillan	"	2			3	"
O 164 John McMillan	"					"
O 165 John McMillan	"					"
O 166 Ewen Kennedy	"	1	2		1	"
O 167 Alexander McLeod	"		3		2	"
O 168 Malcolm McCouag	"	2	1	2	3	"
O 169 Malcolm McCouag	"		3		2	"
O 170 Duncan McKinnon	"		1	2		"
O 171 John Kennedy	Catholic	5		2		Glengarry
O 172 Ronald McDonell	"	3	2		7	"
O 173 Duncan McDonell	"	2	1	1	1	"
O 174 Angus McDonell	"		3		2	"
N 175 Margaret McQuen	"	2				"
N 176 Catherine McLaughlin	"		2	1		"
O 177 Christy McDonell	"	1	1	1	1	"
O 178 John McDonell	"	2	2	2	2	"

Names	Religious Denomination	No. of persons in their families Males above 14yrs	under 14yrs	Females above 14yrs	under 14yrs	Place from whence they came
O 179 Angus McLaughlin	"	2		3	2	"
O 179 John McMillan	"	1				"
O 180 Donald McDonald	"	1			1	"
O 181 Dugald McLaughlin	"	1	2			"
O 182 John McDonell	"					"
O 183 Alexander Cameron	"	3		3		"
O 184 Angus McDonald	"	2		2		"
O 185 John McDonell	"					"
O 186 Roderick McDonell	"					"
O 187 Alexander McDougall	"					"
O 188 Donald McDonell	"		2		3	"
O 189 Ronald McDonell	"				1	"
O 190 Archibald McDonell	Catholic				1	Glengarry
O 191 Angus Kennedy	"					"
O 192 Allan Kennedy	"					"
O 193 Angus McGillis	"					"
N 194 Lauchlin Cameron	"	2	1		2	"
O 195 Duncan McMillan	"					"
O 196 John McGillivray	"	1		1		"
N 197 Andrew McGillivray	"					"
N 198 Duncan Morrison	"					"
O 199 William McGillivray	"					"
O 200 Dougald McMillan	"					"
N 201 Angus McGillivray	"	1				"
O 202 Angus McDonnell	"	2		2	2	"
O 203 Angus McDonnell	"	5		2		"
O 204 Donald McDonnell	"					"
O 205 Donald McDonnell	"					"
N 206 Finlay McDonnell	"					"
N 207 Hugh McDonnell	"					"
O 208 Alexander Kennedy	"					"
O 209 John McDonnell	"					"
N 210 Huigh McDonnell	"					"
N 211 Dougald McDonnell	"		3		2	"
O 212 John Corbet	"	1	1	1	2	Scotland
N 213 William Corbet	"					"
O 214 Donald McPherson	Protestant		3		1	"
N 215 John Morrison	"					"
O 216 John McGillivray	"					"

Names	Religious Denomination	No. of persons in their families				Place from whence they came
		Males above 14yrs	under 14yrs	Females above 14yrs	under 14yrs	
N 217 John McCuaig	"					"
N 218 Hugh McBean	"					"
N 219 William Fraser	"					"
220 John McDonald	Catholic					"
221 Roderick McLennan	Protestant					"
222 Donald Cameron	"					"
223 Peter Davies	"	6	3	1		"
224 Allen Cameron	"	7				"
225 Duncan Dewar	"		1			"
226 John Dewar	"					"
227 Duncan Dewar	"					"
228 Donald Dewar	"					"
229 Alexander Dewar	"					"
230 Donald McGregor	"					"
231 Roderick McDonald	Catholic					"
Duncan McDougall	"				1	"
Donald McArthur	Protestant					"

* Kings T. S. may refer to the King's Royal Regiment of New York.

"Our countrymen have a great aversion to going on new land. They are afraid to encounter fresh difficulties and they live among their friends [in Glengarry], formerly settled in the country, who encourage them as they find them useful in clearing their land without considering that they are losing time for a bare subsistence."[28]

McMillan probably had not anticipated Glengarry's amazing pulling power. Many years earlier, in 1790, when the *British Queen* had arrived in Québec with eighty-seven destitute Inverness-shire emigrants, they had insisted on being taken to Glengarry.[29] This was in spite of an offer made by a Mr. P.L. Panet, who agreed to accommodate them "immediately upon his seigneury of Argenteuil, in the district of Montréal without any assistance from the government excepting the loan of six

Encampment of Loyalists at New Johnstown (later Cornwall) in Stormont County. New Johnstown was named after Sir John Johnson who supervised the resettling of Loyalists along the upper St. Lawrence in 1784. Although he had a grand house built at Williamstown in Glengarry County, named after his father William, Johnson spent most of his time in Montréal. Watercolour by James Peachey, June 6, 1784. *Courtesy of Library and Archives Canada C-002001.*

bateaux...to transport them from Quebec to his estate."[30] Nonetheless, the new arrivals were determined to settle further upriver "near Johnstown, above Montreal." Although the distance was greater, the Québec Executive Council agreed to their demand.[31] The imminent departure of the *Ajax* with 500 souls from the Islands of Skye and Lewis for North Carolina may have influenced the Council's decision. After all, the 1790 arrivals were "a valuable acquisition," who might be lost to the United States if they did not get their own way.[32]

In spite of Glengarry's undoubted appeal, McMillan looked set to entice substantial numbers of Highlanders away from it, and he also obtained a good response from Scotland. Although his list of 233 families, which he compiled in 1806, revealed the loss of around 25 per cent of the initial applicants, it also shows that he obtained most of his recruits from areas in and near Glengarry in Upper Canada and Scotland. Each provided around 100 names, while the remaining 30 or so families came from Montréal (Table 2).[33] Also evident are the relatively large number of Roman Catholics who represented 60% of the total.

McMillan moved to Grenville Township in 1810, hoping that by doing so he might have greater success in persuading other Highlanders to join him. "I mean to set the example myself, having come to a resolution to reside among them, considering that step as most effectual to forward the settlement."[34] Opposite Hawkesbury Mills was a substantial log house

which became known as "the Old Abbey," because of its isolated position in the woods. McMillan moved into it and adopted the ways of a
Highland gentleman.[35] Shortly after his arrival there, he received a commission as major in the Argenteuil battalion of the local militia, which
was largely composed of Lochaber emigrants. He led his unit in battle
during the War of 1812–14, and, upon returning to Grenville, accepted
more public appointments.[36]

However, moving to Grenville did not in itself resolve McMillan's
difficulties. He had to deal with the "opposition made by the Gentlemen of the Upper Province whose interest is to put a stop to the progress
of a Scotch settlement in the Lower Province."[37] Competition from
Upper Canada Scots, who sought to attract all Highland newcomers to
their localities, was a serious enough obstacle, but, in addition to this,
McMillan also had to contend with bureaucratic idiosyncrasies not of
his making. The Executive Council ruled that the 75 settlers on his 1806
list "should adduce proof that he or she has cleared and fenced three
acres, and that the same is fit for immediate cultivation, and that he or
she has also erected thereon a log hut of twenty-five feet by twenty,"
while the 209 people on his 1804 list were not bound by these regulations.[38] When these differences were discovered, a row broke out and
many people on both lists threatened to withdraw their names.

Another contentious development was McMillan's sudden demand for
the payment of land fees. Complaining that few of his settlers were "coming forward to fulfil their engagements, though they partly dragged me
into the business," McMillan was adamant that his settlers should finance
their own land fees.[39] He "visited Glengarry [in 1807] and called a public
meeting of the emigrants, which came under his protection, and declared
to them that the government had made each of them a grant of 200 acres"
and unless they were prepared to pay "the sum of four pounds for each
and every lot they must relinquish their rights."[40] But £4 was a considerable sum to find and at least 41 householders relinquished their rights rather
than pay these fees.[41] At the time they assumed that "the relinquishments"
would fall to the government." but some twenty years later, after it became
known that "Major McMillan had assumed to himself the ownership and
rights to those lands," John Corbet and the others petitioned Earl Dalhousie, the governor-in-chief, to have possession "of the former grants made
to them," which were mainly in Lochaber and Templeton townships.[42]

Figure 7: Scots in Papineau, Argenteuil and Terrebonne Counties

① Glen Almond
② Thurso
③ Scotch Road
④ Scotch settlement (Dalesville)
⑤ Lachute
⑥ St. Andrews
⑦ Lakefield
⑧ New Glasgow Concession
⑨ Paisley Concession
⑩ McMillan Corners
⑪ Williamstown
⑫ Côte St. George
⑬ Coteau-du-Lac

N

Underlining denotes a township or Seigneury with significant Scottish settlement

Upper Canada

County boundary

Meanwhile, in spite of his many difficulties, McMillan could report to his agent in 1807 that there were "50 to 60" Gaelic-speaking settlers who were making their way to his settlements.[43] It would appear that such numbers actually did arrive in Montréal, although they came two years later. Originating from Perthshire, some sixty people left Dundee in 1809 with "20 bagpipes and nearly as many fiddles."[44] And he was understandably optimistic about the economic potential of his site, "being situated on the banks of the Grand or Ottawa River through which the trade to the North West [Company] is carried on, and that company will always give the settlers the Montreal prices for their produce at their doors, for their flour, pork, butter, etc."[45] In addition to being on an important fur trade route, McMillan's townships were also ideally placed to contribute to Québec's burgeoning timber exports to Britain that began to grow from 1812, onward.

McMillan's holdings were in well-forested areas, veined with river and streams, through which "timber may be floated down…to the Ottawa" River.[46] It soon became clear to him that he could make profits far more readily from lumbering than from farming and he invested heavily in the timber trade. By 1816 he had seven sawmills and employed many Highlanders as lumberjacks and as workers in his mills. And by 1821 he had established a general store in Grenville and traded goods with a number of major Montréal firms, including John and Thomas Torrance, Gillespie, Moffat and Company, the Bank of Montreal and John Molson and Sons. However his timber business suffered during an economic depression in the early 1820s and following another depression in 1827, he was forced to cease trading.[47]

To add to his economic woes, McMillan was also failing to meet the settlement conditions that were being imposed on him by the Executive Council. Having allowed the timber trade to absorb most of his time and energy, he failed to recruit sufficient settlers, and, by 1821, was in serious risk of having his land grants confiscated by the government. In a desperate attempt to find more settlers for Lochaber Township, Archibald McMillan's son, Alexander, who lived in Montréal, advertised in a French newspaper in August 1823 that *"terres en bois de bout, de 100 acres chacune, situées sur la Grand Rivière des Outawas dans le township de Lochaber, et joignant la seigneuries de la Petite Nation"* could be purchased.[48] This attempt to recruit French-Canadian settlers clearly failed to produce sufficient settlers since McMillan lost all of his lands by 1825. Returning to Montréal three years later, he died of cholera in 1832, three days before his son's death.

McMillan's poor reputation and many setbacks might suggest that his colonization ventures were a sorry failure, but this was not the case.[49] Substantial Scottish concentrations were established through his efforts along the north side of the Ottawa River and they eventually spread far beyond the boundaries of his own townships. An unknown and possibly small proportion of the people on his original settler lists actually farmed his land. And, further recruits probably arrived from Glengarry in Upper Canada and from Scotland once it became clear that his settlements had a viable future. His prediction that Grenville would "become one of the most popular townships in the province" was overly optimistic, but this was where he achieved his greatest success.[50]

By 1815 "very little of Lochaber Township has yet been cultivated."[51] Nonetheless, judging from its Presbyterian congregation of two hundred and seventeen people by the mid-1820s, "the middle settlement of Lochaber"[52] had reached a substantial size. A few years later it was seeking financial aid from the Glasgow Colonial Society to enable it "to support a minister for a few years."[53] A report from Reverend Walter Roach, a Presbyterian missionary, who had some knowledge of the area, reveals that Scottish colonizers had also established themselves in the adjoining Buckingham Township. The Glen Almond settlement,[54] on the Rivière du Lièvre at Buckingham's northern extremity, probably denotes the Perthshire origins of its early settlers.[55] Having received

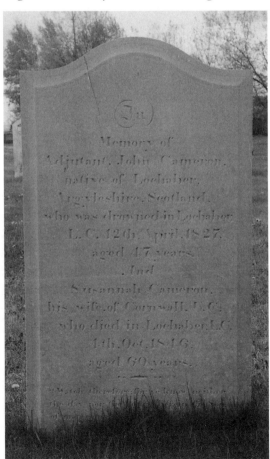

Tombstone of Adjutant John Campbell (1780–1827), "native of Lochaber, Argyleshire, Scotland." His tombstone in Thurso cemetery is the only visible reminder left today of the area's former links with Lochaber. *Photograph by Geoff Campey.*

Tombstones of Robert Sutherland (1824–1908) and his wife (1819–1874) in Thurso cemetery. *Photograph by Geoff Campey.*

"pressing invitations" from people in both townships, Reverend Roach decided that a visit would be of little use," since "the settlers are almost wholly Highlanders," and he did not speak Gaelic.[56] According to him, their combined congregation in 1828 consisted of "ten Episcopalians, thirty Roman Catholics and two hundred and fifty Presbyterians," the latter being "extremely destitute of religious instruction."[57] The 1831 Census reveals that Presbyterians were spread fairly equally between the two townships. They represented 54% of Lochaber's two hundred and thirty-six inhabitants, while they accounted for only 20% of the Buckingham's population, which was two-and-a-half times greater.

By the late 1820s Lochaber's middle settlement was struggling to maintain a Presbyterian minister. An 1827 petition, signed by the combined inhabitants of Lochaber and Buckingham and offering support to Lord Dalhousie's beleaguered administration, reveals one hundred and fifty families of British/American and French descent, with the latter representing about one-third of the total. Just under a quarter can be identified as Scottish names with Camerons, Grahams and Campbells being particularly well represented.[58] This was also the year when the forty-one Glengarry petitioners, led by John Corbet, sought their former land grants. Possibly some of them did return although it is doubtful whether Lochaber's Highland population had ever exceeded fifty or sixty families. When Joseph Bouchette visited it in 1832, he found that little land clearance had taken place beyond the river frontages, and that a similar situation existed at Templeton.[59]

Much later emigrants from Caithness, who settled in Lochaber Township, decided that it was their turn to have their homeland commemorated. At the suggestion of Robert Sutherland, Lochaber was renamed Thurso in 1886 after Sutherland's birthplace in Caithness. He and his wife, who was also born in Caithness, are still remembered in the Thurso cemetery.

Although Scottish concentrations in Lochaber and Templeton were relatively small, their influence extended a considerable distance. Hull Township, just to the west of Templeton, became a major Irish stronghold, having been acquired by the great settlement promoter and timber baron, Philemon Wright.[60] However, townships to the north and west of Hull in Papineau County attracted many emigrant Scots (Figure 7). Settling in townships on either side of the Gatineau River, they arrived soon after their areas were opened up for colonization. Eardley Township had large number of Scottish and Irish settlers by 1819 and later census evidence reveals that Masham and Wakefield townships, to the north of Eardley and Hull, also attracted a significant number of Scots.[61] Low Township, to the north of Masham, had particular appeal to Highlanders, although even as late as 1856 it still was "a forest with few patches cleared."[62]

Ronald Rankin knew of people on Lord MacDonald's estate in Moidart (Inverness-shire) who were preparing to leave for Low Township in 1850 where land "will be sold at 8 shillings per acre in four instalments…the lots are generally of 100 acres.[63] Wishing he "could get a map of Canada on a large-scale," he clearly did not realize that Low was located many miles inland up the Gatineau River.[64] But he knew that it had "a priest who speaks Gaelic and it is well-watered and most fertile." Knowing "some of the Moidarts" who had already settled in Glengarry "and got employment there," he wished "that most of the Moidart people were along with them. The prospects at home are very gloomy indeed."[65] The Potato Famine had hit the Highlands by this time and large-scale depopulation was following in its wake. With this crisis came a large increase in emigration, some of which was compulsory, and most of which was financially assisted by landlords.[66] Rankin believed that there was "no alternative but emigration. Let the emigration be directed to Canada and the people behind will continue to follow."[67]

Archibald McMillan's colonizing efforts were far more successful in Grenville Township, although additional factors were at work along this stretch of the Ottawa River. Chatham, just to the east of Grenville, acquired its first Highlanders in the late eighteenth century when former soldiers, who had served in the Royal Highland Emigrants Regiment during the American War of Independence, took possession of free land grants offered by the government. Malcolm Fraser, owner of the Mount Murray seigneury, obtained his ex-officer's grant of 3,000 acres in Chatham three years after the war ended, and there were probably others like him. There was also an additional proprietor in the area who favoured Scots. Sir John Johnson, had fled from New York to Montréal during the American Revolution with the large group of Highlanders who went on to found the Glengarry settlements. Becoming the owner of the Argenteuil seigneury, lying just to the east of Chatham Township, he was apparently "ever on the alert to invite the attention of the newcomers to the advantages and the attractions of his domain" and such people were invariably Scottish.[68]

When he came to Grenville in 1832, Joseph Bouchette was full of praise for the emigrant Scots who had "improved and cultivated a large portion" of it.[69] And the *"Augmentation de Grenville,"*[70] which represented a later extension of the township's western boundary, had also become another magnet for Scots, receiving its first arrivals in 1816.[71] Lying just to the north of the major Highland settlements in Glengarry, Grenville could be regarded as a close neighbour, while Lochaber and Templeton townships, being far more distant, were remote outposts. In this way, Glengarry's success and enormous pulling power probably benefited Grenville. At the time of Bouchette's visit, its total population was five times greater than Lochaber's.[72]

Grenville's major Scottish settlements developed along the still recognizable "Scotch Road," which runs inland from Grenville Bay to Harrington Township (Figure 7). Harrington, lying just to the north of Grenville, also experienced a sizeable Scottish influx. By 1861 an amazing eighty per cent of its inhabitants had Church of Scotland affiliations. Davisville, or "the Scotch settlement,"[73] to the north of Brownsburg in Chatham, had acquired its first Scots by 1820 and twelve years later

Chatham's population had reached 1,073.[74] The Reverend William Mair became the first Presbyterian minister of the combined congregation of Grenville and Chatham in 1833. He "had two substantial stone churches erected but while they were being built, he received little or nothing from his people in the way of stipend."[75] However, his congregation, "the oldest in the district," was later said to be "composed of a great number of farmers in easy circumstances."[76] The congregation seemed to suit him and he served as minister until his death in 1860. In addition to the Church of Scotland worshippers, both townships also had some Scottish Catholics. When, in 1827, the French inhabitants of the Petite-Nation seigneury appealed for a resident priest, Archibald McMillan called a meeting of the Irish and Scottish Catholics in Grenville and Chatham. They agreed to help support a priest, while McMillan went a stage further and donated land for a Catholic church.[77]

Meanwhile, by the early 1800s, the nearby seigneury of Argenteuil was acquiring its Scottish communities at St. Andrews and Lachute. The first footholds had been established under Major James Murray, who owned the seigneury before Sir John Johnson obtained it in 1814. Murray actively sought Scottish compatriots and John Cameron, from Inverness, was his first recruit at St. Andrews.[78] Arriving in 1802, he was followed two years later by two brothers from Glasgow, although afterwards St. Andrews mainly attracted Highlanders.[79] A few Scottish Lowlanders had settled in Lachute by 1809 and they were followed nine years later by a larger group of Paisley weavers.[80] They were some of the first arrivals from the Glasgow and Paisley textile districts in Scotland. The introduction of power looms and the growing influx of poorly paid migrant workers to the Clyde region had created catastrophic conditions for hand-loom weavers. Having been faced with very low wage rates or redundancy, many of them were emigrating.[81]

Scottish concentrations grew even further under Johnson's period of tenure.[82] Given that he only offered feudal tenancies, it seems surprising that that his land became so attractive to emigrant Scots. Generally, they wanted to be owner and master of their own farms. Nonetheless, for those people with little capital, seigneurial tenure had its advantages. Only nominal rents were charged and it was the seigneur who took on the burden of providing buildings, roads, mills and other amenities. The McOuat and Bilsland families, who originated from Dunbartonshire and Stirlingshire, were typical of the emigrant farmers who settled in this seigneury.[83] Arriving in 1818, they and their extended families settled in and around Lachute and Upper Lachute, while one family went to Brownsburg, just to the south of Davisville, in the neighbouring Township of Chatham.

Lachute soon acquired "a small colony of thrifty, industrious farmers…, who brought not only the best system of agriculture practised in the Lothians,…but who also brought the best and most improved agricultural implements…and in a short time the desert…blossomed as the rose."[84] The Reverend Archibald Henderson, a Presbyterian minister from Edinburgh, was installed at St. Andrews in 1818. He remained there for some forty-nine years, while Lachute acquired Reverend William Brunton, its first minister, in 1831.[85] "There was now an abundance of clerical provisions for, on the same day with Mr. Henderson and in the same building, the Reverend Joseph Abbott of the Church of England began his labours. For a time the two congregations held their services at different hours on the Lord's Day in the village schoolhouse, the Presbyterians meeting in the forenoon and the Episcopalians in the afternoon."[86]

Sir John Johnson (1741–1830), born near Amsterdam, New York. During the American Revolution he raised and commanded the King's Royal Regiment of New York, whose members included the Inverness-shire Scots who later settled at Glengarry. Johnson owned beautiful manor houses at Argenteuil and Monnoir (to the east of Chambly) and accumulated considerable property in both Upper and Lower Canada. Portrait by an unknown artist. *Courtesy of Library and Archives Canada C-088436.*

When Joseph Bouchette came to the seigneury in 1832, he found a population of 2,800, "who were chiefly Episcopalians and Presbyterians." The concessions in St. Andrews, along the Ottawa River, were "the most numerous and perhaps the best cultivated" but the area to the north around Lachute also "exhibited strong indications of a thriving industry."[87] Gore Township, immediately to the north of Argenteuil seigneury, had not yet been surveyed. One of its early settlers, who was of Scottish/Irish descent, could remember when he and his family first arrived from St. Andrews East. "Father was induced to go up north...and locate a new home" in order to provide for his large family.[88] The family went on to establish a farm in Lakefield and "lumbering being the chief industry, my father and brothers logged during the winter months"[89] (Figure 7). Making his way to Lakefield, probably sometime in the 1850s, he walked the 15-mile distance with his parents and grandfather, who "carried a feather bed...Uncle Richard walked [also] and Granny carried the baby and a sword."[90]

Terrebonne seigneury, located to the east of Gore, also attracted Scots and once again the driving force behind their presence was a Scottish proprietor. An additional factor in Terrebonne's appeal was its proximity to Montréal, the operational centre of the North West Company's fur trade business, which was dominated by Scots. Purchasing Terrebonne seigneury in 1802, Simon McTavish, the head of the North West Company, turned it into a major supply centre for fur trade canoe brigades.[91] He established a store, two flour mills and a factory which supplied biscuits to the North West Company. Eventually, much of Terrebonne's industry was devoted to satisfying the provisioning requirements of the brigades. McTavish also invested in the timber

Simon McTavish (1750–1804). Born near Inverness, he was the son of a lieutenant in the Fraser's Highlanders. Rising from humble beginnings, he became the leading light of the North West Company and was Lower Canada's most important businessman during the second half of the eighteenth century. His elegance and cleverness earned him the nickname of "Marquis." This early 20th century copy is by Donald Richings Hill. *Courtesy of McCord Museum of Canadian History, Montréal M1587.*

trade, setting up a sawmill and encouraging the manufacture of barrels.[92]

Terrebonne seigneury was later purchased by another Scottish fur trader, Roderick Mackenzie. Having lived in Terrebonne since the early 1800s, he purchased it in 1814 from the estate of Simon McTavish, although he had to relinquish it eight years later following a legal challenge by McTavish's widow. Mackenzie, who like McTavish was born near Inverness, had previously worked as an assistant to his first cousin, the explorer Sir Alexander Mackenzie of the fur trading company of Gregory, MacLeod and Company. When the firm joined the North West

Company, Roderick Mackenzie's career quickly progressed. He was put in charge of Fort Chipewyan at the southwestern end of Lake Athabaska, and by 1795 was made a partner of the North West Company.[93] By this time he had married a Native woman "according to the custom of the country," by whom he had at least three children. He later married Marie-Loiuse-Rachel Chaboillez the Roman Catholic daughter of fur trader, Charles Jean Baptiste Chaboillez. They had at least five children.[94] His arrival in Terrebonne marked the end of his fur trading days and the beginning of a new life managing the affairs of his estate.[95]

When Joseph Bouchette visited Terrebonne in 1815, he noted the "150 well built houses of wood and stone, beside the church and parsonage house, the seigneural house and the mansion of Roderick Mackenzie, which is worthy of remark for the elegance of its construction; indeed there are several houses in a very superior style to be found in this village, it being a favoured spot, where many gentlemen, who have realized large fortunes in the North West Company fur trade retire to enjoy the comforts and luxuries of private life."[96] He also observed that Terrebonne was "a place of some traffic, occasioned by the continued influx of persons bringing grain to the mills from distant parts and by large exports of flour that annually take place; in consequence many of the residents are traders and artizans whose commercial concerns impose a degree of consequence upon the village."[97] It clearly was a thriving, well-populated place.

Scots had almost certainly gone to live in the seigneury during the period when Simon McTavish owned it. Given the well-known clannishness of Scots, the British element of his workforce was probably entirely Scottish. A substantial Scottish influx occurred in 1820 when large numbers of former weavers arrived from Glasgow and Paisley. Wishing to save the expense of a long journey and learning that Roderick Mackenzie had a large tract of unoccupied land in the northern part of Terrebonne, they applied for it in one group and were successful.[98] By 1824 some sixty-seven householders had settled on both sides of the Rivière L'Achigan, over a distance of six miles.[99] There were few roads and the nearest mill was nine miles away.[100] However, when Joseph Bouchette visited the area eight years later, he noticed that it "is settling fast."[101] The present site of New Glasgow and the two Paisley Concessions to the south west of it,[102] commemorate the geographical origins of these early settlers. A petition in support of Lord Dalhousie, which was signed in 1827 by the

inhabitants of New Glasgow,[103] reveals a predominance of Scottish surnames among the 200 family heads listed (Appendix II).

The combined efforts of Scottish-born proprietors and ex-servicemen
helped to create the conditions which gave townships along the north
side of the Ottawa River and north of Montréal their Scottish communities. Highlanders had been attracted to the banks of the Ottawa River
and to the St. Andrew's area, while Lowlanders had settled at and around
Lachute and Terrebonne seigneury.[104] Although they were clustered
together in distinct groups, they rarely survived as the dominant element in a township. By 1861 the Terrebonne Scots were a tiny proportion
of the total population, and, by this time, New Glasgow had become
Ste Sophie. Grenville's Presbyterian Scots accounted for just under 30
per cent of its population while in Lochaber, Chatham, Masham and
Wakefield they represented only around 20 per cent of the inhabitants.[105]
Archibald McMillan succeeded in bringing many Highlanders to Lower
Canada, but Glengarry always had the greater appeal.[106]

As the spread of settlement moved south and west of Montréal, Scots
streamed into the townships and seigneuries in the Chateauguay Valley. Its accessibility, good land and timber trade opportunities made it
a highly desirable location and as economic conditions in Scotland
declined with the ending of the Napoleonic Wars, Scots came in large
numbers. The region's timber collecting rivers and bays would soon
acquire their many distinctive Scottish communities.

Four

SOUTH AND WEST OF MONTRÉAL

In 1818 a beginning was made, and the experiences of the venturing spirits who led the way were eagerly read. Their letters were passed from family to family in the parishes they had left. They told of good land in the west, where every man could win a farm by hard work. Repugnance to emigration wore away and gave place to eagerness to begin life anew beyond the Atlantic.[1]

WITH THE ENDING OF THE Napoleonic Wars in 1815, much of Scotland was gripped by a severe economic depression. Glowing reports from people who had emigrated earlier of the opportunities to be had in British America became a powerful inducement to the many Scots who wished to escape from their poverty. The initial exodus, beginning from the late eighteenth century, had been directed primarily to the eastern Maritimes, but by the early 1820s eastern Upper Canada was rapidly gaining in popularity. Glengarry had been attracting Highlanders for decades while the government-sponsored military settlements, which were established in the nearby Rideau Valley from 1815, created enduring emigrant streams which drew Scots in their hundreds to this one region.

The continuing search for land soon led emigrant Scots to the Chateauguay Valley lying a short distance to the east. Here they would be won over by "the general goodness of the land, the variety of timber of every description, among which oak, elm, pine and beech are in great quantities," the extensive waterways through which felled timber could be brought to the St. Lawrence and the "easy access by main roads" to the United States.[2] They came in small groups, over a period of twenty to thirty years, settling in the broad belts of land along which lumbering operations could be carried out, thereby establishing their "Petite Écosse."[3] Becoming concentrated in large stretches of Huntingdon County and the Beauharnois seigneury, they settled primarily along the banks of the Trout, Chateauguay and St. Louis rivers, and along the major tributaries which flowed into them (Figure 8).[4]

The Scottish influx had begun in 1802 with the arrival of settlers from Fife. Before this time the Chateauguay region had been attracting most of its new inhabitants from the New England states of Vermont, New Hampshire and Massachusetts. Forming scattered communities, they had settled as squatters on the vast expanse of wilderness to be found west of

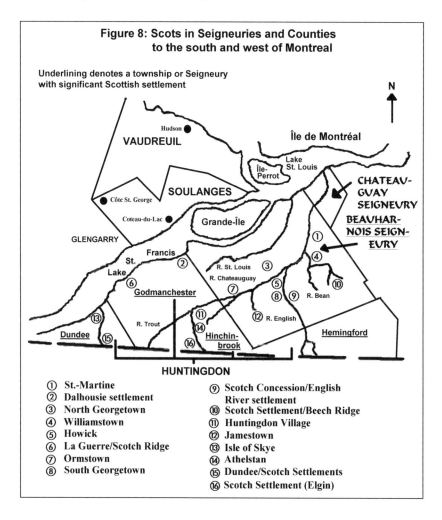

Figure 8: Scots in Seigneuries and Counties to the south and west of Montreal

Underlining denotes a township or Seigneury with significant Scottish settlement

① St.-Martine
② Dalhousie settlement
③ North Georgetown
④ Williamstown
⑤ Howick
⑥ La Guerre/Scotch Ridge
⑦ Ormstown
⑧ South Georgetown
⑨ Scotch Concession/English River settlement
⑩ Scotch Settlement/Beech Ridge
⑪ Huntingdon Village
⑫ Jamestown
⑬ Isle of Skye
⑭ Athelstan
⑮ Dundee/Scotch Settlements
⑯ Scotch Settlement (Elgin)

the Richelieu River.[5] Few of them had come as Loyalists. The British government's policy of keeping British settlers out of French-held territory
had prevented it from adopting its normal practice of moving Loyalists
to vulnerable boundary areas. Following their arrival from the United
States to the province during the American War of Independence, most
Loyalists had been moved on to Upper Canada. The few who did remain
had moved west from the banks of the Richelieu River and made clear-
ings for themselves in the eastern part of Huntingdon County, thus
establishing small hamlets in what would become Hemingford Township.[6] However, the government had also made a half-hearted attempt to
attract loyal British settlers to the empty expanses in Huntingdon County
with the granting of much of Godmanchester Township and a part of
Hinchinbrook Township to veterans of the American War, although very
few of these ex-soldiers actually took up their grants and settled.[7]

The Fife settlers, who had arrived in 1802, originated from an area
of the eastern Lowlands where "the spirit of emigration to America"
had taken hold.[8] Because of the "stagnation of almost every branch of
trade," Dundee's linen exports had declined sharply and the resulting
economic crisis was causing great numbers of people in the region to
emigrate.[9] The exodus from Fife to the Chateauguay Valley, probably
fuelled by these adverse conditions, brought some of the first British
settlers to the region. They purchased farms from earlier settlers and,
having knowledge of advanced agricultural methods, they soon created
successful settlements along stretches of the Chateauguay River.[10] After
the increase in transatlantic fares, which took effect in 1803, and the
onset of the Napoleonic Wars in that year, Scottish emigration declined
sharply. And when the United States actually invaded Canada in 1812,
it was stopped dead in its tracks.

While most of the War of 1812–14 was fought in the interior regions
of Upper Canada, a major American offensive against Montréal had
taken place in 1813 along the Chateauguay River between Ormstown
and Howick. Although this, the so-called Battle of Chateauguay, ended
in defeat for the United States, before this battle the Americans had
looked set to win the war.

The loyalty of the large American populations in Upper and Lower
Canada was always in doubt since it was felt that they were likely to
welcome invading American troops as liberators. Moreover, because

Battle of Chateauguay—reproduced in *Le Journal de Dimanche*, June 24, 1884.
Courtesy of Library and Archives Canada C-003297.

Britain was engaged in the Napoleonic Wars, its military response had to be limited to the forces at hand in North America. But of crucial importance to Britain's eventual success was the loyalty of the French Canadians. Despite attempts made by French agents to rouse French Canada to favour the Americans, it staunchly supported Britain's war effort.[11] The much-acclaimed Voltigeurs Canadiens, the first French-Canadian regiment of regular soldiers, which was raised under the leadership of Charles-Michel de Salaberry, a Canadian lieutenant-colonel in the British Army, played a crucial role in the war. Scots were also prominent in the militia raised before and during the conflict, with the most conspicuous being the Glengarry Light Infantry Fencible Regiment, composed almost entirely of Inverness-shire Scots.[12] Clothed as British units in green uniforms, but equipped with muskets, they were particularly effective skirmishers.[13]

The turning point in the war came with the battles fought in the autumn of 1813 at Chateauguay in Lower Canada and at Crysler's Farm, near present-day Morrisburg in Upper Canada. A small but efficient army, consisting of British, English-Canadian and French-Canadian regulars as well as local militia, repelled the advancing forces.[14] The Voltigeurs Canadiens fought under de Salaberry's command in both battles. Lieutenant-Colonel George Macdonell led the Glengarry Regiment to the Chateauguay region to fight alongside the other forces.[15]

George Macdonell (1780–1870) —known as "Red George," because of his fiery temperament. He led the assault at Ogdensburg in 1813 which ended its occupation by American forces and supported de Salaberry in the Battle of Chateauguay fought on 26th of October, 1813. A Roman Catholic, he married the Honourable Lady Arundel in 1820 and lies buried at the Arundel mansion, known as New Wardour Castle, in Wiltshire, England. Portrait by an unknown artist. *Courtesy of Library and Archives Canada C-019719.*

Together they stopped a determined attempt by the Americans to cut the St Lawrence River supply lines between Montréal and Upper Canada and in so doing changed the course of the war.

Although many armed forces had fought in the Battle of Chateauguay, some later French historians, like Sir Joseph Amable Thomas Chapais, declared that the outcome had been a French victory: "It was ours and no-one can take it from us…Chateauguay was the assertion of our undeniable loyalty and ardent patriotism. Chateauguay was an heroic illustration of our national spirit…Salaberry, and his gallant men, gave to English arms a thing of no small glory—a French victory."[16]

Once peace returned to the Canadas and the Napoleonic Wars had ended, hundreds of Scots began arriving in eastern Upper Canada. Bleak economic conditions in Scotland were stimulating emigration as were the considerable inducements to emigrate being offered by the government. Having nearly lost its North American colonies to the United States, the government was desperate to minimize the continuing threat from the south by moving loyal British civilians to key defensive areas. Departing from its normal policy of requiring emigrants to be self-financing, the government introduced a subsidized emigration scheme in 1815, which was targeted specifically at Scots. Seven hundred people, almost all Scots, received free transport, free provisions and free land so that they would relocate themselves in the newly surveyed Rideau Valley military settlements and the more long-established Glengarry communities lying to the east of them. Similar schemes were offered to Scots in 1818 and in the early 1820s, although these were far less generous.[17]

Even though the government refused adamantly to subsidize further emigration, the influx to eastern Upper Canada grew rapidly. While the Rideau Valley, being an untamed wilderness, had extensive tracts to offer settlers, most of the land in the Glengarry area had already been allocated and what was left was often inferior. Since Lower Canada could be reached by simply going to the opposite side of Lake St. Francis, it soon attracted attention from land-hungry settlers (Figure 8). The seventeen families from Duirinish on Lord MacLeod's estate in Skye, who arrived in Glengarry in 1816, were one of the first Scottish groups to seek land across the Upper Canada border.[18] In their 1818 petition to the government they complained that "the situation of such lands as they could then obtain…in [eastern] Upper Canada" was "very inconvenient."[19] However, when nine of the families discovered that they could lease land in Lower Canada, in "the Indian reservation, …which extended from the village of St. Régis[20] to the western limit of the town of Godmanchester," they decided to move and found a new settlement.[21]

Seven of the Skye families accepted leases of 100-acre lots from the Indian Chiefs along the Salmon River, in an area which came to be known as "the Indian reservation of Kintail."[22] A prime attraction had been "the magnificent timber that fringed the Salmon River…for oaks 5 feet across, and pines unequalled in quality elsewhere, grew upon the knolls that bordered it."[23] The initial family heads: William Campbell, Angus McGillis, John Tolmie, Ranald McDonell, Angus MacDonald, Norman McDonell and William McPhie[24] were joined in 1820 by Roderick Murchison, Duncan Stewart, Duncan McNicol and three McMillans. Together they, with their families, established the Isle of Skye settlement[25] along the lakeshore on the 1st concession of what became Dundee Township (Huntingdon County). With the exception of the Tolmie and McGillis families, the founding Skye families remained in the area.[26]

Assistance was provided to the Skye settlers by their Glengarry neighbours who "often came over to help by bees."[27] When the Perthshire-born John Davidson came to the area he established himself as a storekeeper and soon dominated the area's economic life. His business associations with Dundee in Scotland, which he developed before emigrating, led to the Dundee name being given to the township and to the other Scottish communities, that formed later along the Salmon River near the

American border (Figure 8). Two prominent settlements were founded, one at Dundee Centre and the other at Aubrey's Corners,[28] a short distance away, while Scots also established hamlets at Bittern Island and La Petite-Chenail at the western end of Dundee Township.

Dundee Township almost certainly attracted further Skye settlers after 1820. Ship arrivals at Québec from Tobermory, the principal Western Isle port, were regular occurrences throughout the 1820s and 1830s. The general economic depression and the collapse of traditional kelp markets by the mid-1820s was stimulating a growing exodus from the Western Isles.[29] The impoverished inhabitants of Lord MacLeod's estate in Bracadale, in Skye, were seeking financial help from the government to emigrate in 1825–26 and four years later the *Mary* of Newcastle actually called at Loch Snizort in Skye for passengers to take them to Québec.[30] Some of the *Mary*'s passengers were probably destined for the Skye settlements in Dundee Township. This may have prompted Donald Murchison's request to the Colonial Office for free grants of land "for each family head and a son of each family" in either Cape Breton or Québec.[31] Representing a group from Bernisdale, in Duirinish parish, he described "the reduction of our circumstances [which] induces us to banish ourselves and families from our native and lovely country to these distant colonies of the Kingdom, entirely unknown to us, with the sole view of supporting our numerous offspring."[32] Although his request for help would have been refused, the large number of Murchison tombstones in the Isle of Skye cemetery[33] suggests that Donald Murchison eventually found the means to emigrate to Lower Canada.[34]

The settlements in Dundee Township became sufficiently well-established to attract a resident Presbyterian minister, who came through the auspices of the Glasgow Colonial Society. Having been born in the Highlands but educated in Glasgow, the Reverend Duncan Moody had the essential talent of being able to speak Gaelic.[35] He arrived in 1832 and tended to his congregation even though "the people were too poor to build a church and even if they had been able, it would have been of little service, for the roads were such that they were rarely fit for travel."[36] The Reverend Moody suffered "under the disadvantage of no church being built and having four different stations at which to officiate," and regularly made arduous journeys from one end of the township to the other as well as to the neighbouring Township of Godmanchester.[37] Having met initially in Malcolm Smith's house, the congregation built its first church in 1839 on lot 8 of the 2nd concession:

> It was a plain, frame building, and all the congregation was able to do was to enclose it. The seats were slabs laid out on four water-beech legs and the only one that had a back was the pew for the minister's family…. In the forenoon the service was in Gaelic, the English in the afternoon, and both [being] extremely long, which was rather trying where the seats were so contrived that they neither supported the back nor rendered a few winks possible.[38]

The Reverend Moody coped well with his straggling congregation although, "being city-bred, he knew nothing about farming" and when he wanted a horse Mrs. Moody had to harness it.[39] "He could make little use of the animal in his rounds for the roads, except in the driest times or in winter, were only passable on foot."[40] His furthest preaching station at La Guerre (Godmanchester Township)[41] required a "most fatiguing journey."[42] There he spoke to the settlers of the so-called "Scotch Ridge," which had become established on the west side of La Guerre (Figure 8).[43] In addition he probably also made occasional visits to the "Scotch Settlement" at Beaver Creek, in southwest Godmanchester.[44] He received little financial support from his congregation, apart from "presents of produce and aiding in bees," and thus "was no burden to his people." Not surprisingly he is remembered as having done "more to recommend the gospel to his people by his daily life than by his preaching."[45]

A winter scene in Chateauguay, painted by John Philip c. 1838–41. *Courtesy of Library and Archives Canada C-011855.*

By the early 1820s thousands of people from the Lanarkshire and
Renfrewshire textile districts in Scotland were pouring into eastern
Upper Canada. The introduction of power looms and falling wage rates
had created appalling conditions for hand-loom weavers and many of
them were emigrating. Acting collectively by forming themselves into
emigration societies, whole communities raised money from local bene-
factors and the government to fund their resettlement costs. The schemes
which supported them were aimed at bringing people to the military
settlements being established in the Rideau Valley.[46] However, former
weavers with the means to finance their own emigration costs could act
independently and some of them sought the better land prospects which
the Chateauguay Valley could offer.[47]

Godmanchester Township (Huntingdon County) began attracting
former weavers and tradesmen from 1820. Twenty-one heads of households, who originated mainly from Glasgow and Paisley, were the first
to arrive.[48] Having already refused Roderick Mackenzie's offer of land
in Terrebonne, because "they could not obtain an absolute title and would
have to pay a small perpetual rent," and rejecting the Eastern Townships because "desirable lands" there were held by companies who asked
extortionate prices," the emigrants opted for the shoreline along Lake
St. Francis.[49] On Joseph Bouchette's advice they squatted in the area
between Port Lewis and Hungry Bay, where they hoped eventually to
get secure lots once the township was surveyed. There they founded the
Dalhousie settlement named after Lord Dalhousie, in recognition of his
help and support.[50]

James Hamilton had first visited an uncle in Vermont before joining
the Dalhousie settlement.[51] "We thought very little of Vermont. On coming back to Montreal and hearing where our friends had gone we
determined to join them."[52] Because all of the lake frontage was already
occupied, they had to go inland south of Teafield, where they settled on
the 4th concession:

> We raised a shanty, and fitted the ground for a crop by hewing down
> trees, lopping off the branches, and planting potatoes and corn
> between the logs. We had bought potatoes in Glengarry and corn in
> Fort Covington [United States]. As we had to carry everything on
> our backs, neither horse nor ox being able to pass Teafield, we cut

the potatoes into seed, to make the burden less. As it was, we sank to our knees in water in places. My brother carried a grindstone on one of our trips, the heaviest load ever so brought.[53]

After a disastrous fire that destroyed their shanty, the Hamilton family moved further south to the Hinchinbrook side of the Chateauguay River, becoming the first British settlers in the area. Meanwhile, the newly established inhabitants of the Dalhousie settlement were being forced to leave their farms. To their dismay they discovered that most of Godmanchester Township had been acquired by Edward Ellice as a result of purchases made by his father of the vast tracts of land, which had been granted previously by the government to American War veterans. A fur baron, merchant banker and property speculator, Ellice was a formidable opponent.[54] His Montréal agents told the Dalhousie settlers that "they had either to buy or leave."[55] Having "no money," the settlers left in 1823 and, with Lord Dalhousie's help, they acquired new lots further south in what would later become Elgin Township.[56] "Thus ended in disaster the Dalhousie settlement,[57] whose early days were so promising...furnishing an early warning...of allowing Crown lands to pass into the hands of other than actual settlers."[58]

By 1824 the "Scotch Settlement"[59] in Elgin Township was taking shape. Thomas Danskin, the son of a Cumbernauld (Dunbartonshire) weaver and one of eleven brothers, joined the group in 1827 and became the area's first schoolmaster. "He entered upon his duties at once and, until a schoolhouse could be built, he moved from one neighbour to another...teaching a week in each shanty, the scholars following him."[60] Elgin soon acquired Clyde's Corners, named after William Clyde who settled there in 1826. A number of other hamlets with Scottish names also sprouted up, including Beith, named after an Ayrshire parish, Kelso named after a Roxburghshire parish and Kelvingrove named after an area of Glasgow. Such place names reflect the predominantly Lowland origins of the early inhabitants.[61] By 1861 over half of Elgin Township's population had Presbyterian affiliations.

Having moved to Hinchinbrook Township (Huntingdon County), James Hamilton and his family were unaffected by the demise of the Dalhousie settlement. As one of the earliest settlers in the area, James was having to cope with the burdensome demands of pioneer life:

In November I went to Pointe Claire for a cow, which a relation of my wife's, Robert Benning, had secured for me, and this I led by a rope of withes, carrying a load of 16 lbs. on my back, and driving a ewe lamb. Such was the state of the road, or rather track, that it was after dark when I reached Dewittville.... The night was so dark that I could only tell where I was by throwing chips into the river and being guided by the sound of their splashes.[62]

As James Hamilton would soon discover, Edward Ellice owned his land as well, but, having acquired capital, he was able to pay the $360 being demanded for it. This was a sizeable sum although, as an anonymous letter writer pointed out in a Dumfriesshire newspaper, the land "on the banks of the Chateauguay River" was particularly fertile.[63] "In all my travels, no place has appeared where the land and situation are so good...or where farms can be purchased at so cheap a rate."[64] Reports like this helped to generate a steady influx of Scots to the region and by the time of the 1831 Census an amazing 90 per cent of Hinchinbrook's population had Presbyterian affiliations.

However, Hinchinbrook did not please everyone. James Aitcheson, the 24-year-old son of an affluent Edinburgh brewer, who had been sent to Hinchinbrook to experience pioneer farming, was disappointed by the poor state of the roads and by the sight of tree stumps that "are left standing in the fields."[65] His father's hope that his son would come to appreciate the benefits of life on a farm did not materialize and he soon floundered. After leaving Hinchinbrook, he made a faltering attempt to establish a farm in Tilbury, Upper Canada, then launched a number of businesses all of which failed, fell into debt and, to escape imprisonment, fled to the United States.[66]

With such a rapidly growing Scottish population in Hinchinbrook, it is hardly surprising that the Reverend W. Montgomery Walker would have "the largest flock of any in this quarter—his commanding talents as a popular preacher have increased his congregation to an extent beyond the accommodation of the church lately built."[67] In addition to his principal church at Huntingdon village,[68] Walker also preached at Athelstan[69] and the "Scotch settlements" at Elgin.[70] The full extent of the Scottish presence in the area can be seen in the 1827 petition offering support to Lord Dalhousie. Most of the combined inhabitants of

Hinchinbrook, Godmanchester and St. Regis (Dundee), who signed this document, had Scottish surnames (see Appendix III).[71]

Scots had flocked to the Beauharnois seigneury[72] in spite of its apparent drawbacks of only offering leasehold lots to settlers and being owned by Edward Ellice.[73] Robert Sellar claimed that Scots would only settle in townships "where British and not French laws prevailed," but that was clearly not the case. And however much emigrant Scots may have blamed Ellice for the downfall of the Dalhousie settlement, it did not affect their willingness to rent his land. They were attracted by the prospect of settling along a fine river like the Chateauguay or one of its tributaries, and benefiting from the region's good farming opportunities and booming timber trade. The revenue from cut timber or potash would tide people over "until the

Miniature by William Charles Ross of Katherine Jane Ellice (1814–1864), wife of Edward Ellice's only son Edward (1810–1880). Edwardstown in Beauharnois seigneury (now Ste-Clotilde) was named after him. *Courtesy of Library and Archives Canada C-131638.*

clearing yielded enough to maintain the settler's family."[74] The favourable terms which Ellice offered, of a three-year rent-free period followed by an annual rent of $10, were added inducements as was his investment in buildings, which included mills, schools, churches, post offices, taverns, and a court house.[75] His funding of road construction and a model farm complete with imported breeding stock were further benefits.

By the 1830s the seigneury's Scottish population was sufficiently large to support two resident Presbyterian ministers. The Presbyterian church at South Georgetown, "one of the prettiest country churches in the province," was being built entirely at Ellice's expense. It was "a gift to the Protestants of this densely peopled Catholic country," which, according to their minister Reverend Walter Roach, "cannot be too highly praised."[76] And Ellice also gave Ormstown's Presbyterian congregation a 50-acre grant "for the benefit of a Clergyman in connection with the Church of Scotland. A sum was subscribed by the people amounting to £100…In June last, accordingly, the exterior of the building was commenced, and in the beginning of September the interior part; so that it is now comparatively commodious; but not yet seated. Each family has provided for itself a moveable bench. It is a wooden building, plastered inside, and stands 48 by 38 feet."[77]

By 1832 some three hundred and thirty-six Scottish families were living in the Beauharnois seigneury.[78] Lowlanders were to be found at Ormstown, Jamestown,[79] North and South Georgetown,[80] the English River settlement and Williamstown, while a Highland community had formed at Beechridge. The so-called "Scotch Concession"[81] in the English River settlement, which was founded in 1821–22 by "intelligent and industrious" tradesmen and shepherds, held its first ploughing match by 1827.[82] Donald Cameron's family, from Argyll, were among the first Scots to settle along the Bean River at Williamstown, arriving in 1832. His son, Archibald, could remember how "the settlement grew rapidly during the three years after we arrived...My father set up a forge and got all the work he could do, while the other settlers did fairly well. A great quantity of potash was made, and neighbouring settlers sold their ashes to those who dwelt on the Bean River, from their facilities for leaching. The river was not the shallow stagnant creek it now is but had water enough to float large timber down."[83]

When Joseph Bouchette reported that some parts of the seigneury were "entirely British," he really meant that they were almost entirely Scottish.[84] Having to travel to many preaching stations, Reverend Roach had a good appreciation of the extent of the Scottish influx:

No part of the Lower Province is more thickly populated with the Scotch than the Chateauguay [River], which taking its rise in the State of New York, winds its course through upwards of 60 miles of the most rich and fertile lands of Lower Canada, till it falls into the waters of the Saint Lawrence, a little above Montréal.... Georgetown, Ormstown, Huntingdon, Hinchinbrook and Trout River are following one another in regular succession...all of them wholly peopled with Scotch with a few exceptions of Americans....

Within six miles of Huntingdon alone there are not fewer than two hundred families who at present have not suitable instruction...in Hemingford, according to the Census of 1831 there were 1557 souls, of whom the great majority are Presbyterians...in Beechridge and places adjoining there are not fewer than 150 families firmly attached to the Scottish Kirk, for whom the majority being Highlanders, a

Gaelic preacher is prerequisite. In Ormstown there are not fewer than one hundred and twenty families, Presbyterians who have commenced building a church. All this I have from observation, that whole tract of country, comprising not less than one thousand square miles, having been mostly travelled over by myself.[85]

The Reverend Roach's congregation was "scattered over 9 miles on the Chateauguay River and 11 miles on the St. Louis River,"[86] while Reverend James Anderson's Ormstown congregation,[87] "computed as eighteen square miles, contained 120 families.… They have a chapel of their own, and occasional service from a catechist who resides about 24 miles distant from Ormstown. Many of the people attend our church when they have no service of their own. The number of Roman Catholics is very small. Our people are chiefly Scotch."

In addition to conducting services at their own churches, Reverend Roach and Reverend Anderson took turns tending to the spiritual needs of some 167 Highlanders who lived further to the east at Beechridge:

In their zeal and anxiety to obtain a Minister they have swelled their subscription list to the amount of £75. But alas would it ever be realized? And yet…as must such a congregation be continually destitute of pastoral instruction. The people in that quarter have in a special manner a claim on our sympathy. Surrounded by Roman Catholics and infested with Methodist preachers from the [United] States, and many of the younger families displaying much ignorance in the doctrines and

The Seigneury of Beauharnois, in 1838, painted by Katherine Jane Ellice. *Courtesy of Library and Archives Canada C-013370.*

scriptural facts of the Bible. Yet bound by all the hereditary attachment characteristic of Highlanders to the Church of Scotland, they claim an interest in our endeavours and in our prayers.[88]

By 1837 the Beechridge congregation was "fitted up" with a Gaelic minister in the person of Mr. McPherson."[89] Most of the people were, in fact, Highland migrants from Chambly who had relocated themselves to the Beauharnois seigneury in 1816. Having sailed on the *Neptune* from Loch Nevis, near Fort William in 1802, they had parted from the main group, who had settled at Glengarry, and moved to Sir John Johnson's Chambly seigneury, lying just to the east of Montréal. According to Lord Selkirk, who met Johnson a year later, some twenty to thirty families had been "induced" to go to Chambly.[90] However, "the land was so wet that the Highlanders could make nothing of it," so they moved. Some rejoined their family and friends at Glengarry while others went to Beauharnois, where they founded the "Scotch settlement" at Beechridge.[91] Surviving tombstones reveal the McCuaigs and McGillivarys who came from Glenelg (Inverness-shire), the McRaes, from Kintail (Wester Ross) the McLennans and Finlaysons from Lochalsh (Wester Ross) and the McLeods from Skye.[92]

Sir John Johnson's popularity with the 1802 *Neptune* arrivals had also enabled him to attract another group of Highlanders to his Monnoir seigneury, which adjoined Chambly. Twenty-one Highland families, thus settled, petitioned Sir Robert Shore Milnes, the Lieutenant-Governor of Lower Canada, in 1804 for financial support to be given to Norman McLeod, a schoolmaster, whose services Johnson had procured for them.[93] Having "kept a school for many years" in Glengarry and providing lessons "in their own language," he was set to do the same at Monnoir.[94] Some thirty-four Francophone settlers added their signatures to the Highlanders' petition, demonstrating remarkable solidarity between the two communities. When McLeod later moved to Beechridge, he "continued to hold school in his own house, so that the rising generation was more favoured in this than in any of the early settlements."[95]

Another group of Inverness-shire emigrants, who settled apart from their compatriots at Glengarry, opted for Lachine on the south side of Montréal Island. Forty-two of them sailed from Oban to Québec in 1804 on the brig *Commerce,* each paying relatively steep fares of £10. 10s.[96]

Lachine in 1865, painted by George Harlan White. *Courtesy of Toronto Public Library (TRL) J. Ross Robertson Collection: MTL 3025.*

After "a pleasant passage of seven weeks," John Cameron and his family travelled to his brother-in-law's house at Sorrel, where they stayed over the winter before settling at Lachine.[97] Leasing a farm "for about £30 yearly rent," Cameron wrote home stating that he now lived in "a better country for poor men than Lochaber. We are very happy here; we have a Scotch settlement here amongst the Canadians."[98] Some thirty years later Lachine had "a splendid Presbyterian Church" with the Reverend John Taylor as their minister.[99]

Meanwhile Vaudreuil County also acquired small groups of Scots, particularly at Saint-Justine, Saint-Redempteur, Saint-Marthe and Rigaud, although little is known of their geographical origins.[100] James Halcro came to Côte St. Henry, in the Rigaud seigneury, in 1813, while Peter Spence arrived in 1819. Both men originated from the Orkney Islands.[101] Given the close association between Orcadians and the fur trade, it is possible that they were former fur trade workers who decided to retire to the Montréal area.[102] And in choosing Rigaud they had come to a seigneury where the men were "chiefly voyageurs."[103] Several "Scotch and Orkney people" were certainly living in or near Montréal at the time, who were apparently "all blessing the day they left their native country."[104] While Côte St. Henry mainly attracted English settlers from Cumberland, during the 1830s it acquired two further Orcadians and four settlers from the nearby north of Scotland mainland.[105] Possibly, this was a close circle of family and friends who were being drawn to Rigaud by favourable reports.

The Chateauguay region received most of its Scots from the Low-lands. The Highland communities, which did form, owed their origins to the early and sustained popularity of Glengarry. As Glengarry filled up, the on-going search for land took Highlanders across the border into Lower Canada, some merely crossing Lake St. Francis and settling on the opposite side, while others went much further afield. The spill-over effect from Glengarry also generated the substantial Highland settlements which developed at Côte St. George and Coteau-du-Lac in Soulanges County. However, these trends were about to come to an abrupt end. As Upper Canada's interior became more accessible, it became the favoured choice of most immigrants, including Scots. Mean-while Lower Canada's continuing intake of Scots would come almost entirely from the Western Isles.

Five

THE EASTERN TOWNSHIPS

We should not be sad; rather we should be philosophical. The early settlers from the isle of Lewis were improving their lot in coming to a new country, and their children were emulating their example in cutting the umbilical cord and apron strings in seeking a new life in the more prosperous parts of the country. And, it has been said and is still repeated that most of them were and are highly regarded wherever they choose to make their abode.[1]

THE LEWIS SETTLERS OF THE Eastern Townships[2] deserve special recognition for their heroic colonization feats. Originating from near treeless peat bogs, they had few of the practical skills which would be required of them. Arriving in 1838, they were the first-time clearers of the massive forests which greeted them and within these fearsome woods they built their first houses and early communities. And in spite of the huge difficulties which they faced in adapting to their strange and forbidding surroundings, the initial Lewis settlers were optimistic about their prospects and wrote favourable reports back home. Thus began one of the largest, sustained influxes from a Hebridean island to a single area of British North America. Because huge tracts of land were available to them, whole communities were able to move and transplant themselves in their new world locations. By the 1860s Lewis settlers had colonized large swathes of land between the St. Francis River and Lake Megantic, establishing communities which stretched across six townships in two counties (Figure 9).

However, these Lewis emigrants were not the earliest Hebridean arrivals into the Eastern Townships. Inverness Township, in Megantic

County, had acquired a small group of Arran settlers in 1829, some nine years before the Lewis communities first became established. William Hendry, one of the Arran emigrants, found Inverness "very lonely to live in; sometimes you see nothing but the woods and the sky above. The winter is long and cold...."[3] Having just left the moors and rugged mountains of his homeland, it is hardly surprising that his new surroundings seemed so alien and claustrophobic. But despite his obvious homesickness, Hendry preferred his new location and hoped other members of his family would follow him. He and the other Arran settlers adapted readily to the ways of the New World and soon became land-owning farmers. The many tombstones to be found in Inverness, carrying the inscription "a native of Arran," are an on-going reminder of the immense importance which these settlers placed on their Scottish identity.

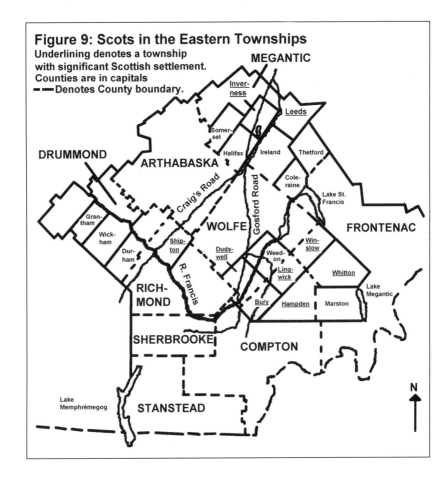

Figure 9: Scots in the Eastern Townships
Underlining denotes a township
with significant Scottish settlement.
Counties are in capitals
➖➖Denotes County boundary.

The influx from Arran had its roots in the deteriorating economic conditions which were being experienced throughout the Hebridean Islands. A general economic depression had set in with the ending of the Napoleonic Wars in 1815, but a bad situation became critical when the Hebridean kelp industry collapsed in the mid-1820s.[4] Many people faced extreme destitution. The 10th Duke of Hamilton, the proprietor of Arran, responded to these distressing conditions by clearing his estates to make way for sheep farms, a process which began in 1825. The first evictions were not accompanied by any emigration schemes, but, in 1829, when the north of the island including Glen Sannox was being cleared, the Duke offered his displaced tenants financial help to emigrate.[5] Many Arran people accepted his offer. Over the next few years some four hundred of them would settle in Baie-des-Chaleurs in New Brunswick,[6] while another three hundred would choose the Eastern Townships.

Although his tenants must have felt bitter about being uprooted, those who saw benefit in seeking better economic conditions abroad could not have had a better advocate for their cause than the Duke of Hamilton. A year before the evictions of 1829, he had written to the government seeking free land, as well as seeds and farm implements for his tenants, explaining that, although "no emigration has as yet taken place from the Island of Arran, my property," many more would follow.[7] "There are a thousand of them disposed in the hope of bettering their condition to emigrate next Spring, and in all probability many of those who remain will follow the example of their countrymen."[8] In the end the government offered free land but no other aid.

The Duke of Hamilton paid half of the fares of an initial group of twenty-six householders who would each obtain free grants of land (Table 3).[9] "Having been brought up near to the seashore," the Duke believed that his tenants were likely to want a river location. Requesting Crown land for his tenants in the Rideau Valley in Upper Canada, he was later informed that they would be granted lots along the Ottawa River in Horton Township (Renfrew County).[10] With the arrangements having been made, some seventeen Arran families (or 117 people), all from the north side of the island, set sail for Québec in the Spring of 1829. Twelve families sailed on the *Caledonia,* four on the *Albion* and one on the *Newfoundland.*[11]

TABLE 3
List of twenty-six tenants from the Duke of Hamilton's estate in Arran who are to emigrate, 1829
[PRO CO 384/22 ff. 3-5]

Family Head	No. in family	Former residence
Archibald McKillop	9	Lochranza
Archibald McKillop	7	Lochranza
Charles Murdoch, shoemaker	9	Lochranza
Archibald Kelso	8	Glen
Donald McKillop	8	Sannox
Neil McKillop	8	North Sannox
Alexander Kelso	8	North Sannox
John McKenzie	5	North Sannox
William McKenzie	6	North Sannox
Francis Logan	6	North Sannox
Robert Kelso	8	Loggantwine
Margaret Kelso, widow McMillan	3	Loggantwine
Angus Brodie	7	Loggantwine
William Kelso	7	Mid Sannox
Dugald McKenzie	4	Mid Sannox
Neil McMillan	8	South Sannox
Peter Sillars	8	South Sannox
Catherine Kelso, widow McKillop	4	Corrie
James Fullarton	7	Corrie
Peter McKillop	9	Corrie
Bill Crawford	2	Corrie
Archibald McKenzie	2	Corrie
Donald Stewart	9	Late in Margarioch
Donald McIntyre	6	Slidderie
Mrs Murchie	2	Corrie
Peter McKenzie	5	Sannox

The Arran families[12] were met at the Port of Québec by Archibald Buchanan, the immigration agent at that time, who wasted no time in "encouraging them to remain in the Lower Province."[13] They were apparently influenced by Buchanan's tales of "the prevalence of fevers in the Upper Province" and reports of the availability of good farm land near Québec City. Because of its substantial population, the city would give them markets for their farm produce. Lieutenant-Governor, Sir John

Colborne, suspected that the Arran arrivals had simply fallen prey to "a few merchants of Québec and speculators in land" who wanted "to detain all industrious settlers near their own property." While they were undoubtedly being targeted by such people, the Arran emigrants had the good sense to test out Buchanan's advice. Archibald McKillop, their leader, together with William Kelso, actually travelled to Inverness Township and, having viewed it, returned saying they were "very much satisfied."[14]

There certainly was an element of truth in Colborne's remarks. Because of the predominance of French culture, many British emigrants were reticent about settling in Lower Canada. Gaelic-speakers from Arran were oblivious to French/English differences and were therefore more susceptible to Buchanan's persuasive powers. The *Québec Gazette* could hardly contain its excitement when it learned that "several industrious families, lately arrived from Scotland, had...been forwarded to Inverness by the resident agent."[15] And it hoped more would follow. "Taking into consideration the good roads by which Leeds and Inverness [townships] can be reached, together with the shortness of the distance from Québec, the character of the soil and healthiness of the climate, we do not think a more eligible situation could be found."[16] The article, which was reprinted a month later in the *Inverness Journal,* may have helped to stimulate further arrivals from the Highlands. Buchanan's 1835 report included a reference to the "few industrious Highlanders from Islay" who had established a settlement at St. Croix seigneury, just to the north of Inverness Township.[17] "I would designate it "New Argyle," as I have good reason to believe it will increase rapidly in numbers by the friends and followers of the present founders."[18]

There was yet another factor which might have influenced the Arran settlers to move to the Eastern Townships. Nine "Scotch settlers," who had probably originated from the Hebridean island of Mull,[19] had been some of the first British settlers to arrive in the adjoining township of Leeds (Megantic County). Having successfully petitioned the government for land in 1811, while being "resident in the United States," Malcolm McLean, Neil McLean, Neil Ferguson, Angus Mclean, Archibald McLean, Archibald McKinnon, Angus Kennedy, Archibald McDonnel and Dougald McDonell, would have established themselves on farms on the 7th and 8th concessions of Leeds Township.[20] Archibald McKillop may have received reports from this earlier group and thus may have had some knowledge of local conditions. He certainly impressed the Québec immigration officials, coming

Archibald McKillop's name lives on in the road sign for "Chemin McKillop," which runs along the east side of Lake Joseph. *Photograph by Geoff Campey.*

across as "an intelligent person" who was "possessed of some capital."[21] Being "a chief among men…taller than the majority of his fellow emigrants," McKillop "could converse intelligently on many subjects and present his views with great readiness and facility of speech."[22]

Having decided to settle in Inverness, McKillop and the other householders each took up their 100-acre grants on the 2nd, 3rd and 4th concessions to the west of Lake Joseph, where they founded "New Hamilton"(Figure 10). Although it later became known as the "Scotch settlement," "Chemin Hamilton" still survives as a road name.[23] A second smaller group arrived from Arran the following year, having obtained the same terms as the 1829 group. "The men quickly became expert in the use of the axe, and seemed to take naturally to the work of chopping trees and clearing land, which was all the more remarkable since this kind of labour was new to the colonists." [24]

Being Congregationalists, the settlers began building an "old log Meeting House," completing it by 1832, and this became their first church.[25] By then, "the colony" was reported to be "now settled at Inverness…and with every prospect of success and prosperity,"[26] having "fifty dwelling houses and barns, 129 head of cattle and a large supply of wheat for sale."[27] However, a descendent of Mrs. John McKillop, who arrived with her family in 1829, paints a very different picture: "Severe hardships were suffered here the first winter as they had no idea of how cold a winter in Québec could be, so were nearly frozen to death in their hastily built houses. In fact, they would have starved to death had it not been for the kindness of the United Empire Loyalists who had settled in Maple Grove a few years previous."[28]

Thirty-five families arrived from Arran in 1831, but instead of obtaining free grants they were being required to purchase their lots (Table 4).[29] The Colonial Office refused to change its policy, in spite of strenuous efforts made by the Duke of Hamilton to have this ruling overturned.[30] The Arran settlers were being denied preferential treatment, because it was argued that granting "indulgences…in favour of the Duke of Hamilton's tenantry must operate injuriously to the interests of the Crown." Quite simply, other settlers would feel unfairly treated if they had to pay for land while the Arran emigrants continued to receive their land free of charge.[31]

TABLE 4

List of thirty-five heads of families from Arran who emigrated to Inverness Township, 1831
[PRO CO 384/28 ff.24-6]

Name	Location	Name	Location
Dugald McAllan	Lochranza	Andrew McIntyre	Slidderie
Hugh Kerr	Urinbeg	Duncan Sillars	Monyguil
Widow McKillop	Do	Peter Hamilton	Do
John Kerr	Do	John McKinnon Elder	Slidderie
Angus Robertson	Do	William Hamilton	Cloined
Archibald McKenzie	Glen	Alexander Cook	Do
Donald Kerr	Nanachar	Daniel Nicol	West Bennan
William McKenzie	Lochranza	John Cumming	Largymeanoch
John Kelso	Corrie	William Hamilton	Glenloig
Widow McKillop	Do	Archibald Fullarton	Brodick
James Stewart	North Kiscadale	Alexander Fullarton	South Blairmore
Archibald Cook	Mid Kiscadale	William Murchie	Ballymiehail
Alexander Stewart	Corriecravie	Donald Henry	Corrygills
Duncan McKelvie	Knockew	John Sillars	Maryquil
Donald Hendry Preacher		John Robertson	Kilpatrick
Alexander McKinnon	Corriecravie	Donald McDonald	Glaister
John McKinnon	Do	Donald Sillars	Maryquil
Daniel McKinnon	Do		

Many of the 1831 arrivals came from the south side of the island although they included Donald Hendry, a Congregational preacher, who originated from the north side. As the Congregationalists grew in strength and numbers, they built a second more substantial church in 1840, which was located at the intersection of the 3rd Concession and Gosford Road.[32] Donald Hendry served as their minister until his death in 1847.[33]

The Arran colonists continued to attract further emigrants from their homeland and by 1840 more than 300 Arran immigrants were living in

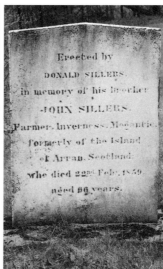

Memorials to John McKillop (1805–1871) and John Sillers (1793–1859), both from Arran, in the cemetery of the former Congregational Chapel on Chemin du Cimetière. *Photographs by Geoff Campey.*

Inverness Township.[34] They soon extended their territory to the 6th Concession, which became the site of Inverness village, the 8th Concession, which became Campbell Corners, and the 11th Concession, located to the south of Chemin Hamilton, which became Adderley (Figure 10).

Meanwhile the Presbyterian congregation in Inverness had been relying on regular visits from Glasgow Colonial Society ministers who resided in the immediate area. The Reverend Duncan Macaulay, who was based in Leeds Township, visited them in 1833 but left the area in the following year. His replacement, the Reverend James Geggie, regularly ministered to the Presbyterian Highlanders who were living in what would become Inverness village (6th Concession) and Adderley (11th Concession).[35]

Having informed the Glasgow Colonial Society Secretary in 1839 that Inverness was "a populous and destitute place" where many people "require a minister acquainted with the Gaelic," Reverend John Clugston had ensured that the Inverness congregation would acquire its own minister.[36] The Reverend Simon Fraser was duly appointed in the following year and, according to Reverend Clugston, was "doing well." Apparently, he was "very clamorous for books" written in Gaelic.

"He is persuaded that he would find them very useful among his Highland people and that the value of them would be returned. There are other Highland settlements, at least more or less twenty, in which books as well as the Scriptures and Latin books are demanded in Gaelic."[37] However, despite this promising start, Reverend Fraser could not bear "the fatigue and the privations" of his new post and was replaced by Reverend John Crombie, who served as resident minister of Inverness from 1856 to 1869.[38]

Plaque commemorating the former site of Adderley Presbyterian Church, which was built in 1873. It is located on Gosford Road between the 10th and 11th concessions. *Photograph by Geoff Campey.*

The Presbyterian congregation built their "Old Kirk" in 1839, in the centre of Inverness village. There were no pews. The congregation sat "on planks, or boards, resting on stones."[39] "The windows did not open and for some years the two [people] on each side of the pulpit had to be taken bodily out for a breath of fresh air."[40] The Old Kirk was replaced by St. Andrew's Church in 1862, but this second church was demolished by 1900.

At the time that Inverness Township was acquiring its many Highlanders, the surrounding area was also attracting other Scots whose geographical origins are largely unknown. Having emigrated to Leeds Township in the late 1820s with only £1. 16s, "a man from Aberdeen…was fast emerging from the pressure of supporting a small family that can yield as yet no assistance."[41] Great strides were clearly

Memorial to William McKenzie (1786–1855) and his wife Mary (1785–1870), both natives of Arran, in St. Andrew's Presbyterian Cemetery, intersection of Gosford and Dublin roads, Inverness village. *Photograph by Geoff Campey.*

being made by this man and his neighbours. "The road-side where I am at present…is nearly all cleared from the River St Lawrence to twenty miles above me." This area may have acquired more Aberdeen settlers in 1835. Having travelled to Craig's Road "to inspect the townships," some "respectable farmers possessing considerable capital" from Aberdeen, were planning "to settle there if found satisfactory."[42] Many more Scots came to Megantic County in small groups such as this and then became assimilated into mixed communities. Although their numbers are difficult to quantify, there is no doubt that they were present in substantial numbers.

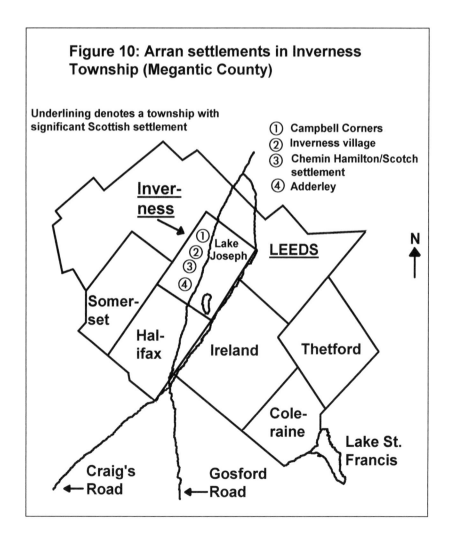

Figure 10: Arran settlements in Inverness Township (Megantic County)

Underlining denotes a township with significant Scottish settlement

① Campbell Corners
② Inverness village
③ Chemin Hamilton/Scotch settlement
④ Adderley

In his 1833 visit to Megantic County and the area just to the north of it, Reverend Clugston, had observed for himself that "the Scotch population is great." But he had also noticed "the considerable numbers of Irish Presbyterians."[43] "Three-fourths" of the population of the St. Giles seigneury "is of the Presbyterian persuasion" and three townships in the area apparently had "a multitude of Presbyterians."[44] Eight years later Scots were also to be found at nearby St. Sylvestre, at La Belle on the Kennebec Road (along the Chaudière River) and at the Portneuf and Jacques Cartier seigneuries, on the north side of the St. Lawrence River.[45] Meanwhile the Reverend David Brown had been established as the resident Presbyterian minister of the village of Valcartier in the St. Gabriel seigneury, some 17 miles northwest of Québec City. [46]

In his tour of 1833, Reverend Macaulay had preached within the seigneury of St. Giles, about 30 miles south of Québec City, as well as in the townships of Leeds, Inverness and Ireland" in Megantic County (Figure 10). Later, "one of the oldest inhabitants at Leeds" stated "that he had never seen so great an assemblage of people there for any purpose, as he saw that Sabbath assembled in the school house, to hear the word of God and join in his service."[47]

At the time of Reverend Macaulay's momentous visit, the St. Giles congregation was building "a very neat church which will hold about five hundred people." Apparently, "it was intended for the Church of England" but the Trustees, having realized that "the majority of the people inclined towards the Presbyterian form of worship," later joined forces with the Presbyterians.[48] Of particular concern to the congregation was the prospect of acquiring a library. "They cannot in present circumstances do anything themselves for establishing one" but Reverend Macaulay "promised to give them thirty or forty volumes—part of those sent out lately. The prospect of such a thing seemed to delight many of the people." The people most likely to be campaigning for a library were Scottish weavers. They were especially well known for their intellectual pursuits and healthy appetite for reading books.[49] Having emigrated from the Glasgow and Paisley areas in considerable numbers, most settled in Upper Canada although some smaller groups had gone to the Chateauguay Valley and to districts along the north side of the Ottawa River.[50] It seems that yet another group found their way to the Eastern Townships. Perhaps they were among the twenty-one

"Scotch" families (130 people) who are known to have settled in Megantic County in 1831.[51] Claiming that they could not obtain suitable land
in Godmanchester Township (Huntingdon County), or its neighbourhood, an area which had previously drawn many weavers, they were
directed to Megantic County by Archibald Buchanan.

Although not present in great numbers, emigrant Scots also settled
in the western stretches of the Eastern Townships. Many of them were
ex-soldiers, who acquired land in Grantham and Wickham townships
(Drummond County) as a reward for their services in the War of 1812–14
(Figure 9). The closely fought war had brought home the necessity of
improving Canada's defence capability. The British government's belief
that this aim could best be achieved by introducing disbanded soldiers
to act as a civilian resistance in one or two strategic areas, led to the
establishment of Rideau Valley military settlements in Upper Canada,[52]
and the Drummondville military settlement in Lower Canada.

By 1815 Frederick George Heriot, a Scottish military officer, had been
placed in overall charge of the Drummondville settlement.[53] Demobi-
lized soldiers, who arrived that same year, began the task of establishing
their farms within the St. Francis River valley. However, life in a military settlement had its difficulties. Although the ex-soldiers received
free land, log cabins, farm implements and food, they also had to accept
the personal constraints and rigours of living under military rule. Moreover, militarily important sites did not necessarily have good land.
Nevertheless, by 1816 a settlement of houses, a hospital, school and military barracks were being laid out and the community was taking shape.[54]
In the following year advertisements began appearing in some Scottish
newspapers stating that prospective emigrants could have the "great
advantage" of obtaining "grants of land and other indulgences" at settlements "now forming in Drummondville."[55] And the *Lord Middleton*
of North Shields, which was due to sail to Québec from Leith in May
1817, would actually be stopping at Trois Rivières, near Drummondville,
to disembark passengers.[56] However, the suggestion that special help
might be available to ordinary emigrants was totally misleading, since
financial aid was only being given to ex-servicemen.

Those who did accept the government's offer of land grants were
generally disappointed with the quality of their land and many left the
area. As a consequence, the Drummondville settlement failed to attract

much interest and by the end of 1819 only 235 people were living there.[57] Joseph Findlay, originally a member of the Forfar County Scottish Militia, who had fought with the 2nd Battalion of the 49th Regiment of Foot in the War of 1812–14, was probably fairly typical. Having taken up his 100 acres in Wickham Township when the war ended, he later sought better land farther down the St. Francis River. After selling his farm in Wickham, by 1831 he had moved to another farm in Durham Township, in what is now L'Avenir.[58] He was certainly not alone. "In the era, 1815–20, Durham Township received a good number of people from Drummondville, in the person of many soldiers, who were not satisfied with their terms in Grantham and Wickham Townships."[59] Joseph Findlay was clearly part of an on-going migration which was moving southward along the St. Francis River.

By 1821, the Township of Shipton (Richmond County), to the southeast of Durham, had acquired "100 families, three grist and three sawmills, three distilleries for making whisky from potatoes, several schools, but had neither a clergyman nor a magistrate."[60] They included the family of James Murdoch, a weaver from Kilmarnock (Ayrshire) who had arrived a year earlier. In less than a year Murdoch had "bought one pair of oxen, built our barn and began to reap."[61] He soon concluded that "there is plenty of land and work here for thousands but without money or a friend, a poor man is ill off."[62] And he certainly found plenty of work. A job "to superintend a woollen works near Boston" had been offered to him but, before this he had been offered another job "in the first carpet works in this part of the world on the River Connecticut," which he had accepted.[63] While Murdoch and his family almost certainly moved to the United States, plenty of Scots remained. Having obtained land near the town of Richmond in 1824, Andrew Glen was looking forward to his "place of abode" in an area "settled with Scotsmen who were Presbyterians."[64] The 1861 Census would show a modest Scottish presence in the townships of Shipton, Melbourne and Cleveland. Shipton Township eventually acquired its "Scotch Hill" along Craig's Road on the 5th Concession, south of present-day Danville (Figure 9). "The two families from Greenock," who were noted by the Quebec immigration agent in 1842 as being on their way "to join friends in Shipton," were probably heading for this settlement.[65]

TABLE 5
List of the Highland families who petitioned for land in the Township of Upton (Bagot County) in 1819
[LAC RG1 L3 ff. 66355-60]

No of Family	Age	No. in each family	No of Family	Age	No. in each family
1 Norman MacLeod - head	59		6 Catherine MacRae – wdow	60	
Alexander MacLeod	28		Farquhar MacRae	22	
William MacLeod	22		Nelly MacRae	20	2
Kenneth MacLeod	19				
Donald MacLeod	14		7 Norman Stewart – head	58	
Mary MacLeod	19		Norman Stewart Jnr.	24	
Vera MacLeod	9	6	John Stewart	20	
			Kenneth Stewart	19	4
2 Alexander MacLeod – head	54				
Olave MacLeod	19		8 Donald Stewart – head		
Angus MacLeod	17		James Stewart	4	
Alexander MacLeod	16		Norman Stewart	2	
Donald MacLeod	15		Nancy Stewart	7	3
Mary MacLeod	12				
Margaret MacLeod	8		9 John Stewart – head	36	
Penelope MacLeod	2	7	Donald Stewart	12	
			Saly Stewart	10	
3 John MacLeod – head	38		Hamish Stewart	8	
Martin MacLeod	3		Ann Stewart	6	
Norman MacLeod	2		Harriet Stewart	2	5
Betsey MacLeod	1	3			
			10 Alan McLeod – head		
4 Donald Finlayson – head	30		Hugh McLeod	25	
Catherine MacLeod	1	1	Sally McLeod	16	
			Roderick McLeod	12	3
5 Duncan MacLellan – head	42				
Archibald MacLellan	21		11 Finlay McCuaig – head		
Christy MacLellan	19		Duncan McCuaig	25	
Mary MacLellan	17		Angus McCuaig	23	
John MacLellan	13		Mary McCuaig	20	3
Nancy MacLellan	11				
Duncan MacLellan	9				
Jenny MacLellan	2	7			

No of Family	Age	No. in each family	No of Family	Age	No. in each family
12 Duncan MacCuaig – head			18 John MacLennan		
Donald MacCuaig	12		John MacLennan	18	
Kelly MacCuaig	11		Duncan MacLennan	14	
John MacCuaig	7		Malcolm MacLennan	12	
Jenney MacCuaig	5		Bell MacLennan	9	
Duncan MacCuaig	3		Donald MacLennan	6	
Mary MacCuaig	1	6	Catherine MacLennan	3	
			Farquhar MacLennan	1	7
13 John MacLenan					
John MacLenan	21		19 John MacRae		
Christy MacLenan	18		Farquhar MacRae	23	
Nancy MacLenan	16		Nancy MacRae	20	
Flory MacLenan	14		Catherine MacRae	19	
Elizabeth MacLenan	12		Donald MacRae	9	
Mary MacLenan	10		Janet MacRae	7	
Catherine MacLenan	8	7	Martha MacRae	5	
			Coll MacRae	1	7
14 Finlay MacLenan					
Christian MacLenan	24		20 Christopher MacRae		
Bell MacLenan	22	3	Alexander MacRae	2	1
15 Farquhar MacLenan			21 Angus MacIntosh & wife		2
Nancy MacLenan	7				
Alexander MacLenan	5		22 Duncan MacRae		
John MacLenan	3	3	Catherine MacRae	20	
			Nancy MacRae	18	
16 Widow MacCuaig – head			Peggy MacRae	14	
Martin MacPherson	30		Catherine MacRae	8	
Angus MacPherson	28		John MacRae	6	5
Hugh MacPherson	26				
Murdoch MacPherson	24	4	23 John Donaldson		
			John Donaldson	21	
17 John Finlayson – head			George Donaldson	19	
Donald Finlayson	20		Lucy Donaldson	16	
Isabella Finlayson	14		Josetti Donaldson	14	
Alexander Finlayson	12		Francis Donaldson	12	
Nancy Finlayson	9		Charles Donaldson	9	
Finlay Finlayson	5		James Donaldson	3	7
Archibald Finlayson	2	6			
			24 Mark Donaldson & wife		

No of Family	Age	No. in each family	No of Family	Age	No. in each family
25 Murdoch McGillivray			32 Norman McLeod		
Duncan McGillivray	28		Olave McLeod	3	1
Donald McGillivray	26				
Mary McGillivray	22		33 Margaret Campbell- widow		
Margaret McGillivray	18	4	John McPherson	28	
			Murdoch McPherson	26	
26 Lauchlin Stewart			Malcolm McPherson	24	
Janet Stewart	19		Mary McPherson	22	4
an infant son	1	2			
			34 Christopher MacRae		
27 Donald MacKinnon			Duncan MacRae	2	
an infant girl	1	1	Christian MacRae	1	3
28 John MacCallum			35 Donald MacLenan		
John MacCallum	16		Alan MacLenan	4	
James MacCallum	7		Mary MacLenan	2	
an infant daughter	1	3			
			36 Norman MacDonell		
29 Mary Cameron – widow			Angus MacDonell	27	
Martin Cameron	21		Ronald MacDonell	20	
Catherine Cameron	17		Jannet MacDonell	25	3
Nancy Cameron	15				
Angus Cameron	14		37 William McPhee		
John Cameron	12		Hamish McPhee	13	
Mary Cameron	10	6	Sally McPhee	11	
			Mary McPhee	5	
30 Duncan McLennan					
Ann McLennan	12		38 Neil Chisholm		
Isabella MacLennan	10		John Chisholm	3	1
John MacLennan	8				
Catherine MacLennan	6		39 Sally Campbell – widow		
Alexander MacLennan	4		Alan Campbell	27	1
Finlay MacLennan	2	6			
			40 William Campbell		
31 Donald McLean			John Campbell	5	
Sally MacLean	19		Norman Campbell	3	2
Roderick MacLean	15				
Mary MacLean	11		41 Angus Gillis & wife		
John MacLean	8				
Nancy MacLean	3				
Catherine MacLean	1	6			

No of Family	Age	No. in each family
42 James Blackburn & mother		
Janet Blackburn	17	
Margaret Blackburn	15	
Jane Blackburn	12	
Anne Blackburn	10	
Mary Blackburn	8	6
43 Farquhar MacRae		
John MacRae	14	
Marion MacRae	16	
Catherine MacRae	3	
Kenneth MacRae	1	4
44 James Struthers		
John Struthers	18	
a daughter grown		2
45 Joseph Simmons		
Joseph Simmons Jr.	20	1
46 Donald MacLeod & wife		
47 William MacLeod & wife		
48 Samuel Morrison		
Norman Morrison	24	
Kenneth Morrison	22	
49 David Higgins		
Philip Higgins	8	
Benjamin Higgins	6	
Charles Higgins	4	
Mary Ann Higgins	2	
Nancy Higgins	1	5
50 Charles Gordon		
1 child	7	1

No of Family	Age	No. in each family
51 Samuel Gordon		
Rachel Gordon	9	
Sally Gordon	7	
Hannah Gordon	5	
John Gordon	3	4
52 William Muir		
William Muir	17	
Anne Muir	15	
Margaret Muir	13	
Barbara	9	
Kelly Muir	7	
Mary Muir	4	
Pellin Muir	3	7
52 Nicholas Hogan		
53 Archibald Muir		
54 James Tyffe		
David Tyffe		
Donald Tyffe		
55 David Stewart		
56 James Lang		
57 John Stoddard		
Betsey Stoddard	2	
58 Peter Montgomery		
Charles Montgomery	7	
Alexander Montgomery	12	
Eliza Montgomery	10	3
59 William Knight & wife		
60 Joseph Simpson		

No of Family	Age	No. in each family	The undersigned are single young men who support themselves by their labour. Viz:
			Donald MacMillan
61 Samuel Morrison			Murdoch MacKenzie
John Morrison	20		Roderick McCuaig
William Morrison	17		Hugh Cameron
Mary Morrison	10		John McInnes
Malcolm Morrison	8		John McLeod
Janet Morrison	6		Alexander McLeod
Norman Morrison	3	6	John Tolmie
			Neil McDonell
62 Donald MacRae & wife			John Chilly
			George Gun
63 Donald Cameron & wife			Dominic McRae, Taylor
			Duncan MacRae
64 John MacGregor			John McDonald
Betsey MacGregor	12		Donald Grant
Kelly MacGregor	10		Duncan McKenzie
Mary MacGregor	8		Kenneth MacKenzie
Ann MacGregor	6	4	Donald Campbell
			Lauchlin Campbell
65 Donald Ross			Malcolm Campbell
1 son	14		Finlay Campbell
1 daughter	16	2	Alexander McMillan
			John MacMillan
Widow Stewart - head			Angus Grant
John Stewart	28		Hugh MacMillan
Angus Stewart	26		John Bui McCuaig
Neil Stewart	23		Alan Grant
William Stewart	20		John McDonald
Marion Stewart	17		John Finlayson
Roderick Stewart	15		William MacLeod
Mary Stewart	13		Alexander MacLeod
Alexander Stewart	10		Donald Murchison
Isabella Stewart	7	9	Simon Murchison
			Kenneth Murchison
Donald McLeod – head	35		Alan Fraser
Christian McLeod	17	1	William Montgomery

TABLE 6

Petition of Highlanders wishing to settle in Bury and Dudswell townships, 1819
[LAC RG1 L3 ff. 66361-64]

Norman MacLeod	Duncan MacLennan	Samuel Gordon
Alexander MacLeod	Funlay MacLennan	Donald Grant
William MacLeod	Farquhar MacLennan	Duncan McKenzie
Kenneth McLeod	John MacLenan	Donald Campbell
Alexander McLeod	Alan Campbell	Lauchlan Campbell
Alan McLeod	Donald McLean	Malcolm Campbell
Angus McLeod	John McRae	Finlay Campbell
Alexander McLeod	Farquhar McRae	Alexander MacMillan
Norman McLeod	Christopher McRae	Donald MacMillan
Donald McMillan	Duncan McRae	John MacMillan
Finlay McCraig		Angus Grant
Duncan McCuaig	Alexander Cameron	Hugh MacMillan
Angus McCuaig	Simon Murchison	Alan Grant Snr.
Donald Finlayson	Kenneth Murchison	Alan MacDonell
Duncan MacCuaig Snr.	James Blackburne	Simon Fraser
John Roy MacLennan	Joseph Simmons Snr.	Alan Fraser
John MacLennan Jnr.	Joseph Simmons Jnr.	John Tolmie
Duncan McLellan	Archibald Campbell	Donald MacDonald, Kintail
Archibald McLellan	Farquhar McRae	DonaldMurchison
Murdoch McGillivray	William Montgomery	Donald Finlayson
Angus MacIntosh	Martin MacPherson	
John MacCallum	Angus MacPherson	John MacGregor
John MacCallum	Hugh MacPherson	John Finlayson
William Knight	Murdo MacPherson	John Stewart
James Lang	Malcolm Cameron	John Donaldson
Duncan MacGillivray	John MacInnes	Mack Donaldson
Norman Stewart Snr.	Duncan MacRae Taylor	John Donaldson
Donald Stewart	Alan Cameron	George Donaldson
Kenneth Stewart	Hugh Cameron	Murdoch MacKenzie
John Stewart	Alexander McLeod,	Ludovick McCuaig
John Stewart	- Glengarry	John McLeod Taylor
Norman Stewart Jnr.	Donald Ross	John McLeod
Lauchlan Stewart	Daniel Higgins	John McCuaig
Donald McGillivray	William Muer	Donald Cameron
Donald MacKinnon	David Stewart	James Struthers
Alan MacLeod	Nicholas Hogan	Duncan McRae
Neil MacLeod	Archibald Muer	John MacPherson
Hugh MacLeod	James Tuffe	Murdo MacPherson
Duncan MacRae	Charles Gordon	Malcolm MacPherson

John MacLauren	Donald McLeod	Alexander McLeod
Michael Thompson	Kenneth McLeod	John MacLeod
William MacLeod	Rory McLeod	John McLeod
Alexander MacLeod	Kenneth McLeod	Donald Rory McLeod
William McLeod	John Urquhart	

Emigrant Scots were also finding their way to more westerly parts, near the Lake St. Peter end of the St. Francis River. By 1819 sixty-five Highland families were petitioning the Executive Council for land in Upton Township, on the St. Francis River in Bagot County (Table 5).[66] Following them was another even larger group, who petitioned for lots much further inland in the adjoining Township of Bury, in Compton County, and Dudswell in Wolfe County (Figure 9).[67] They were the 130 families who had emigrated "upwards of fourteen years past and are now scattered in different parts of the Province on seigniorial lands, where they could find locations"[68] (Table 6). Clearly part of the much larger group who had emigrated from west Inverness-shire and Wester Ross in the early 1800s in the hope of obtaining land grants in Glengarry, they had dispersed to various locations. Now the families, which included large numbers of MacLeods, MacCuaigs, MacRaes and MacLennons, were seeking to settle together on "the waste lands of the Crown."[69] If the government obliged them, they would be joined by "other settlers now in and about Montréal, whose means are inadequate" to fund their transport to Upper Canada."[70] Promising to "form a settlement of useful, industrious, loyal Protestant subjects," they almost certainly obtained their grants in Bury and Dudswell townships.[71] Organizing their petition had been Norman MacLeod, the versatile "schoolmaster," who, having initially lived in Glengarry, moved to Sir John Johnson's Monnoir seigneury, and then relocated himself to Edward Ellice's Beauharnois seigneury, running a school in each location.[72]

Colonization efforts in the Eastern Townships remained sporadic and largely uncoordinated until the creation of the British American Land Company in 1834. Modelled after the Canada Company, founded eight years earlier to promote the colonization of vast tracts of Upper Canada, it actively recruited British settlers for its lands. The Company bought large tracts of land and sold them on to *bona fide* settlers, on the understanding that they would be provided with an infrastructure of buildings and roads within which to develop their communities. Over 850,000 acres of land were acquired. The so-called St. Francis Tract, consisting of 596,000 acres of unsurveyed Crown land, was located between Lake Megantic and the St. Francis River, while a second section consisting of 250,000 acres of surveyed land lay in Shefford, Stanstead and Sherbrooke counties.[73]

The British government's on-going defence concerns had made it receptive to the company's highly focused and commercially-driven plans. Through its efforts, large numbers of loyal British people would be moving into the Eastern Townships, thereby providing extra security close to the American border, where it mattered most. Moreover, the government was coming under mounting pressure to open up the Eastern Townships to British settlers. The region's good farmland, situated relatively close to Québec City, made it a prime candidate for large-scale colonization. The Maritime provinces were fast filling up and the long distances involved in reaching Upper Canada did not suit everyone because of the extra costs involved in travel. Consequently, the policy, advocated some decades earlier of designating the Eastern Townships solely for the use of French-Canadian settlers, was reversed and preference was now being given to British settlers.

The company invested large amounts of capital in roads, bridges and buildings in the hope of realizing good profits from land sales. Cleared land was offered at from $10 to $12 per acre although uncleared land, laid out in lots from 50 to 200 acres, could be purchased from as little as $1.50 to $2.50 per acre.[74] Leaflets and posters were produced, which were intended to attract tradesmen, agricultural labourers and farmers with at least enough capital to fund their emigration costs.[75] Typical of these was the pamphlet written by Mr. W.G. Mack, which was published in Glasgow. Extolling what he saw as the many virtues of the Eastern Townships, he contrasted the "fever and ague"[76] of Upper Canada with the Eastern Townships' healthy environment.[77] While Upper Canada was flat and uninteresting, Lower Canada was "highly picturesque." Lamenting the fact that there were "almost no Scotch in the country yet," he hoped that this "may not long be the case as, laying prejudice aside, they are perhaps the quietest and most useful settlers we could have."[78] Although the pamphlet gave the impression of expressing the unbiased observations of a casual visitor, it was actually a highly contrived piece of promotional literature which was almost certainly being sponsored by the land company.

The British American Land Company faced stiff competition from the Canada Company and always had an uphill struggle to find settlers. As the Quebec immigration agent had noted in his report to the 1826 Emigration Select Committee: "Many of them [emigrants] dislike Lower Canada, on account of the French language and laws; the peasantry all speak French, and the emigrant is quite lost among them."[79] However, the company soon appreciated that it should look to the masses of Gaelic-speaking people in the Highlands and Islands for its recruits. Most of them were enduring appalling poverty and, were they to emigrate, the prevalence of the French language would have no more consequence than the prevalence of English. They had their own language and culture and would keep themselves apart from everyone else.

As severe destitution became widespread throughout the Highlands and Islands, Highland landlords increasingly turned to emigration as the obvious solution to their own and their tenants' plight. Emigration relieved them of their surplus tenantry while at the same time it offered their tenants an escape from their poverty and the prospect of a better life abroad. Thus large-scale emigration was being advocated on many Highland estates, but the high costs involved in moving large numbers of destitute people across the Atlantic proved to be a major stumbling block. In 1837, Colin Duncan McDougall, a former inspecting field officer of the Nova Scotia militia, advocated a subsidized emigration scheme which would relocate 5000 Highland families (25,000 people) to company land in the Eastern Townships. But the government refused to pay the £227,500 that the scheme was going to cost and so it was abandoned.[80] Hopes were raised that emigrants from Mull would settle on company land, but, failing to get financial aid from the government, this proposed scheme also came to nothing.[81] However, the company did begin co-operating with Scottish landlords, like Stewart MacKenzie of Seaforth.[82]

Conditions could not have been worse on the Seaforth estates on the Island of Lewis. With the rapid decline of the kelp industry, poverty and deprivation were sweeping through the island. By the late 1830s eighty percent of the entire population was reported to be in a desperate state and the estate was mired in debt.[83] MacKenzie of Seaforth had hoped to get financial aid from the government to finance emigration from his

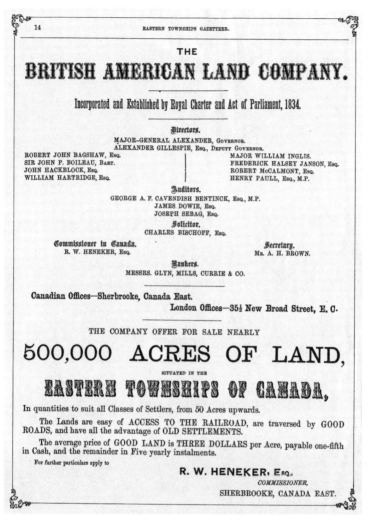

Advertisement for sale of land by the British American Land Company which appeared in *The Eastern Townships Gazetteer and General Business Directory, 1867. Courtesy of Eastern Townships Research Centre, Bishop's University, Lennoxville, Québec.*

estate, but this was not forthcoming.[84] In these dire circumstances he was faced with having to foot the bill himself. And he spent his money wisely, by entering into an arrangement with the British American Land Company. Under the agreed plan, MacKenzie paid his tenants' transport costs, while the company provided them with land on easy terms and provisions during their first winter, thus giving them some support while they

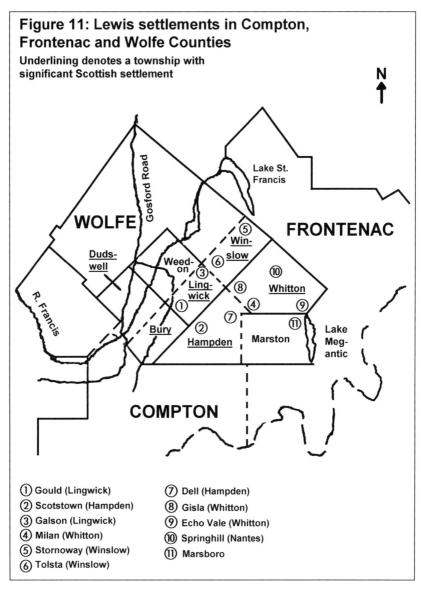

Figure 11: Lewis settlements in Compton, Frontenac and Wolfe Counties

Underlining denotes a township with significant Scottish settlement

① Gould (Lingwick)
② Scotstown (Hampden)
③ Galson (Lingwick)
④ Milan (Whitton)
⑤ Stornoway (Winslow)
⑥ Tolsta (Winslow)
⑦ Dell (Hampden)
⑧ Gisla (Whitton)
⑨ Echo Vale (Whitton)
⑩ Springhill (Nantes)
⑪ Marsboro

settled in. The scheme swiftly led to a large influx of Lewis settlers to the St. Francis Tract. From 1838 they began colonizing Bury, Lingwick and Winslow townships and by the early 1850s they were moving into Whitton, Marston and Hampden townships (Figure 11).[85]

The first group of Lewis emigrants set sail for Québec in 1838.[86] Fifteen Lewis families (70 people), all of whom originated from Uig parish on the west of the island,[87] sailed on the *Energy* of Dundee from

Stornoway.[88] In charge of the contingent was John MacKenzie, whose son Colin, "late of Galson," having gone to live "some years at Calcutta" and later settled in Canada, was now returning to Lewis to guide the emigrants to their new homes.[89] A larger group of 130 passengers, who originated from the mainland parish of Loch Broom (Wester Ross), also sailed on the same ship, having had their fares paid by their landlord.[90]

Archibald Buchanan, the Quebec immigration agent, found the Lewis families to be "all in good health," on their arrival. They were "proceeding immediately to Port St. Francis [on the St. Lawrence] on the route to the company's lands" and according to Buchanan, "they will prove a valuable acquisition to that part of the country."[91] After reaching their destinations, the emigrants were provided with houses and provisions for their first winter, which they were going to have to repay by taking up employment on

Gould Pioneer Cemetery, Lingwick Township: Memorial to Neil McKay (1822–1904) from Lewis, and Christina Rose (1826–1897), his wife, from Loch Broom. Christina Rose was almost certainly in the group who sailed from Loch Broom in 1838. *Photograph by Geoff Campey.*

one of the land company building projects. In the Spring of the following year, a government inspector was able to report that they "were succeeding well, having already cut down and burned off from two to three acres each family."[92] The Loch Broom settlers also appear to have adapted readily to their new surroundings. Evander McIver, their former estate manager, would later tell the 1841 Select Committee that he had "a letter from my relation very lately saying they are very comfortable and that they never were so well off in Loch Broom."[93] Most of the 1838 arrivals established themselves in the townships of Bury and Lingwick (Compton County) and Winslow (Frontenac County).[94] While the Lewis settlers attracted a steady stream of followers from their homeland over many decades, the Loch Broom settlers failed to attract any subsequent migration to the region.

A much larger group of 223 Lewis emigrants arrived in the Eastern Townships in 1841, having sailed from Stornoway in the *Charles* (145 passengers)

The magnificent Memorial Gate at Gould Pioneer Cemetery, Lingwick
Township, built in 1962. "In recognition of the courage and integrity of
the Presbyterian pioneers from the island of Lewis, Scotland, this gate is
dedicated to their memory." *Photograph by Geoff Campey.*

and *Lady Hood* (78 passengers).[95] Most of them originated from Barvas
parish[96] on the north of the island, especially from Tolsta, Dell and Galson
and from Uig parish on the west, especially from Brenish and Crowlista.[97]
The Quebec immigration agent noted that the *Lady Hood* of Stornoway
passengers were "very poor," having arrived "in great distress for want of
provisions," while the *Charles* passengers were nearly as destitute. Most of
them intended to join their fellow countrymen
in Bury and Lingwick townships.[98]

Memorial in Gould Pioneer
Cemetery, Lingwick Town-
ship, to John E. MacLeod
(1811–1893) and Dorothy
MacAskill (1816–1893) his
wife, both from Lewis. *Photograph by Geoff Campey.*

By 1841 the land company was close to
bankruptcy, and, to deal with its massive
debts, it was forced to hand over 500,000 acres
of the St. Francis Tract to the government.[99]
Settlers were then able to obtain 50-acre por-
tions of the land, which had been relinquished
by the company, as free grants from the government. But although the 1841 arrivals could
acquire their land, they did not receive any
financial support from the land company, and
during their first winter they were depend-
ent on donations raised by the inhabitants of
Sherbrooke and Montréal. The Quebec
immigration agent also provided them with
200 pounds of oatmeal, while Dr. Thomas
Rolph, Upper Canada's great colonization

Tolsta Pioneer Cemetery, Winslow Township. The cemetery
is located some distance from the entrance, which is marked
by a simple iron archway. *Photograph by Geoff Campey.*

promoter, roused the public to donate further funds of around £250 to
help the group to survive its first winter.[100] He firmly believed them to
be in "imminent risk," having arrived so late in the season "when labour
was not in demand."[101]

Another contingent of 133 Lewis settlers arrived in 1842 on the *St.
Andrew* of New Brunswick, some of whom were reported to be "very
poor."[102] Many joined some of the earlier 1838 Lewis arrivals who had
settled at Gould in Lingwick Township.[103] Little wonder that, by 1869,
"the adult inhabitants of Lingwick" were said to be "nearly all natives
of the Island of Lewis."[104] And the Lewis predominance soon began to
have an impact on local place names. Galson and Tolsta, both Lewis
names, became separate settlements in Lingwick and Winslow townships (Figure 11). It would seem also that Lake McIver, lying a short
distance to the south east of Tolsta, owes its name to the many McIvers
from Lewis who settled in this area during the 1840s and 1850s.[105]

Gould's commercial life was given a strong boost in 1845 when James
Ross, who originated from Fearn in Ross-shire, established his potash
and pearl ash business.[106] By this time Gould's growing Scottish community had formed a Free Church congregation and built a church.[107]
Soon after this the congregation was in receipt of financial aid from the
Edinburgh Ladies Association, a fundraising body that primarily supported Presbyterian churches in Cape Breton.[108] Thanks to their efforts
three Presbyterian missionaries visited the township in the following
year. Although the Glasgow Colonial Society had wanted to extend its

brand of Presbyterianism to this region[109] there was no prospect that it would succeed since the Lewis settlers were Free Church adherents who had no time for the established church.[110]

Meanwhile the land company soldiered on. Although it had lost most of its land, it was left with the St. Francis Tract's most valuable and readily accessible lands in Bury, Lingwick and Weedon townships. Promotional literature and posters proclaimed "the improved farms with buildings...in any quantity from 50 acres upward," together with the 50-acre lots, which were being offered "at the low price of 10s. per acre" to "respectable persons of small means"[111] And for 50-acre lots paid in advance, the company threw in the added inducement in March 1844, of "a free passage from Scotland," although this offer was rescinded a month later, having been a brief, short-term measure to stimulate "a greatly increased demand" for its lands.[112]

The next large influx from Lewis occurred in the 1850s. Sir James Matheson had purchased the island from MacKenzie of Seaforth by this time, and was coping with the devastating effects of the "Potato Famine" which first struck in 1846. With the passing of the 1845 Poor Law Amendment Act, landlords like Matheson had become legally responsible for the welfare of their tenants and, as conditions worsened during the Highland Famine years from 1846 to 1856, forced evictions, coupled with assisted emigration schemes, were becoming commonplace on Highland estates. Lewis was no exception. John Munro MacKenzie, the estate chamberlain, explained Matheson's removal terms to the people, but it was he who determined who would emigrate and who would remain.[113] People who resisted the order to emigrate risked being evicted without any form of assistance if they fell into arrears; so there was an element of coercion.[114] Even so, Matheson's funding was very generous. When he met the Lewis settlers at Québec, Archibald Buchanan could not help but contrast their fit and healthy condition with the miserable state of Gordon of Cluny's Barra and South Uist tenants, who kept arriving with insufficient provisions.[115] All in all, Matheson spent over £10,000 in funding the removal costs of some 2,337 Lewis people, who emigrated between 1851 and 1855.[116]

Originating mainly from the northern and western parts of Lewis, a total of 1,554 Lewis emigrants made their way to Québec in 1851 aboard six ships: the *Wolfville* of Ardrossan (69), *Barlow* (287), *Prince George* of

Alloa (203), *Islay* (68), *Marquis of Stafford* (500) and *Urgent* of Belfast
(370).[117] According to the *Inverness Journal,* which reported their departure that summer, "many had friends and relatives before them in
comfortable circumstances."[118] However, details of where they actually
settled are confused and sketchy. Around 500 (109 families) of them
opted for Upper Canada, where they founded "the Lewis settlement"
in Huron Township, Bruce County.[119] Another 600 Lewis people are
known to have made their way to the Eastern Townships, but the final
destination of the remaining 450 is not known.[120] Many of the 1851
arrivals to the Eastern Townships went to Lingwick and Winslow, townships where substantial Lewis communities had already formed.[121]

Others Lewis settlers established new communities in the townships
of Hampden (Compton County), Marston and Whitton (Frontenac
County). Two communities, Gisla and Dell, were named after places in
Lewis, the former being in Uig parish on the west side of the island and
the latter lying at the northern end in Barvas parish. Adapting well to
their new surroundings, the settlers sent a series of glowing letters to
the *Inverness Advertiser,* extolling the abundance of well-paid construction jobs. One person wrote that, "I am very sorry because you are not
here with us, as this country is promising to be better for poor people
than the old and poor country…we are working at the railroad for 4s.
6d, the first month and the next month 5s. a day…there is plenty money
here now that we are working."[122]

Meanwhile, forty Scottish families, "settlers of ten years standing"
who were farming land in nearby Weedon Township (Wolfe County),
still under the control of the British American Land Company, objected
to the high prices being demanded of them and moved to Winslow
Township in 1849, where they could acquire free government land.[123]
Another group of fifty-four Scottish families moved from Lingwick to
Winslow in 1851 for the same reason. And two years later Winslow
received another seventy-three Lewis emigrants.[124] Marston Township
(Frontenac County) also received Scottish migrants from Lingwick, but
as it was in a totally undeveloped state, relocating to it was difficult and
arduous. William MacLeod, Rory MacIver and Murdo MacIver
acquired their new lots in Marston in 1852, and, four years later, led
their families on a "long and tedious journey through the forest."[125]
Arriving in Marston, "thirteen settlers built thirteen houses in thirteen

days."[126] There were no roads initially, just "blazed trails" through dense forests. Carts and sleds could not be used and so people had to carry their supplies long distances on their backs. "I have seen Murdo MacIver carry 180 pounds of flour on his back for 6 miles, settling it down for a rest at the end of every mile."[127]

Predictably the Scottish-born population of Winslow rose rapidly, increasing from 166 in 1851 to 422 in 1861 while Lingwick's population fell by sixty per cent in that same period.[128] As Winslow's population grew, the village of Bruceville developed at the intersection of two important roads, one being the east/west artery of the Gosford Road and the other being the southern extension of the Lambton Road.[129] Later renamed Stornoway, after the major town in Lewis, it became the commercial centre of the many Scottish communities within Winslow and Whitton townships (Figure 11).[130] Colin Noble, a Scot from Inverness, was in charge of the first general store in 1852 and he quickly became one of the most important and influential businessmen in the area.[131] One year earlier, Stornoway's Free Church of Scotland congregation had built a log church just west of the village, on the road to Tolsta. Reverend Ewen McLean, who apparently had been "sent by Lady Matheson" from Lewis, was their first minister.[132] The log church was replaced in 1878 by the much larger St. John's Church, however, with declining numbers, its services were discontinued by 1921 and two years later it was sold.[133]

Memorial in Stornoway Pioneer Cemetery, Winslow Township, to Donald McLeod (1800–1884) and Rachel McLeod (1811–1886) from Barraglom, Great Bernera, Lewis, who emigrated to Whitton Township in 1851. The cemetery is opposite the Roman Catholic Church of Saint-Alphonse. *Photograph by Geoff Campey.*

Another 453 Lewis emigrants set sail for Québec in 1852 on the *Blanche* of Liverpool, and after a three-year gap, a further contingent of 330 people sailed on the *Melissa* from Stornoway in 1855. Both groups settled mainly in western Upper Canada and the Eastern Townships, although their precise distribution is unknown.[134] Two hundred people in the 1855 contingent went to the Eastern Townships and mainly settled in the Township of Whitton which was reported to have forty-six Scottish families by 1861.

Their communities were to be found at Sandy Bay (renamed Echo Vale), Springhill (renamed Nantes) and Marsden (renamed Milan).[135]

Following the failure in 1863 of the oats crop in Galson, on the northwest side of the island, forty Lewis families came to the region.[136] Perhaps they were the inspiration behind the Galson village, which sprouted in Lingwick, although given that this township was among the first to acquire Lewis settlers, it is likely that it already existed as a community by this time.[137] Another thirty-five Lewis families arrived in the early 1870s, with most settling in Lingwick, Marston, Hampden and Whitton townships.[138] Marston township acquired its first Presbyterian church at Marsboro in 1872[139] and by 1914 there would be "approximately two thousand five hundred Gaels in Marsboro alone"[140] (Figure 11). A local man recalled "that he did not know that there was any other language in the world but Gaelic until he was seven years old."[141] And four years later, Gisla had its St. Luke's Presbyterian Church, which served the Scottish population of North Whitton and Hampden.[142] After being destroyed by a cyclone in 1917, it was replaced by a new St. Luke's Church which was located in Milan.[143] Until 1944 services were held "in English in the evening, and in Gaelic in the morning."[144]

Around this time the village of Agnes, at the north end of Lake Megantic, was founded, having acquired its name as a consequence of Sir John A. MacDonald's visit to the area. It was named after his second wife, Susan Agnes Bernard.[145] The sawmill town of Scotstown also began to emerge near the junction of Bury, Hampden and Lingwick townships. Even this far inland, the timber trade, both overseas and with the United States, was vital to the town's livelihood, with most settlers being engaged in some aspect of timber felling or transport, particularly

St. Paul's Presbyterian Church in Scotstown. Constructed in 1926, it replaced St. Andrew's Church which had been built in 1881. *Photograph by Geoff Campey.*

Memorial in Stornoway Pioneer Cemetery, Winslow Township, to Kenneth McLeod (1811–1894), who was "born in Lewis." Part of the inscription is in Gaelic. *Photograph by Geoff Campey.*

during the winter months.[146] Scotstown had its first Presbyterian church by 1881 and twenty years later Reverend R. MacLeod, an itinerant preacher, would be holding regular prayer meetings there for the benefit of the "Isle of Lewis settlers."[147]

When John Ramsay of Kildalton, the proprietor of the island of Islay,[148] travelled from Lingwick Township to Stornoway, and then on to Lake Megantic in 1870, he observed that "nearly all the settlers in this neighbourhood for many miles have come from Lewis"; but he also discovered that some people had originated from North Uist.[149] In addition, there were some settlers who had come from Harris.[150] And other residents, like Malcolm MacAulay and Donald MacIver, although initially from Lewis, had come to the Eastern Townships via Cape Breton.[151] Most of the Cape Breton arrivals were Roman Catholics who "changed to Presbyterians because they didn't get a Gaelic-speaking priest."[152] "Language was so important" to Arthur MacDonald's mother that, in spite of being Roman Catholic, her family attended the local Presbyterian church in Lingwick parish because its services were in Gaelic. "Here they felt at home."[153]

During his travels, John Ramsay met many Lewis people who "gave me the same favourable report of the country and though some older men I met expressed their preference for their native land, they all admitted, after some conversation, that they had been in better circumstances after their arrival than they had been at home." However, James Ross, the Gould entrepreneur, felt that people should be induced to come to the Eastern Townships "from parts of Scotland where the system of agriculture is better" than in the Outer Hebrides, and it was hoped that they would "stimulate the Highlanders to further improvement, as too many of them are ready to rest satisfied as soon as they have attained to a comfortable subsistence and live on in the log house rather than labour more to get a better dwelling or otherwise to add to their wealth."[154]

Maybe so, but what Ross failed to appreciate was that these poor Highlanders had displayed amazing qualities of fortitude and endurance in coping with the deprivations and isolation of pioneer life. They had built their successful communities and they were content with modest strides in their living standards and did not need lessons from anyone on how to better themselves.

Having first arrived in 1838, Lewis settlers had emigrated to the Eastern Townships with great regularity over a period of thirty-five years. While another sizeable influx was experienced after the First World War, the people who left Lewis this time were mainly young people seeking employment abroad in towns and cities.[155] By 1881 the largest concentrations of Lewis settlers were to be found in Lingwick, Hampden, Marston and Whitton townships.[156] People of Scottish ancestry accounted for 82 per cent of the population in both Lingwick and Hampden.[157] Nonetheless, Scottish predominance was reaching its peak by this stage and would begin its slow decline during the early twentieth century.

By 1941 Lingwick's Scots accounted for only 28 percent of its total population while only 1.5 per cent of Winslow's population were Scottish.[158] During this period, the Hebridean component of the overall population had plummeted from twenty per cent in 1881 to five per cent in 1941.[159]

Robert Sellar viewed these developments with alarm, believing that the British exodus and subsequent takeover of the Eastern Townships by French farmers had been masterminded by the French-Catholic establishment.[160] However, the arrival of French-Canadian families followed in the wake of the British exodus. They had not caused it. British settlers began leaving the area at a time when people of British ancestry still predominated. The driving force behind the exodus was the prospect of the better economic

Stornoway Vous Accueille— the road sign, at the town line of Stornoway. Once the heart of a large Scottish community, Stornoway's population today is entirely French-speaking. *Photograph by Geoff Campey.*

opportunities that western Canada and the United States had to offer. This led to the steady drift of Hebridean Scots out of Lower Canada, an exodus which began in 1850. In their place came the French and by 1911 they outnumbered the Scots and others of British ancestry. By the 1970s they accounted for 80 per cent of the total population.[161] All that is left today of the former Scottish communities are the beautifully kept cemeteries, occasional road signs and dark patches of new forest which mark the places where Hebridean settlers once cultivated their land.

Emigrant Scots had also made substantial inroads in the Gaspé region, although their settlements here were not nearly as widespread as they had been in the Eastern Townships. The Gaspé was a great forested region, having a timber trade, that offered great benefits to fledgling pioneer settlements. And, being particularly well represented among the early arrivals, Scottish communities were to be found at or near the main timber bays. Yet, as is the case in the Eastern Townships, a modern-day visitor would be astonished to learn that these Scottish settlements had ever existed.

Six

THE GASPÉ SCOTS

Below Quebec is the old settlement of Gaspé, a long neglected quarter where upon the authority of the Crown Agent himself, the great majority are of the Church of Scotland.[1]

WHEN THE REVEREND WALTER ROACH, a Glasgow Colonial Society minister, visited the Gaspé in 1833, many Protestant settlers of British descent were living in scattered farms and communities along the southern and eastern sides of the peninsula. He noted that emigrant Scots were highly visible. Various French-Canadian settlements had sprouted along both coastlines, while two major Mi'kmaw communities were concentrated near the mouth of the Restigouche River [2] and at Cascapédia (Maria) on the north side of Baie des Chaleurs. Had Reverend Roach arrived in 1800 he would have noticed a great many British settlers but few French Canadians. A present-day visitor would find this hard to believe. Now the Gaspé is almost entirely peopled by French Canadians, and apart from occasional place names like New Carlisle and Douglastown, there are few reminders of its former British past.

After Britain lost the American War of Independence, Loyalist ex-servicemen had been moved to the Gaspé to bolster its population because of its strategic location at the entrance to the Saint Lawrence. As a consequence, the Gaspé suddenly acquired four hundred settlers of British descent, who arrived as Loyalists in 1784.[3] Being relocated at public expense, they were allocated land on the north side of the Baie des

Chaleurs, along the border between Lower Canada and New Brunswick. Establishing themselves initially at New Richmond and New Carlisle, the Gaspé Loyalists went on to found a third stronghold at Douglastown on the east side of the peninsula (Figure 12). However, relatively few Scots went to Douglastown, with most settling along the north side of the bay between Restigouche and New Carlisle. Already present along this same stretch of coastline were the Acadian communities at Tracadièche (now Carleton),[4] Bonaventure and Paspébiac, which had been founded some thirty years earlier.[5] Having been forcibly expelled from Nova Scotia in 1755, along with many thousands of other Acadians, they were some of the very few who had escaped deportation.[6] Finding a safe haven by the shores of Baie des Chaleurs, they then attracted further waves of followers. Also present were groups of French-speaking Protestants from the Channel Islands of Jersey and Guernsey. Arriving from 1764, they had established fisheries and settlements along the east side of the peninsula between New Carlisle and Rivière-au-Renard.[7]

The Gaspé Loyalists need to be seen in the wider context of the government's overall relocation scheme which had brought 35,000 Loyalists to the Maritime provinces.[8] While the Gaspé had acquired four hundred Loyalists and a few more had settled on the Island of St. John (later Prince Edward Island) and Cape Breton, most of the Loyalist influx had been concentrated in the Bay of Fundy area further to the south.[9] Therefore, this relatively small number of Gaspé Loyalists was merely the northern flank of the huge intake of Loyalists that had been experienced in the Maritime region. Taken together they had doubled the population of peninsular Nova Scotia and swelled the population on the New Brunswick side of the Bay of Fundy by fivefold.[10]

Having acquired its Loyalists in 1784, the Gaspé had to wait another thirty years for its next large influx of British settlers. The turning point was the establishment of the region's timber trade, which grew dramatically from 1815. Four ships arrived to collect timber in 1818, but seven years later some sixty ships "were engaged in the trade," which stimulated the region's economy, attracting settlers from Britain in increasing numbers.[11] Substantial Protestant clusters had developed along the south side of the peninsula by 1825, especially in New Carlisle, Paspébiac, Hope Town, New Richmond and Restigouche[12] (Table 7). Three years later, large sections of the Gaspé were said to be principally inhabited by British settlers.[13] All the while, Scottish entrepreneurs had been investing in the local timber industry and eventually they were the ones who came to dominate timber felling operations on both sides of the Baie des Chaleurs.[14]

TABLE 7
Population in the Baie-des-Chaleurs c. 1825
[NAS GD 45/3/153]

	No of heads of Families	Total no. of inmates at a place	children under 14	Males over 14	Females over 14	Prot-estants	Acres in cultivation
Port Daniel	47	279	149	66	55	42	195
Hope Town	54	334	152	108	74	146	435
Paspébiac	43	471	127	267	68	190	448
New Carlisle	98	607	255	183	169	429	1020
Bonaventure	85	518	156	170	143	26	848
New Richmond	79	446	165	175	103	181	1009
Maria	75	476	214	134	127	12	1463
Carleton	80	546	251	176	146	13	1930
Maguasha Seigneury	19	121	58	31	42	17	183
Restigouche	16	109	33	54	22	99	369
Indians:				Males	Females		
Restigouche	60	269		132	137		
Cascapédiac	22	112		50	62		

Although the major focus of the timber trade lay on the New Brunswick side of the bay, it was nevertheless a compelling factor in the Gaspé's intake of new settlers from Scotland.[15] Scottish merchants ran their businesses with and for the benefit of fellow Scots and thus immigrant Scots were particularly well-placed to benefit from the region's growing timber trade. Being some of the earliest arrivals, they could choose the best locations along the coast near to the timber-collecting bays and along river frontages and their tributaries. Hence, in a great timber producing region like the Gaspé, the progress of Scottish settlements and the timber trade were closely linked.

View of the Gaspé Basin, c. 1866, from Pye *Canadian Scenery: District of Gaspé Montréal, 1866. Courtesy of Toronto Public Library (TRL).*

As the Reverend Walter Roach had observed, there was an unmistakable concentration of Scots along the north side of Baie des Chaleurs in the early 1830s. Nearly fifty per cent of the population living between Restigouche and Carleton were Church of Scotland adherents,[16] and there were also large concentrations of Scots to the east of Carleton at New Richmond.[17] Although they originated from many parts of Scotland, "a considerable number of emigrants from the Highlands" were inhabiting the region.[18] Because of their large numbers, John Deans, a local businessman, advised the Glasgow Colonial Society that "a clergyman who could preach the Gaelic would be preferred by them." However, given that "they all speak English and their children are taught in the English language," Deans doubted whether the ability to speak Gaelic was all that necessary.[19] Certainly, when the Glasgow Colonial Society sought a minister for the fast-growing Presbyterian congregation at New Richmond a few years later, it was careful to point out that "Gaelic was not required."[20]

When he visited the area in 1826, Lord Dalhousie had noted that New Richmond "is thinly settled and chiefly by Scotch Presbyterian families [who are] doing tolerably well."[21] He met "a party of very stout, healthy, hard-working Scotchmen" who came on board his ship when it docked at New Richmond, to ask for help in acquiring a Presbyterian minister, a schoolmaster and funds to build a flour mill.[22] Eight years later a visiting Glasgow Colonial Society missionary counted the one hundred and fifty people at New Richmond who were "professing the tenets of the Established Church of Scotland, although he also noted that their "spiritual wants" were not being met. [23] While "the zealous inhabitants" had built a chapel and schoolhouse, "no regular services are held and the school master is a Roman Catholic," who was "under the control of the Roman [Catholic] priest."[24]

Another factor in New Richmond's popularity with Scots was its location. Lying almost directly opposite New Mills in Restigouche County, New Brunswick, it was at the heart of a major Scottish stronghold, which straddled both sides of Baie des Chaleurs. New Mills had acquired its Scots in a large and sudden influx in 1829–30, when around four hundred settlers from the island of Arran came to the area. They joined a long-established community of Scots at Athol (now Atholville) just south of Campbellton, whose fishing and timber interests were being managed by the Perthshire-born Robert Ferguson. Having arrived in the area in 1796, he was known for his entrepreneurial flair that helped to attract fellow-Scots to the area, making this a Scottish enclave long before the Arran settlers arrived at New Mills.[25]

Like the other emigrants from Arran who had relocated to the Eastern Townships at this time,[26] they too received financial help to emigrate from their landlord, the Duke of Hamilton.[27] Arriving just as the local timber trade was expanding rapidly, they spearheaded a steady Scottish influx into the region.[28] Scots soon colonized the area to the west of New Mills as far as Campbellton and by 1851 they represented sixty percent of the total immigrant population of Restigouche County.[29] As was the case with New Richmond, a visiting Presbyterian missionary later found New Mills to be in "a desolate condition" owing to "the want of the preaching of the Gospel."[30]

Meanwhile, New Carlisle was also booming and settlers were apparently "rushing" to it in 1827.[31] When he visited five years earlier, Lieutenant-Colonel Sir Francis Cockburn, superintendent of the Upper Canada military settlements, had observed it to be in a "good state of cultivation and plentifully stocked with cattle."[32]

Douglastown, on the other hand, was struggling. Lord Dalhousie thought it to be "a most wretched hovel" where people "were poor in

View of New Carlisle c. 1866 from Pye *Canadian Scenery: District of Gaspé Montréal, 1866. Courtesy of Toronto Public Library (TRL).*

the extreme."[33] Having only a small timber trade, its economy relied heavily on a "large fishing establishment.[34] Yet it had some affluent residents. Daniel McPherson of Cluny (Inverness-shire), a Loyalist from Philadelphia, established a business at Douglastown and also purchased the seigneury of Crane Island (Île aux Grues), situated some distance away to the southwest of the Gaspé.[35] Having recruited settlers for his seigneury, McPherson moved to Crane Island, leaving his son John in charge of his Douglastown operations. When Joseph Bouchette visited Crane Island and nearby Goose Island (Île aux Oies) in 1815, he observed that they were "inhabited by about forty families [whose] land was well-cultivated, producing wheat beyond their own consumption."[36]

By the time that McPherson took this initiative, the north shore of the Gaspé was just beginning to attract colonizers. Although most of the arrivals were French Canadians, some Scots were establishing themselves at the northwestern end of the peninsula. The attraction was the seigneury of Métis which had been acquired by the Scottish-born John McNider. Scottish colonists first arrived in 1818, having sailed to Québec on McNider's timber vessels, one of which was the *Rebecca*[37] (Figure 12). Five years later Métis was reported to have forty Scottish families, who had taken up their lots on two concessions lying close to the shore. The 2nd Concession is still recognizable today as "Rang des Écossais."

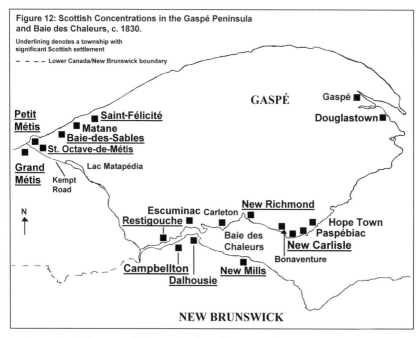

Figure 12: Scottish Concentrations in the Gaspé Peninsula and Baie des Chaleurs, c. 1830.

Born in Kilmarnock (Ayrshire), John McNider came to Québec as a young man. Becoming a successful merchant and founder member and vice-president of the Quebec Savings Bank, he purchased the Métis seigneury from his cousin Matthew McNider in 1807; his cousin, in turn, had acquired it five years earlier from Antoine Joubin dit Boisvert.[38] Extending his land holdings to the west of Montréal, he also acquired five stone-built stores on Rue Fabrique, in Québec City.[39] He then built a country estate for himself at Sillery, near to his shipyards, which he named Kilmarnock, to commemorate his Scottish roots. This was where he built his ships and sent his timber cargoes to Britain. To support him in his various ventures was his wife Angelique, daughter of Murdoch Stuart of Québec who had originated from Tain (Easter Ross).[40]

The settlers originated from diverse parts of Scotland, with some being disbanded ex-servicemen who had fought in the War of 1812–14.[41] Also included in their number was a Scottish family who had moved to the seigneury from Québec City.[42] By the time that the Reverend Clugston visited the region in 1839, Métis had clearly developed into a substantial Scottish community. His overall impression was that the people were all Presbyterians, who originated principally from the north of Scotland:

John McNider, seigneur of Métis. A copy made in the twentieth century by Messrs William Notman and Son for Messrs Scott and Sons. *Courtesy of McCord Museum of Canadian History, Montréal View-26111.*

Mr. McNider, the seignior of Métis has I believe done what he could to induce Scotch men to settle there. If I mistake not there are in all about 30 Presbyterian families or more. They are not able to support a Minister…. No minister had visited them for two to three years. I preached in the school house on the Sabbath to nearly 100 people.[43]

When they arrived, the settlers had been given rent-free accommodation for their first two years and were also provided with food, clothing and farm implements. After this initial period they then paid 12s. 5d. rent for each farm of 140 to 200 acres. The focal point of their settlement was McNider's manor house at Petit Métis, from which he ran his many business interests. But his and Angelique's real home was a modest cottage in Grand Métis which seemed "the pleasantest situation in the world" to Angelique until she discovered Petit Métis in the summer of 1822:

Little Métis is one of the prettiest places that I ever saw; it is like an island. The house is built on the Point and all the buildings which are built around it makes it appear as a little Villa surrounded with water. They have no garden which is a great shame as the soil seems very rich.[44]

As McNider's construction work was underway at the time, Angelique was being "very well entertained to see so many men at work."[45] There were "millwrights, carpenters, masons, carters for the stones, etc."[46] Meeting some of her husband's tenants, she found them "very happy to see their seigneuresse." Their cottages were "very comfortable and clean" and they were in good health, there being "no need of doctors at Métis."[47]

However, Lord Dalhousie's assessment of the seigneury some six years later was less flattering. Although "the soil appears excellent" and thus "tempting to settlers," its distance from Québec markets and poor roads were limiting its economic development."[48] But it had "very superior timber."[49] This would become the seigneury's prime asset. Having abundant quantities of hard wood and extensive pine forests,[50] it attracted the attention of the timber baron, William Price, who joined forces with McNider in exploiting the region's rich forest resources. Price established large sawmills to replace McNider's smaller ones, and timber exports soared. Consequently, when Joseph Bouchette called in 1832, Métis had the trappings of a well-settled community. The river frontage was fully cleared and there were "some tolerably good farms.[51] In addition to the manor house at Petit Métis, there were "mills and stores" together with "dwelling houses intended for the reception of travellers."[52] The settlers were concentrated at Grand Métis, which was about five miles to the west of Petit Métis and linked to it by a beach road which was "passable." "Seigneurial mills" had been constructed "about one mile below Grand Métis" and McNider had also built a schooner to provide himself with a regular shipping service to Québec.[53]

The many Scottish surnames, appearing on local tombstones, provide evidence of an enduring Scottish presence at Métis. Names such as Astle, Blue, Brand, Campbell, Crawford, Ferguson, McEwing, McGougan, McLaren, McMillan, McNider, Shaw, Sims and Turriff, were almost certainly some of the surnames of the original settlers.[54] Being a small enclave in a predominately French-Canadian region, they would have been forced to make major cultural, and even spiritual, adjustments as they came to terms with the world around them. Lacking funds in the early days to have a Presbyterian church and minister of their own, they would have grabbed opportunities for religious worship where they could. Hence, a visit from a Roman Catholic Bishop was a major event to be relished and celebrated. Angelique McNider, who may have been Roman Catholic herself, could hardly contain her excitement:

His eminence made his appearance in his barge, accompanied by four priests; they fired guns and we answered from our fort; as the tide was low we sent a carriage for his Lordship, who arrived in safety.

Never was there such a sight at Métis before; all the ladies of the neighbourhood in their best attire, came to pay their homage, and ask the
Bishop's benediction....[55]

This happened in 1822[56] and, when he came to Métis two years later,
the Anglican Bishop, Dr. George Mountain, could not have been "more
thankfully received."[57] Although they were all Presbyterians, "the public prayers, the psalm singing, the preaching of the word had all the zest
for these people of a rare and unexpected occurrence."[58]

While the Métis Scots had employed a Presbyterian schoolmaster for
a period, they had not been able to retain him. The Reverend Clugston,
having "found Mr. Paul the former teacher at Métis" during his 1839
visit to Rimouski, discovered that he had taken charge of a general store
which was owned by a Québec lumbering company:

> He [Mr. Paul] regrets having been compelled to leave Métis and seems
> to have had pleasure in his labours there. I doubt not that he would
> return provided sufficient encouragement were held out. The peo-
> ple in Métis are much scattered and Mr. Paul told me that at some
> particular seasons of the years when children at a distance could not
> well attend school or in cases where parents manifested indifference
> to their children's attendance at School he itinerated—that is he went
> from settlement to settlement teaching in each for a week more or
> less as circumstances seemed to require.[59]

Of course it was just a matter of time before the Métis Scots would
become absorbed by the rapidly-growing French-Canadian communities around them. Métis itself acquired a major influx of French
Canadians from the more long-established settlements at Kamouraska
and Rivière-Ouelle, further to the south along the St. Lawrence.[60] This
had followed on the heels of the new colonization road which was completed in 1832, at a cost of $29,000, to provide the vital overland link
between Métis and Lac Matapédia[61] (Figure 12). Attracted by the construction jobs that had suddenly become available, French Canadians
arrived in considerable numbers. The colonization road, named after
Governor Sir James Kempt,[62] eventually opened up the hill country to
the south, thus creating the 3rd Concession on which was founded

St-Octave-de-Métis. Predictably, the Kempt Road became a settlement magnet and eventually the settlement became the principal population centre for the entire area. A Presbyterian church was in place by 1847,[63] and a Catholic church was built eight years later.[64] Therefore, Reverend Jean-Baptiste Blanchette, their first priest, had to cope with a mixed community of French Canadians and Scots:

> There are…. Catholics and Protestants, [mainly] Presbyterians. There is a Catholic church and a Catholic curé [priest], a Protestant Chapel and a Protestant minister. There are not more than three hundred Scots. These Protestants give me little trouble and do not interfere with the Catholics in the practice of their religion. Their minister, the Reverend McAllister, always conducts himself, as a gentleman should, in his dealings with the Catholics.[65]

The support that he gave to the building of the Kempt Road was one of John McNider's most impressive legacies.[66] However, he never witnessed the benefits which it brought to the area, since he had died three years before its completion. So too had Angelique. Since there were no children from their union,[67] the Métis seigneury was transferred after their death to John's nephew, Adam Lymburner McNider.[68] He extended his uncle's road-building program and, as more settlers were attracted to the area, he requested the government to survey the neighbouring township. It was duly opened and named after the McNider family.[69] Following Adam's death in 1840, his two sons, William and John then inherited the seigneury. When William McNider, a Montréal physician, died in 1846 the property then passed to the remaining heir, John, who sold it to Archibald and David Ferguson of Montréal. Archibald acquired the Grand-Métis section,[70] on the west side of the Kempt Road while David had the Petit-Métis section on the east side of the road.[71]

Although Métis became the primary focus for Scots living on the north shore, there were other much smaller groups living in widely scattered communities. In his 1839 tour, the Reverend Clugston had ventured much further north of Métis to Matane and encountered "two families of Presbyterians." He arrived on the day when a ship from Ireland had gone aground near the shore and found himself with a ready-made congregation:

There were a great many emigrants on board, principally Presbyterians from the north of Ireland. Many of them came on shore the following day to the service so that I had rather (accidentally) a large congregation. Many of them seemed to value the opportunity, so unexpected, of hearing the word and all the circumstances gave a peculiar interest to the service.[72]

Just beyond Matane was the settlement of Sainte Félicité, which had attracted Scottish colonizers during the early 1800s. Becoming totally assimilated into Francophone communities by 1860, the descendents of these colonizers had names like Hamilton, Harrison and MacMalan (probably derived from MacMillan), but little else of their Scottish culture survived.[73] Yet another Scottish community had sprouted just to the west of Matane at Baie-des-Sables in this same period, and it too succumbed to similar demographic pressures.[74]

Although they had been a tiny minority in 1800, French Canadians quickly became the Gaspé's dominant ethnic group. By 1861 people of either English or Scottish origin accounted for only seventeen per cent of the population, and forty years later they were only 7 per cent of the total. Irish population trends were similar.[75] By 1935 Métis had only 180 people who could trace their ancestry back to the first Scottish settlers and this pattern was repeated throughout the Gaspé.[76] Although there was some migration, the French-Canadian propensity of the time for large families was the major cause of the rapid growth in their population. Three sisters from Rivière-au-Renard, on the north coast, who between them produced a total of 50 children, are a particularly outstanding example.[77] Meanwhile, Scots, who were faced with growing French predominance and a steadily deteriorating timber trade, had been leaving for Upper Canada where better land and job prospects awaited them.

The Scottish influx to the Gaspé and other parts of Lower Canada only gained ground when affordable sea crossings became a reality. The choice of shipping routes and the frequency of service varied widely from one end of the country to the other. Transport opportunities influenced the regional direction of emigration and of particular importance was the growth of the North American timber trade, which revolutionized the scale and costs of transatlantic shipping.

Seven

THE ATLANTIC CROSSING

The day arrived at last in which we were to sail. Friday of all days in the week.
Friday April 16th, 1853 at eleven a.m. with all on board the good three-masted
sailing ship Berbice. [We] set sail from Aberdeen Dock, and great and loud
were the lamentations of the crew and not a few curses at Captain Elliot for
sailing on a Friday and predicting all sorts of calamities which were to a great
extent fulfilled ere we landed in Quebec.... From April 16th to June 9th is a
good long voyage, being seven weeks and five days, the voyage now being made
in about the five days without the seven weeks.[1]

I T SHOULD HAVE BEEN A good crossing. The *Berbice* of Aberdeen
was a top-quality, recently-built ship.[2] Her generous proportions
would have enabled her to comfortably accommodate the one hundred and forty three passengers who sailed away from Aberdeen on
that fateful Friday.[3] With her slim hull, she offered better than average
sailing speeds and her highly experienced captain, James Elliot, had been
sailing the Atlantic with passengers for about twenty years.[4] Yet, the
Berbice had a difficult crossing. Perhaps there was something in the
sailor's superstition about setting sail on a Friday. It was supposed to be
unlucky and, as events would show, the *Berbice*'s crew and passengers
endured more than their fair share of bad luck.

Charles Peterkin, who was on board with his father and six brothers and sisters, recalled the voyage in later life. It had begun well. After
the "tug with the pilot" had steered the ship safely out of Aberdeen harbour the passengers assembled on the deck:

all enjoying the fresh sea air and the warm sunshine and lovely ocean view which was very calm—and as you would look away...it seemed as if the water was as a mountain towering above the ship away in the distance; and thus we sailed along in the sunshine every one gay and happy in the anticipation of the good things awaiting them in the new land to which we were all journeying, as the days went by so pleasantly with little change one from the other—the captain said he thought it was going to be a record voyage for time, as everything had gone so smoothly, but one day it darkened...[5]

As the storm approached Captain Elliott told his passengers "not to be afraid as he had been out in this ship in some of the worst storms on record" At sea everything depended on a captain's navigational skills and his were about to be put to the test. The storm came and went but it soon became clear that the *Berbice* had been badly damaged:

...Remarks were being made that the pumps were being tested very often with the result that that there seemed too much water for just an ordinary bilge or leakage and the crew were unable to keep the water down—and it was gaining on them fast; it was then that every man was ordered to report for duty at the pumps and they were divided into watches with so many of the sailors on each watch and all the pumps kept going night and day steady for fourteen days and nights when we reached Newfoundland at St. John's.[6]

Fortunately the sea remained calm after the storm. "If it had been stormy and rough" the ship might have sunk and "not likely one would have been left to tell the tale." After a ten-day sojourn at St. John's for repairs, the *Berbice* set sail once again and eventually entered the Saint Lawrence but a fresh problem loomed. Having been caught in unfavourable winds, she ran aground on a large rock. "A sudden heavy jar was felt and the ship suddenly stopped." Rocks were a familiar hazard along this stretch of coastline just off Île du Bic[7] and the local light-house keeper was well-used to dealing with stranded ships:

The captain went ashore to the light-house keeper and consulting with him it was decided to take all the women and children ashore;

so when the captain returned to the ship preparations, [we] were immediately made to transfer the women and children to the Island by the vessel's boats, also some boats belonging to the lighthouse, and continued until all had been taken ashore...the captain himself was helping the women and children over the side of the ship into the boats, a steady stream from about three thirty in the afternoon until after twelve o'clock at night...[8]

Captain Elliott's organizational skills were now being put to the test as were his passengers' resilience and self-reliance:

Each one [passenger] had to provide their own mattress in the shape of brush which grew in many places; accommodation was provided for some of the feebler persons in the [light-house keeper's] house. There was plenty of government flour in stock also lots of so-called coffee so it was not long before there was plenty of good bread to eat after the large oven of the fine stove had been put into commission and for tea they used nothing but a weed that grew in abundance on the Island....Then there was an enormous number of gulls on the Island and their eggs could be seen in holes in the rocks and the eggs were good to eat if not over ripe, some risk was incurred in getting them...there must have been hundreds of dozens collected and eaten as there was no meat to be had...[9]

The *Berbice*, having settled on her side at low tide, righted herself as the tide rose and was free of the rock. Captain Elliot set sail for Québec to have his ship repaired once again but without his passengers. Having seriously reduced the sea gull population of Île du Bic by greatly depleting their eggs, they were taken on a steamer to Québec. Most of them would be making their way to Upper Canada or the United States. However, Charles Peterkin's family suffered yet another setback when they reached Kingston. Having mistakenly got on a steamer for Rochester, Charles' father became separated from "seven youngsters standing on the steamer" bound for Toronto.[10] More bad luck, but thanks to the kindness and help of the crew on the Toronto steamer the family were eventually re-united and they ultimately reached their destination.

View of the busy Port of Québec in 1840. A lithograph by Thomas Picken based on
a drawing by Captain Benjamin Beaufoy. *Courtesy Metropolitan Toronto Reference
Library, J. Ross Robertson Collection, JRR 2014.*

Even without gales, there were plenty of difficulties to be faced by
emigrants when crossing the Atlantic. Accommodation in the steerage
was basic to say the least. Temporary wooden planking was hammered
over cross beams and temporary sleeping berths were constructed along
each side of a hold. There were no portholes, nor any means of ventila-
tion beyond the hatches. And, in stormy seas, the hatches could be kept
battened down for days. Conditions had been even more primitive eighty
years earlier when the Scottish influx to British North America had first
begun. Shipowners regarded emigrants as just another commodity to be
shipped and paid little regard for their creature comforts although the
ships themselves were usually sea worthy. It would not be until the steam
ship era, beginning in the 1850s, that custom-built accommodation would
become available for passengers. Until then passenger needs would have
a low priority with shipping services being primarily geared to the
stowage requirements of the goods being exported. Yet for emigrants
who could not afford the privacy and comforts of a cabin, travelling in
the hold was the only practical means they had of crossing the Atlantic.

Scotland's overseas commerce had grown rapidly from the late eighteenth century partly because Scots had been quick to appreciate the

new fields for enterprise which were emerging across the Atlantic. The combined effects of the Scottish-dominated Saint Lawrence fur trade and the relocation from the United States of Loyalists, following the American Rebellion, drew a large pool of merchants, of Scottish ancestry, into Québec and Montréal. With this headstart Scots achieved a level of economic supremacy by the early 1800s which was out of all proportion to their numbers.[11] Scottish firms soon dominated the import and export business of the St. Lawrence and commanded the major share of the shipping services which operated from Montréal and Québec.[12]

Among the many Scottish firms which had established early trade links with Québec and Montréal was the Ayrshire firm of McKnight and McIlwraith. Using John MacDonald, who "lives at Québec during the season the river is open" as its Lower Canada agent, the company became regular exporters of potash and wheat.[13] One of their ships, the *Eagle,* made frequent Atlantic crossings with small numbers of passengers and this is probably why an unnamed emigrant contractor approached McKnight and McIlwraith in 1803.[14] The firm was asked to provide a ship which could take two hundred emigrants from the Clyde to Québec. The *Eagle* was offered:

I conjoin the dimensions of the Ship *Eagle*[15] in order you may judge how far my calculations are accurate. You'll observe the ship is pretty deep and I think she will carry 200 passengers, allowing 6 feet by 18 inches for each berth, two feet of passage between every two tier of berths besides a general passage up the middle fore to aft. As there is always a great waste and leakage of water every precaution must be used to have plenty of that article. Therefore casks must be made on purpose that will stow to allow two heights of passengers....[16]

Three pricing options were put forward. For 200 passengers, with water and provisions supplied, the total cost would be £1150, plus two thirds of all port charges and pilotage.[17] An additional £50 had to be given to the captain, "to provide himself with stewards to attend the passengers for provisions."[18] The second option was for 150 passengers to be taken on the same terms. This would cost £1000 and only £25 would be paid to the captain. As a third option the firm would charge £300 to have the *Eagle* "manned and victualled for fourteen men for three months." However, it "will not provide coal, water, cambousses [caboose[19]]" nor take charge of provisions, fit up berths etc.."[20] None of these options found favour. Nevertheless, McKnight and McIlwraith did secure a contract to take 200 passengers, but not in the *Eagle*. They concluded a deal that same year with Lord Selkirk who hired the *Oughton,* one of their other ships, to take 200 Western Isle emigrants to Prince Edward Island. Being part of a much larger group of 800 Highlanders, they would eventually found the Belfast settlements there.[21]

So, the *Eagle* made her normal crossing to Québec in the Spring of 1803 but without passengers. If 200 passengers had sailed in her hold they would have endured extremely over-crowded conditions. The sleeping berth space allowance of six feet by eighteen inches was bad enough, but according to the Passenger Act of 1803, which specified that one person should be carried for every two tons burthen, the 179 ton *Eagle* was woefully over her legal space limit.[22] But the *Eagle* was going to be refurbished with "new masts and spars, a complete set of new sails and running rigging"[23] and she did have an "A1" rating from Lloyd's of London.[24]

McKnight and McIlwraith wanted the *Eagle* to leave in early March "in order that she may make a second voyage this season," the winter in Canada "having been moderate."[25] Early Spring departures were much favoured by shipowners because it enabled them to schedule at least two round trips a year across the Atlantic. Yet they could be perilous for the crew and passengers since ships could easily become ensnared in the large ice-fields to be found near Newfoundland and Cape Breton. Irrespective of such risks, Captain David Nicolson was to "lose no time in getting under sail, using every exertion prudent to make a North Channel passage and a quick direct voyage to Québec."[26] He would hopefully obtain "a cargo of plump clean wheat" and was given twelve days to get 10,000 bushels on board. If he exceeded this time he had to provide a voucher stating that it was not his fault "signed by Messrs McDonald & Co, who I dare say will not detain you as long, knowing that you must make another voyage this season or ruin your owner."[27] He was warned to "watch over the boys that they do not run off" in Québec and to choose his homeward route carefully since the war with France was about to begin.

McKnight and McIlwarith's export trade at this time was primarily in wheat and potash. The *Eagle* carried staves, that were five and a half inches

The King's Wharf in the old Port of Québec c.1827–41. Trade was booming by this stage. All exports such as wheat, potash and timber passed through this harbour as did thousands of immigrants. A watercolour by Fanny Amelia Bayfield (1814–91). *Courtesy of Library and Archives Canada C-002671.*

wide by one inch thick, as "dunnage," but these were only loose pieces of wood which had been inserted in the hold to secure the cargo. The timber trade was of little interest to them. They were seeking "an old vessel of large dimensions to bring oak logs from Québec" although this was only a one-off speculative venture.[28] But as the Napoleonic Wars (1803–15) progressed, North American timber would suddenly acquire a much higher status and value. The blockade of 1806, which effectively barred British ships from the Baltic, forced timber merchants to look to Québec and the Maritimes for their supplies. Then, when the already high duties on Baltic timber were nearly doubled in 1811, thus pricing it out of the market, timber exports rose greatly in importance. Because the disadvantage of greater distance had been effectively removed, North American timber became the cheaper option.[29]

Although wheat and potash remained major components of the Lower Canada economy, lumber and timber products soon constituted an increasing proportion of the value of exports from Québec and a major surge in shipbuilding followed.[30] Ships which were specifically designed to carry timber cargoes and cope with the severe conditions to be found in the North Atlantic were built in ever greater numbers. Vessels like the *Ardgour* of Fort William, the *Morningfield* of Aberdeen and the *Rebecca* of Greenock were offered to emigrants in 1816–1817 almost immediately after they were built (Appendix IV) Far from travelling in the old vessels, which McKnight and McIlwarith had once sought, emigrants mainly crossed the Atlantic in these new purpose-built timber ships which were being produced in British and North American shipyards. As competition brought down fares, emigrant travel became affordable to the masses. Transatlantic crossings became regular occurrences primarily because of the timber trade and without these timber ships the early Scottish influx to British North America could not have happened.

An over-riding priority for emigrants was to have low fares. Shippers wanted high volume and to achieve this many would lower their fares. Six hundred people had been packed into the hold of the 308-ton *Neptune* of Greenock when she sailed from Loch Nevis, near Fort William to Québec in 1802. No doubt the emigrants had negotiated cheap fares but in doing so, they endured very over-crowded conditions. The *Neptune* was four times over her legal limit when judged against the terms of the 1803 Passenger Act, which required two tons per person. While the 1803 legislation did reduce over-crowding for a period, its space requirements were relaxed in 1817, to one and one half tons per person, as a result of pressure from shipowners and agents. Ten years later the passenger to tonnage ratio was set at three passengers for every four tons in 1828 and it was made slightly more generous in 1835, when it was increased to three passengers for every five tons.[31]

The emigrant's desire for cheap fares and the shipper's desire for high volume certainly kept prices down. Steerage fares for passengers, supplying their own food, averaged £3.10s. in the 1820s and fell in the following decade to around £2. 10s.[32] However low fares were often achieved at the expense of overcrowding. In the absence of any regulatory body the space limitations were largely unenforceable and were frequently ignored. The evidence from the emigrants themselves suggests that they were prepared to put up with overcrowded ships to have affordable fares.[33] As a consequence, the avarice of shippers was not

View of Stornoway Harbour c. 1820. In 1816, the newly built *Morningfield* of Aberdeen carried 63 emigrants from Stornoway to Québec. The *John and Samuel* of Liverpool also called at Stornoway that same year to collect 82 Skye emigrants, some of whom settled at Dundee Township in Huntingdon County. William Daniell, *Voyage Round Great Britain* Volume IV (1820) *Stornoway, in the Isle of Lewis. Courtesy of Birmingham Central Library, United Kingdom.*

necessarily always to blame for the excess numbers which were occasionally carried on vessels. While they might have flouted the legislation, shipowners, who wanted repeat business, had to be responsive to the needs of their passengers. At this time a good personal recommendation from an emigrant was far more effective in checking unsavoury practices than was the legislation. That was the emigrant's principal weapon.

By the late 1840s emigrants could travel on large and streamlined ships like the 340-ton *Berbice* of Aberdeen. The sharpness of the hull and sheer lines, which helped to reduce wave-making resistance, all contributed to greater speed.[34] Having a floor to ceiling space between decks of seven feet and an "AE1" rating from Lloyd's of London, she was a popular choice. Her spacious height between decks was a considerable improvement on McKnight and McIlwarith's *Eagle* which probably offered no more than five and one half feet.[35] Given that the average male height at the time was somewhere between five feet five inches and five feet seven inches, this would have been miserly accommodation.[36] Nevertheless, while she offered more space and speed than was possible with earlier ships like the *Eagle*, the *Berbice* was still limited by

Notice to Passengers for Quebec.

T HE Fine, Fast-sailing, Copper-fas-
tened Barque and Regular Trader,
B E R B I C E,
A 1, 400 Tons Register,

J A M E S E L L I O T, Commander,

Is soon expected to arrive from the above Port, and will again be
despatched from hence for QUEBEC about the 24th of July.
Has excellent accommodation for Cabin and Steerage Passen-
gers, to whom every attention will be paid.
For Freight or Passage, apply to
RICHARD CONNON & CO., Brokers,
58, Marischal Street.
ALEXANDER DUTHIE, Footdee.
Aberdeen, 15th June, 1852.

Public Sale of Quebec Timber and Staves.

There will be exposed for sale, by public roup, on the LINKS,
adjoining the Aberdeen Rope and Sail Company's Works,
on SATURDAY *the 7th of August,*

T HE Entire Cargo of TIMBER and
STAVES, just now landing ex the Barque
" Berbice," from Quebec—consisting of
12,700 Feet YELLOW PINE
2,900 „   RED PINE
2,200 „   ROCK ELM
1,800 „   OAK
300 „   ASH
2 RED PINE MASTS, 63 X 16½, and 73 X 16½
300 Pieces SPRUCE DEALS
2,000 STANDARD STAVES
2,600 W. O. W. I. PUNCHEON ditto

The whole of the above Cargo is of the very best quality, having
been carefully selected at Quebec.
The Sale of Staves will commence at Eleven o'clock Forenoon,
on Waterloo Quay, and that of the Timber at Twelve o'clock Noon,
on the Links, as above mentioned.
Apply to   ALEXANDER DUTHIE, Footdee.
WILLIAM ROSS, Auctioneer.
Aberdeen, 27th July, 1852.

These 1852 newspaper advertisements reveal the *Berbice* of Aberdeen's two-
way trade in timber and passengers (*Aberdeen Herald,* June 19, July 31, 1852).
Between 1848 and 1855, she carried nearly 1,200 people to Québec.

the forces of nature. Sailing still depended on catching the wind in sails and on the vagaries of the weather.

On the whole, most emigrant crossings ran smoothly, although as happened with the *Berbice* in 1853, there were occasional mishaps. Disease could flare up at any time and most people succumbed to long bouts of seasickness. The *Caledonia*, which carried some of the Arran settlers to Québec in 1829 was buffeted by a severe storm "and though little damage was done all passengers including hardy fishermen became violently seasick."[37] But far more serious were the frequent cholera outbreaks which claimed many lives. Infectious diseases like cholera, smallpox and typhus often travelled with poor immigrants. Rudimentary medical facilities were in place at the Port of Québec by 1819. These were managed by the Quebec Emigrant Society, which was having to cope with thousands of immigrants, some of whom required medical care. Funds, together with charitable donations of "clothing, firewood and provisions," were raised from the general public to cover the running costs of the hospital, which treated around 500 sick people in its first year.[38] Having sent back some of the "deluded and helpless beings" who arrived in 1819, the Society wrote to the Colonial Office stating that it should warn British immigrants of the perils of abandoning their homes "in a vague expectation of relief" when they reached Québec.[39] However, little notice was taken of their warnings and Québec continued to be inundated with penniless immigrants.

With the passing of the Quarantine Act in 1832, which introduced an immigrant tax of five shillings, payable by each overseas passenger, quarantine and other medical facilities were built at Grosse Île, near Québec City.[40] Predictably, the new immigrant tax was bitterly opposed by shipowners and agents, who claimed that it would deter people from emigrating.[41] As anticipated, emigration numbers fell sharply from the following year and only began to rise again in the early 1840s (Table 8).

Although the quarantine facilities were intended to enable the authorities to contain the spread of disease, 1832 proved to be a particularly disastrous year for cholera deaths. That year there were 2,723 cholera-related deaths in Québec City, 2,547 deaths in Montréal and countless more people died elsewhere in the nearby countryside.[42] Even with incomplete statistics, the mortality rate reached five per cent of the population in that one year.[43] One French-Canadian commentator pinned the blame for the epidemic on the holders of economic power in the province—the so-called "Scottish rabble," whose links with the devil apparently made them immune to the disease.[44] Understandably, strong emotions were being unleashed at the time:

> When friends meet they bid each other adieu as though they will never see each other again. Day and night wagons are seen carrying bodies to the cemetery; sorrow and terror reign on every face, and the continuing spectacle of death and the tears and sobbing of those who have lost relatives or friends are enough to sadden the hearts of the most callous.[45]

***

TABLE 8

British immigrant and other arrivals at the Port of Québec, 1829–55

[Annual Reports of the Immigration Agent at Québec, 1831–55 (note: PP 1837–38(175)XLVII contains figures for 1829–36)]

Year	England	Ireland	Scotland	Europe	Maritime Provinces	Total
1829	3565	9614	2634	—	123	15945
1830	6799	18300	2450	—	451	28000
1831	10343	34133	5354	—	424	50254
1832	17481	28204	5500	15	546	51746
1833	5198	12013	4196	—	345	21752
1834	6799	19206	4591	—	339	30935
1835	3067	7108	2127	—	225	12527
1836	12188	12590	2224	485	235	27722
1837	5580	14538	1509	—	274	21901
1838	990	1456	547	—	273	3266
1839	1586	5113	485	—	255	7439
1840	4567	16291	1144	—	232	22234
1841	5970	18317	3559	—	240	28086
1842	12191	25532	6095	—	556	44374
1843	6499	9728	5006	—	494	21727
1844	7698	9993	2234	—	217	20142
1845	8883	14208	2174	—	160	23375
1846	9163	21049	1645	896	—	32753
1847	31505	54310	3747	—	—	89562
1848	6034	16582	3086	1395	842	27939
1849	8980	23126	4984	436	968	38494

Year	Maritime England	Ireland	Scotland	Europe	Provinces	Total
1850	9887	17979	2879	849	701	32292
1851	9677	22381	7042	870	1106	41076
1852	9276	15983	5477	7256	1184	39176
1853	9585	14417	4745	7456	496	36699
1854	18175	16156	6446	11537	857	53183
1855	6754	4106	4859	4864	691	21274

In one instance, two years later, the quarantine arrangements appeared to be doing more harm than good. Having arrived at Grosse Île in a perfectly healthy state some 368 Scots were detained for two weeks, because of a bureaucratic mix-up over the payment of their emigrant tax. Soon after leaving the quarantine station 53 of them contracted cholera and later died.[46] Despite the imposition of quarantine regulations and the best efforts of local medical authorities, the second cholera outbreak ran its course and further outbreaks were experienced in 1845, 1851, 1854 and 1867. And many thousands of mostly Irish immigrants would perish in the dreadful typhus and dysentery epidemic which gripped Grosse Île and Québec City in 1847. The port had been exceptionally busy that year, with the 1847 arrival numbers being three times greater than normal (Table 8). Around 17,500 Irish emigrants died either on board ship, or shortly after landing. Never before or since had such misery and suffering been witnessed.[47] By this time Irish immigrants accounted for some sixty per cent of the total arrivals at Québec.[48]

With the continued development of the timber trade, regular passenger services had become fully established at the main Scottish ports by the 1830s.[49] While there had been just over fifty ship crossings from Québec to Scotland in 1816, double this number were arriving twenty years later.[50] "Regular traders," as they were called, were now crossing the Atlantic at least twice a year, sometimes three times, usually under the helm of the same captain. Vessels like the *Favourite* of Montréal, *Brilliant* of Aberdeen and the *Canada, Corsair* and *Arabian*, all of Greenock, proved to be particularly popular with emigrants during the 1830s, while the *Berbice* of Aberdeen, *St. Lawrence* of Aberdeen and *Caledonia* of Greenock were favourites in the 1840s and 1850s (Appendix IV). These

View of the Quarantine Station at Grosse Île in 1850. Oil painting by Henri Delattre (1801–1876). *Courtesy of Library and Archives Canada C-120285.*

ships always followed the same Atlantic route between their home and foreign ports and brought an element of continuity to the local service. Designed to meet specific cargo needs, they usually carried both steerage and cabin passengers.[51] Some may have had large-sized cabins which could have accommodated up to thirty or forty passengers.[52] The needs of the timber trade were still paramount although some semblance of a transatlantic passenger service was being offered.

TABLE 9

Emigrant Departures to Québec from Scottish Ports, 1831–55

[PP, Annual Reports of the Immigration Agent at Québec]

Scottish Port	Emigrant Totals
Glasgow	28238
Greenock	18008
Aberdeen	10409
Highlands & Islands*	10081
Misc. Small Ports#	5459

Scottish Port	Emigrant Totals
Leith	4411
Stornoway	3362
Dundee	2294
Dumfries	394
Children under 1 year	292
Cabin Passengers	1152

*Excludes Stornoway
#For example, Alloa, Annan, Ayr, Irvine, Montrose, Peterhead and Stranraer

TABLE 10
Two-way crossings between Québec/Montréal and Scottish ports, 1836 to 1838

The list below shows the sequence of crossings made by ships which carried passengers from Scotland to Québec/Montréal and timber and other cargos on the return voyages to Scotland during the three year period from 1836 to 1838. The data for eastward crossings from Québec/Montréal to Scottish ports is taken from PP 1840(75)XLIV—"Return of Vessels cleared at the British Northern Colonies, 1836, 1837 and 1838." Passenger numbers carried on westward crossings are taken from the *Québec Mercury*.

1836

Amity of Aberdeen
Sailings: (1) April, Aberdeen to Québec with 13 settlers.
(2) June, Québec to Dundee with cargo.
(3) August. Québec to Dundee with cargo.
Vessel details: brig, 312 tons built 1825, New Brunswick; dimensions: 98' 6" x 27' x 19' 2".

Annandale of Aberdeen
Sailings: (1) April, Aberdeen and Kirkwall to Québec with 4 settlers and 3 cabin passengers.
(2) June, Québec to Dundee with cargo.
(3) September, Québec to Aberdeen with cargo.
Vessel details: brig, 254 tons, built 1828, New Brunswick; dimensions: 91' 10" x 25' 2" x 17' 3".

Betsey Miller
Sailings: (1) June, Glasgow to Québec with 12 settlers.
(2) August, Montréal to Glasgow with cargo.
Vessel details: brig, 142 tons, built 1816, Saltcoats; dimensions: 73′ 4″ x 21′ 1″ x 12′ 4″.

Brilliant of Aberdeen
Sailings: (1) April, Aberdeen to Québec with 67 steerage and 13 cabin passengers.
(2) June, Québec to Aberdeen with cargo.
(3) August, Aberdeen to Québec with 24 steerage and 4 cabin passengers.
(4) November, Québec to Aberdeen with cargo.
Vessel details: ship, 332 tons, built 1814, Aberdeen; dimensions: 97′ 2″ x 28′ 8″ x 19′ 3″.

Canada of Greenock
Sailings: (1) June, Montréal to Greenock with cargo.
(2) July, Greenock to Québec and Montréal with 35 steerage and 17 cabin passengers.
(3) October, Montréal to Greenock with cargo.
Vessel details: ship, 330 tons, built 1831, Greenock; dimensions: 107′ 8″ x 26′ 1″ x 18′ 2″.

Cherokee of Glasgow
Sailings: (1) June, Montréal to Greenock with cargo.
(2) August, Greenock to Québec and Montréal with 10 steerage and 6 cabin passengers.
(3) October, Montréal to Glasgow with cargo.
Vessel details: 278 tons, built 1831, Greenock; dimensions: 98′ 3″ x 25′ 5″ x 17′ 5″.

Circassian of Aberdeen
Sailings: (1) July, Aberdeen to Québec with 117 settlers.
(2) September, Québec to Leith with cargo.
Vessel details: brig, 180 tons, built 1835, Aberdeen; dimensions: 82′ 9″ x 22′ 6″ x 15′ 4″.

Clansman of Glasgow
Sailings: (1) August, Glasgow to Sydney, Cape Breton and Québec with 206 settlers of whom six landed at Québec.
(2) November, Québec to Greenock with cargo.
Vessels details: barque, 348 tons, built 1823, New Brunswick; dimensions: 104′ x 27′ 7″ x 19′ 6″.

Deveron of Glasgow
Sailings: (1) June, Saint John New Brunswick to Greenock with cargo.
(2) August. Loch Indaal (Isaly) to Québec with 174 settlers.
(3) November, Québec to Greenock with cargo.
Vessels details: brig, 333 tons, built 1824, Nova Scotia; dimensions: 102′ 6″ x 27′ 8″ x 19′ 6″.

Favourite of Montréal
Sailings: (1) March, Greenock to Québec with 43 steerage passengers.
    (2) June, Québec to Greenock with cargo.
    (3) June, Greenock to Québec/Montréal with 29 steerage passengers.
    (4) September, Montréal to Greenock with cargo.
Vessel details: brig, 296 tons, built 1825, Montréal; dimensions: 101' 0" x 26' 0" x 17' 6".

Globe
Sailings: (1) April, Montrose to Québec with 15 settlers.
    (2) June, Québec to Montrose with cargo.
Vessel details: 227 tons, built 1833, Montrose; dimensions: 87' 1" x 24' 8" x 16' 6".

Harmony
Sailings: (1) April, Troon to Québec with 10 settlers.
    (2) July, Québec to Irvine with cargo.
    (3) October, Bathurst, New Brunswick to Irvine with cargo.
Vessel details: 166 tons, built 1813, Ayr; dimensions: 28' 5" x 22' 7" x 14' 2".

Henry
Sailings: (1) July, Greenock to Québec with 58 steerage and 2 cabin passengers,
    (2) September, Montréal to Glasgow with cargo.
Vessel details: 238 tons, built 1833, Nova Scotia; dimensions: 89' 1" x 24' 9" x 5' 10" between decks.

Hercules of Aberdeen
Sailings: (1) June, Aberdeen to Québec with 155 steerage and 5 cabin
    passengers.
    (2) September, Québec to Aberdeen with cargo.
Vessel details: barque, 250 tons, former whaling ship, built 1781, Stockton;
dimensions: 88' 6" x 26' 2" x 6' 3" between decks.

Highlander of Aberdeen
Sailings: (1) July, Cromarty to Québec with 150 settlers.
    (2) September, Québec to Perth with cargo.
Vessel details: brig, 174 tons, built 1817, Aberdeen; dimensions: 79' 1" x 22' 11" x 14' 11".

Iris
Sailings: (1) April, Greenock to Québec with 14 settlers.
    (2) July, Québec to Greenock with cargo.
Vessel details: barque, 296 tons, built 1826, New Brunswick; dimensions: 97' 4" x 26' 2" x 18' 4".

Lord Sidmouth
Sailings: (1) April, Greenock to Québec with 6 settlers.
    (2) July, Québec to Port Glasgow with cargo.
    (3) November, Saint John, New Brunswick, to Port Glasgow with cargo.
Vessel details: barque, 595 tons, built 1835, Québec; dimensions: 133' 2" x 31' 5" x 22' 5".

Mariner of Sunderland
Sailings: (1) June, Miramichi, New Brunswick, to Port Glasgow with cargo.
(2) July, Thurso and Loch Eriboll to Québec with 145 settlers.
(3) October, Miramichi, New Brunswick, to Port Glasgow with cargo.
Vessel details: 255 tons, built 1799, Stockton; dimensions: 179′ 9″ x 26′ 5″ x 18′ 9″.

Monarch of Glasgow
Sailings: (1) April, Greenock to Québec with 4 steerage and 11 cabin
passengers.
(2) June, Montréal to Glasgow with cargo.
(3) August, Glasgow to Québec and Montréal with 23 settlers.
(4) November, Montréal to Glasgow with cargo.
Vessel details: barque, 316 tons, built 1835, Greenock; dimensions: 103′ 3″ x 26′ 8″ x 16′ 3″.

Osprey of Leith
Sailings: (1) April, Greenock to Québec with 12 settlers.
(2) July, Québec to Leith with cargo.
Vessel details: ship, 382 tons, built 1819, Greenock; dimensions: 103′ 6″ x 29′ x 20′.

Palmona
Sailings: (1) August, Greenock to Québec with 9 steerage and 6 cabin
passengers.
(2) June, Québec to Greenock wirh cargo.
(3) October, Québec to Leith with cargo.
Vessel details: ship, 359 tons, built 1810, Greenock; dimensions: 105′ 7″ x 28′ x 19′ 3″.

Rebecca of Greenock
Sailings: (1) August, Greenock to Québec with 11 steerage and 13 cabin
passengers.
(2) November, Québec to Greenock with cargo.
Vessel details: ship, 305 tons, built 1816, Greenock; dimensions: 97′ 8″ x 26′ 10″ x 17′ 9″.

Romulus of Greenock
Sailings: (1) July, Greenock to Québec with 8 steerage and 5 cabin passengers.
(2) September, Québec to Greenock with cargo.
Vessel details: barque, 467 tons, built 1831, Miramichi, New Brunswick; dimensions: 117′ 7″ x 30′ 1″ x 26′ 6″, 8 feet between decks, (*IJ* 8 July, 1836).

Shakespeare of Aberdeen
Sailings: (1) May, Aberdeen to Québec with 84 settlers.
(2) August, Québec to Aberdeen with cargo.
Vessel details: snow, 179 tons, built 1825, Aberdeen; dimensions: 75′ 9″ x 20′ 6″ x 14′ 11″.

Sir William Wallace of Aberdeen
Sailings: (1) April, Aberdeen to Québec with 13 steerage and 4 cabin
    passengers.
    (2) June, Québec to Montrose with cargo.
    (3) August, Aberdeen to Québec with 17 steerage and 1 cabin
    passengers.
    (4) October, Québec to Aberdeen with cargo.
Vessel details: brig, 183 tons, built 1835, Aberdeen; dimensions: 79' 9" x 22' 11" x 14' 5".

Sophia of Greenock
Sailings: (1) June, Montréal to Greenock with cargo.
    (2) August, Greenock to Québec with 8 settlers.
    (3) November, Montréal to Greenock with cargo.
Vessel details: brig, 266 tons, built 1825, Greenock; dimensions: 93' 3" x 25' 5" x 17' 3".

Victoria of Dundee
Sailings: (1) April, Dundee to Québec and Montral with 4 settlers.
    (2)November, Montréal to Dundee with cargo.
Vessel details: snow, 252 tons, built 1832, Dundee; dimensions: 93' 0" x 24' 9" x 16' 6".

Viewforth of Kirkaldy
Sailings: (1) June, Cromarty to Québec with 150 settlers.
    (2) August, Québec to Leith with cargo.
Vessel details: barque, 289 tons, built 1830, Shields; dimensions: 91' 9" x 27' 1" x 6' 2" between
decks.

1837

Andromeda
Sailings: (1) March, Dundee to Québec with 4 settlers.
    (2) June, Québec to Dundee with cargo.
Vessel details: brig, 384 tons, built 1824, New Brunswick; dimensions: 100' 8" x 27' 11" x 20'.

Arabian of Greenock
Sailings: (1) May, Greenock to Québec and Montréal with 81 settlers.
    (2) July, Montréal to Greenock with cargo.
    (3) August, Greenock to Québec with 28 settlers.
    (4) October, Montréal to Glasgow with cargo.
Vessel details: barque, 330 tons, built 1837, Greenock; dimensions: 105' 3" x 22' 9" x 17' 3".

Brilliant of Aberdeen
Sailings: (1) April, Aberdeen to Québec with 40 settlers.
    (2) June, Québec to Aberdeen with cargo.
    (3) August, Aberdeen to Québec with 12 settlers.
    (4) October, Québec to Aberdeen with cargo.
Vessel details: see 1836 above.

Canada of Greenock

Sailings: (1) April, Greenock to Québec and Montréal with 22 steerage and 6
    cabin passengers.
    (2) May, Montréal to Greenock with cargo.
    (3) October, Montréal to Greenock with cargo.
Vessel details: see 1836 above.

Cherokee of Glasgow

Sailings: (1) April, Glasgow to Québec with 32 steerage and 12 cabin
    passengers.
    (2) June, Montréal to Glasgow with cargo.
    (2) October, Montréal to Glasgow with cargo.
Vessel details: see 1836 above.

Corsair of Greenock

Sailings: (1) June, Greenock to Québec with 29 settlers.
    (2) September, Québec to Greenock with cargo.
Vessel details: brig, 273 tons, built 1823, New Brunswick; dimensions: 92' x 26' x 18' 7".
"High and roomy between decks" (*IJ* 27 May, 1831)

General Graham of Alloa

Sailings: (1) April, Alloa to Québec with 9 settlers.
    (2) June, Québec to Grangemouth with cargo.
    (3) October, Miramichi, New Brunswick to Grangemouth with cargo.
Vessel details: ship, 426 tons, built 1811, Hull; dimensions: 116' 6" x 29' 5" x 6' 1" between decks

Isabella of Glasgow

Sailings: (1) April, Greenock to Pictou with 190 settlers.
    (2) July, Greenock to Sydney, Cape Breton and Pictou with 124
    settlers.
    (3) October, Québec to Grangemouth with cargo.
Vessel details: bk, 376 tons, built 1821, New Brunswick.

Pacific of Aberdeen

Sailings: (1) April, Aberdeen to Québec with 48 steerage and 2 cabin
    passengers.
    (2) June, Québec to Dundee with cargo.
    (3) November, Dalhousie, New Brunswick, to Dundee with cargo.
Vessel details: barque, 386 tons, built 1826, Aberdeen; dimensions: 102' x 26' 2" x 18' 7".

Princess Victoria

Sailings: (1) April, Ayr to Québec with 10 settlers.
    (2) June, Québec to Ayr with cargo.
    (3) September, Québec to Ayr with cargo.
Vessel details: 251 tons, built 1835, Sunderland; dimensions: 87' 8" x 25' 11" x 17' 3".

Québec Packet of Aberdeen
Sailings: (1) June, Aberdeen to Québec with 35 settlers.
        (2) August, Québec to Montrose with cargo.
Vessel details: brig, 196 tons, built 1822, Aberdeen; dimensions: 82′ 2″ x 23′ 11″ x 15′ 4″.

Royal Adelaide of Greenock
Sailings: (1) June, Greenock to Québec with 152 settlers.
        (2) August, Québec to Greenock with cargo.
Vessel details: barque, 417 tons, built 1830, Miramichi, New Brunswick;
dimensions: 109′ 1″ x 29′ 6″ x 19′ 9″.

Sir William Wallace of Aberdeen
Sailings: (1) April, Aberdeen to Québec with 7 settlers.
        (2) June, Québec to Aberdeen with cargo.
Vessel details: see 1836 above.

Victoria of Dundee
Sailings: (1) April, Dundee to Québec with 14 settlers.
        (2) June, Montréal to Dundee with cargo.
        (3) November, Québec to Dundee with cargo.
Vessel details: see 1836 above.

1838

Arabian of Greenock
Sailings: (1) June, Montréal to Greenock with cargo.
        (2) August, Greenock to Québec with 11 steerage and 5 cabin
        passengers.
        (3) November, Montréal to Greenock with cargo.
Vessel details: see 1837 above.

Brilliant of Aberdeen
Sailings: (1) April, Aberdeen to Québec with 24 steerage passengers.
        (2) June, Québec to Dundee with cargo.
        (3) November, Québec to Dundee with cargo.
Vessel details: see 1836 above.

Canada of Greenock
Sailings: (1) June, Montréal to Greenock with cargo.
        (2) July, Greenock to Québec with 28 steerage and 13 cabin
        passengers.
Vessel details: see 1836 above.

Corsair of Greenock
Sailings: (1) July, Tobermory to Sydney, Cape Breton, and Québec with 250 settlers of whom
155 left at Sydney.
　　　　　(2) October, Québec to Aberdeen with cargo.
Vessel details: see 1837 above.

Eliza of Ayr
Sailings: (1) July, Greenock to Québec with 42 settlers.
　　　　　(2) September, Québec to Ayr with cargo.
Vessel details: brig, 237 tons, built 1836, Nova Scotia; dimensions: 87′ 6″ x 22′ 6″ x 18′.

Pilgrim of Aberdeen
Sailings: (1) June, Aberdeen to Québec with 77 steerage and 4 cabin passengers.
　　　　　(2) August, Québec to Aberdeen with cargo.
Vessel details: brig, 170 tons, built 1828, Aberdeen; dimensions: 75′ 6″ x 22′ 10″ x 14′ 3″.

Superb of Greenock
Sailings: (1) June, Greenock to Québec with 17 settlers.
　　　　　(2) September, Québec to Greenock with cargo.
Vessel details: barque, 599 tons, built 1837, Miramichi, New Brunswick; dimensions: 125′ 6″ x
29′ 7″ x 20′ 9″.

During the 25 year period from 1831 to 1855 over 92,000 emigrants
sailed from Scottish ports to Québec, with the majority leaving from
the Clyde ports of Glasgow and Greenock (Table 9). However, only a
small percentage of these people ever settled in Lower Canada. While
nearly a third of the British arrivals who came to Québec between 1819
and 1825 remained in Lower Canada, after 1835 the proportion
decreased to around four per cent. Nearly half of the arrivals went to
Upper Canada and the remainder went to the United States.[53]

Because vessel crossings from British North America were strictly
monitored from 1836 to 1838, lists survive of all of the ships which sailed
to Scottish ports from Québec during this three-year period.[54] On average, ships from Scotland made 100 crossings each year to Québec. Of
the ships which arrived in 1836 to collect cargoes only 28 had carried
passengers from Scotland, while in 1837 the proportion had decreased
to 14 per cent, and a year later it was only 8 per cent (Table 10).[55] Thus
the passenger trade was concentrated around a few ships and they generally carried very few passengers.[56] The *Cherokee* of Glasgow's ten

Customs House, on Rue Saint-André in the Old Port area of Québec. Built in 1860, it replaces an earlier Customs House which was constructed in 1793. *Photograph by Geoff Campey.*

steerage and six cabin passengers, the *Romulus* of Greenock's eight steerage and five cabin passengers and the *Annandale* of Aberdeen's four steerage and three cabin steerage passengers are typical examples. Each returned directly to Scotland with a cargo. There were a few regular traders like the *Brilliant* of Aberdeen and the *Corsair, Arabian* and *Canada,* all of Greenock, which brought sizable numbers of emigrants each year to Québec, and there were others like the *Pacific* of Aberdeen, and the *Québec Packet* of Aberdeen which made only occasional round trips across the Atlantic with passengers. What these ships all had in common were spacious proportions and an experienced captain.[57]

Ships like the *Circassian* of Aberdeen and the *Royal Adelaide* of Greenock, came only once to Québec with emigrants during this entire three year period and, when they did, they brought very large numbers. Once all of their passengers had disembarked at Québec, they collected their cargoes, with the *Circassian* returning to Leith and the *Royal Adelaide* to Greenock. Some ships like the *Deveron* of Glasgow followed a more circuitous route. Having left Saint John, New Brunswick, with a timber cargo in June 1836, the *Deveron* sailed to Greenock. Two months later she called at Loch Indaal in Islay to collect 174 emigrants and, having taken them to Québec, she then returned to Greenock with yet another cargo. The *Mariner* of Sunderland, having sailed in the same year from Miramichi in New Brunswick to Port Glasgow with a timber cargo, then collected 145 emigrants at Thurso and Loch Eriboll in the north of Scotland and took them to Québec. She then sailed from

the Miramichi to Port Glasgow later in the year with yet another timber cargo (Table 10).

Other ships like the *Viewforth* of Kirkcaldy in 1836, the *Swift* of Sunderland and *Margaret Bogle* of Leith in 1837, occasionally arrived at
Québec with large contingents of emigrants which had been collected
at Cromarty. Situated as it was midway between the Dornoch and Moray
firths and having an excellent harbour, Cromarty became a major collecting point for emigrants in the northeast Highlands. Because it had
no appreciable foreign timber trade there was no question of ships making round trips with passengers one way and timber the other way. These
were merely opportunistic one-off collections by passing timber ships,
which had sailed from east coast ports like Aberdeen and Leith. But,
although the ships made fleeting appearances at Cromarty, the emigration agents who procured them were more permanent fixtures.
Acting as middlemen, these agents provided a succession of ships, which
had the appearance of a purpose-built shipping fleet, although, of course,
they had no common owner and rarely did the same journey more than
once. But the agents sought a consistent standard of shipping since their
repeat business depended on a good recommendation from passengers.
This meant that they were under pressure to provide good ships and
reliable captains.[58]

Somehow emigrant sea crossings always seem to conjure up lurid
imagery of brutal captains, leaky ships and wretched conditions. Travelling by sea at this time did come with many perils and discomforts.
Nonetheless, the key question is whether emigrants were offered as good
a service as the primitive state of sea travel would allow. That is the ulti-
mate test. One crucial factor was the quality of shipping used. Dating
back to the late eighteenth century, the *Lloyd's Shipping Register* offers
a unique and highly reliable indicator of the quality of ships in use year
by year.[59] This source reveals that emigrant shipping was not, as is generally believed, concentrated on the poorest ships. Quite the reverse. The
data for the Québec arrivals, although incomplete, shows that emigrants
generally sailed on good quality ships.[60]

As major insurers, Lloyd's of London needed reliable shipping intel-
ligence, which it procured through the use of paid agents in the main
ports in Britain and abroad. Vessels were inspected by Lloyd's survey-
ors and assigned a code according to the quality of their construction

and maintenance.[61] An honest and open inspection was vital to the insurer's risk assessment, and the ship owner's ability to attract profitable trade hinged on the classification given to his ships. Shipowners actually complained that the codes were too stringent, particularly in the way a ship's age and place of construction could affect its classification.[62] Today these codes provide hard data on the quality of construction of the ships which carried emigrant Scots to Québec during the late eighteenth and nineteenth centuries.

Because of gaps and inconsistencies in shipping sources, the identification of shipping codes can never be an exact science.[63] Shipping codes have been located for 58 per cent of the 512 ships known to have carried emigrants from Scotland to Québec during the seventy year period covered in this study (Appendix V). One hundred and fifty-four of the 294 ships with known codes were first class ships ("A1" code) while 76 were ranked just below as "AE1." The latter had no defects, but their age put them just beyond the reach of an "A1" designation.[64] Overall a total of 230 ships, representing 78 per cent of the ships with known codes, were of the highest quality. All of the remaining 64 ships had an "E," or second-class ranking, signifying that they were seaworthy, although they had minor defects. No examples were found of unsuitable ships. A similar pattern emerges when the most frequently-used ships are analyzed. There were 76 ships which carried 300 or more passengers, either in a single crossing or in several journeys. Codes are known for 64 ships of which 27 had an A1 ranking while 24 were graded AE1. In other words 51 ships, or 80 per cent of the most frequently-used ships were of the highest quality. The remaining 13 ships had a E1 rating. The popular image of leaky and substandard vessels is simply not borne out by the evidence.

Nor were good ships the prerogative of the affluent emigrant. Although they were extremely poor, the Lewis emigrants who settled in the Eastern Townships, had generally sailed on good ships. Their landlords, Stewart MacKenzie of Seaforth, followed by Sir James Matheson who financed their relocation costs, had not skimped. Ships like the *Lady Hood,* which carried the 1841 Lewis contingent, the *Wolfville* of Ardrossan, *Barlow, Prince George* of Alloa and *Urgent* of Belfast, which sailed in the next year, and the *Blanche* of Liverpool in 1850, and the *Melissa* in 1855, all had "A1" or "AE1" ratings (Appendix V). There are few surviving accounts of their sea crossings. People recalled the babies who "were born on the boat" but little else.[65] The only recurring impressions, which lingered on, concerned the reluctance of the first settlers to leave Scotland. An obvious conclusion is that the Lewis settlers had crossed the Atlantic without mishap or incident. In this respect they were no different from the many thousands of other emigrant Scots who sailed to Québec safely.

Appendices IV and V provide overwhelming evidence that most Scots sailed to Québec in good ships under experienced captains. However, irrespective of the soundness of the ship or experience of the captain, crossing the Atlantic in a sailing ship was always going to be a perilous undertaking. Storms could create havoc and disease was an ever-present problem. There were many discomforts and anxious moments, but they were relatively minor when compared with what lay ahead for the emigrant. Coping with the rigours, privations and uncertainties of pioneer life would be a far greater challenge. The sea crossing was the first of many hurdles which the emigrant had to overcome—but it certainly was not the most difficult.

Eight

QUÉBEC'S SCOTTISH HERITAGE

When I was a child there were French and there were Scotch.... We associated with French kids; we played with them; we chatted. And there were French families that learned to speak the Gaelic![1]

IN HIS REMINISCENCES OF THE Scotstown he had known as a young boy, Bill Young of Lennoxville reminds us that cultural retention works both ways. I felt this sense of a shared heritage when I visited the magnificent pioneer cemeteries to be found in the Stornoway area of the Eastern Townships. Through their tombstone memorials the once-flourishing Hebridean communities remain highly visible to passing visitors and most of all, to the local population, which is almost entirely French. The cemeteries are being kept in an immaculate condition and reflect the high esteem in which the early settlers are held. As is evident from publications like Carl Beaulieu's *L'Alliance Écossaise au Québec*, which describes the Scots of Charlevoix County and the Saguenay region, and Albert Gravel's *La Pousse Gaelique Écossais dans les Cantons de l'Est,* which deals with the Eastern Townships, French Canadians are keen to learn more about their region's Scottish past. After all, some of them are themselves descendents of the province's Scottish pioneers.

The shared experiences of the early settlers transcended ethnic boundaries. In 1995, when the Town of Megantic, now entirely French, held a weekend festival to pay *hômmage aux premiers arrivants Écossais,* the focus of the proceedings was the centenary of the death of Donald Morrison.[2] The son of Lewis immigrants, Morrison, otherwise known as the "Megantic Outlaw," had been the town's most famous man. Having gone west to the prairies in 1888 to earn money to pay off his father's debt to a money lender, he found, on his return, that the money lender denied receiving payment and had sold his father's farm to a French family. The enraged Morrison went on the rampage and shot dead the man who came to arrest him. Becoming a fugitive, Morrison was sheltered by both Hebridean and French families, some of whom were imprisoned. He was later arrested and sentenced to 18 years in prison but was released five years later suffering from tuberculosis and died within hours of being freed.[3] These were hard times and tales of Morrison's suffering and fate, which had been passed down Hebridean and French families, still struck a chord one hundred years later.

Margaret Bennet, author, folklorist and singer of traditional Gaelic songs contributed to the festival along with her son Martyn:

> By the end of the weekend, the festival had given thousands of Québecois a chance to hear the story of Megantic's first settlers, to enjoy Gaelic songs and music on bagpipe and fiddle, to taste their Scotch whisky, tea and scones, and to share hospitality together.... As their guests, my son Martyn (the main musician) and I were deeply moved to watch the appreciation of our music and songs, especially of the old-time French fiddlers (one in his eighties) almost in tears as they jigged their feet to the tunes of *le jeune Écossias*. One old-timer shouted loudly for "Beeg John MacNeil" and when he instantly got the tune he wanted he was ecstatic; for the only language he and Martyn had in common was *le musique du violon*.[4]

The affinity felt between emigrant Scots and French Canadians, which Margaret Bennett describes with such poignancy, also struck me during visits to pioneer cemeteries and in studying the documentation relating to the pioneers. Scottish and French settlers were clearly comfortable with each other. As some of the earliest British arrivals in the province, the men of the Fraser's Highlanders Regiment played an important role in cementing these good relations. Steeped in the traditions of the *auld alliance*, which sometimes included being partly educated in France, they blended effortlessly into French society.

St. Andrew's Presbyterian Church, Québec City. Built in 1810 and enlarged in 1823, its congregation was initially composed of former members of the Fraser's Highlanders Regiment, which was disbanded in Lower Canada in 1763. *Photograph by Geoff Campey.*

There were early Scots like Hugh Finlay, whose fluency in French smoothed his introduction to Québec City's mercantile community in 1763 and secured his appointment as the province's first postmaster.[5] In his tour of the province in 1803, Lord Selkirk had noticed how French Canadians were "socially disposed" to the Scots. When two Highland children, living at Sir John Johnson's Chambly seigneury, were lost in the woods "all the [French] Canadians turned out to assist in seeking them" while "not one of the Americans." lifted a finger to help them. "The children were at last found by two Indians…who tracked them from the place where they entered the woods."[6]

However, ethnic tensions did develop, particularly during periods of economic crisis. A source of great disquiet, felt by French Canadians, was the immense influence and economic power which men of British ancestry enjoyed in the province. And when it came to power and influence few could outperform the Scots. Pierre Berton attributed their astonishing success to the Scottish work ethic:

For the Scots it was work, save and study; study save and work. The Irish outnumbered them, as did the English, but the Scots ran the country. Though they formed only one-fifteenth of the population they controlled the fur trade, the great banking and financial houses, the major educational institutions and, to a considerable degree, the government.[7]

Having been amongst the earliest arrivals, Scots had an enormous influence on all aspects of the province's development, particularly in business, education and politics, and this influence was out of all proportion to their numbers.[8] In 1871 they represented a mere four per cent of Québec province's population.[9]

The merchants of Scottish ancestry, who moved to Montréal from the United States after the American Revolutionary War, quickly found a niche for their entrepreneurial talents in the Montréal fur trade. In so doing they brought their business acumen and much-needed capital to Montréal. Arriving from New York in 1775, Simon McTavish became a giant of the fur trade as did James McGill, who transferred his business interests from the southern colonies in the previous year.[10] Unlike many of his contemporaries, James Dunlop, a Glasgow-trained merchant from Virginia, shunned the fur trade. Establishing himself as a general merchant in Québec City from 1779, he later moved to Montréal, the main economic centre, and amassed his fortune by exporting large quantities of potash, grain and timber to the Clyde.[11]

Scots were a dominant force in the province's early economic life. Included among Montréal's leading merchants and industrialists were: the Perthshire-born William Dow, who established a brewing company,

A view of Montréal, October 1784. Scottish merchants and entrepeneurs were already well ensconced by this time and were dominating much of Montréal's growing business community. Watercolour by James Peachey. *Courtesy of Library and Archives Canada C-002002.*

Simon McTavish House, St. Jean
Baptiste Street, Montréal c. 1900.
Watercolour by Walter Baker.
*Courtesy of Toronto Public Library
(TRL) J. Ross Robertson
Collection: MTL 2244.*

Angus McDonald, from Aberdeenshire, who became a pioneer of paper manufacturing; John Redpath, born in Earlston, near Edinburgh,[12] who founded a sugar refinery; Sir William Christopher Macdonald, of Highland stock,[13] who became a tobacco manufacturer; the Renfrewshire-born Robert Anderson, who founded a glass and china company and Joseph and Edward MacKay, from Kildonan in Sutherland, who founded a dry goods firm. Peter McGill, who originated from Wigtownshire, rose to the top of Montréal's business community and was president of the Bank of Montreal by 1834—the bank itself having been established in 1817 mainly by Scots.[14] The Ayrshire-born Sir Hugh Allan, together with his sea captain father and brothers founded the "Allan Line," which dominated trade between the Clyde and Montréal. He always made a point of speaking French and used this to advantage in business.[15] Like so many Scots he was a self-made man. There were countless other Scots, simply too numerous to mention, who attained great wealth and status.[16]

John Bell's shipbuilding business is a more modest example of Scottish enterprise. His firm constructed large ships in Québec, one of which, the *Triton,* made three crossings with emigrants from Leith to Québec in the early 1830s.[17] Bell clearly prospered and diversified into property, having "two houses of three stories and cellars" which he expected to rent for £50 a year. However his primary asset was his shipyard and wharf "that divides my property and Mr. [James] McCallum's...of 395 feet in length."[18] A factor in their success was the Scottish tendency to work within collective groupings. Their tightly controlled coteries ensured that Scots would choose fellow-Scots as their business partners, clerks and ship masters. The Ayrshire-born Thomas Porteous, a grain merchant and co-founder of the Bank of Montreal, moved to Montréal

St. Gabriel Street Church, the first
Presbyterian Church in Montréal c.
1885. It was built in 1792 with money
raised by wealthy Scottish merchants.
Watercolour by Alfred Worsley
Holdstock. *Courtesy of Library and
Archives Canada C-040117.*

with his brother John in 1762, having previously settled in New
Brunswick.[19] John Porteous' nephew John Mure, also from Ayrshire,
having become a prominent fur trader by the 1790s, entered into part-
nerships with other Scots, some of whom shared his Ayrshire origins.
Thus was formed the Montréal firm of Parker, Gerrard and Ogilvy,
which by 1800 was the leading exporter of Lower Canada potash.[20]

Alexander Leslie, a Glasgow merchant, had business interests throughout the early 1800s in Leslie McNaught & Co. in Glasgow, Duncan
McNaught & Co. in Greenock, Irvine McNaught & Co. in Québec City,
and Irvine Leslie & Co. in Montréal, the latter being managed by his son,
Alexander Junior. All of these firms were engaged in the lucrative
import/export trade between the St. Lawrence and the Clyde. Meanwhile,
William Liddell, a Glasgow-based timber merchant and brother-in-law
of one of the McNaughts, formed a partnership with the Scottish-born
Edward Mortimer, who rose to the top of the Pictou timber trade.[21] And
so it went on. Scottish cliques were everywhere. Even James Thomson,
a humble baker's apprentice from Aberdeen, had a network of Scottish
contacts to guide him when he first reached Montréal in 1844. Recover-
ing from the initial shock of seeing Montréal's "wooden wharfs, streets,
houses, churches and steeples," after being accustomed to the granite of
Aberdeen, he looked for a job.[22] Almost immediately he found employment at a bakery run by Mr. McDougal and Mr. Morrison, the latter being
"a native of Huntly [Aberdeenshire]." He then located a room "at a lodg-
ing house kept by Mr. McHardy, who twelve years ago was a coach guard
on the Deeside Road [Aberdeen]" and later visited the baker from
Aberdeen, who lived on Côte des Neiges.[23]

Hugh Brodie, another Ayrshire Scot, achieved fame as an agriculturalist and "was several times appointed a judge at the New York State agricultural exhibitions."[24] He also exemplifies the bookish and intellectual traditions of the hand-loom weaving community from which he had originated.[25] Having been raised "without the advantages of an early education," he dedicated himself to the establishment "of good schools in Lower Canada."[26] At the other end of the spectrum, was the extremely wealthy James McGill who endowed a Montréal university bearing his name.

Scots had obvious entrepreneurial talents, but they also had a strong sense of identity and self-belief, which contributed to their success. In recognition of the importance they placed on their traditions and customs, Bishop Alexander Macdonell of Glengarry and leading lights of the North West Company, including William McGillivray, formed the Highland Society of Canada in 1818.[27] An offshoot of the Highland Society in London,[28] which had been founded in 1778, the Society sought to preserve what was left of "the language, martial spirit, dress, music and antiquities of the ancient Caledonians."[29] Simon McGillivray, brother of William, who was the London agent for the North West Company, was a past president of the

View of Lower Market Place, Québec, from McCallum's Wharf in July 1829. James McCallum (1762–1825), a second-generation Scot, was a prominent businessmen and landowner. Watercolour by James Pattison Cockburn. *Courtesy of Library and Archives Canada C-150737.*

Portrait of James McGill (1744–1813). Born in Glasgow, he made a fortune from the fur trade and was
a member of the Scottish-dominated Beaver Club of
Montréal. He married Charlotte Trottier Desriv-
ières, a Roman Catholic widow, in 1776 and they
had two sons, one of whom became his partner and
principal heir. Painting c. 1800 by Louis Dulongpré.
*Courtesy of McCord Museum of Canadian History,
Montréal M970X.106.*

Highland Society of London.[30] Although several of its members were Mon-
tréal-based fur barons, meetings of the Highland Society of Canada were
held in Glengarry, the region's principal Highland stronghold. At a general meeting held each year "to celebrate the anniversary of the Battle of
Waterloo" members would appear "in the garb of Highlanders," and dis-
pense provisions to needy Highlanders living in Upper Canada.[31]

While kilts were a symbol of martial endeavour and Highland identity, they were also the military uniforms of regular soldiers. When the
Cameron Highlanders (79th Regiment) marched into the Jesuits' Barracks at Québec City in November 1825, they excited "surprise and
admiration, not unmixt with sentiments of pity from the softer sex, at
the bare idea of the sufferings even these hardy mountaineers might
endure if exposed to the rigour of a Canadian winter." But reassurances
were given that they would wear garments "more suitable to the climate of these frozen regions" during the winter.[32] Their circumstances
were somewhat different from the wealthy businessmen who donned
their kilts at fancy dress gatherings. These were men who, having abandoned the harsh economic realities of the Highlands, sought the better
life which North America could offer. They had probably been induced
to join the regiment by the offer of "a grant of land" after seven years
service.[33] While the grandees of the Highland Society may have once
experienced harsh realities, those days had long since past.

The St. Andrew's Society of Montréal, which was founded in 1835 by
Scottish business leaders and fur traders to assist poor immigrant Scots
newly arrived in the province, continues to raise funds for charitable

purposes. However, the Highland Society of Canada ceased to function by 1870 and in more recent times the Montréal Highland Games have given Scottish culture new life, although they bear little relation to the province's actual Scottish traditions.[34] But, the same can be said of the cultural symbolism which abounds in Scotland. The Highland symbols which came into vogue are modern inventions. They began appearing in the nineteenth century when Scotland was seeking a more distinctive national identity. Adopting the cultural emblems of its poorest region, the Highlands and Islands, Scotland redefined its heritage and gave itself a rich panoply of pipe bands and tartans. This same process also happened in the New World.[35]

William McGillivray (1764–1825). A Highlander, he rose from humble origins to become head of the North West Company, succeeding Simon McTavish, who was his uncle. The company's headquarters, Fort Kaministiquia, was renamed Fort William in his honour in 1807. He too was a member of the select Beaver Club, formed in Montréal in 1785 by fur traders, and served on Lower Canada's Legislative Council from 1814 to 1825. The artist of this watercolour is not known. *Courtesy of Library and Archives Canada C-095779.*

The traditions and customs which the pioneer Scots brought to Lower Canada were often centuries old. The Highland tradition of working to the accompaniment of music lived on for some time in the Eastern Townships. Hebridean settlers would measure out their land grants to the strains of the Twenty-third Psalm ("The Lord's My Shepherd") sung in Gaelic. As they marked the boundaries of each family's plot, "they'd sing that [the psalm] over so many times, and they'd keep time walking through the woods."[36] The making of maple sugar also had musical accompaniment. In April of each year Hebridean families would gather at "sugaring-off parties" held at the Oddfellows Hall in Milan, in Whitton Township,[37] part of the Eastern Townships (Figure 11). They would "bring a sample of their season's syrup" and when it turned into "a kind of toffee" in the fresh snow outside, people enjoyed "their hard-earned treats." The evening ended with Scottish dancing, although local Presbyterian stalwarts "frowned on such frivolity."[38]

The Arran settlers of Megantic County arrived in 1829–31, "well-stocked with bibles [written in] both English and Gaelic" although their Congregationalist preacher, Donald Hendry, would only ever preach to them in Gaelic.[39] However, the situation was very different in the Gaspé Peninsula, where the dominance of the English language had forced the relatively small numbers of Highlanders, who came as Loyalists, to abandon their Gaelic and learn English. Hence, even though the Gaspé attracted a great many Highlanders over the years, the Gaelic language never took root there. How different this was from the situation in the Eastern Townships where vast areas had nothing but Gaelic-speakers, although even here the language eventually went into decline. Angus Mackay, (Oscar Dhu), who was raised in the rich Gaelic tradition of spoken song and verse, lamented the widespread abandonment of Gaelic which was taking place in the Eastern Townships by the 1890s. His "Guard the Gaelic" poem[40] exhorted his fellow Highlanders to preserve their language, but his pleas went unheeded:

"Some gay natives of the soil
Cross "the line" [into the United States] a little while
And returning, deem it style
to deny the Gaelic.
Lads and lassies in their teens
Wearing airs of kings and queens—
Just a taste of Boston beans
Makes them lose their Gaelic!
They return with finer clothes
Speaking Yankee through their nose!
That's the way the Gaelic goes—
Pop! goes the Gaelic."[41]

But Gaelic had not been totally lost. During the 1920s "probably two hundred" people would fill the Oddfellows' Hall in Scotstown to hear a Gaelic concert. The older people "loved the old songs," although the younger generation, who could not speak Gaelic, "became sick and tired of the length of the Gaelic songs!"[42] And Gaelic traditions, like the *ceilidh,* lived on in the Eastern Townships as neighbourhood gatherings:

Night after night, during the long winter evenings, people would gather, first in one place, then at the other. Around a cracking bush fire they would congregate and would swap stories, joke and sing the folk songs of their old homeland...[Some evenings] the women quilted...[other times] all the moveable pieces of furniture would be thrust out of the way, and, and as the fiddlers ground out their gay Scottish melodies, all hands would temporarily abandon their cares to join in joyful dances.[43]

In the lumber camps of the late 1920s "songs, stories, jokes and the occasional fiddle tune and step-dance" were often the only respites from back-breaking and lonely work.[44] Some of the Scottish fiddle tunes found their way into Québec music and acquired French names.

However, it was through curling that Scots had their most stunning success in imparting their culture to Québec province. After the siege of Québec, the Fraser's Highlanders apparently "found ideal conditions in the hard Canadian winters" to indulge in curling.[45] "A group of Scots who were identified with the fur trade" formed Canada's first curling club, the Royal Montréal Curling Club in 1807 and used the St. Lawrence River as their rink.[46] Choosing Trois Rivières as a half-way point, the Montréal club played a match with the Québec Curling Club in 1835, with some members arriving at the match on their own sleighs.[47] Curling clubs can now be found from one end of the province to the other and are particularly noticeable in the St. Lawrence Valley, Ottawa Valley and Eastern Townships, regions where Scottish communities had once been widespread. And shinty was another Scottish first. Having been imported to Canada by Scots, it became the forerunner of ice hockey.[48] Shinty was first played in Montréal "by a club of McGill College students, one of whose number had played it in Glasgow."[49] It is widely believed that the first game of ice hockey was played in Montréal in 1875. Scots, particularly McGill students, were the main participants.[50]

Scots brought their fighting skills and work ethic to the province, but they also came with a strong sense of history in their bones. The *auld alliance* made them uniquely qualified to act as mediators during the first stages of the province's development after the conquest. They mixed easily with the French population and were the essential bridge between them and the English rulers back in Britain. The Fraser's Highlanders,

Lachine Ladies Curling Club, Montréal, 1903. The club was founded in 1898.
Courtesy of McCord Museum of Canadian History, Montréal II-147881.

the province's earliest military settlers, and the waves of pioneer Scots who followed them, cared little for ethnic boundaries. Unlike the other British immigrants who nearly always went to the newly created townships, which had been set aside specifically for them, many Scots headed for the French seigneuries. Scots chose locations for their proximity to fellow Scots or for their economic advantages. French versus English was not an issue for them.

The original policy of allowing two cultures to grow side by side was bound to create deep-seated ethnic tensions. However, if it had not been for the first governor's inspired interpretation of the *auld alliance* would we still have a Canada? It took a Scot, in the shape of General James Murray, to understand and recognize that Britain's North American interests would best be served by tolerating both French culture and the Church of Rome.

When Upper and Lower Canada came under attack from the United States in 1812–14, the entire population, including the French, fought on the British side and Canada's future was thus secured. The long-standing affinity between *les Écossais* and the French Canadians was a vital factor in this decisive victory.

Appendix I

Passenger Lists for the *Helen* of Irvine, *Jean* of Irvine and *Friends of John Saltcoats,* which sailed from Fort William to Québec in June, 1802.
[NAC MG24 I183 File 2, 7-9, 11; Fleming, *The Lochaber Emigrants to Glengarry*, 5-11; MacMillan, *Bygone Lochaber*, 239]

Passengers who Boarded at Fort William

Alex. McPhee,	Aberchalder		25 his Wife	
Alex. McPhee	Do.		Alex'r Scot	
Catherine McPhee	"		Dun. Scot	
Mary McPhee	"		Janet Scot	
5 Margt McPhee	"		Mary Scot & 2 Children	
Anny McPhee & 1 Child	"			
			30 Dun: Kennedy	Aberchalder
Don'd McPhee	Do.		His Wife & 3 Children	
Anne Kennedy }	"			
Janet Marshall }	"		Don'd Kennedy	Achluachrach
10 McPhee's wife & ~~1 Child~~	"		Mrs. Kennedy	
			~~Mary McDonald~~ & 5 Children	
Ewen Kennedy	Aberchalder			
His wife			35 Alex'r McDonell	Laggan
Don'd Kennedy	Kinlochlochy		Mrs. McDonell & 2 Children	
4 Children				
			John McDonell	Leck
Don. Cameron	Drumnasallie			
15 His Wife			Don'd Kennedy	Laddy
			Mrs. Kennedy & 2 Children	
John Corbet	Ardachy			
Mrs Corbet			40 Don'd McDonell	Laddy
~~Mary Corbet~~			John McDonell	
Wm. Corbet			Dun: McDonell	
20 Christy Corbet & 1 Child			Catherine McDonell	
			~~McDonell~~	
John McDonald	Inchlagan		Mary Kennedy	
His Wife				
Don'd McDonald & 2 Children			45 Allan McDonell	Munergy
			Mrs. McDonell	
Don'd Scot	Aberchalder		Margaret McDonell taken in No. 298	

Passengers who Boarded at Fort William

Catherine McDonell
Donald McDonell & 2 Children
———————
Don'd McDougald Ft Augustus
50 Mrs. McDougald
Marjery McDougald
Alex'r McDougald
John McDougald
———————
Alex'r Stewart
& 1 Child   Ft Augustus
55 Don'd Fraser   Leck
Mrs. Fraser & 1 Child
———————
Mary McAlpin   Greenfield
Mary Cameron   Letterfinlay
Catherin McAlpine   Do.
60 Eliz. Grant   Drumnadrochit
———————
Alex. Grant   Achnaconeran
Mrs. Grant
John Grant & 4 Children
———————
Don'd Grant   Dalcattaig
65 Mrs. Grant
———————
Mary Grant   Duldreggan
Flory Grant
Isabella Grant
Anne Grant   Livisie
70 John Grant & 1 Child
———————
James Mcdonell   Balmean
Mrs. McDonell
Kath: McDonell
Allan McDonell & 4 Ch.
———————
75 Don'd McDonell   Inchlagen
His Wife
Mary McDonell
———————
Janet McDonell
Catherine McDonell
80 Peggy McDonell
Allan McDonell & 4 Ch.
———————
Alex'r McDonell   Boline
his Wife
Dun: McDonell
85 Don'd McDonell
Cath. McDonell & 4 Ch.
———————
John McDonell   Invervigar
Dugald McDonell
Catherine McDonell
90 Flora McDonell
Peggy McDonell

Don'd McDonell & 1 Ch.
———————
Arch'd McLean   Laddy
Angus McLean
———————
95 John Kennedy   Invervigar
His Wife
Dun: Kennedy
Alex'r Kennedy
———————
Don'd Kennedy   Inchlagen
100 Angus Kennedy
Alex'r Kennedy
Allan Kennedy
Mrs. Kennedy & 2 Children
———————
John Kennedy   Inchlagen
105 his Wife
Ewen Kennedy
Mary Kennedy
Alex'r Kennedy
Janet Kennedy
110 Angus Kennedy & 3 Children
———————
John McDonell   Ardnabie
His Wife & 1 Child
Alex'r Cameron
His Wife
———————
115 John Stewart   Boline
Mary Stewart
Catherine Stewart
———————
Ran'd McDonell   Achteraw
Alex'r McKinzie   Urquhart
120 John McDonell   Divach
Alex'r Scot   Urquhart
———————
Chas. McArthur   Inverskilroy
John McArthur
Sarrah McArthur
125 Lizie McArthur
Donald McArthur
———————
Dun: McKinnon   Donie
His Wife & 6 Children
———————
Effy Kennedy   Caum
130 Archy McMillan
Mary McMillan
Kath: McMillan
Miles McMillan
Dun: McLean & Wife
135 Alex'r McKinnon
His Wife & 3 Childrem
Dun: McKinnon
———————

Passengers who Boarded at Fort William

Jas. McIntosh   Kerrowdoun
Catherin McIntosh
140 Mary McDonell
Mary McDonell
_____

Don Kennedy   Lewiston
Marg't Kennedy & 3 Children
_____

145 John Cameron   Glenturret
Angus Cameron his Bro.
Catherine Cameron   Leck
Mary Gillis
Mary Cameron
150 Marjory Cameron 2 Ch.
_____

Don Cameron   Kenlocharkaig
His Wife & 2 Children
_____

John Cameron   Kenmore
His Wife
155 John Cameron
Donald Cameron
Ewen Cameron
_____

Dun: McMillan   Shanvail
His Wife
160 Catherine McMillan
Effy McMillan
4 Children
_____

John McMillan   Shanvail
His Wife
Alex'r McKay & 3 Children
_____

165 Kath: McMillan   Shanvail
Mary McMillan
Peggy McMillan & 1 Child
_____

Angus McPhee   Crieff
170 His Wife & 3 Children
_____

John McDon'd   Kenlochnasale
His Wife
Alex'r McDonald
Don'd McDonald
_____

175 Peggy McDonald
Mary McGilvray
_____

Don: McMillan   Tomdoun
His Wife & 4 Children
_____

E. McMillan   Corrybuy
180 his Wife & 4 Children
Arch'd McMillan
_____

Ewen McMillan   Craigalachie
His Wife & 1 Child
_____

John McMillan   Corsuck
His Wife
185 Ewen McMilland
5 Children
_____

John McMillan   Muick
His Wife
Mary McMillan
190 Marg: McMillan
Catherin McMillab
_____

Ewewn McMillan   Coinich
his Wife & 3 Children
_____

John McMillan   Glenpean
195 his Wife
Dun: McMillan
Dug'd McMillan
Bell McMillan
Alex'r McMillan
1 Child
_____

200 John McMillan   Camusine
3 Children
_____

John McMillan   Coinich
His Wife
Dun: McMillan
Betty McKinnon
205 Alex'r McDonell
Mary McMillan   Munerigy
3 Children
_____

Alex'r McMillan   Callich
His Wife & 1 Child
_____

Ewen McMillan   Quarter
210 Cath: McMillan
_____

Angus McMillan   Arkaig
His Wife & 2 Children
_____

Angus McDonald   Invervigar
His Wife
215 Duncan McDonell
Katherine McDonell
Mary McDonell
Alex'r McDonell
John McDonell
_____

220 Don' McMilland   Achintore
& his Wife
_____

John McDon'd   Doers

Passengers who Boarded at Fort William

John McDon'd for his Broyr	Inchlagen		Mary McLean Katherin Mclean	Laddy
Donald McDonell 225 & his Wife	Leck		265 Dun: McLean His Wife Angus McLean Duncan McLean Janet McLean & 1 Child	Munergy
Dun Gillis Moread McMillan Mary Kennedy Mrs. Gillis 4 Children	Aberchalder		270 Mary McMaster Anne Cameron	Glenpean Muick
230 Don'd McDonell His Wife Anne McDonell Dun McDonell Ewen McDonell 2 Children	Aberchalder		Ewen McMillan His Wife Mary McMillan 275 Peggy McMillan Donald McMillan Ewen McMillan	Lubriach
235 W'm Fraser His Wife & 2 Children	F. Augustus		Cath McLean	Caum
Alex'r Fraser His Wife	F Augustus		John Cameron 280 his Wife Don: Cameron	Achnacarry
Alex'r Rankin 240 his Wife [Blank Line] & 2 Children	Carnach		Mary Chisholm Anne Chisholm	Strathglass Do
			Don: McDonald 285 His Wife & 2 Children	Inchlagan
Arch'd Henderson His Wife 245 [Blank Line] & 1 Child	Glencoe		Dugald McMillan His Wife & 1 Child	Inchlagan
Ewen McLean His Wife Don. McLean 250 Cathr. McLean Mary McLean 4 Children	Aberchalder		Ewen Kennedy His Wife 290 Christy McLean Peggy Kennedy	Invergarry
Don: McMillan His Wife John McMillan 255 Marg't McMillan Marg't McDonell & 3 Children	Aberchalder		Don: McMillan His Wife & 2 Children	Paisley
			Annie McMillan	Paisley
Don: McDonell	Thornhill		295 Alex'r Kennedy His Wife & 2 Children	Laddy
His Wife & 3 Children			Alex'r Cameron	Lochielhead
Alex'r Cameron 260 his Wife & 2 Children	Thornhill		Marg't McDonald See no 45: Omitted in that family	Munergy
Arch. McDonell His wife	Paisley		Dun: McLean's Wife Nr 134 Omitted	

Passengers who boarded at Saltcoats near Irvine.

Archibald McMillan	Murlaggen	Angus McKay	Shanvall
His Wife & 5 Children		Kenneth McLean	Mull
Thamsina Gray	Maryburgh	Donald McLellan	Glenelg
———————		Mary McMaster	Oban
Allan McMillan	Glenpean	Alex McMillan	Late Soldier,
His wife Margaret &			Lochaber
Children – Ewen, John,			Regiment
Alexander, James, Donald,		Angus McMillan	Callich
Archibald, Helen, Janet		Don: McMillan	Callop, Glen-
———————			finnan
Alexander Cameron	Gortenorn	Donald McMillan	Rellen
Alexander Cameron	Sallachen	Dugald McMillan	Oban
Alexander Cameron	Arkaigside	James McMillan	Knoydart
Donald Cameron	Kirkton	John McMillan	Callich
Duncan Cameron	Drimnasallie	Murdoch McPherson	Noid, Badenoch
John Cameron	Kinlochiel	Dun: McRae	Glenshiel, Kintail
John Cameron	Muick	Gilchrist McRae	Lianish, Kintail
Margaret Cameron	Glengarry	Norman Morrison	Glenelg
John Campbell	Glenelg	John Wright	Millwright, from
Alex: McDonald	Moy, Glen Spean		Ayrshire
Duncan McDonell	Aviemore		

Appendix II

List of the inhabitants of New Glasgow who signed a petition in support of the Earl of Dalhousie, 1827.
[NAS GD 45/3/534/12]

Many of the names listed in the manuscript are difficult to read and thus some spellings may be inaccurate.

Niel Livingston
Donald Stevenson
John Laverty
William Locker
Richard Locker
Patrick Stanton
Robert Keall
Philip Shevland
Thomas Shaveland
William Young
Francis Cox
James Morrison
James Morison
John McIvin
John Campbell
Robert Campbell
James Campbell
George Kater
Matthew Young
Peter MacMillan
Donald MacMillan
Archibald Henderson
John Henderson
William Foulds
Richard Hayter
John Meickle
Joseph Nichols
John Meldram
Charles Meldram
John Meldram
Robert Meldram
Thomas Meldram
William Meldram
Joseph Meldram
Abraham Nichols
Richard Fortune
William Ross

Nathaniel Cairey
William Hamilton
Alexander Hamilton
Thomas Hamilton
Willam Hamilton of Jura
John Frazer
William Frazer
Francis Frazer
Thomas Frazer
Joseph Wright
James Robertson
John Hunter senior
John Hunter junior
Robert Hunter
James Gunn
William Gunn
Robert Periman
William Ginnigan
Murdoch McDonall
Lauchlin McNeill
Patrick Cox
William Hunt
James Hunt
Richard Guin
William Guin
James Halfpenny
Bryan Memaham
Owen Memaham
James Memaham
John English
Nicholas Woods
Albert Hunter
William Hunter
John Cameron
Alexander Cameron
Malcolm Cameron
Richard Cameron

Malcolm MacCall
Duncan MacCall
James Black
Duncan McIntyre
Malcolm MacIntyre
Daniell MacIntyre
Thomas Hume
Walter Hume
John Hume
John McIntyre
Joesph McIntyre
James McIntyre
Edward Heslam
John MacIntyre
Duncan MacIntyre
Donald MacIntyre
Neal MacIntyre
Peter MacIntyre
Guillan McLean
Archibald Sievwright
William Langton
John Langton
John Stormont
Ralph Stephenson
Joshua Brown
Peter Stormont
John Stormont
Alexander MacGregor
John Cogle
Daniel Cogle
John Cogle jumior
Thomas Stapleton
John Monkman
John McIntosh
Robert Hamilton
Thomas Morrison
John Morrison

James Morrison
William Morrison
John Neale
Edward Neale
James Neale
Charles Neale
Samuel McBride
Frederick Cook
James Rennie
John Rennie
Alexander Neale
Alexander Neale junior
Thomas Liverwright
Dennis Morrison
John Gunn
Robert McMallan
Stewart Smeley
Robert Cairns
Archibald Stewart
James Sturgin
Samuel Cairns
Francis Berrisford
George Brook
James Brook
John Brook
Alexander Brook
John Monteath
Thomas Deardon

William Turnbull
Robert Brook
William Craig
William Sherwood
George Reburn
James Beatty
Thomas Hodge
Luke Reburn
William Davis
David Lloyd
Arthur Campbell
Arthur Campbell
George Holland
Wesley Holland
Alexander Simpson
Hugh Miller
William Palmer
John Kelly
Alexander Grant
James Grant
David Grant
James Wollay
Frederick Wollay
Niel Gilles
Robert Reid
John Dick
John Livingston
John Grant

James Blake senior
James Blake junior
George Blake
Neil Chisholm
William Shephard
Daniel Caley
John Holland
Robert Holland
Andrew Holland
William Bayne
John Bayne
Peter Lawson
Alexander Crear
Alexander Bayne
John Johnston Beers
William Beers
James Crawford Beers
L. Preston
Richard Blake
Henry Harvey
John Wilson
James Wilson
William McCredie
William Bayne senior
William McDowall
David Lloyd junior
John Lloyd
Robert Lloyd

Appendix III

List of the inhabitants of Hinchinbrook, Godmanchester and the St. Regis Indian Reservation lands who signed a petition in support of the Earl of Dalhousie, 1827.
[NAS GD 45/3/534/8]

Many of the names in the original manuscript are difficult to read and twenty-eight names are indecipherable.

William Bowman	Henry Bagley	Frederick Sorven
John Davidson	John Davis	John McGibbon
James Davidson	Robert Holmes	Charles March
Alexander Davidson	Nelson Bagley	John Cunningham
Robert Adam	James Ferguson	Patrick Banman
James Black	John Campbell	Horatio Brunson
Peter Cameron	James Denyer	Horace Brunson
Lo. Myers	Jean Baptiste Lefloune	John McCrea
Thomas McLeod	Joseph Monoir	Duncan McCrea
Robert McEwen	John McIver	Alexander McCrea
Adam McMaster	John Ashburne	John McCrea
William Leonusny	John Filomond	John Spink
John Grant	Frederick Delisle	Joseph Spencer
Donald Grant	John Handley	Alexander Gordon
Joseph Richards	George Waudley	William Aubery
James Summers	John Waudley	Peter Buchanan
John Empey	William Waudley	Alexander McRea
Louis Dufresner	Daniel Wallis	John McMillan
John Parker	William Wallis	Allan McMillan
Ignace La Gambe	John Todd	Alexander McRea
William Empey senior	William Lamb	Duncan McRea
William Empey junior	Andrew Anderson	Laughlan McBain
William Grant	Duncan McPhee	Angus McDonald
Peter Arquit	George Salamie	Norman McDonald
Olivier La Combe	Malcolm Dessier	Donald McKinnon
Daniel Ward	Robert Leathem	Ronald McDonald
John Clark	George Kenedy	William McPhee
John Cunningham	William Kennedy	Robert England
John Murchison	Abraham Letreau	Michael Gray
Jacob Murchison	George Woods	John Finyard
David Morris	Michael Riley	Angus MacDonald
Angus McGilles	William McFarland	Archibald MaDonald
Donald Murchison	Hugh Cameron	Robert Fortune
Murdoch Murchison	Ewen Smith	Duncan Stewart
James Gray	James Hughes	James Stewart
James Farlinger	John Murray	Alexander Stewart

Donald Stewart
William Stewart
John McLean
William Campbell
Neil Chisholm
Peter McLean
Neil Ferguson
Andrew Thomson
Edward Smith
John Smith
Alexander McLaughlin
Donald Rankin
Duncan Rankin
Alexander Cameron
Hugh McLean
Donald McMillan
Hugh McMillan
Duncan McNicol
John McNichol
Donald Cameron
Duncan Levingston
Chester Wilson
Archibald Hudson
David Milne
George Barnard
Edward Nutting
William Wallis
James Andersson
Robert Todd
Archibald Henderson
Edward Maudley
John Hayes
George Hayes
Thomas Monaghan
Patrick McFaull
John McFaull
John Robertson
John McGill
Donald McFee
Alexander MacFee
Finley Fisher
James Fisher senior
George Fisher

John Fisher
Richard Fisher
James Fisher
John Hennagin
Isaac Laing
Alexander Ogilvie
Joseph Davies
John Harvie
William Brooke
John Hammington
John Hythe
John Hythe junior
Hugh Hythe
Patrick Curran
John Kerr
John Grant
William Campbell
Angus McPherson junior
Angus McPherson senior
Angus McIntosh
Thomas Mun
David Grey
Alexander McBain
William Caldwell
Peter Caldwell
Andrew Caldwell
William Caldwell
James Caldwell
Alexander Caldwell
James Gordon
Elijah Walker
Richard Prevost
Hiram Prevost
Robert Harris
John Telford junior
John Harris
Claudius Burrow
Thomas Smith
John Smith
James Smith
John Hunter senior
John Hunter junior
David Hunter

J I Kingston
Thomas Kingston
L I Kingston
Edward Charles senior
Matthew Charles
Edward Charles junior
Thomas Charles
Allan Munro
Cornelius Munro
John Munro
Frederick Munro
Kenneth Lewis
Benjamin Lalane
Robert Parks
Benjamin Burnside
John Wallis
James Robb
Thomas C Colburn
William Wallace
Hugh Cameron
William Henderson
Roger Robertson
Aaron Smith
Peter McDougall
Angus McEisac
Claudius Henessy
Widow Higgins
William Brophy
Patrick Furlong
John McCarty
John O'Harra
James Stewart
Isaac Proper
Nelson Proper
Simon Piclott
Walter Connick
James Brownlie
Joseph Smith
Truman Christcall
William Christcall
George Christcall

Appendix IV

Ship Crossings from Scotland to Québec, 1785–1855

The list is restricted to ship crossings with a minimum of 15 passengers. Unless otherwise stated, the passenger numbers refer only to Québec arrivals. In those crossings where passengers also disembarked at Pictou and other Maritime ports, the figures for these, which are additional to the Québec numbers, are given in the comments field. Vessels that carried passengers who were destined for Upper Canada have been excluded from the list (for Upper Canada Ship crossings see Campey, *Scottish Pioneers of Upper Canada*, 216-67).

Passenger figures have been obtained from a wide variety of documentary sources. Some passenger figures are approximations and some are ambiguous. Uncertainties arise as to whether passenger numbers include all adults (not just heads of households) and children and infants. For details of the ships which carried the emigrants see Appendix V.

Year	Mth	Vessel	Master	Psgr. Nos.	Departure Port
1800	04	*Eliza* (1)	n/k	43	Port Glasgow
Bumsted, *Peoples Clearance*, 224					
1801		*Fame* (1)	Forrest, F.	79	Grnk
Bumsted, *Peoples Clearance*, 225					
1801		*Union*	n.k	55	Grnk
Bumsted, *Peoples Clearance*, 225					
1802	06	*Eagle* (1)	Conolly, N.	21	Grnk
QG Sept. 11.					
1802	06	*Helen* of Irvine	Service, G.	166	Fort William
psgr list: [NAC] MG 24 I183 file 2 , 7, 9-11; McLean, *Glengarry*, 142-4. Glengarry settlers.					
1802	06	*Jean* of Irvine	MacDonald, J.	250	Fort William
psgr list: [NAC] MG 24 I183 file 2, 7,9-11; *QG* Sept. 9; McLean, *Glengarry*, 142-4. Glengarry settlers.					
1802	06	*Neptune* of Greenock	Boyd	600	Loch Nevis (near Fort William)
QG Sept. 11; McLean, *Glengarry*, 136-9. Glengarry settlers.					
1802	07	*Albion* (1)	Service, G.	167	Fort William
QG Sept. 9.					

Year	Mth	Vessel	Master	Psgr. Nos.	Departure Port
1802	07	*Friends of John Saltcoats*	Hen, John	136	Fort William

psgr list: [NAC] MG 24 I183 File 2 7, 9-11; *QG* Sept. 15; McLean, *Glengarry*, 142-4. Glengarry settlers.

| 1804 | 07 | *Emily* | Murphy, John | 16 | Port Glasgow |

QG Aug. 30

| 1804 | 08 | *Commerce* | London | 42 | Oban |

[NAS] GD202/70/12

| 1805 | 04 | *Jean* of Irvine | Wilson | 24 | Grnk |

QM May 18; *GA* April 5

| 1806 | 08 | *Hope* (2) | Henry, M. | 47 | Port Glasgow |

QM Oct. 30; *GA* Aug. 20. Called at Halifax.

| 1809 | 05 | *Albion* (2) | Kidd, R. | 60 | Dundee |

QG July 6

| 1810 | 04 | *Dunlop* | Stevenson, Allan | 54 | Glasgow |

QG June 14

| 1810 | 04 | *Johns* | Cochran, John | 47 | Grnk |

QG May 31

| 1810 | | *Ocean* | n/k | 17 | Grnk |

Bumsted, *Peoples Clearance*, 227

| 1811 | 04 | *Betsey* | Gordon, J. | 15 | Grnk |

QG July 11

| 1812 | 05 | *Cambria* of Aberdeen | Perie, James | 33 | Aberdeen |

E 504/1/24 Some of the 33 passengers left at Halifax.

| 1812 | 06 | *Betsey* | Gordon, J. | 15 | Grnk |

QG July 11

| 1814 | 05 | *Montréal* | Allen | 18 | Grnk |

QG July 14

| 1815 | 04 | *Carolina* of Aberdeen | Dunoon, A. | 24 | Aberdeen |

E 504/1/25

| 1815 | 07 | *Margaret* of Peterhead | Shand, J. | 16 | Leith |

E 504/22/70

| 1815 | 08 | *Union* | Henry | 15 | Grnk |

QG Sept. 21

| 1816 | 03 | *Carolina* of Aberdeen | Duncan, A. | 25 | Aberdeen |

E 504/1/26

| 1816 | 03 | *Mary* of Greenock (1) | Moore, A. | 15 | Grnk |

QM May 24; E504/15/111

| 1816 | 04 | *Mary* of Aberdeen | Clayton, J. | 21 | Aberdeen |

QM July 23; E 504/1/26

172   APPENDIX IV

Year	Mth	Vessel	Master	Psgr. Nos.	Departure Port
1816	04	*Prescott* of Leith	Young	26	Leith
		QM June 21; E504/22/72			
1816	04	*Rothiemurchus* of Leith	Watson, G.	28	Leith
		QM May 31; E504/22/72			
1816	05	*Caledonia* of Irvine	Reid, J.	30	Grnk
		E504/15/112			
1816	05	*Fancy* of Aberdeen	Struthers, J.	15	Grnk
		QM Aug. 20; E504/15/112			
1816	05	*Greenfield*	Holmes, J.	28	Grnk
		QM Aug. 27; E504/15/112			
1816	07	*Lady of the Lake*	Primrose, D.	27	Grnk
		QM Sept. 10; E504/15/112			
1816	08	*Britannia*	Spence, C.	36	Grnk
		QM Sept. 27; E504/15/113			
1816	08	*Fame* (2)	Abrams	17	Grnk
		QM Sept. 17; E504/15/113			
1816	08	*Hibernia* of Aberdeen	Lamb, R.	42	Stornoway
		E504/33/3			
1816	08	*Isabella and Euphemia*	Middleton, J.	32	Stornoway
		QM Nov. 5; E504/33/3			
1816	08	*Jane* of Sunderland	Rogers, J.	16	Grnk
		E504/15/113			
1816	08	*John and Samuel* of Liverpool	Cook, F.	82	Stornoway
		E504/33/3; [PRO] CO 42/358 ff.113-5			
1816	08	*Morningfield* of Aberdeen	Perie, J.	63	Stornoway
		QM Sept. 20; E504/33/3			
1816	08	*Perseverence* of Aberdeen	Philip, J.	52	Stornoway
		E504/33/3			
1817	03	*Renown* of Kirkaldy	Watts, J.	20	Leith
		QM June 10; E.504/22/76			
1817	04	*Rothiemurchus* of Leith	Watson, G.	105	Leith
		QM June 3; E.504/22/76			
1817	04	*Juno* of Aberdeen	Henderson, J.	20	Dundee
		QM June 17			
1817	04	*Mary* of Greenock (1)	Moore	26	Grnk
		QM June 3; *GA* Mar. 7			
1817	04	*Nancy* of South Shields	Allan, R.	34	Leith

QM Aug. 1; J S. Martell, *Immigration to and Emigration from Nova Scotia, 1815-1838,* (Halifax, N.S.: PANS 1942), 43. 130 passengers left at Halifax.

Year	Mth	Vessel	Master	Psgr. Nos.	Departure Port
1817	04	*Neptune* of Ayr	Neil	22	Grnk

QM June 10

| 1817 | 04 | *Prompt* of Bo'ness | Coverdale | 133 | Leith |

QM July 8; E.504/22/77; Martell, Ibid, 43; *GA* Mar. 21; *KM* June 26. 60 left at Halifax.

| 1817 | 04 | *Rebecca* of Greenock | Harvey | 29 | Grnk |

QM June 3

| 1817 | 05 | *Agincourt* of Leith | Matheson | 73 | Leith |

QM Aug. 11; *SM* LXXIX, 477. 127 passengers left at Halifax.

| 1817 | 05 | *Alexander* of Bo'ness | Henry, J. | 44 | Leith |

QM July 22; E.504/22/77; *SM* LXXIX, 477

| 1817 | 05 | *Harmony* (1) | Abrams | 136 | Grnk |

QM July 18

| 1817 | 05 | *James* | Jack, W. | 24 | Grnk |

QM Aug. 11

| 1817 | 05 | *Jessie* of Aberdeen | Thomson, J. | 21 | Aberdeen |

QM Aug. 1; E 504/1/27

| 1817 | 05 | *John* of Bo'ness | Mitchell, J. | 118 | Leith |

QM Aug. 19; E.504/22/7

| 1817 | 05 | *Lord Middleton* of North Shields | Kerr, G. | 163 | Leith |

QM July 22; E.504/22/77; *SM* LXXIX, 477; *DC* May 23; *KM* May 12

| 1817 | 05 | *Tods* of Perth | McPherson, W. | 42 | Dundee |

QM July 22; E504/27/14; *DC* Apr. 25; *PC* Apr. 24

| 1817 | 05 | *Trafalgar* of London | Mitchell, J. | 100 | Leith |

QM Aug. 1; E.504/22/77; *PC* May 29; *KM* May 12

| 1817 | 06 | *Ardgour* of Fort William | Lillie, W. | 108 | Fort William |

QM Sept. 9; E504/12/6

| 1817 | 06 | *Minerva* of Aberdeen | Strachan, W. | 26 | Fort William |

E504/12/6

| 1817 | 06 | *Peace* | Seator | 85 | Grnk |

QM July 18; *GA* Apr. 22

| 1817 | 07 | *Cambria* of Aberdeen | Wilson, J. | 15 | Aberdeen |

QM Sept. 9; E504/1/27

| 1817 | 07 | *General Goldie* of Dumfries | Smith | 18 | Dumfries |

QM Sept. 16; *DGC* June 24. Called at Pictou and Miramichi

| 1817 | 07 | *Pitt* | Hamilton | 37 | Grnk |

QM Sept. 26; *GA* June 27   6

| 1818 | 04 | *Jane* (3) | Murdoch | 18 | Grnk |

QM May 19

Year Mth	Vessel	Master	Psgr. Nos.	Departure Port
1818 04 QM May 19	*Neptune* (1)	Clark	34	Glasgow
1818 05 QM Aug. 7	*Agincourt* of Leith	Mathwin	298	Leith
1818 06 QM July 17	*Camilla*	McCarthy, D.	109	Grnk
1818 06 QM July 17	*Favourite* (1)	Greg	23	Grnk
1818 06 E 504/9/9	*General Goldie* of Dumfries	Smith, W.	30	Dumfries
1818 07 QM Aug. 15	*Agamemnon*	Rogers	192	Leith
1818 07 QM Sept. 8	*Mars*	Blin	253	Mull
1818 07 QM Sept. 10; E504/12/6	*Waterloo* of Fort William	Kendal, J.	108	Fort William

1819 03   *Skeen* of Leith(1)   Mason   37   Leith
Martell, Ibid, 47; *SM* IV 1819, 465. 113 passengers left at Halifax.

1819 04 QM May 14	*Earl of Dalhousie* of Aberdeen	Levie, J.	19	Aberdeen

1819 04   *Mary* (2)   Munro   32   Leith
SM 1819 IV, 465.

1819 04   *Percival* of Leith   Scott   85   Leith
SM IV 1819, 465; *PC* Feb. 25.

1819 04   *Renown* of Kirkaldy   Watts, J.   37   Leith
QM May 18; E.504/22/84

1819 05   *Agincourt* of Leith   Matthews   40   Leith
QM July 27; E.504/22/85; Martell, Ibid, 47; *SM* IV 1819, 465.
133 passengers left at Halifax. According to Scottish customs records, 200 people left Leith.

1819 06 QM Aug. 2	*Jean*	Allan	28	Grnk

1819 06   *Speculation*   Allen   87   Oban
QM Sept. 14; Martell, Ibid, 49; *IJ* June 4. 23 passengers left at Pictou.

1819 07 QM Aug. 24	*Harmony* (1)	Messop, H.	233	Oban
1819 07 QM Aug. 24; E.504/25/3	*Hope* of Greenock	Marden	184	Oban
1819 07 QM Aug. 31	*Paragon*	Mitchell	66	Leith

Year Mth	Vessel	Master	Psgr. Nos.	Departure Port
1819 07 E504/35/2	*Traveller* of Aberdeen	Goldie, J.	143	Tobermory
1819 08 *QM* Sept. 17	*Nelson*	Barrick	19	Leith
1820 04 *QM* June 5	*Alexander*	Young	96	Grnk
1820 04 *QM* May 25	*Enterprise*	Pattin	39	Ayr
1820 04 *QM* May 19	*Jane* (2)	Allen, W.	34	Grnk
1820 04 *QM* May 27; DCA CE 70 11/2; DCA CE 70/11/16	*Psyche* of Dundee	Erskine, T.	38	Dundee
1820 04 *QM* May 25	*Rebecca* of Greenock	McKenzie	42	Grnk
1820 04 *QM* May 21	*Robert*	Neil	44	Grnk
1820 04 *QM* June 8	*Sally*	Cumming	33	Grnk
1820 04 *QM* May 18	*Skeen* of Leith (1)	Bishop	22	Leith
1820 04 *QM* June 3	*Sovereign* (1)	Pearson	49	Leith
1820 04 *QM* May 12	*Traveller* of Aberdeen	Goldie, J.	20	Aberdeen
1820 04 *QM* June 5	*True Briton*	Reid, J.	54	Grnk
1820 04 *QM* May 26	*Young Norval*	Luck	37	Grnk
1820 05 *QM* June 24	*Earl of Buckinghamshire*	Johnson, J.	200	Grnk
1820 05 *QM* June 30	*Minerva* (1)	Williamson	60	Grnk
1820 05 *QM* July 15; E.504/22/90	*Sir J H Craig*	Dease, J.	100	Leith
1820 05 *QM* June 30	*Speculation*	Douglass	120	Grnk
1820 06 *QM* July 21	*Benlomond*	Rattray, H.	218	Grnk

Year	Mth	Vessel	Master	Psgr. Nos.	Departure Port
1820	06	*Betsey* of Greenock	Wither	78	Oban

QM Aug. 15; E504/25/3

1820	06	*Commerce* of Greenock	Coverdale, N.	402	Grnk

QM Aug. 5.
Passengers included emigration society members destined for Upper Canada.

1820	06	*Martha*	Denwood	43	Dumfries

DWJ June 20

1820	07	*Alexander*	Ferguson	112	Grnk

QM Sept. 5

1820	07	*Argus* (1)	Wilkinson	88	Dumfries

QM Aug. 14; *DWJ* June 13

1820	07	*Duchess of Richmond*	Cook	266	Oban

QM Aug. 17

1820	07	*Glentanner* of Aberdeen	Murray	18	Tobermory

QM Aug. 25; E504/35/2. 123 passengers left at Cape Breton.

1820	07	*Hope* (1)	Duncan	44	Grnk

QM Aug. 14

1820	08	*Rebecca* of Greenock	Harvey	50	Grnk

QM Oct. 11

1821	04	*Earl of Dalhousie* of Aberdeen	Levie, J.	15	Aberdeen

QM May 15

1821	04	*Helen* of Dundee	Erskine, T.	55	Dundee

QM June 12; *DC* Jan. 12

1821	04	*Neptune* (2)	Bell	63	Leith

QM June 8

1821	05	*Kent*	Stirling	50	Grnk

QM June 26

1821	06	*Benson*	Rowe, W.	287	Grnk

QM July 27

1821	06	*Catherine* (1)	Daysdale	63	Leith

QM Aug. 11

1821	08	*Ann* (1)	Henry	37	Grnk

QM Sept. 14

1821	08	*John Howard*	Smith	100	London

QM Sept. 24. 100 settlers from Anticosti who were saved from the brig *Earl of Dalhousie* of Greenock, which sailed from Fort William. The remainder were picked up by the *Dolphin*.

1821	09	*Thistle* of Aberdeen	Allen, R.	43	Tobermory

QM Oct. 19; *IJ* June 22

Year	Mth	Vessel	Master	Psgr. Nos.	Departure Port
1822	04	*True Briton*	n/k	28	Grnk
QM June 7					
1822	05	*Rose*	Johnson	45	Leith
QM June 11					
1822	05	*Thompsons Packet* of Dumfries	Lookup	40	Dumfries
QM July 9; Martell, Ibid, 53. Ninety-three passengers left at Pictou.					
1822	07	*George* (1)	McAlpin, J.	42	Grnk
QM Aug. 13					
1822	07	*Ossian* of Leith	Block	127	Fort William
QM Aug. 23; *IJ* 29 June 1821					
1822	07	*Pilgrim*	Smith	62	Tobermory
QM Aug. 23					
1823	04	*Ann* (1)	Maclean	38	Glasgow
QM May 23					
1823	04	*Helen* of Dundee	Erskine, T.	20	Dundee
QM May 23					
1823	05	*Roscius*	McClaren	47	Grnk
QM June 15					
1823	06	*Eleanor*	Wallace	96	Workington
QM June 19					
1823	06	*Jane* (2)	Snowden	63	Grnk
QM June 19					
1823	06	*Pilgrim*	Smith	77	Grnk
QM Aug. 12					
1823	07	*Emperor Alexander* of Aberdeen	Watts, A.	49	Tobermory
QM Oct. 7; *IJ* Jan 30, 1824. One hundred and eleven passengers left at Sydney, Cape Breton. Campey, *After the Hector*, 217-9.					
1823	07	*Monarch*	Crawford	259	Tobermory
QM Aug. 19					
1823	07	*Québec Packet* of Aberdeen	Anderson	16	Aberdeen
QM Sept. 23					
1823	08	*Rebecca* of Greenock	Harvey	25	Grnk
QM Sept. 26					
1824	04	*Culloden*	Leyden	19	Leith
QM June 5					
1824	04	*Jean* of Ayr	Allan	16	Grnk
QM June 5					

Year Mth	Vessel	Master	Psgr. Nos.	Departure Port
1824 04 QM June 1	*Rebecca* of Greenock	Harvey	22	Grnk
1824 05 QM June 16	*Margaret Bogle* of Leith	Boyd	17	Glasgow
1824 06 QM July 10	*Active* (1)	Johnson	84	Whitehaven
1824 06 QM Aug. 10	*Aurora*	Hodson	61	Whitehaven
1824 06 QM Aug. 3	*Jane Wright*	n/k	50	Grnk
1824 07	*Dunlop*	Mandell	131	Grnk

QM Aug. 31; Martell, Ibid, 54. Ninety-six passengers left at Sydney, Cape Breton.

| 1824   07 | *Gratitude* of Dundee | Gellatly, J. | 55 | Fort William |

QM Sept. 14; DCA CE 70/11/1. Includes 20 settlers who boarded ship at Baie-des-Chaleurs.

1824 08 QM Sept. 11	*Commerce* of Greenock	Wittleton	15	Grnk
1824 08 QM Sept. 28	*Duchess of Richmond*	McClashen	20	Grnk
1825 05 QM July 16	*George Stewart*	Stewart	57	Grnk
1825 07 QM Sept. 6	*Margaret* (1)	Boyd	20	Grnk
1825 07 QM Aug. 24	*Tamerlane* of Greenock	McKillop	30	Grnk
1825 08 QM Sept. 20	*Corsair* of Greenock	McAlpine	30	Grnk
1826 04 QM May 20; E504/15/155	*Favourite* of Montréal	Allan	22	Grnk
1826 04 QM May 20; E504/15/155	*General Wolfe*	Johnston	32	Grnk
1826 04 QM May 13	*Québec Packet* of Aberdeen	Anderson	19	Aberdeen
1826 06 QM July 29; E504/15/156	*Gleniffer*	Stevenson	42	Grnk
1826 06 QM Aug. 5; E504/15/156	*Margaret* (1)	Boyd	22	Grnk
1826 06	*Tamerlane* of Greenock	McKillop	55	Grnk

QM Aug. 5; E504/15/156. Called at Sydney, Cape Breton.

Year	Mth	Vessel	Master	Psgr. Nos.	Departure Port
1826	07	*Highland Lad*	Vickerman	16	Tobermory

QM Sept. 23; Martell, Ibid , 57. Called at Nova Scotia.

| 1826 | 07 | *Ythan* | Cairns | 20 | Grnk |

QM Sept. 12

| 1826 | 08 | *Rebecca* of Greenock | Laurie | 20 | Grnk |

QM Oct. 7; E504/15/156

| 1826 | 08 | *Sophia* of Greenock | Neil | 43 | Grnk |

QM Oct. 7; E504/15/157

| 1826 | 08 | *Welcome* | McColl | 15 | Grnk |

QM Oct. 10; E504/15/157

| 1826 | 09 | *Favourite* of Montréal | Allan | 17 | Grnk |

QM Oct. 14; E504/15/157

| 1827 | 04 | *Caledonia* | Miller | 79 | Grnk |

QM June 2; *GA* March 16

| 1827 | 04 | *Percival* of Leith | Johnson | 47 | Leith |

QM May 19

| 1827 | 04 | *Rebecca* of Greenock | n/k | 20 | Grnk |

QM May 5

| 1827 | 05 | *George Canning* | Callender | 164 | Grnk |

QM June 23; *GA* April 6

| 1827 | 05 | *Harmony* of Whitehaven | Young | 36 | Stornoway |

QM Sept. 1; Martell, Ibid , 59. 200 passengers left at Halifax.

| 1827 | 05 | *Lord Byron* | Robinson | 26 | Grnk |

QM July 21

| 1827 | 06 | *Forth* | Robinson | 150 | Grnk |

QM July 17

| 1827 | 06 | *Warner* | Crawford | 43 | Grnk |

QM July 24; *GA* May 8

| 1827 | 07 | *Indian* | Matthias | 69 | Grnk |

QM Sept. 7; *GA* June 8

| 1827 | 08 | *Active* (2) | Walker, A. | 40 | Tobermory |

QM Sept. 21; E504/35/2. Vessel called at Cape Breton.

| 1827 | 08 | *Earl of Dalhousie* | Boyd | 20 | Grnk |

QM Oct. 9

| 1828 | 03 | *Brilliant* of Aberdeen | Barclay, A. | 20 | Aberdeen |

QM May 17

| 1828 | 03 | *Harmony* (2) | Young | 79 | Leith |

QM May 20

Year Mth	Vessel	Master	Psgr. Nos.	Departure Port
1828 04 QM May 17	*Ariadne*	McCall	20	Grnk
1828 04 QM May 31	*Caledonia*	Miller	90	Grnk
1828 04 QM May 17	*Favourite* of Montréal	Allan	40	Grnk
1828 04 QM May 31	*Mary* (1)	Dunlop	206	Grnk
1828 05 QM June 24	*George Canning*	Callender	180	Grnk
1828 06 QM Aug. 9	*Majestic*	Black	60	Leith
1828 07 QM Aug. 19	*Duchess of Richmond*	McClashan	106	Grnk
1828 08 QM Sept. 30	*Favourite* of Montréal	Allan	60	Grnk
1829 04	*Caledonia*	Miller, Donald	130	Grnk

QM June 23; carried 12 families (86 people) from Arran who settled in Megantic County. Captain Miller was a native of Arran.

Year Mth	Vessel	Master	Psgr. Nos.	Departure Port
1829 04 QM May 12	*Cherub*	Miller	15	Grnk
1829 04 QM May 23	*George Canning*	Callender	103	Grnk
1829 04 QM May 30	*Mary* (1)	Duck	161	Grnk
1829 06	*Albion* of Aberdeen	n/k	n/k	Grnk

McKillop, *Annals of Megantic County*, 21. Passengers included four Arran families who settled in Megantic County.

Year Mth	Vessel	Master	Psgr. Nos.	Departure Port
1829 06 QM Sept. 8	*Corsair* of Greenock	Hamilton	38	Grnk
1829 06 QM Aug. 1	*Foundling*	McLeod	170	Grnk
1829 06 QM Aug. 4	*Scotia*	Simpson	33	Grnk
1829 07 QM Aug. 29	*Amity* of Glasgow	Ray	17	Glasgow
1829 07 QM Aug. 15	*Huntley*	Wilson	176	Grnk
1829 07 QM Aug. 15	*Regent*	Steel	16	Leith

Year	Mth	Vessel	Master	Psgr. Nos.	Departure Port
1829	08	*Favourite* of Montréal	Allan	40	Grnk

QM Sept. 29

| 1830 | 03 | *Sprightly* | n/k | 60 | Dundee |

PC Mar. 3.

| 1830 | 04 | *Brilliant* of Aberdeen | Barclay, A. | 20 | Aberdeen |

QM May 24

| 1830 | 04 | *Margaret Balfour* of Dundee | n/k | 63 | Dundee |

QM June 8; *PC* Mar. 1831.

| 1830 | 04 | *Nailer* | n/k | 120 | Grnk |

QM June 8

| 1830 | 04 | *Neptune* (2) | n/k | 144 | Leith |

QM June 8

| 1830 | 05 | *Brittannia* | n/k | 19 | Leith |

QM June 19

| 1830 | 06 | *Canada* | Potts | 244 | Cromarty from Leith |

QM Aug. 19; *IC* June23 & Oct. 6; *IJ* Nov. 6

| 1830 | 06 | *Cartha* | Smith | 144 | Grnk |

QM July 24

| 1830 | 06 | *Duchess of Richmond* | Alexander | 129 | Grnk |

QM Aug. 7

| 1830 | 06 | *George Canning* | Callender | 140 | Grnk |

QM July 27; McKillop, *Annals of Megantic County*, 38. Passengers included Arran emigrants who settled in Megantic County.

| 1830 | 06 | *Hope* (3) | McFarlane | 25 | Leith |

QM July 16

| 1830 | 06 | *John* | Mann | 120 | Cromarty |

QM Aug. 10

| 1830 | 06 | *Stirling Castle* of Greenock | Fraser | 224 | Grnk |

QM Aug. 10

| 1830 | 07 | *Deveron* of Glasgow | McGill | 117 | Grnk |

QM Aug. 14

| 1830 | 07 | *Malay* | Coverdale | 50 | Tobermory |

QM Sept. 11. An additional 220 passengers disembarked at Sydney, Cape Breton (see Campey, *After The Hector*, 259).

| 1830 | 07 | *Mary* of Newcastle | Jacobson | 64 | Loch Snizort, |

QM Sept. 4; *IJ* Dec. 10. Left Scotland with 330 passengers. Additional Skye passengers probably disembarked at Charlottetown, P.E.I. (see Campey, *Very Fine Class of Immigrants*, 80-9).

Year	Mth	Vessel	Master	Psgr. Nos.	Departure Port
1830	07 QM Aug. 14	*Triton*	McClean	64	Leith
1831	04	*Brilliant* of Aberdeen	Barclay, A.	75	Aberdeen

Fowler, *Journal of a tour through British North America*, 5-42.

Year	Mth	Vessel	Master	Psgr. Nos.	Departure Port
1831	04 QM May 17	*Dalmarnock*	McFarlane	28	Grangemouth
1831	04 QM May 26	*Donegall*	Matches	164	Maryport
1831	04 QM May 28	*George* (2)	Thompson	23	Maryport
1831	04 QM May 24	*Molson* of Dundee	Law	143	Dundee
1831	04 QM May 31	*Nailer*	McColl	65	Grnk

McKillop, *Annals of Megantic County*, 47. Includes passengers from Arran who settled in Megantic County.

Year	Mth	Vessel	Master	Psgr. Nos.	Departure Port
1831	04 QM May 28	*Neried*	Whitehead	49	Dumfries
1831	04 QM May 17	*Rebecca* of Greenock	Laurie	50	Grnk
1831	04 QM May 28	*Sarah Mariana*	Archibald	164	Maryport
1831	04 QM May 19	*Triton*	McClean	33	Leith
1831	04 QM May 21	*True Briton*	Balderston	43	Glasgow
1831	05 QM June 23	*Amity* of Glasgow	Ray	30	Glasgow
1831	05 QM June 14	*Elizabeth and Anne*	Wright, J.	296	Grnk
1831	05 QM June 2	*Experiment*	Collins	32	Maryport
1831	05 QM June 23	*George Canning*	Callender	300	Grnk

McKillop, *Annals of Megantic County*, 47. Included Arran emigrants who settled in Megantic County.

Year	Mth	Vessel	Master	Psgr. Nos.	Departure Port
1831	05 QM June 21	*Hope* (4)	Middleton	73	Maryport
1831	05 QM June 7	*Sally*	Cumming	40	Ayr

Year	Mth	Vessel	Master	Psgr. Nos.	Departure Port
1831	05 QM July 9	*Salmes*	Royal, H.	250	Inverness
1831	05 QM June 4	*Skeen* of Leith (2)	Bennett	118	Leith
1831	05 QM July 5	*William Shand*	Hunter	299	Berwick
1831	06 QM July 19	*Atlas*	Scott	52	Dundee
1831	06 QM Sept. 8	*Baronet*	Rankin	187	Cromarty
1831	06 QM July 19	*Foundling*	McKenzie	161	Grnk
1831	06 QM Aug. 7	*Sophia*	Neil	36	Grnk
1831	07 QM Sept. 8	*Brilliant* of Aberdeen	Barclay, A.	68	Aberdeen
1831	07	*Corsair* of Greenock	Scott, J.	57	Cromarty

QM Aug. 30; Martell, Ibid, 70; *IJ* May 27. 161 passengers left at Pictou.

Year	Mth	Vessel	Master	Psgr. Nos.	Departure Port
1831	07 QM Aug. 27	*Deveron* of Glasgow	McGill	302	Grnk
1831	07 QM Sept. 29; *IJ* June 24	*Industry*	Carr	57	Cromarty
1831	07 QM Aug. 30	*Iris*	Frank	240	Grnk
1831	07 QM Aug. 27	*Margaret*	Wallace	160	Leith
1831	07 QM Aug. 18	*Rival*	Wallace	333	Grnk
1831	07 QM Aug. 20	*Tamerlane* of Greenock	Black	377	Grnk
1831	07 QM Aug. 27	*Zealous*	Reed	182	Leith
1831	08 QM Sept. 8	*Annandale* of Aberdeen	Anderson	23	Aberdeen
1831	08 QM Sept. 22	*Canada* of Greenock	Allan	25	Grnk
1831	08 QM Sept. 8	*Cleopatra*	Morris, J.	246	Cromarty

Year Mth	Vessel	Master	Psgr. Nos.	Departure Port
1831 08 *QM* Sept. 8	*Dalmarnock*	McFarlane	27	Grnk
1831 08 *QM* Sept. 22	*Earl of Dalhousie*	Boyd	20	Grnk
1831 08 *QM* Sept. 22	*Rebecca* of Greenock	Laurie	39	Grnk
1832 03 *QM* May 17	*Brilliant* of Aberdeen	Barclay, A.	175	Aberdeen
1832 03 *QM* May 16; *DC* Dec. 22 1831	*Isabella* of Dundee	Donaldson, J.	43	Dundee
1832 03 *QM* May 17; *DC* Mar. 8	*Margaret Balfour* of Dundee	Gellatly, J.	25	Dundee
1832 03 *QM* May 16; *DC* Dec. 29, 1831 & Feb. 9, 1832	*Molson* of Dundee	Elliot, J.	49	Dundee
1832 03 *QM* May 14	*Prince George* of Alloa	Morison	16	Alloa
1832 03 *QM* May 16	*Rebecca* of Greenock	Laurie	43	Grnk
1832 04 *QM* June 6	*Agnes Primrose*	Johnson	40	Glasgow
1832 04 *QM* May 19	*Aimwell* of Aberdeen	Morrison	24	Aberdeen
1832 04 *QM* May 19	*Annandale* of Aberdeen	Anderson, A.	61	Aberdeen
1832 04 *QM* May 28	*Betsey Howe*	n/k	42	Leith
1832 04 *QM* June 1	*Donegall*	Matches	138	Maryport
1832 04 *QM* May 23	*Dykes* of Maryport	Cockton	156	Maryport
1832 04 *QM* June 4	*Fisher*	Kay, T.	69	Stranraer
1832 04 *QM* June 3	*Hedleys* of Newcastle	n/k	209	Cromarty
1832 04 *QM* May 23	*Helen* of Aberdeen	Anderson	18	Aberdeen
1832 04 *QM* May 27	*Jane* (1)	Wilson	65	Leith

Year Mth	Vessel	Master	Psgr. Nos.	Departure Port
1832 04 QM June 3	*Maria* (1)	Hewitt	136	Maryport
1832 04 QM May 19; *PC* Mar. 1	*Nailer*	McColl	172	Grnk
1832 04 QM June 6	*Nicholson*	Craig	183	Maryport
1832 04 QM June 2	*Sarah* (1)	Marianne	165	Maryport
1832 04 QM May 27; *DC* Mar. 20	*Traveller* of Dundee	Wighton	42	Dundee
1832 05 QM July 26	*Amity* of Glasgow	Mercer, J.	39	Grnk
1832 05 QM June 24	*Ann* (2)	Moore	136	Maryport
1832 05 QM June 2	*Catherine* (2)	Davidson	37	Irvine
1832 05 QM July 2; *KM* Feb. 7, 1833	*Dalmarnock*	McFarlane	227	Berwick
1832 05 QM July 9	*Lawther*	Pewley	121	Workington
1832 05 QM July 2; "Ships to Megantic County," Clan Donald Centre. Includes passengers from Arran who settled in Megantic County.	*Margaret* (2)	Mathewson	110	Campbeltown
1832 05 QM June 21	*Margaret Thompson*	Ogilvy, J.	125	Leith
1832 05 Psgr List: *QM* June 13.	*Portaferry*	Pollock, J.	216	Grnk
1832 05 QM July 26; Martell, Ibid, 73; *IJ* Apr. 20. 196 passengers left at Pictou.	*Sylvanus* of North Shields	Lawson	41	Cromarty
1832 05 QM July 10	*Tamerlane* of Greenock	Black	210	Grnk
1832 06 QM July 10, Aug. 30	*Albion* of Glasgow	Boyd, J.	84	Glasgow
1832 06 QM Aug. 20; Martell, Ibid, 73; *IJ* May 18. Some passengers left at Pictou.	*Blagdon*	Thomson	132	Cromarty
1832 06 QM Aug. 22; Martell, Ibid, 73. 130 passengers left at Pictou.	*Canada*	Hunter	111	Cromarty
1832 06 QM July 26	*Chieftain* of Kirkaldy	Scott, A.	210	Leith

Year Mth	Vessel	Master	Psgr. Nos.	Departure Port
1832 06 QM July 18	*Duchess* of Richmond	McGlashen	240	Grnk
1832 06 QM Aug. 5	*Gleniffer*	Dunlop	152	Grnk
1832 06 QM July 8; *DC* Apr. 12	*Industry*	Chapman, J.	130	Dundee
1832 06 QM July 16	*Iris*	Welsh	164	Grnk
1832 06 QM Aug. 6	*Magnet*	Goulder	146	Whitehaven
1832 06 QM July 25	*Oxford*	Davidson	300	Leith
1832 06 QM Aug. 13	*Sharp*	Almond	206	Cromarty
1832 06 QM Aug. 5; *DC* May 10; DCA CE 70/11/3	*Victoria* of Dundee	Berrie, J.	126	Dundee
1832 07 QM Sept. 16; Martell, Ibid, 72. 59 passengers left at Pictou.	*Albion* of Glasgow	McMaster	181	Loch Eriboll
1832 07 QM Aug. 27	*Crown*	Howie	75	Grnk
1832 07 QM Aug. 10	*Elizabeth*	McAlpine	74	Clyde
1832 07 QM Aug. 20	*Roger Stewart*	Kerr	123	Grnk
1832 08 QM Oct. 4	*Favourite* of Montréal	Allan	22	Grnk
1832 08 QM Sept. 29	*Robertson*	Neil	19	Grnk
1832 09 QM Oct. 19	*Sophia*	Easton	19	Grnk
1833 03 QM May 9	*Favourite* of Montréal	Allan	73	Grnk
1833 03 QM May 9	*Robertson*	Neil	36	Grnk
1833 04 QM June 16	*Bethea*	n/k	20	Glasgow
1833 04 QM May 17	*Brilliant* of Aberdeen	Duthie	64	Aberdeen

Year Mth	Vessel	Master	Psgr. Nos.	Departure Port
1833 04 *QM* May 21	*Charles Forbes*	Beveridge	47	Kirkaldy
1833 04 *QM* June 12	*Dykes* of Maryport	n/k	33	Maryport
1833 04 *QM* June 15	*Elizabeth* of Leith	n/k	15	Leith
1833 04 *QM* June 20	*European* (1)	n/k	155	Leith
1833 04 *DC* Feb. 7, 1834; DCA CE 70/11/2	*Fairy* of Dundee	Ritchie, D.	50	Dundee
1833 04 *QM* May 19	*Gleniffer*	n/k	31	Grnk
1833 04 *QM* June 4	*Hedleys* of Newcastle	Morris, J.	138	Cromarty
1833 04 *QM* May 27; *DPC* Feb. 1	*Isabella* of Dundee	Donaldson, J.	22	Dundee
1833 04 *QM* June 2	*Isabella* of Irvine	Miller	102	Grnk
1833 04 *QM* June 6; *KM* Feb. 28	*Lancaster*	Creighton	137	Dumfries
1833 04 *QM* May 24; *KM* Feb. 7	*Margaret Bogle* of Leith	n/k	68	Leith
1833 04 *QM* May 29; *PC* Feb. 28	*Nailer*	McColl	22	Grnk
1833 04 *QM* May 29	*Panmore*	n/k	24	Ayr
1833 04 *QM* May 25; *MG* 30 May	*Portaferry*	Pollock, J.	103	Grnk
1833 04 *QM* May 18	*Sir William Wallace* of Aberdeen (1)	Anderson, D.	28	Aberdeen
1833 04 *QM* June 5	*St. George*	Thomson	26	Maryport
1833 04 *QM* June 1; *PC* Feb. 21	*Triton*	McClean	71	Cromarty
1833 05 *QM* July 25	*Agnes*	Outerbridge	24	Grnk
1833 05 *QM* July 11	*Betsey* of Dundee	n/k	131	Leith

Year	Mth	Vessel	Master	Psgr. Nos.	Departure Port
1833	05	*Grace*	n/k	132	Whitehaven
QM July 16					
1833	05	*Sovereign* (2)	n/k	44	Grnk
QM June 13					
1833	05	*Stranraer*	n/k	75	Stranraer
QM July 10					
1833	05	*William & Ann*	n/k	24	Glasgow
QM July 2					
1833	06	*Amity* of Glasgow	n/k	91	Glasgow
QM Aug. 10					
1833	06	*Argus* (2)	n/k	115	Maryport
QM Aug. 3					
1833	06	*Balfour* of Whitehaven	Bee	272	Whitehaven
QM July 28					
1833	06	*Economist* of Newport	Stokeham	47	Cromarty
QM Aug. 25; Martell, Ibid, 76; *IJ* May 17. 42 passengers left at Pictou.					
1833	06	*Jane Kay*	Toft, D.	66	Cromarty
QM Aug. 12; Martell, Ibid, 75; *IJ* May 17. 106 passengers left at Pictou.					
1833	06	*Marjory*	Stocks, J.	24	Thurso
QM Aug. 29; *IJ* June 7, 14 & 21					
1833	06	*Minerva* (2)	Adamson	59	Leith
QM Aug. 5					
1833	06	*Molson* of Dundee	Elliot, J.	108	Dundee
QM Aug. 1; *DC* May 3					
1833	06	*Tamerlane* of Greenock	Martin	278	Grnk
QM July 28; *PC* Apr. 18					
1833	06	*Zephyr*	Tucker	99	Cromarty
QM Aug. 21; Martell, Ibid, 76; *IJ* May 31. 51 passengers left at Pictou.					
1833	07	*Cartha*	Morrison	51	Grnk
QM Aug. 22; *PC* June 13					
1833	07	*Favourite* of Montréal	Burns	47	Grnk
QM Aug. 20					
1833	07	*Retrench* of Greenock	Cooper	299	Grnk
QM Aug. 22					
1833	07	*Robert & Margaret*	n/k	66	Cromarty
IJ May 14, June 21					
1833	08	*Adrian*	Forster	106	Tobermory
QM Oct. 5					

Year Mth	Vessel	Master	Psgr. Nos.	Departure Port
1833 08 *QM* Oct. 1	*Brilliant* of Aberdeen	Duthie	84	Dundee
1833 08 *QM* Sept. 29	*Gleniffer*	Dunlop	21	Grnk
1833 08 *QM* Oct. 1	*Prince George* of Alloa	Morrison	48	Leith
1833 08 *QM* Sept. 14	*Robertson*	Neil	31	Grnk
1834 04 *QM* May 15	*Brilliant* of Aberdeen	Duthie	137	Aberdeen
1834 04 *QM* May 8; *PC* Apr. 17	*Canada* of Greenock	Allan	51	Grnk
1834 04 *QM* May 17	*Cherokee* of Glasgow	Miller	52	Glasgow
1834 04 *PC* Apr. 17	*Cherub*	n/k	24	Grnk
1834 04 *QM* May 15	*Cyrus*	Scott	33	Dundee
1834 04 *QM* May 13	*Fairy Queen*	Ritchie, D.	28	Dundee
1834 04 *QM* May 8; *PC* Apr. 17	*Favourite* of Montréal	Burns	31	Grnk
1834 04 *QM* May 17	*General Graham* of Alloa	Craigie	66	Alloa
1834 04 *QM* May 13	*Hercules* of Aberdeen	Walker, D.	75	Aberdeen
1834 04 *QM* May 17	*Margaret Bogle* of Leith	Smith	41	Leith
1834 04 *QM* May 13	*Springhill* of Irvine	Auld	16	Grnk
1834 04 *QM* May 24	*Stranraer*	Irvine	72	Stranraer
1834 04 *QM* May 15	*Victoria* of Dundee	Berrie	34	Dundee
1834 05 *QM* June 10	*Rosebud*	Roy	80	Glasgow
1834 06 *QM* July 15	*Alfred*	n/k	243	Leith

Year Mth	Vessel	Master	Psgr. Nos.	Departure Port
1834 06 QM July 8	*Amity* of Glasgow	Mercer, J.	33	Grnk
1834 06 QM July 20	*Cartha*	Morrison	184	Grnk
1834 06 QM July 29	*Conference* of Newcastle	Buchan	112	Leith
1834 06 QM July 12	*Favourite* (2)	Girvan	33	Ayr
1834 06 QM July 17	*Henry*	Anderson	154	Glasgow
1834 07 QM Aug. 14	*Bowes*	Faulkner	172	Cromarty
1834 07 QM Aug. 14	*Fame* (3)	Wright	35	Grnk
1834 07 QM Aug. 26	*Favourite* of Montréal	Burns	87	Grnk
1834 07 QM Aug. 7	*Gleniffer*	Watson	181	Grnk
1834 07 QM Aug. 14	*John & Mary*	Nicholson	79	Leith
1834 07 QM Aug. 14	*Portia*	Hirst	171	Grnk
1834 07 QM Aug. 19	*Stirling Castle* of Greenock	Fraser	358	Islay
1834 08 QM Sept. 30	*Canada* of Greenock	Allan	46	Grnk
1834 08 QM Sept. 20	*Hercules* of Aberdeen	Walker, D.	133	Aberdeen
1834 08 QM Sept. 13	*Janet Izat* of Alloa	n/k	100	Tobermory
1834 09 QM Oct. 7	*Brilliant* of Aberdeen	Duthie	169	Aberdeen
1834 09 QM Oct. 7	*Cherokee* of Glasgow	Miller	26	Grnk
1835 04	*Amity* of Aberdeen	Rae, W.	39	Aberdeen

QM June 6. "Respectable farmers with considerable capital." PP w/e June 6. Some intend to view townships along Craig's Road (Eastern Townships).

Year Mth	Vessel	Master	Psgr. Nos.	Departure Port
1835 04 QM May 30	*Berwick on Tweed*	Muers	20	Berwick

Year Mth	Vessel	Master	Psgr. Nos.	Departure Port
1835 04 QM May 29	*Cyrus*	Scott	33	Leith
1835 04 QM June 18, *AH* April 18	*Hercules* of Aberdeen	Walker, D.	70	Aberdeen
1835 04 QM May 23	*Lother*	Murphy	29	Annan
1835 04 QM May 19	*Victoria* of Dundee	n/k	19	Dundee
1835 05 QM June 6	*Carleton* of Aberdeen	Anderson	64	Aberdeen
1835 05 QM June 4	*Caroline*	Lowergran	50	Berwick
1835 05 QM June 18	*Favourite* of Montréal	Burns	39	Grnk
1835 05 QM June 27	*Pacific* of Aberdeen	Morrison, J.	24	Aberdeen
1835 06 QM July 11	*Cartha*	n/k	48	Grnk
1835 06 QM Aug. 1; PP w/e Aug. 22. Smallpox aboard.	*Maria* (2)	Davieson	111	Cromarty
1835 07 QM Aug. 4	*Chieftain* of Kirkaldy	Spark	85	Cromarty
1835 07 QM Aug. 22	*Gleniffer*	Wilson	31	Grnk
1835 07 QM Aug. 22	*Hector*	Davison	49	Islay
1835 07 QM Aug. 4	*Pilgrim* of Aberdeen	Allan, G.	49	Aberdeen
1835 07 QM Aug. 4	*Retreat*	Hamilton	92	Grnk
1835 08 QM Sept. 24	*Canada* of Greenock	Allan	70	Grnk
1835 08 QM Sept. 19	*Robert McWilliam* of Aberdeen	Williamson	25	Aberdeen
1835 09 QM Oct. 13	*Brilliant* of Aberdeen	Duthie	70	Aberdeen
1835 09 QM Oct. 27. 54 passengers left at Pictou.	*Paragon*	Goodchild	46	Cromarty

Year	Mth	Vessel	Master	Psgr. Nos.	Departure Port
1836	03	*Favourite* of Montréal	Allan, B.	43	Grnk
QM May 17; *IJ* March 5					
1836	04	*Brilliant* of Aberdeen	Duthie	80	Aberdeen
QM June 4; *AH* April 16					
1836	04	*Cyrus*	Nicoll	33	Leith
QM June 18					
1836	04	*Globe*	Lindsay	15	Montrose
QM May 31					
1836	04	*Monarch* of Glasgow	Welsh	15	Grnk
QM May 28					
1836	04	*Pacific* of Aberdeen	Morrison, J.	122	Aberdeen
AH April 23					
1836	04	*Robertson*	Neil	25	Grnk
QM May 17					
1836	04	*Sir William Wallace* of Aberdeen (2)	Anderson, D.	17	Aberdeen
QM May 28; *AH* April 23					
1836	05	*Augusta* of Aberdeen	Rae, W.	46	Aberdeen
QM June 22					
1836	05	*Corsair* of Greenock	Ritchie	95	Grnk
QM July 16					
1836	05	*Shakespeare* of Aberdeen	Rosie	84	Aberdeen
QM July 19					
1836	06	*Albion* of Scarborough	Hicks, M.	28	Cromarty
QM Sept. 16; Martell, Ibid, 84; *IJ* 10 June, 1 July. 75 passengers left at Sydney, Cape Breton.					
1836	06	*Favourite* of Montréal	Allan, B.	29	Grnk
QM Sept. 10					
1836	06	*Hercules* of Aberdeen	Walker, D.	158	Aberdeen
QM Aug. 27; *AH* June 18					
1836	06	*Tweed*	Slocombe	245	Cromarty
QM July 19; *EC* May 20					
1836	06	*Viewforth* of Kirkaldy	Elden	150	Cromarty
QM July 19; *EC* May 20					
1836	07	*Belmont* of Greenock	Ford	77	Grnk
QM Aug. 25					
1836	07	*Canada* of Greenock	n/k	52	Grnk
QM Sept. 22					
1836	07	*Circassian* of Aberdeen	Ritchie, T.	117	Aberdeen
QM Sept. 3					

Year Mth	Vessel	Master	Psgr. Nos.	Departure Port
1836 07 *QM* Sept. 6	*Henry*	Gibson	60	Grnk
1836 07 *QM* Aug. 19	*Highlander* of Aberdeen	Fluckhart	150	Cromarty
1836 07 *QM* Sept. 6; *IJ* July 1; *JJ* July 1; *PP* w/e 10 Sept. Sixty seven of the 145 passengers had intended to disembark at Pictou.	*Mariner* of Sunderland	Collins	145	Loch Eriboll
1836 08 *QM* Oct. 6	*Brilliant* of Aberdeen	Elliot, J.	28	Aberdeen
1836 08 *QM* Sept. 27	*Cherokee* of Glasgow	Miller	16	Grnk
1836 08 *QM* Oct.13	*Deveron* of Glasgow	Anderson	174	Loch Indaal (Islay)
1836 08 *QM* Oct. 11	*Monarch* of Glasgow	Welsh	23	Glasgow
1836 08 *QM* Oct. 6	*Palmona*	Morison	15	Grnk
1836 08 *QM* Oct. 6	*Rebecca* of Greenock	Galetly	24	Grnk
1836 08 *QM* Sept. 27	*Sir William Wallace* of Aberdeen (2)	Anderson	18	Aberdeen
1837 04 *QM* May 23	*Brilliant* of Aberdeen	Elliot, J.	40	Aberdeen
1837 04 *QM* May 6	*Canada* of Greenock	Allan, B.	28	Grnk
1837 04 *QM* June 7	*Cherokee* of Glasgow	Miller	44	Glasgow
1837 04 *QM* May 30	*Jane Christie*	Scott	34	Leith
1837 04 *QM* May 30	*Richibucto* of Aberdeen	Ganson, H.	45	Grnk
1837 05 *QM* June 7	*Arabian* of Greenock	Allan	81	Grnk
1837 05 *QM* June 18	*Blackness* of Dundee	Paton	49	Leith
1837 05 *QM* July 1; *JJ* Mar. 31, Apr. 14 & May 26; *EC* Apr. 21.	*Margaret Bogle* of Leith	Smith	179	Cromarty
1837 05 *QM* May 30	*Pacific* of Aberdeen	Thompson	50	Aberdeen

Year	Mth	Vessel	Master	Psgr. Nos.	Departure Port
1837	06	*Corsair* of Greenock	Ritchie	29	Grnk

QM Aug. 11

| 1837 | 06 | *Hercules* of Aberdeen | Walker, D. | 42 | Stornoway |

QM July 27; Martell, Ibid, 86. Seventy passengers left at Pictou.

| 1837 | 06 | *Norfolk* | Harrison | 41 | Berwick |

QM July 27

| 1837 | 06 | *Québec Packet* of Aberdeen | Stephen | 35 | Aberdeen |

QM July 22

| 1837 | 06 | *Royal Adelaide* of Greenock | Dewar | 152 | Grnk |

QM July 27

| 1837 | 06 | *Swift* of Sunderland | Beveridge | 215 | Cromarty |

QM July 27; *EC* Apr. 28. Steerage fare for adults was 52 shillings.

| 1837 | 07 | *Thomas Worthington* | Morrison | 96 | Grnk |

QM Aug. 31

| 1837 | 08 | *Arabian* of Greenock | Allan | 28 | Grnk |

QM Oct. 5

| 1838 | 04 | *Ann* (3) | Wallace | 20 | Leith |

QM May 26

| 1838 | 04 | *Brilliant* of Aberdeen | Elliot, J. | 24 | Aberdeen |

QM May 12

| 1838 | 04 | *Carleton* of Aberdeen | Anderson, A. | 32 | Aberdeen |

QM May 22

| 1838 | 06 | *Pilgrim* of Aberdeen | Allan | 81 | Aberdeen |

QM Aug. 19

| 1838 | 06 | *Superb* of Greenock | Shannon | 17 | Grnk |

QM Aug. 19

| 1838 | 07 | *Canada* of Greenock | Allan, B. | 41 | Grnk |

QM Sept. 8

| 1838 | 07 | *Corsair* of Greenock | Ritchie | 95 | Tobermory |

QM Sept. 18; Martell, Ibid, 90. 155 passengers left at Sydney, Cape Breton.

| 1838 | 07 | *Eliza* (2) | McEwen | 42 | Grnk |

QM Aug. 21; PP w/e 25 Aug. Emigrants had considerable capital.

| 1838 | 08 | *Arabian* of Greenock | Allan | 16 | Grnk |

QM Sept. 21

| 1838 | 08 | *Energy* of Dundee | Fleming | 210 | Stornoway |

PP w/e Sept. 29, *QM* Sept. 24. To settle on British American Land Company's land in the Eastern Townships. "A valuable acquisition."

| 1839 | 04 | *Cruickston Castle* of Greenock | McKinlay | 47 | Grnk |

QM May 14.

Year	Mth	Vessel	Master	Psgr. Nos.	Departure Port
1839	06	*Kilmuir*	Blair	18	Grnk
QM Aug. 24					
1839	06	*Kincardineshire* of Aberdeen	Goven	55	Aberdeen
QG Aug. 31; MT Sept. 3.					
1839	06	*Sir William Wallace* of Aberdeen (2)	Tulloch, J.	19	Aberdeen
QM Aug. 24					
1839	08	*Canada* of Greenock	Allan	35	Grnk
QM Sept. 10					
1840	04	*Caroline* of Aberdeen	Marsh, J.	16	Aberdeen
PP w/e May 23					
1840	04	*Cruickston Castle* of Greenock	McInlay	18	Grnk
PP w/e May 23					
1840	04	*Henry* of Montrose	Ross	30	Dundee
PP 1841 (369) xv					
1840	04	*Osprey* of Leith	Kirk	90	Cromarty
IC Aug. 5; JJ Apr. 10; EC Apr. 3. 60 passengers left at Pictou.					
1840	04	*Sarah* of Aberdeen	Allan	29	Aberdeen
PP 1841 (369) xv					
1840	04	*Victoria* of Dundee	Peters, G.	21	Leith
PP w/e May 23					
1840	05	*Ann Grant* of Sligo	Murdoch	72	Glasgow
PP w/e July 18					
1840	05	*Hercules* of Aberdeen	Davidson	42	Aberdeen
PP w/e July 11					
1840	05	*Leven Lass* of Glasgow	Wright	59	Glasgow
PP w/e July 18					
1840	05	*Sisters* of Aberdeen	Hull	41	Aberdeen
PP w/e July 18					
1840	06	*Westmorland*	Duncan	76	Leith
PP w/e Aug. 22. One family intend to settle in Leeds, Lower Canada.					
1840	07	*Brilliant* of Aberdeen	Elliot, J.	23	Aberdeen
PP w/e Sept. 12					
1840	07	*British King* of Dundee	Brown, A.	20	Cromarty
IC Aug. 5; PP w/e Aug. 22; JJ May 29. Brought capital of £7,000 to £8,000. 137 passengers left at Pictou.					
1840	07	*Jamaica* of Glasgow	Martin	58	Grnk
PP w/e Aug. 29					
1840	07	*Lord Panmure* of Dundee	McNeill, J.	22	Dundee
PP w/e Sept. 19					

Year	Mth	Vessel	Master	Psgr. Nos.	Departure Port
1840	07	*Québec Packet* of Aberdeen	Stephen	60	Cromarty

IC Aug. 5; JJ June 26; PP w/e Sept. 12. Passengers had £800 to £1,000 in gold.

1840	07	*Sarah* of Aberdeen	Allan, G.	22	Aberdeen

PP w/e Sept .19

1840	08	*Canada* of Greenock	Allan, B.	31	Grnk

PP w/e Sept. 19

1841	04	*Alarm* of Cork	Brown, J.	133	Glasgow

PP 1842 (301) xxxi

1841	04	*Brilliant* of Aberdeen	n/k	82	Aberdeen

PP 1842 (301) xxxi

1841	04	*Duke of Buccleugh*	Blair, J.	41	Dumfries

PP 1842 (301) xxxi; *DT* Mar. 22

1841	04	*Fairy* of Dundee	Peters, G.	123	Cromarty

PP 1842 (301) xxxi; *JJ* March 12

1841	04	*Favourite* of Greenock	Bannerman	42	Glasgow

PP 1842 (301) xxxi

1841	04	*Mohawk* of Greenock		37	Glasgow

PP 1842 (301) xxxi

1841	04	*Pacific* of Aberdeen	Morrison, J.	171	Thurso

PP 1842 (301) xxxi; *JJ* Feb 5. 22 passengers left at Pictou.

1841	04	*Sarah Botsford* of Glasgow	Wallace, M.	219	Glasgow

PP 1842 (301) xxxi

1841	05	*Ann and Mary*	n/k	87	Banff

PP w/e July 17; PP 1842 (301) xxxi

1841	05	*Isabella* of Irvine	Miller, D.	33	Grnk

PP 1842 (301) xxxi

1841	06	*Andrew White* of Sunderland	Clark, B.	138	Glasgow

PP w/e Aug. 28

1841	06	*Bon Accord* of Aberdeen	Sim, J.	70	Aberdeen

PP w/e Sept. 4; *EC* June 11

1841	06	*Hants* of Greenock	Neill, W.	71	Glasgow

PP w/e Sept 4; PP 1842 (301) xxxi

1841	06	*Independence* of Belfast	n/k	245	Liverpool

PP w/e Aug. 14; PP 1842 (301) xxxi

1841	06	*Lady Grey* of North Shields	Grey, W.	105	Cromarty

IJ June 25; PP w/e Aug. 28; PP 1842 (301) xxxi. 135 passengers left at Pictou.

1841	06	*Margaret Bogle* of Leith	Smith, W.	117	Thurso and Loch Laxford

PP w/e July 24; PP 1842 (301) xxxi; *IJ* June 4; *JJ* April 30.

Year	Mth	Vessel	Master	Psgr. Nos.	Departure Port
1841	06	*Patriot*	n/k	19	Leith

PP w/e Aug. 28

| 1841 | 06 | *Saphiras* of Whitby | Brown, R. | 202 | Loch Laxford |

PP 1842 (301) xxxi; *IJ* June 4

| 1841 | 06 | *Taurus* of Aberdeen | n/k | 134 | Aberdeen |

PP w/e July 17; PP 1842 (301) xxxi

| 1841 | 06 | *Wanderer* | Cowan, F. | 141 | Glasgow |

PP w/e Aug 21; PP 1842 (301) xxxi. 58 (8 families) assisted by their landlord, Neill Malcolm.

| 1841 | 07 | *Canada* of Greenock | Allan. B. | 115 | Glasgow |

PP w/e Sept. 4

| 1841 | 07 | *Charles* | n/k | 145 | Stornoway |

PP 1842 (301) xxxi. Carried Lewis emigrants destined for the Eastern Townships.

| 1841 | 07 | *Jessy Logan* | n/k | 27 | Grnk |

PP w/e Sept. 4

| 1841 | 07 | *John Walker* of Liverpool | n/k | 49 | Skye |

PP w/e Aug. 28

| 1841 | 07 | *Lady Hood* of Stornoway | n/k | 78 | Stornoway |

PP w/e Sept. 4. Carried Lewis emigrants destined for the Eastern Townships.

| 1841 | 07 | *Stillman* | Williamson, C. | 60 | Glasgow |

PP 1842 (301) xxxi

| 1841 | 08 | *Caledonia* of Greenock | n/k | 54 | Grnk |

PP w/e Sept. 11

| 1841 | 08 | *Favourite* of Greenock | Bannerman | 34 | Glasgow |

PP w/e Sept. 25; PP 1842 (301) xxxi

| 1841 | 09 | *Universe* of Aberdeen | n/k | 19 | Thurso |

PP w/e Oct. 9. 105 passengers left at Pictou.

| 1842 | 03 | *Bowling* of Glasgow | Gentle,R. | 157 | Glasgow |

PP w/e June 11; SRA T/CN-21(2). Included members of Glasgow emigration societies.

| 1842 | 03 | *Harper* | Murphy | 235 | Glasgow |

PP w/e June 11; SRA T/CN-21(2). 29 passengers were members of Glasgow emigration societies.

| 1842 | 03 | *James Dean* of Greenock | Wilson | 29 | Glasgow |

PP w/e May 28; SRA T/CN-21(2)

| 1842 | 03 | *Kent* | Gardner, J. | 54 | Glasgow |

PP w/e May 28; SRA T/CN-21(2)

| 1842 | 03 | *Mohawk* of Greenock | Miller | 45 | Glasgow |

PP w/e May 21; SRA T/CN-21(2); *GH* Mar. 4. See comments for *Favourite* of Greenock (1842/04).

Year	Mth	Vessel	Master	Psgr. Nos.	Departure Port
1842	03	*Monarch* of Glasgow	Allan	36	Glasgow

PP w/e May 21; SRA T/CN-21(2); *GH* Mar. 4. See comments for *Favourite* of Greenock (1842/04).

| 1842 | 03 | *Queen of the Isles* of Stromness | Leask | 105 | Glasgow |

PP w/e June 18; SRA T/CN-21(2); *GH* Mar. 4

| 1842 | 04 | *Apollo* of Dundee | Walker, H. | 48 | Dundee |

PP w/e May 28; DCA CE 70/11/6.

| 1842 | 04 | *Blonde* of Montréal | Crawford | 396 | Glasgow |

PP w/e July 2; SRA T/CN-21(2); *GH* Mar. 18. Passengers had considerable capital.

| 1842 | 04 | *Brilliant* of Aberdeen | Elliot, J. | 32 | Aberdeen |

PP w/e May 28; *AH* Mar. 19, Apr. 23.

| 1842 | 04 | *Emma* of Dundee | Innis | 18 | Dundee |

PP w/e June 4

| 1842 | 04 | *Favourite* of Greenock | Bannerman | 88 | Grnk |

PP w/e May 21; SRA T/CN-21(2). "Farmers and respectable mechanics in good circumstances." Two families to join friends in Shipton in the Eastern Townships.

| 1842 | 04 | *Feronia* | Grant, R. | 87 | Glasgow |

PP w/e July 2; SRA T/CN-21(2); *GH* Apr. 22. Passengers had considerable capital.

| 1842 | 04 | *General Graham* of Alloa | n/k | 27 | Alloa |

PP w/e May 28

| 1842 | 04 | *Leven Lass* of Glasgow | Wright | 39 | Glasgow |

PP w/e June 11; SRA T/CN-21(2)

| 1842 | 04 | *Pacific* of Aberdeen | Morrison, J. | 89 | Cromarty |

PP w/e June 4; *IJ* Mar. 11; *AH* Mar. 19; *JJ* Feb. 11. Called at Orkney Islands.

| 1842 | 04 | *Sarah* of Aberdeen | Allan, G. | 28 | Aberdeen |

PP w/e May 28; *AH* Apr. 23.

| 1842 | 04 | *St. Lawrence* of Aberdeen | Tulloch, J. | 25 | Aberdeen |

PP w/e May 28; *AH* Mar. 5.

| 1842 | 05 | *Elizabeth* of Leith | Stocks | 15 | Leith |

PP w/e June 11

| 1842 | 05 | *Mahaica* of Greenock | Jump, W. | 145 | Glasgow |

PP w/e July 9; SRA T/CN-21(2); *GH* May 20

| 1842 | 05 | *Pactolus* | Lloyd, T. | 182 | Glasgow |

PP w/e Aug. 6; SRA T/CN-21(2); *GH* May16. 51 psgrs aided by public & private contributions.

| 1842 | 05 | *Robert Morrow* of Kirkaldy | n/k | 60 | Leith |

PP w/e June 25

| 1842 | 05 | *Superior* of Peterhead | Manson | 191 | Cromarty |

PP w/e July 9; *JJ* Mar. 18, 25, July 29. 52 passengers left at Pictou.

Year	Mth	Vessel	Master	Psgr. Nos.	Departure Port
1842	05	*Troubadour* of Irvine	McDowell, J.	224	Glasgow

PP w/e Aug. 6; SRA T/CN-21(2); *GH* Apr. 22

| 1842 | 05 | *Wexford* of Wexford | Slatterly, J. | 200 | Grnk |

PP w/e July 9; SRA T/CN-21(2). 130 passengers were members of Emigration Societies.

| 1842 | 06 | *Alice* of Milford | Rees, S. | 107 | Glasgow |

PP w/e Aug. 20; SRA T/CN-21(2); GH May 20

| 1842 | 06 | *Joseph Green* of Peterhead | Volum, J. | 239 | Cromarty |

PP w/e July 23; *IJ* March 25. 38 passengers received financial help.

| 1842 | 06 | *Margaret Wilkie* of Greenock | Miller, J. | 111 | Grnk |

PP w/e Sept. 17; SRA TCN-21(2); *GH* June 17

| 1842 | 06 | *Royal Bride* of Dundee | Welsh, G. | 78 | Dundee |

PP w/e Aug. 13; DCA CE 70/11/6; *DC* May 13

| 1842 | 06 | *St. Andrew* of New Brunswick | Leith, J. | 133 | Stornoway |

PP w/e Aug. 6; *IJ* Aug. 19. Some "very poor". Passengers to settle in the Eastern Townships.

| 1842 | 06 | *William Glen Anderson* of Glasgow | Gillespie | 152 | Aberdeen |

PP w/e Aug. 13; *AH* June 18

| 1842 | 07 | *Bellona* of Glasgow | Mitchell, R. | 18 | Grnk |

PP w/e Oct. 1; SRA T/CN-21(2); *GH* July 22

| 1842 | 07 | *Caledonia* of Greenock | Allan, B. | 86 | Glasgow |

PP w/e Aug. 27; SRA T/CN-21(2); *GH* June 20

| 1842 | 07 | *Elephanta* of Glasgow | Ross, D. | 130 | Grnk |

GH June 13; PP w/e Aug. 27.

| 1842 | 07 | *Gem* of Aberdeen | Ross, P. | 30 | Leith |

PP w/e Aug. 27; *AH* June 4

| 1842 | 07 | *Hercules* of Liverpool | Postill, F. | 59 | Lochmaddy |

PP w/e Sept. 17; *IJ* Aug. 19

| 1842 | 07 | *James Campbell* of Glasgow | Miller, J. | 27 | Glasgow |

PP w/e Sept. 17; SRA T/CN-21(2); *GH* June 13

| 1842 | 07 | *Jane Brown* of Glasgow | Wylie, J. | 30 | Glasgow |

PP w/e Oct. 1; SRA T/CN-21(2); *GH* June 13

| 1842 | 07 | *Lady Falkland* | Parker | 361 | Port Glasgow |

PP w/e Sept. 3; *GH* June 24

| 1842 | 07 | *Merlin* | Thompson, D. | 185 | Grnk |

PP w/e Sept. 3; *GH* June 10

| 1842 | 07 | *Mohawk* of Greenock | Bannerman | 62 | Glasgow |

PP w/e Sept. 17; SRA T/CN-21(2)

| 1842 | 07 | *Sir William Wallace* of Aberdeen (2) | Anderson, R. | 78 | Thurso |

PP w/e Aug. 20; *IJ* June 3; *AH* June 4; *JJ* June 10.

Year Mth	Vessel	Master	Psgr. Nos.	Departure Port
1842 08 PP w/e Oct. 15	*Apollo* of Dundee	Walker, H.	20	Dundee
1842 08 PP w/e Oct. 15	*Brilliant* of Aberdeen	Elliot, J.	32	Aberdeen
1842 08 PP w/e Oct. 15; SRA T/CN-21(2)	*Favourite* of Greenock	Greenhorn, A.	62	Glasgow
1842 08 PP w/e Oct .1; *IJ* June 10, Sept. 30. 86 passengers left at Pictou.	*Lady Emily* of Sunderland	Smith, J.	64	Loch Laxford
1842 08 PP w/e Oct. 15	*Sarah* of Aberdeen	Allan	25	Aberdeen
1843 04 PP 1844 (181) xxxv	*Ann and Mary*	n/k	29	Banff
1843 04 PP 1844 (181) xxxv; *DC* Feb. 24	*Apollo* of Dundee	n/k	42	Dundee
1843 04 PP 1844 (181) xxxv	*Brilliant* of Aberdeen	Barr, R.	23	Aberdeen
1843 04 PP 1844 (181) xxxv	*Caledonia* of Greenock	n/k	171	Glasgow
1843 04 PP 1844 (181) xxxv	*Commodore*	Miller, J.	27	Glasgow
1843 04 PP 1844 (181) xxxv; *IC* Mar. 15	*Eagle* (2)	Morton, R.	94	Glasgow
1843 04 PP 1844 (181) xxxv; *DC* March 3	*Emma* of Dundee	n/k	34	Dundee
1843 04 PP 1844 (181) xxxv	*Essex*	n/k	29	Glasgow
1843 04 PP 1844 (181) xxxv	*Favourite* of Greenock	n/k	78	Glasgow
1843 04 PP 1844 (181) xxxv	*Flora* of Dundee	n/k	57	Dundee
1843 04 PP 1844 (181) xxxv	*Hector*	n/k	16	Glasgow
1843 04 PP 1844 (181) xxxv	*Heroine* of Aberdeen	n/k	48	Aberdeen
1843 04 PP 1844 (181) xxxv	*James Redden* of Dumfries	n/k	31	Dumfries
1843 04 PP 1844 (181) xxxv	*Jane Brown* of Glasgow	Wylie, J.	23	Glasgow

Year	Mth	Vessel	Master	Psgr. Nos.	Departure Port
1843	04	*Jeanie Deans*	Miller, D.	75	Glasgow
PP 1844 (181) xxxv; PP w/e June17.					
1843	04	*Mahaica* of Greenock	Jump, W.	39	Glasgow
PP 1844 (181) xxxv; PP w/e June 17.					
1843	04	*Mohawk* of Greenock	Bannerman, G.	17	Glasgow
PP 1844 (181) xxxv					
1843	04	*New York Packet*	n/k	80	Grnk
PP 1844 (181) xxxv					
1843	04	*Pacific* of Aberdeen	n/k	39	Thurso
PP 1844 (181) xxxv					
1843	04	*Robert Murrow*	n/k	41	Leith
PP 1844 (181) xxxv					
1843	04	*Sarah* (2)	McLean, W.	58	Glasgow
PP 1844 (181) xxxv; *GSP* Apr. 23.					
1843	04	*Sarah* of Aberdeen	n/k	33	Aberdeen
PP 1844 (181) xxxv					
1843	04	*Springfield*	n/k	42	Glasgow
PP 1844 (181) xxxv					
1843	04	*St. Lawrence* of Aberdeen	n/k	32	Aberdeen
PP 1844 (181) xxxv					
1843	04	*Superb* of Greenock	n/k	194	Glasgow
PP 1844 (181) xxxv					
1843	04	*Symmetry*	n/k	110	Thurso
PP 1844 (181) xxxv; PP w/e July 1. 18 passengers left at Pictou and PEI.					
1843	05	*Blonde* of Montréal	n/k	297	Glasgow
PP 1844 (181) xxxv; PP w/e June 24.					
1843	05	*Caspian*	n/k	35	Glasgow
PP 1844 (181) xxxv					
1843	05	*Catherine* (2)	McKechney	22	Tobermory
PP 1844 (181) xxxv; PP w/e Oct. 14. 275 steerage passengers, ship wrecked; transhipped on *John & Robert*; all but 22 landed at Cape Breton.					
1843	05	*Hamilton* of Glasgow	Dick, J.	283	Grnk
PP 1844 (181) xxxv; PP w/e July 15; *IC* May 10.					
1843	05	*Jean Baptiste* of Glasgow	n/k	15	Glasgow
PP 1844 (181) xxxv					
1843	05	*Lady Kinnaird* of Dundee	n/k	65	Dundee
PP 1844 (181) xxxv; PP w/e July 1; *DC* Apr. 7.					
1843	05	*Margaret Bogle* of Leith	n/k	70	Leith
PP 1844 (181) xxxv; PP w/e July 1.					

Year	Mth	Vessel	Master	Psgr. Nos.	Departure Port
1843	05	*Roger Stewart*	n/k	56	Grnk

PP 1844 (181) xxxv; PP w/e June 24

| 1843 | 06 | *California* of Greenock | Auld | 328 | Glasgow |

PP 1844 (181) xxxv; PP w/e July 15; *IC* May 24.

| 1843 | 06 | *Canada* of Greenock | McArthur, J. | 43 | Glasgow |

PP 1844 (181) xxxv

| 1843 | 06 | *George* of Dundee | Hanley, F. | 120 | Loch Laxford |

PP 1844 (181) xxxv; PP w/e Sept. 16; *DC* Apr. 28. 95 passengers left at Pictou.

| 1843 | 06 | *John Cumming* | n/k | 83 | Glasgow |

PP 1844 (181) xxxv

| 1843 | 06 | *Margaret* of Greenock | McBride, A. | 238 | Glasgow |

PP 1844 (181) xxxv; *IC* June 14.

| 1843 | 06 | *Menapia* | Queen, J. | 183 | Glasgow |

PP 1844 (181) xxxv; PP w/e July 29.

| 1843 | 06 | *Messenger* | Mather, W. | 42 | Glasgow |

PP 1844 (181) xxxv

| 1843 | 06 | *Monument* | n/k | 87 | Glasgow |

PP 1844 (181) xxxv

| 1843 | 06 | *Navarino* | n/k | 27 | Glasgow |

PP 1844 (181) xxxv

| 1843 | 06 | *Rose* of Aberdeen | n/k | 94 | Aberdeen |

PP 1844 (181) xxxv

| 1843 | 06 | *Tay* of Glasgow | Langwell | 327 | Grnk |

PP 1844 (181) xxxv; PP w/e August 5. Included 118 emigrants who were assisted by their landlords.

| 1843 | 06 | *Wilson* | n/k | 21 | Grnk |

PP 1844 (181) xxxv

| 1843 | 07 | *Albion* of Aberdeen | Leslie, A. | 16 | Aberdeen |

PP 1844 (181) xxxv

| 1843 | 07 | *Blackness* of Dundee | n/k | 58 | Dundee |

PP 1844 (181) xxxv; *DC* May 12.

| 1843 | 07 | *Hector* of Dundee | Anderson, W. | 92 | Glasgow |

PP 1844 (181) xxxv; PP w/e Sept. 16.

| 1843 | 07 | *Henry Kneeland* | n/k | 19 | Glasgow |

PP 1844 (181) xxxv

| 1843 | 07 | *Jean Hastie* of Grangemouth | Robertson, J. | 44 | Thurso |

PP 1844 (181) xxxv; *DC* June 2.

| 1843 | 07 | *Octovara* | n/k | 59 | Glasgow |

PP 1844 (181) xxxv

Year	Mth	Vessel	Master	Psgr. Nos.	Departure Port
1843	08	*Acadian* of Glasgow PP 1844 (181) xxxv	n/k	26	Grnk
1843	08	*Apollo* of Dundee PP 1844 (181) xxxv; *DC* July 7.	n/k	26	Dundee
1843	08	*Brilliant* of Aberdeen PP 1844 (181) xxxv; PP w/e Sept. 23.	n/k	36	Aberdeen
1843	08	*Caledonia* of Greenock PP 1844 (181) xxxv; PP w/e Sept. 16.	Allan, B.	61	Glasgow
1843	08	*Canmore* of St. John PP 1844 (181) xxxv	n/k	23	Glasgow
1843	08	*Entaw* PP 1844 (181) xxxv	n/k	54	Glasgow
1843	08	*Favourite* of Greenock PP 1844 (181) xxxv	Greenhorn, A.	53	Glasgow
1843	08	*Jane Brown* of Glasgow PP 1844 (181) xxxv	Wyllie, J.	41	Glasgow
1843	08	*Margaret Pointer* PP 1844 (181) xxxv	Miller, J.	51	Glasgow
1843	08	*Warsaw* PP 1844 (181) xxxv	n/k	31	Glasgow
1843	09	*Jupiter* PP 1844 (181) xxxv	n/k	18	Glasgow
1843	09	*Perdonnet* PP 1844 (181) xxxv	n/k	37	Glasgow
1843	10	*Herald* of Greenock PP 1844 (181) xxxv	Coubro	319	Grnk
1844	04	*Messenger* *QM* June 8	Miller	18	Glasgow
1844	04	*St. Lawrence* of Aberdeen *AH* Apr. 27	Tulloch, J.	139	Aberdeen
1844	05	*Ann Henzell* *QM* July 3	Henzell	75	Glasgow
1844	05	*Brilliant* of Glasgow *QM* June 20	Barr	219	Glasgow
1844	05	*Congress* *QM* June 27	Greig	22	Leith
1844	05	*Hector* *QM* July 3	Anderson	134	Glasgow

Year Mth	Vessel	Master	Psgr. Nos.	Departure Port
1844 06 *QM* July 23	*Abigail*	Daly	341	Glasgow
1844 06 *QM* Aug. 3	*Canada* of Greenock	McArthur, J.	118	Glasgow
1844 06 *QM* July 23	*St. Nicholas*	Morgan	29	Inverness
1844 06 *QM* July 23	*William Hutt*	Rankin	138	Glasgow
1844 07 *QM* Aug. 27	*Caledonia* of Greenock	Allan	45	Glasgow
1844 07 *QM* Sept. 10	*Papineau*	Morland	28	Glasgow
1844 07 *QM* Aug. 27	*Tay* of Glasgow	Longwell	146	Grnk
1844 07 *QM* Aug. 27	*Watermillock*	Conner	34	Glasgow
1844 08 *QM* Sept. 24	*St. Lawrence* of Aberdeen	Tulloch, J.	76	Aberdeen
1845 03 *QM* May 27	*St. Lawrence* of Aberdeen	Tulloch, J.	17	Aberdeen
1845 04 *QM* May 20	*Apollo* of Dundee	Walker, H.	33	Dundee
1845 04 *QM* June 5	*Brilliant* of Glasgow	Barr	39	Glasgow
1845 04 *QM* May 15	*Favourite* of Greenock	Crawford	30	Glasgow
1845 04 *QM* May 27	*Margaret Boyle*	Scott	20	Leith
1845 05 *QM* July 1	*Abercrombie*	Louttef	27	Glasgow
1845 05 *QM* June 28	*Agitator*	Henry	33	Glasgow
1845 05 *QM* July 10	*Blonde* of Montréal	Crawford	226	Glasgow
1845 05 *QM* June 7; *AH* May 10.	*Brilliant* of Aberdeen	Elliot, J.	37	Aberdeen
1845 05 *AH* May 24, 31; *QM* July 15.	*Heroine* of Aberdeen	Walker, D.	70	Aberdeen

Year Mth	Vessel	Master	Psgr. Nos.	Departure Port
1845 05 QM July 1	*Jeanie Deans*	Miller	36	Glasgow
1845 05 QM July 12	*Mary* of Greenock (2)	Harrison, J.	25	Glasgow
1845 05 AH May 10	*St. Lawrence* of Aberdeen	Tulloch, J.	98	Aberdeen
1845 06 QM Aug. 5	*Afghan*	Black	229	Grnk
1845 06 QM July 31	*Canada* of Greenock	McArthur, J.	110	Glasgow
1845 06 QM June 28	*Lerwick*	Giffney	83	Dundee
1845 06 QM July 19	*Messenger*	Miller	48	Glasgow
1845 06 QM July 31	*New York Packet*	Hossack	108	Glasgow
1845 06 QM July 22	*Romulus*	Sangster	86	Glasgow
1845 06 QM July 15	*Romulus* of Greenock	Esson	58	Glasgow
1845 07 QM Aug. 30	*Caledonia* of Greenock	Greenhorn, A.	50	Glasgow
1845 07 QM Sept. 4	*Erromanga* of Greenock	Kelso	38	Glasgow
1845 07 QM Sept. 11	*European* (2)	McBride, A.	91	Glasgow
1845 07 QM Aug. 26, *IC* May 28, July 16.	*John Hutchison*	Harrison	76	Thurso
1845 07 QM Sept. 9	*Lord Seaton* of Aberdeen	Talbot, W.	64	Aberdeen
1845 08 QM Sept. 25	*St. Lawrence* of Aberdeen	Tulloch, J.	52	Aberdeen
1845 09 QM Oct. 21	*Mary Sharp*	Woolf	17	Glasgow
1846 04 QM June 9	*Cambria* of Greenock	Kelso	19	Glasgow
1846 04 QM June 13	*Fame* (4)	Miller	27	Glasgow

Year	Mth	Vessel	Master	Psgr. Nos.	Departure Port
1846	04	*Favourite* of Greenock	Grant	39	Glasgow

QM May 14. "Ships to Megantic County", Clan Donald Centre. Carried Arran emigrants who settled in Megantic County.

1846	04	*Lord Seaton* of Aberdeen	Talbot, W.	18	Thurso

IC April 1; *QM* May 19

1846	04	*Norway*	Hughes	22	Glasgow

QM June 20

1846	04	*St. Lawrence* of Aberdeen	Tulloch, J.	97	Aberdeen

QM May 19

1846	05	*Ianthe*	Hunter	37	Glasgow

QM July 17

1846	05	*Jamaica* of Glasgow	Martin	76	Glasgow

QM July 7

1846	06	*Blonde* of Montréal	Crawford	374	Glasgow

QM July 7. "Ships to Megantic County", Clan Donald Centre. May have carried Arran emigrants who settled in Megantic County.

1846	06	*Brilliant* of Aberdeen	Brown	164	Grnk

QM Aug. 15

1846	06	*Heroine* of Aberdeen	Walker, D.	132	Aberdeen

QM Aug. 25

1846	06	*Mary* of Glasgow	Harrison, J.	42	Glasgow

QM July 28

1846	07	*Albion* of Greenock	Allan	70	Glasgow

QM Aug. 15

1846	07	*Caledonia* of Greenock	Greenhorn, A.	30	Glasgow

QM Aug. 31

1846	07	*Kate* of Newcastle	Taylor, T.	43	Cromarty

IC June 17; *QM* Sept. 8. The shipping agent, John Sutherland, was also the northern agent for the British American Land Company which had land for sale in the Eastern Townships.

1847	03	*Albion* of Greenock	Allan, B.	18	Glasgow

PP 1847-48 (964) xlvii

1847	03	*Caledonia* of Greenock	Greenhorn, A.	15	Glasgow

PP 1847-48 (964) xlvii

1847	04	*Belleisle* of Glasgow	Reid	33	Glasgow

PP 1847-48 (964) xlvii

1847	04	*Cambria* of Greenock	Birnie, W.	19	Glasgow

PP 1847-48 (964) xlvii

1847	04	*Earl Powis* of Dundee	n/k	52	Dundee

PP 1847-48 (964) xlvii

Year	Mth	Vessel	Master	Psgr. Nos.	Departure Port
1847	04	*Favourite* of Greenock	Crawford, M.	79	Glasgow
PP 1847-48 (964) xlvii					
1847	04	*Glenswilly* of Glasgow	Henderson, T.	43	Glasgow
PP 1847-48 (964) xlvii					
1847	04	*Mary* of Greenock (2)	Shotton, J.	36	Glasgow
PP 1847-48 (964) xlvii					
1847	04	*St. Lawrence* of Aberdeen	n/k	55	Aberdeen
PP 1847-48 (964) xlvii					
1847	05	*Charlotte Harrison* of Greenock	McIntyre	305	Grnk
PP 1847-48 (964) xlvii. 66 assisted from parish & private funds.					
1847	05	*Clansman* of Glasgow	Peck	218	Grnk
PP 1847-48 (964) xlvii					
1847	05	*Lord Panmure* of Dundee	Henderson, J.	116	Glasgow
PP 1847-48 (964) xlvii					
1847	05	*Peruvian* of Glasgow	Boyd, J.	35	Glasgow
PP 1847-48 (964) xlvii					
1847	06	*Ann Rankin* of Glasgow	McArthur, J.	336	Glasgow
PP 1847-48 (964) xlvii					
1847	06	*Britannia* of Newcastle	Simpson	388	Glasgow
PP 1847-48 (964) xlvii					
1847	06	*Euclid* of Liverpool	Bainbridge, G.	330	Glasgow
PP 1847-48 (964) xlvii; *GH* May 31.					
1847	06	*Heroine* of Aberdeen	n/k	81	Aberdeen
PP 1847-48 (964) xlvii					
1847	07	*Caledonia* of Greenock	Greenhorn, A.	45	Glasgow
PP 1847-48 (964) xlvii					
1847	07	*Cambria* of Greenock	Birnie, W.	67	Glasgow
PP 1847-48 (964) xlvii					
1847	07	*Canada* of Greenock	McArthur, J.	136	Glasgow
PP 1847-48 (964) xlvii					
1847	07	*Erromanga* of Greenock	Ramsay, R.	56	Glasgow
PP 1847-48 (964) xlvii					
1847	08	*Albion* of Greenock	Allan, B.	64	Glasgow
PP 1847-48 (964) xlvii					
1847	08	*Belleisle* of Glasgow	Reid	28	Glasgow
PP 1847-48 (964) xlvii					
1847	08	*Earl Powis* of Dundee	n/k	20	Dundee
PP 1847-48 (964) xlvii					

Year	Mth	Vessel	Master	Psgr. Nos.	Departure Port
1847	08	*Favourite* of Greenock PP 1847-48 (964) xlvii	Crawford, M.	19	Grnk
1847	08	*Lord Metcalfe* of Aberdeen PP 1847-48 (964) xlvii	Bain	51	Aberdeen
1847	08	*Mary* of Greenock (2) PP 1847-48 (964) xlvii	Harrison, J.	20	Glasgow
1847	08	*St. Lawrence* of Aberdeen PP 1847-48 (964) xlvii	n/k	26	Aberdeen
1848	03	*Albion* of Greenock PP 1847-48 (971) xlvii	Allan, B.	17	Glasgow
1848	03	*Caledonia* of Greenock PP 1847-48 (971) xlvii	Greenhorn, A.	20	Glasgow
1848	03	*Royalist* of Alloa PP 1847-48 (971) xlvii	Beveridge	15	Grnk
1848	04	*Berbice* of Aberdeen PP 1847-48 (971) xlvii	Elliot, J.	33	Aberdeen
1848	04	*Cambria* of Greenock PP 1847-48 (971) xlvii	Birnie, W.	31	Glasgow
1848	04	*Circassian* of Greenock SRA T/CN 26/2	Dixon, G.	106	Glasgow
1848	04	*Earl Powis* of Dundee PP 1847-48 (971) xlvii	Walker, H.	34	Dundee
1848	04	*Erromanga* of Greenock PP 1847-48 (971) xlvii	Ramsay, R.	79	Glasgow
1848	04	*Favourite* of Greenock PP 1847-48 (971) xlvii	Wylie, H.	91	Glasgow
1848	04	*Lord Metcalfe* of Aberdeen PP 1847-48 (971) xlvii	Bain	31	Aberdeen
1848	04	*Mary* of Greenock (2) PP 1847-48 (971) xlvii	Harrison, J.	25	Glasgow
1848	04	*St. Lawrence* of Aberdeen PP 1847-48 (971) xlvii	Tulloch, J.	120	Aberdeen
1848	05	*Jessie Stephens* of Irvine PP w/e July 8; SRA T/CN 26/2	Miller, D.	131	Glasgow
1848	06	*Blonde* of Montréal SRA T/CN 26/2	n/k	272	Glasgow
1848	06	*Jamaica* of Glasgow SRA T/CN 26/2	Martin	108	Glasgow

Year	Mth	Vessel	Master	Psgr. Nos.	Departure Port
1848	06	*Rosina* of Campbeltown	n/k	247	Grnk
SRA T/CN 26/2; *IC* May 23					
1848	07	*Albion* of Greenock	n/k	87	Glasgow
SRA T/CN 26/2					
1848	07	*Caledonia* of Greenock	Greenhorn, A.	113	Glasgow
SRA T/CN 26/2					
1848	07	*Tay* of Glasgow	Adams	106	Glasgow
SRA T/CN 26/2; *IC* June 27					
1848	08	*Favourite* of Greenock	Wylie, H.	22	Glasgow
SRA T/CN 26/2					
1849	04	*Berbice* of Aberdeen	Elliot	28	Aberdeen
QM May 29					
1849	04	*Earl Powis* of Dundee	Walker, H.	42	Dundee
QM June 1					
1849	04	*Erromanga* of Greenock	Ramsay, R.	25	Glasgow
QM May 12					
1849	04	*Favourite* of Greenock	Wylie, H.	101	Glasgow
QM May 29					
1849	04	*Helen*	Johnson	18	Montrose
QM May 29					
1849	04	*Lord Seaton* of Aberdeen	Talbot, W.	23	Longhope (Orkney)
IC March 8; *QM* May 22					
1849	04	*St. Lawrence* of Aberdeen	Tulloch, J.	36	Aberdeen
QM May 29					
1849	05	*Blonde* of Montréal	Crawford	300	Glasgow
QM July 3					
1849	05	*Clansman* of Glasgow	Johnston	40	Glasgow
QM June 23					
1849	05	*Lanarkshire* of Glasgow	Turner	80	Glasgow
QM June 23					
1849	05	*Scotia* of Belfast	Carrey	194	Glasgow
QM July 5					
1849	05	*Springhill* of Irvine	Gunn	67	Glasgow
QM June 7					
1849	06	*Champion* of Greenock	Cochrane	219	Glasgow
QM July 29					
1849	06	*Circassian* of Greenock	Dixon, G.	209	Glasgow
PP 1850 (173) xl; *QM* July 10. Seventy died from disease.					

Year Mth	Vessel	Master	Psgr. Nos.	Departure Port
1849 06 QM July 26	*Jamaica* of Glasgow	Martin	158	Grnk
1849 06 *JJ* April 27, June 15; *IC* May 3; *QM* Aug. 14.	*Prince Albert* of Arbroath	Rodger, A.	125	Thurso
1849 07 QM Aug. 14	*Albion* of Greenock	McArthur, J.	81	Glasgow
1849 07 QM Aug. 28	*Caledonia* of Greenock	Greenham	48	Glasgow
1849 07 QM Aug. 14	*Cambria* of Greenock	Harrison, J.	82	Glasgow
1849 07 QM Sept. 1	*Erromanga* of Greenock	n/k	85	Glasgow
1849 08 QM Sept. 11	*Berbice* of Aberdeen	Elliot, J.	56	Aberdeen
1849 08 QM Sept. 13	*Favourite* of Greenock	Wylie, H.	42	Glasgow
1849 08 QM Sept. 15	*Home*	Grey	33	Glasgow
1849 08 QM Sept. 25	*Mary* of Greenock (2)	Munro	25	Glasgow
1849 08 QM Sept. 11	*St. Lawrence* of Aberdeen	Tulloch, J.	17	Aberdeen
1850 04 AH Apr. 13	*Berbice* of Aberdeen	Elliot, J.	45	Aberdeen
1850 04 AH Apr. 20	*St. Lawrence* of Aberdeen	Tulloch, J.	95	Aberdeen
1850 06 PP 1851 (348) xl	*Three Bells* of Glasgow	n/k	262	Glasgow
1850 06 PP 1851 (348) xl	*Wandsworth* of Glasgow	n/k	377	Grnk
1850 08 AH Aug. 3	*Berbice* of Aberdeen	Elliot, J.	60	Aberdeen
1850 08 AH Aug. 3	*St. Lawrence* of Aberdeen	Tulloch, J.	69	Aberdeen
1851 04 QM May 26	*Berbice* of Aberdeen	Elliot	98	Aberdeen
1851 04 SRA T/CN 26/5	*Glencairn* of Glasgow	Allan	57	Glasgow

Year Mth	Vessel	Master	Psgr. Nos.	Departure Port
1851 04 SRA T/CN 26/5	*Mary* of Greenock (2)	Watson	22	Glasgow
1851 04 SRA T/CN 26/5	*Minerva* of Greenock	Stewart	41	Glasgow
1851 04 *AJ* Apr. 23	*Sarah* of Aberdeen	Sim, J.	85	Aberdeen
1851 04 *QM* May 26, *AJ* Apr. 23.	*St. Lawrence* of Aberdeen	Tulloch, J.	139	Aberdeen
1851 05 SRA T/CN 26/5	*Ann Rankin* of Glasgow	Burns	113	Glasgow
1851 05 SRA T/CN 26/5	*California* of Greenock	Gall, R.	103	Glasgow
1851 05 SRA T/CN 26/5; *QM* June 24.	*Clutha* of Greenock	Muir	134	Glasgow
1851 05 *QM* June 24	*Harrison Chilton* of Liverpool	n/k	130	Glasgow
1851 05 Devine, *Highland Famine*, 219. Sir James Matheson's tenants.	*Islay*	n/k	68	Stornoway
1851 05 Devine, *Highland Famine*, 219; *IC* June 12. Sir James Matheson's tenants.	*Marquis of Stafford*	n/k	500	Stornoway
1851 05 SRA T/CN 26/5	*Pekin* of Irvine	Crawford	44	Glasgow
1851 05 PP 1852 (1474) xxxiii; Devine, *Highland Famine*, 325. Sir James Matheson's tenants.	*Prince George* of Alloa	n/k	203	Stornoway
1851 05 SRA T/CN 26/5	*Sappho* of Sunderland	MacDonald	78	Glasgow
1851 05 PP 1852 (1474) xxxiii; *IC* May 29; SRA T/CN 26/5; *QM* July 5.	*Susan* of Glasgow	Taylor	69	Glasgow
1851 05 PP 1852 (1474) xxxiii. Sir James Matheson's tenants.	*Urgent* of Belfast	n/k	370	Stornoway
1851 05 *QM* June 24	*Woodfield*	n/k	69	Glasgow
1851 06 PP 1852 (1474) xxxiii; *QM* July 19; Devine, *Highland Famine*, 220. Sir James Matheson's tenants.	*Barlow*	n/k	287	Stornoway
1851 06 PP 1852 (1474) xxxiii; *QM* Aug. 28. Col. John Gordon's tenants.	*Brooksby* of Glasgow	McEwan	285	Loch Boisdale
1851 06 PP 1852 (1474) xxxiii	*Ellen* of Liverpool	n/k	100	Liverpool

Year	Mth	Vessel	Master	Psgr. Nos.	Departure Port
1851	06	*Jamaica* of Glasgow	Martin	179	Grnk

QM Aug. 5; PP 1852 (1474) xxxiii; SRA T/CN 26/5. 104 passengers were assisted by landlords.

1851	06	*Justyn* of Leith	Thomson, R.	313	Grnk

QM July 5; SRA T/CN 26/5; *JJ* May 16

1851	06	*Sesostris* of Glasgow	Logan	302	Glasgow

QM July 12; PP 1852 (1474) xxxiii; SRA T/CN 26/5. Includes some of Sir James Matheson's Lewis tenants.

1851	06	*Spartan* of Greenock	Morrison	244	Glasgow

QM July 12; SRA T/CN 26/5; JJ June 6

1851	06	*Wolfville* of Ardrossan	McMillan, J.	149	Loch Roag, Lewis

QM July 5; PP 1852 (1474) xxxiii; *IC* July 3; SRA T/CN 26/5. Sixty-nine were Sir James Matheson's Lewis tenants.

1851	07	*Cambria* of Greenock	Harrison, J.	49	Glasgow

QM Aug 16; SRA T/CN 26/5

1851	07	*Canmore* of Saint John	Secyle	104	Glasgow

QM Aug. 16; PP 1852 (1474) xxxiii; SRA T/CN 26/5. 16 passengers assisted by their landlord.

1851	07	*Onyx* of Grangemouth	Hogg	120	Glasgow

QM Aug. 5; SRA T/CN 26/5

1851	07	*Ottawa* of Glasgow	McArthur, J.	32	Glasgow

SRA T/CN 26/5

1851	08	*Berbice* of Aberdeen	Elliot, J.	80	Aberdeen

AJ Aug. 20

1851	08	*Hope* of Glasgow	Kidston	28	Glasgow

SRA T/CN 26/5

1852	04	*Ann Rankin* of Glasgow	Burns	193	Glasgow

PP 1852 (542) xlix; SRA T/CN 26/6, 26/7

1852	04	*Berbice* of Aberdeen	Elliot, J.	115	Aberdeen

QM May 23; *AH* Feb. 21, July 31

1852	04	*Birman* of Greenock	Fuller	29	Glasgow

QM May 5; SRA T/CN 21/7, 10

1852	04	*Empress* of Banff	Leslie	136	Stromness

QM May 25

1852	04	*Mary* of Glasgow	Shearer	16	Glasgow

QM May 15; TCN 21/7, 10; *DGC* June 1; SRA T/CN 26/6.

1852	04	*Retreat* of Alloa	Hudlass	32	Alloa

QM June 6

1852	04	*Sarah* of Aberdeen	Sim, J.	81	Aberdeen

QM June21; *AH* Apr. 24; *JJ* Mar. 12, Apr, 16.

Year	Mth	Vessel	Master	Psgr. Nos.	Departure Port
1852	04	*Springhill* of Irvine	Elliott	96	Ardrossan

QM May 12; *DGC* July 21

| 1852 | 04 | *St. Lawrence* of Aberdeen | Tulloch, J. | 136 | Aberdeen |

QM May 25; *AH* Feb. 21, Apr. 24; *JJ* Mar. 12, Apr. 16

| 1852 | 04 | *Susan* of Glasgow | Wylie | 105 | Glasgow |

PP 1852 (542) xlix; SRA T/CN 26/7

| 1852 | 04 | *Wolfville* of Ardrossan | McMillan, J. | 179 | Glasgow |

PP 1852 (542) xlix; SRA T/CN 26/6, 26/7

| 1852 | 05 | *California* of Greenock | Gall, R. | 194 | Glasgow |

PP 1852 (542) xlix; SRA T/CN 26/6

| 1852 | 05 | *Commodore* of Sunderland | Hall | 15 | Glasgow |

SRA T/CN 26/7

| 1852 | 05 | *Harlequin* of Glasgow | Craig, G. | 272 | Glasgow |

QM June 12; PP 1852 (542) xlix; SRA T/CN 26/6

| 1852 | 05 | *Tay* of Glasgow | Adams | 274 | Glasgow |

QM June 28; SRA T/CN 21/7, 10

| 1852 | 06 | *Abeona* of Glasgow | McArthur, J. | 216 | Glasgow |

PP 1852 (542) xlix; SRA T/CN 26/6, 26/7; *QM* June 28

| 1852 | 06 | *Ann Harley* of Glasgow | MacDonald | 206 | Glasgow |

QM July 10; SRA T/CN 21/7, 10

| 1852 | 06 | *Blanche* of Liverpool | Rudolf, G. | 453 | Stornoway |

QM July 31; PP 1852-53 (1650) lxviii. Sir James Matheson's tenants.

| 1852 | 06 | *Clutha* of Greenock | Bruce, A. | 352 | Glasgow |

QM July 3; PP 1852 (542) xlix; SRA T/CN26/6, 26/7; *IA* June 1; *DGC* June 1

| 1852 | 06 | *Glencairn* of Glasgow | Crawford R. | 245 | Glasgow |

QM July 10; SRA T/CN 21/7, 10; *IA* June 1, 8

| 1852 | 06 | *Marion* of Glasgow | Reid | 265 | Glasgow |

PP 1852 (542) xlix; SRA T/CN 26/6, 26/7

| 1852 | 06 | *Melissa* of Greenock | n/k | 350 | Glasgow |

QM July 10; SRA T/CN 21/7, 10

| 1852 | 07 | *Albion* of Greenock | Barclay | 55 | Glasgow |

QM Aug. 26; SRA T/CN 26/7; PP 1852-53 (113) xcviii; *IA* June 22; *IH* June 19

| 1852 | 07 | *Cambria* of Greenock | Harrison, J. | 99 | Glasgow |

QM Aug. 26; PP 1852-53 (113) xcviii; SRA T/CN 26/6, 26/7; *DGC* June 1

| 1852 | 07 | *Helen* of Montrose | Johnston | 64 | Montrose |

QM Aug. 12

| 1852 | 07 | *Janet* of Glasgow | McIntosh | 190 | Glasgow |

PP 1852 -53 (113) xcviii; SRA T/CN 26/6, 26/7

Year	Mth	Vessel	Master	Psgr. Nos.	Departure Port
1852	07	*Polly* of Glasgow	Wilson	267	Glasgow

PP 1852 -53 (113) xcviii; SRA T/CN 26/6, 26/7; *IA* June 1; *AH* June 19.

| 1852 | 08 | *Caledonia* of Greenock | Hood | 102 | Glasgow |

QM Sept. 20; SRA T/CN 26/7; PP 1852-53 (113) xcviii; *IA* June 22; *AH* June 19.

| 1852 | 08 | *California* of Greenock | Gall, R. | 95 | Glasgow |

QM Sept. 28; TCN 26/6; PP 1852-53 (113) xcviii

| 1852 | 08 | *Erromanga* of Greenock | Watson | 75 | Glasgow |

QM Sept. 20; PP 1852-53 (113) xcviii; SRA T/CN 26/7; *DGC* June 1.

| 1852 | 08 | *Ottawa* of Glasgow | McArthur, J. | 34 | Glasgow |

QM Sept. 10; SRA T/CN26/7; *IA* June 22; *AH* June 19.

| 1852 | 08 | *St. Lawrence* of Aberdeen | Tulloch, J. | 59 | Aberdeen |

QM Sept. 28

| 1853 | 03 | *Caledonia* of Greenock | Wylie | 26 | Glasgow |

QM May 17

| 1853 | 03 | *Empress* of Banff | Leslie | 129 | Stromness |

QM May 28

| 1853 | 03 | *Helen* of Aberdeen | Johnston | 103 | Montrose |

QM May 19

| 1853 | 04 | *Berbice* of Aberdeen | Elliot, J. | 143 | Aberdeen |

QM June 14

| 1853 | 04 | *Clutha* of Greenock | Bruce, A. | 126 | Glasgow |

QM June 2

| 1853 | 04 | *Earl Powis* of Dundee | Walker | 18 | Dundee |

QM May 28

| 1853 | 04 | *Harringer* | Morrison | 170 | Aberdeen |

QM June 7

| 1853 | 04 | *Home* | Kidston | 23 | Glasgow |

QM May 28

| 1853 | 04 | *Jane Boyd* of Aberdeen | Ganson, H. | 134 | Aberdeen |

QM May 31; *IC* Mar. 24.

| 1853 | 04 | *Juliet* | Teulon, J. | 101 | Glasgow |

QM June 4; *IC* Apr. 21.

| 1853 | 04 | *Springhill* of Irvine | Elliott | 16 | Ardrossan |

QM May 28

| 1853 | 05 | *California* of Greenock | Gall | 230 | Glasgow |

QM July 28; *IC* May 19.

| 1853 | 05 | *Glencairn* of Glasgow | Crawford | 274 | Glasgow |

QM June 16

Year	Mth	Vessel	Master	Psgr. Nos.	Departure Port
1853 QM Aug. 16	06	*Albion* of Greenock	Barclay	23	Glasgow
1853 QM Aug. 6	06	*Benlomond*	Meldrum	388	Grnk
1853 QM Aug. 9	06	*Harlequin* of Glasgow	Logan	284	Glasgow
1853 QM Aug. 16; *IC* May 19, Aug. 16	06	*Rosina* of Campbeltown	Gale	375	Glasgow
1853 QM Aug. 13	06	*Shandon*	Greig	33	Glasgow
1853 QM Aug. 6	06	*Susan* of Glasgow	Adams	124	Glasgow
1853 QM July 28	06	*Thornhill*	Bogart	253	Glasgow
1853 QM Sept. 8	07	*Caledonia* of Greenock	Wylie	28	Glasgow
1853 QM Sept. 8	07	*Cambria* of Greenock	Russell	17	Glasgow
1853 QM Sept. 6	07	*Ottawa* of Glasgow	McArthur, J.	29	Glasgow
1853 QM Sept. 6	07	*Polly* of Glasgow	Allan	27	Glasgow
1853 QM Sept. 22	07	*St. Lawrence* of Aberdeen	Tulloch, J.	72	Aberdeen
1853 QM Sept. 6	07	*Three Bells* of Glasgow	Campbell	36	Glasgow
1853 *IC* Oct. 13; Ship wrecked off Vatersay, Barra - 450 lives lost including 100 Glasgow carpenters.	08	*Annie Jane*	n/k	400	Liverpool
1853 QM Oct. 22	09	*Glencairn* of Glasgow	Crawford	52	Glasgow
1854 QM June 10; *AH* Mar. 4	04	*Alexander Hall*	Leslie	172	Aberdeen
1854 QM May 23; *AH* Feb. 4, June 7	04	*Aurora* of Aberdeen	Morison, A.	277	Aberdeen
1854 *AH* Jan. 28	04	*Berbice* of Aberdeen	Elliot, J.	126	Aberdeen
1854 QM May 27	04	*Empress* of Banff	Leslie	152	Stromness

Year	Mth	Vessel	Master	Psgr. Nos.	Departure Port
1854	04	*Erromanga* of Greenock	Watson	16	Glasgow
QM May 23					
1854	04	*Helen Thompson*	n/k	145	Troon

PP 1854-55 (464) xxxix; *AH* June 24. Shipwrecked, 15 passengers reached Québec in brig *Dykes*; 130 taken on board *Sarah* & landed at Richibucto.

Year	Mth	Vessel	Master	Psgr. Nos.	Departure Port
1854	04	*Jane Boyd* of Aberdeen	Ganson, H.	119	Aberdeen
AH Jan. 14					
1854	04	*Marion* of Glasgow	Borland	32	Glasgow
QM May 27					
1854	04	*Mayflower*	Nichol	242	Glasgow
QM May 27					
1854	04	*Renown* of Aberdeen	Walker, W.	115	Aberdeen
QM June 1; *AH* Mar. 11					
1854	04	*Springhill* of Irvine	Anderson	57	Ardrossan
QM June 10					
1854	04	*St. Lawrence* of Aberdeen	Tulloch, J.	300	Aberdeen
AH Jan. 21					
1854	04	*Susan* of Glasgow	Martin	179	Glasgow
QM July 8					
1854	04	*Three Bells* of Glasgow	McCallum	39	Glasgow
QM May 23					
1854	05	*Commodore*	Cove	344	Glasgow
QM July 1					
1854	06	*Bannockburn*	Swan	166	Glasgow
QM Aug. 8					
1854	06	*John Hamilton* of Greenock	Sillers	326	Grnk
QM Aug. 5					
1854	06	*Lord Sidmouth* of Glasgow	McIntosh	306	Glasgow
QM Aug. 10					
1854	06	*Tadmor*	Bovie	387	Glasgow
QM Aug. 1; *IC* June 1					
1854	06	*Wallace* (1)	Wilkie	111	Glasgow
QM Aug. 10					
1854	07	*Berbice* of Aberdeen	n/k	59	Aberdeen
AH June 17					
1854	07	*Champion* of Greenock	Cochrane	278	Glasgow
QM Aug. 24					
1854	07	*Dahlia*	Trobridge	31	Glasgow
QM Aug. 26					

Year	Mth	Vessel	Master	Psgr. Nos.	Departure Port
1854	07	*Glencairn* of Glasgow	Crawford	23	Glasgow

QM Sept. 5. On 3 Aug. stopped by the ship Shandos, of Glasgow, which was on fire. Took on board the crew and passengers, amounting to 65 souls.

Year	Mth	Vessel	Master	Psgr. Nos.	Departure Port
1854	07	*Jane Boyd* of Aberdeen	n/k	126	Aberdeen
AH June 10					
1854	07	*John McKenzie* of Greenock	Tilley	302	Grnk
QM Sept. 5					
1854	07	*St. Lawrence* of Aberdeen	n/k	118	Aberdeen
AH June 17					
1854	07	*Wallace* (2)	Sim, J.	117	Fraserburgh
QM Aug. 12					
1854	08	*Harlequin* of Glasgow	Logan	23	Glasgow
QM Sept. 30					
1854	08	*Hyndeford*	Carmichael	148	Glasgow
QM Sept. 21					
1854	08	*Ottawa* of Glasgow	Wylie	30	Glasgow
QM Oct. 7					
1854	08	*St. Lawrence* of Aberdeen	Tulloch, J.	118	Aberdeen
QM Oct. 10					
1854	08	*Three Bells* of Glasgow	McCallum	44	Glasgow
QM Sept. 23					
1855	04	*Berbice* of Aberdeen	Scott	124	Aberdeen
QM May 16, 17					
1855	04	*Caledonia* of Greenock	Shearer	28	Glasgow
QM May 15					
1855	04	*Helen* of Montrose	Johnston	200	Montrose
QM May 17					
1855	04	*Home*	Poe	31	Glasgow
QM May 19					
1855	04	*Renown* of Aberdeen	Walker	58	Aberdeen
QM June 5					
1855	04	*Sir William Wallace* of Aberdeen (2)	Andrews	98	Aberdeen
QM June 10, 12					
1855	05	*Aurora* of Aberdeen	Morison, A.	340	Aberdeen
QM 19 June					
1855	05	*George Rogers*	Younger	375	Glasgow
QM June 26					
1855	05	*Polly* of Glasgow	Bruce	115	Clyde
QM June 23					

Year Mth	Vessel	Master	Psgr. Nos.	Departure Port
1855 05 QM June 3	*Renown* of Aberdeen	Walker, W.	55	Aberdeen
1855 05 QM June 19	*Sunbeam*	Dow	367	Grnk
1855 06 QM Aug. 7	*Charlotte Harrison* of Greenock	Welsh	264	Grnk
1855 06 QM July 24	*Chieftain* of Glasgow	Scott	303	Glasgow
1855 06 QM Aug. 10	*City of Québec*	Graham	29	Glasgow
1855 06 QM Aug. 10	*Harlequin* of Glasgow	Logan	256	Glasgow
1855 06 QM July 31	*John McKenzie* of Glasgow	Tilley	357	Grnk
1855 06 QM Aug. 9	*Shandon*	Greig	52	Glasgow
1855 07 QM Aug. 28	*Albion* of Greenock	Wylie	25	Glasgow
1855 07 QM Aug. 28	*California* of Greenock	Fowler	25	Glasgow
1855 07 QM Aug. 28	*Helen* of Montrose	Fluckhart	85	Montrose
1855 07 QM Aug. 20. PP 1856 (325) xxiv. Sir James Matheson's former Lewis tenants.	*Melissa*	Reid	330	Stornoway
1855 08 QM Sept. 13	*Acteon*	Benson	28	Port Glasgow
1855 08 QM Sept. 25	*Berbice* of Aberdeen	Scott	134	Aberdeen
1855 08 QM Sept. 25	*Caledonia* of Greenock	Shearer	22	Glasgow
1855 08 QM Sept. 13	*Cambria* of Greenock	Russell	38	Glasgow
1855 08 QM Oct. 11	*Home*	Poe	30	Glasgow
1855 09 QM Oct. 16	*Aurora* of Aberdeen	Morison, A.	93	Aberdeen

Appendix V

Characteristics of Vessels listed in Appendix IV

EXPLANATORY NOTES

Vessel Names

Vessel names often include the port at which the vessel is registered – e.g. *Rebecca* of Greenock. However, the port of registration is not always given. Where several vessels bear the same name – e.g. *Fame*, they are distinguished by a number in brackets – e.g. *Fame* (1), *Fame* (2), etc.

Passenger Data

The number of crossings and cumulative passenger totals are provided for each vessel. For details of the individual crossings see Appendix IV.

Vessel Details

Information on the tonnage, vessel type, year built, place built and the Lloyd's Code have been taken from the *Lloyd's Shipping Register*.

Tonnage

This was a standard measure used to determine customs dues and navigation fees. Because it was a calculated figure, tonnage did not necessarily convey actual carrying capacity. Before 1836, the formula used to calculate tonnage was based only on breadth and length, but after 1836 it incorporated the vessel's depth as well.

Vessel Type

The word "ship" can signify a particular vessel type as well as having a generic usage in denoting all types of sea-going vessels. Sailing ship rigs were many and varied. A major distinction was the alignment of the sails. There were the square-rigged vessels in which the sails were rigged across the vessel and the fore-and-aft rigs which followed the fore-and-aft-line of the vessel. The square rig was normally used on ocean-going vessels:

Brig (bg)	a two masted vessel with square rigging on both masts.
Snow (sw)	rigged as a brig, with square sails on both masts but with a small triangular sail mast stepped immediately towards the stern of the main-mast.
Barque (bk)	three-masted vessel, square rigged on the fore and main masts and fore-and-aft rigged on the third aftermost mast.
Ship (s)	three-masted vessel, square rigged on all three masts.
Schooner (sr)	fore-and-aft sails on two or more masts. Some had small square

topsails on the foremast. They were largely used in the coasting trade and for fishing, their advantage being the smaller crew than that required by square rigged vessels of a comparable size.

Lloyd's Shipping Codes

These were assigned to vessels after periodic surveys according to their quality of construction, condition and age:

A   first class condition, kept in the highest state of repair and efficiency and within a prescribed age limit at the time of sailing.

AE   "second description of the first class," fit for safe conveyance, no defects but may be over a prescribed age limit.

E   second class vessels which, although unfit for carrying dry cargoes, were suitable for long distance sea voyages.

I   third class vessels only suitable for short voyages (i.e. not out of Europe).

The letters were followed by the number 1 or 2 which signified the condition of the vessel's equipment (anchors, cables and stores). Where satisfactory, the number 1 was used, and where not, 2 was used.

Failure to locate vessels in the *Register* does not in itself signify its exclusion from the Lloyd's classification system. To select the relevant vessel from the *Register* it is usually necessary to know the tonnage and captain's name, information which is often elusive and problematic because of gaps in the available shipping and customs records.

Vessel	Type	Tons	Capt.	No. of Voyages	Depart	Psgr Nos	Year built	Place built	Lloyd's Code
Abeona of Glasgow	n/k	611	McArthur, J.	1	Glasgow	216	1847	Québec	n/k
Abercrombie	bk	n/k	Louttef	1	Glasgow	27	n/k	n/k	n/k
Abigail	bk	n/k	Daly	1	Glasgow	341	n/k	n/k	n/k
Acadian of Glasgow	bk	385	n/k	1	Grnk	26	1832	Greenock	A1
Acteon	bk	n/k	Benson	1	Port Glasgow	28	n/k	n/k	n/k
Active (1)	bg	166	Johnson	1	Whitehaven	84	1803	Yarmouth	E1
Active (2)	s	351	Walker, A.	1	Tobermory	40	1826	Nova Scotia	A1
Adrian	s	374	Forster	1	Tobermory	106	1819	Newcastle	E1
Afghan	bk	n/k	Black	1	Grnk	229	n/k	n/k	n/k
Agamemnon	n/k	n/k	Rogers	1	Leith	192	n/k	n/k	n/k
Agincourt of Leith	s	347	Matheson	3	Leith	411	1804	North Shields	E1
Agitator	bk	n/k	Henry	1	Glasgow	33	n/k	n/k	n/k
Agnes	n/k	n/k	Outerbridge	1	Grnk	24	n/k	n/k	n/k
Agnes Primrose	n/k	n/k	Johnson	1	Glasgow	40	n/k	n/k	n/k
Aimwell of Aberdeen	sw	232	Morrison	1	Aberdeen	24	1816	Aberdeen	A1
Alarm of Cork	sr	186	Brown, J.	1	Glasgow	133	1838	PEI	A1
Albion (1)	n/k	n/k	Service, G.	1	Fort William	167	n/k	n/k	n/k
Albion (2)	bg	152	Kidd, R.	1	Dundee	60	1805	Dysart	A1
Albion of Aberdeen	sw	266	Leslie, A.	1	Aberdeen	16	1826	Aberdeen	AE1

Vessel	Type	Tons	Capt.	No. of Voyages	Depart	Psgr Nos	Year built	Place built	Lloyd's Code
Albion of Glasgow	bg	190	Boyd, J.	2	Glasgow	265	1826	Campbeltown	E1
Albion of Greenock	s	414	Allan	9	Glasgow	440	1845	Greenock	A1
Albion of Scarborough	sw	287	Hicks, M.	1	Cromarty	28	1836	Sunderland	A1
Alexander	bg	333	Young	2	Grnk	208	1811	Sunderland	A1
Alexander Hall	n/k	n/k	Leslie	1	Aberdeen	172	n/k	n/k	n/k
Alexander of Bo'ness	n/k	n/k	Henry, J.	1	Leith	44	n/k	n/k	n/k
Alfred	n/k	n/k	n/k	1	Leith	243	n/k	n/k	n/k
Alice of Milford	bg	156	Rees, S.	1	Glasgow	107	1832	Milford	A1
Amity of Aberdeen	bg	312	Rae	1	Aberdeen	39	1825	New Brunswick	E1
Amity of Glasgow	bg	116	Mercer, J.	5	Grnk	210	1827	Bowlg	A1
Andrew White of Sunderland	sw	256	Clark, B.	1	Glasgow	138	1838	Sunderland	A1
Ann (1)	bg	n/k	Henry	2	Grnk	75	n/k	n/k	n/k
Ann (2)	sw	195	Moore	1	Maryport	136	1810	Workington	E1
Ann (3)	bk	n/k	Wallace	1	Leith	20	n/k	n/k	n/k
Ann and Mary	n/k	213	n/k	2	Banff	116	n/k	n/k	n/k
Ann Grant of Sligo	bk	378	Murdoch	1	Glasgow	72	1806	Whitby	AE1
Ann Harley of Glasgow	bk	455	MacDonald	1	Glasgow	206	1844	Miramichi N. B.	AE1
Ann Henzell	bg	n/k	Henzell	1	Glasgow	75	n/k	n/k	n/k
Ann Rankin of Glasgow	s	466	McArthur, J.	3	Glasgow	642	1840	Québec	n/k
Annandale of Aberdeen	bg	254	Anderson, A.	2	Aberdeen	84	1828	New Brunswick	A1
Annie Jane	n/k	n/k	n/k	1	Liverpool	400	n/k	n/k	n/k
Apollo of Dundee	bk	248	Walker, H.	5	Dundee	169	1819	Bristol	AE1
Arabian of Greenock	bk	330	Allan	3	Grnk	125	1837	Greenock	A1
Ardgour of Fort William	sw	166	Lillie, W.	1	Fort William	108	1817	Fort William	A1
Argus (1)	bg	168	Wilkinson	1	Dumfries	88	1805	Workington	E1
Argus (2)	n/k	n/k	n/k	1	Maryport	115	n/k	n/k	n/k
Ariadne	s	n/k	McCall	1	Grnk	20	n/k	n/k	n/k
Atlas	n/k	n/k	Scott	1	Dundee	52	n/k	n/k	n/k
Augusta of Aberdeen	s	417	Rae, W.	1	Aberdeen	46	1828	N. Brunswick	E1
Aurora	n/k	n/k	Hodson	1	Whitehaven	61	n/k	n/k	n/k
Aurora of Aberdeen	s	709	Morison, A.	3	Aberdeen	710	1843	Miramichi N. B.	AE1
Balfour of Whitehaven	bg	310	Bee	1	Whitehaven	272	1809	Whitehaven	E1
Bannockburn	s	n/k	Swan	1	Glasgow	166	n/k	n/k	n/k
Barlow	bk	436	Fraser, P.	1	Grnk	287	1834	Saintt John N. B.	AE1
Baronet	n/k	n/k	Rankin	1	Cromarty	187	n/k	n/k	n/k
Belleisle of Glasgow	s	499	Reid	2	Glasgow	33	1847	Dumbarton	A1
Bellona of Glasgow	s	368	Mitchell, R.	1	Grnk	18	1838	Greenock	A1

Vessel	Type	Tons	Capt.	No. of Voyages	Depart	Psgr Nos	Year built	Place built	Lloyd's Code
Belmont of Greenock	bg	294	Ford	1	Grnk	77	1825	N. Brunswick	AE1
Benlomond	s	345	Rattray, H.	2	Grnk	606	1815	N. Brunswick	A1
Benson	s	265	Rowe, W.	1	Grnk	287	1798	Lancaster	E1
Berbice of Aberdeen	bk	340	Elliot	14	Aberdeen	1225	1847	Miramichi	AE1
Berwick on Tweed	n/k	n/k	Muers	1	Berwick	20	n/k	n/k	n/k
Bethea	n/k	n/k	n/k	1	Glasgow	20	n/k	n/k	n/k
Betsey	bg	148	Gordon, J.	2	Grnk	30	n/k	Prize	E1
Betsey Howe	bg	n/k	n/k	1	Leith	42	n/k	n/k	n/k
Betsey of Dundee	bk	291	n/k	1	Leith	131	1828	Montréal	A1
Betsey of Greenock	sw	205	Wither	1	Oban	78	1803	Scotland	E1
Birman of Greenock	bk	448	Fuller	1	Grnk	29	1840	Greenock	A1
Blackness of Dundee	bk	266	n/k	2	Dundee	107	1835	Dundee	A1
Blagdon	bg	289	Thomson	1	Cromarty	132	1825	Shields	A1
Blanche of Liverpool	s	966	Rudolf, G.	1	Stornoway	453	1850	Saint John, N. B.	A1
Blonde of Montréal	bk	604	Crawford	6	Glasgow	1865	1841	Montréal	A1
Bon Accord of Aberdeen	bk	365	Sim, J.	1	Aberdeen	70	1812	Blythe	AE1
Bowes		n/k	Faulkner	1	Cromarty	172	n/k	n/k	n/k
Bowling of Glasgow	bk	242	Gentle, R.	1	Glasgow	157	1842	Blng	A1
Brilliant of Aberdeen	s	332	Barclay, A.	23	Aberdeen	1518	1814	Aberdeen	AE1
Brilliant of Glasgow	s	428	Barr	2	Glasgow	258	1834	n/k	A1
Britannia (1)	bg	172	Spence, C.	1	Grnk	36	1813	Montréal	A1
Britannia (2)	n/k	n/k	n/k	1	Leith	19	n/k	n/k	n/k
Britannia of Newcastle	s	542	Simpson	1	Glasgow	388	1840	N. B.	AE1
British King of Dundee	bg	239	Brown, A.	1	Cromarty	20	1825	Sunderland	AE1
Brooksby of Glasgow	s	423	McEwan	1	Loch Boisdale	285	1843	Greenock	A1
Caledonia	bg	160	Miller	3	Grnk	299	1806	Scotland	E1
Caledonia of Greenock	s	383	Greenhorn	18	Grnk	944	1841	Greenock	A1
Caledonia of Irvine	n/k	154	Reid, J.	1	Grnk	30	1806	Irvine	E1
California of Greenock	bk	563	Gall, R.	6	Glasgow	975	1841	Miramichi	N. B.A1
Cambria of Aberdeen	bg	120	Perie, James	2	Aberdeen	48	1808	Aberdeen	A1
Cambria of Greenock	s	397	Kelso	9	Glasgow	421	1846	Greenock	A1
Camilla	s	287	McCarthy, D.	1	Grnk	109	1798	New York	E1
Canada	s	269	Hunter	2	Cromarty	355	1811	Montréal	E1
Canada of Greenock	s	330	Allan	14	Grnk	901	1831	Greenock	A1

Vessel	Type	Tons	Capt.	No. of Voyages	Depart	Psgr Nos	Year built	Place built	Lloyd's Code
Canmore of Saint John	bk	264	n/k	2	Glasgow	127	1843	N. B. AE1, 1851	A1
Carleton of Aberdeen	bk	404	Anderson, A.	2	Aberdeen	96	1834	N. B.	AE1
Carolina of Aberdeen	n/k	170	Dunoon, A.	2	Aberdeen	49	n/k	n/k	n/k
Caroline	n/k	n/k	Lowergran	1	Berwick	50	n/k	n/k	n/k
Caroline of Aberdeen	bk	393	Marsh, J.	1	Aberdeen	16	1839	N. B.	A1
Cartha	bg	358	Smith	4	Grnk	427	1827	N. B.	A1
Caspian	n/k	n/k	n/k	1	Glasgow	35	n/k	n/k	n/k
Catherine (1)	bg	n/k	Daysdale	1	Leith	63	n/k	n/k	n/k
Catherine (2)	n/k	448	Davidson	2	Irvine	59	n/k	n/k	n/k
Champion of Greenock	bk	673	Cochrane	2	Glasgow	497	1838	Canada	AE1
Charles	n/k	580	n/k	1	Stornoway	145	n/k	n/k	n/k
Charles Forbes	sw	295	Beveridge	1	Kirkaldy	47	1816	Aberdeen	E1
CharlotteHarrison of Greenock	bk	557	McIntyre	2	Grnk	569	1841	Québec	AE1
Cherokee of Glasgow	bk	278	Miller	4	Grnk	138	1834	Greenock	A1
Cherub	bg	269	Miller	2	Grnk	39	1814	Workington	A1
Chieftain of Glasgow	bk	n/k	Scott	1	Glasgow	303	1842	N. B.	AE1
Chieftain of Kirkaldy	bk	333	Scott, A.	2	Leith	295	1832	Leith	A1
Circassian of Aberdeen	bg	180	Ritchie, T.	1	Aberdeen	117	1835	Aberdeen	A1
Circassian of Greenock	bk	520	Dixon, G.	2	Glasgow	315	1839	N. B.	A1
City of Québec	n/k	n/k	Graham	1	Glasgow	29	n/k	n/k	n/k
Clansman of Glasgow	bk	348	Peck	2	Grnk	258	1823	N. B.	AE1
Cleopatra	bg	267	Morris, J.	1	Cromarty	246	1817	Whitby	E1
Clutha of Greenock	bk	462	Muir	3	Glasgow	612	1839	N. B.	AE1
Commerce	n/k	n/k	London	1	Oban	42	n/k	n/k	n/k
Commerce of Greenock	s	425	Coverdale, N.	2	Grnk	417	1813	Québec	A1
Commodore	n/k	n/k	Miller, J.	2	Glasgow	371	n/k	n/k	n/k
Commodore of Sunderland	n/k	n/k	Hall	1	Glasgow	15	n/k	n/k	n/k
Conference of Newcastle	s	298	Buchan		Leith	112	n/k	Bristol	AE1
Congress	bg	n/k	Greig	1	Leith	22	n/k	n/k	n/k
Corsair of Greenock	bg	273	McAlpine	6	Grnk	344	1823	N. B.	E1
Crown	bg	338	Howie	1	Grnk	75	1824	N. B.	E1
Cruickston Castle of Greenock	bk	382	McInlay	2	Grnk	65	1822	New Brunswick	AE1
Culloden	n/k	n/k	Leyden	1	Leith	19	n/k	n/k	n/k
Cyrus	n/k	n/k	Scott	3	Dundee	99	n/k	n/k	n/k
Dahlia	bk	n/k	Trobridge	1	Glasgow	31	n/k	n/k	n/k
Dalmarnock	s	315	McFarlane	3	Berwick	282	1828	Workington	E1
Deveron of Glasgow	bg	333	Anderson	3	Grnk	593	1824	Nova Scotia	AE1

Vessel	Type	Tons	Capt.	No. of Voyages	Depart	Psgr Nos	Year built	Place built	Lloyd's Code
Donegall	sw	190	Matches	2	Maryport	302	1808	Belfast	E1
Duchess of Richmond	s	324	Cook	5	Grnk	761	1807	Dublin	E1
Duke of Buccleugh	bg	205	Blair, J.	1	Dumfries	41	1829	Leith	A1
Dunlop	bg	331	Stevenson, A.	2	Glasgow	185	1805	Montréal	A1-1810 E1-1824
Dykes of Maryport	n/k	n/k	Cockton	2	Maryport	189	n/k	n/k	E1
Eagle (1)	s	179	Conolly, N.	1	Grnk	21	1791	Whitehaven	A1
Eagle (2)	n/k	n/k	Morton, R.	1	Glasgow	94	n/k	n/k	n/k
Earl of Buckinghamshire	n/k	n/k	Johnson, J.	1	Grnk	200	n/k	n/k	n/k
Earl of Dalhousie	bg	222	Boyd	2	Grnk	40	1826	Scotland	A1
Earl of Dalhousie of Aberdeen	bg	183	Levie, J.	2	Aberdeen	34	1817	Aberdeen	A1
Earl Powis of Dundee	bk	299	n/k	5	Dundee	166	1836	Liverpool	A1
Economist of Newport	bk	324	Stokeham	1	Cromarty	47	1829	PEI	A1
Eleanor	n/k	n/k	Wallace	1	Workington	96	n/k	n/k	n/k
Elephanta of Glasgow	bk	310	Ross, D.	1	Grnk	130	1836	Newport	A1
Eliza (1)	n/k	n/k	n/k	1	Grnk	43	n/k	n/k	n/k
Eliza of Ayr	n/k	n/k	n/k	1	Grnk	42	n/k	n/k	n/k
Elizabeth	n/k	n/k	McAlpine	1	Clyde	74	n/k	n/k	n/k
Elizabeth and Anne	sw	296	Wright, J.	1	Grnk	296	1779	Shields	E1
Elizabeth of Leith	bg	165	n/k	2	Leith	30	1831	Leith	n/k
Ellen of Liverpool	bk	397	n/k	1	Liverpool	100	1834	N. B.	AE1
Emily	n/k	n/k	Murphy, J.	1	Port Glasgow	16	n/k	n/k	n/k
Emma of Dundee	bg	215	Innis	2	Dundee	52	1822	Suffolk	A1
Emperor Alexander of Aberdeen	sw	236	Watts, A.	1	Tobermory	49	1814	Sunderland	A1
Empress of Banff	bk	359	Leslie	3	Stromness	417	1845	N. S.	n/k
Energy of Dundee	bg	224	Fleming	1	Stornoway	210	1832	n/k	n/k
Entaw	n/k	n/k		1	Glasgow	54	n/k	n/k	n/k
Enterprise	n/k	n/k	Pattin	1	Ayr	39	n/k	n/k	n/k
Erromanga of Greenock	bk	351	Ramsay, R.	7	Glasgow	374	1845	Greenock	A1
Essex	n/k	n/k	n/k	1	Glasgow	29	n/k	n/k	n/k
Euclid of Liverpool	bk	501	Bainbridge, G.	1	Glasgow	330	1841	Pictou	AE1
European (1)	n/k	n/k	n/k	1	Leith	155	n/k	n/k	n/k
European (2)	s	n/k	McBride	1	Glasgow	91	n/k	n/k	n/k
Experiment	n/k	n/k	Collins	1	Maryport	32	n/k	n/k	n/k
Fairy of Dundees		248	Ritchie, D.	2	Dundee	173	1801	York	E1
Fairy Queen	bk	n/k	Ritchie, D.	1	Dundee	28	n/k	n/k	n/k

Vessel	Type	Tons	Capt.	No. of Voyages	Depart	Psgr Nos	Year built	Place built	Lloyd's Code
Fame (1)	bg	144	Forrest	1	Grnk	79	1790	Chester	E1
Fame (2)	bg	204	Abrams	1	Grnk	17	1815	Québec	A1
Fame (3)	bk	n/k	Wright	1	Grnk	35	n/k	n/k	n/k
Fame (4)	n/k	n/k	Miller	1	Glasgow	27	n/k	n/k	n/k
Fancy of Aberdeen	bg	141	Struthers, J.	1	Grnk	15	1808	Aberdeen	A1
Favourite (1)	n/k	n/k	Greg	1	Grnk	23	n/k	n/k	n/k
Favourite (2)	n/k	n/k	Girvan	1	Ayr	33	n/k	n/k	n/k
Favourite of Greenock	bk	355	Bannerman	14	Glasgow	780	1839	Montréal	A1
Favourite of Montréal	bg	296	Allan	13	Grnk	550	1825	Montréal	A1
Feronia	n/k	n/k	Grant, R.	1	Glasgow	87	n/k	n/k	n/k
Fisher	bg	175	Kay, T.	1	Stranraer	69	1804	Hrngt	E1
Flora of Dundee	sw	174	n/k	1	Dundee	57	1824	Dundee	AE1
Forth	sw	369	Robinson	1	Grnk	150	1826	Leith	A1
Foundling	bg	205	McKenzie	2	Grnk	331	1810	America	E1
Friends of John Saltcoats	n/k	107	Hen, John	1	Fort William	136	n/k	n/k	n/k
Gem of Aberdeen	bg	186	Ross, P.	1	Leith	30	1839	Aberdeen	A1
General Goldie of Dumfries	sp	61	Smith	2	Dumfries	48	1812	Whitehaven	A1
General Graham of Alloa	s	426	Craigie	2	Alloa	93	1811	Hull	E1
General Wolfe	n/k	n/k	Johnston	1	Grnk	32	n/k	n/k	n/k
George (1)	bg	n/k	McAlpin, J.	1	Grnk	42	n/k	n/k	n/k
George (2)	n/k	n/k	Thompson	1	Maryport	23	n/k	n/k	n/k
George Canning	s	482	Callender	5	Grnk	887	1812	Montréal	A1
George of Dundee	s	676	Hanley, F.	1	Loch Laxford	120	1839	Pictou	n/k
George Rogers	s	n/k	Younger	1	Glasgow	375	n/k	n/k	n/k
George Stewart	n/k	n/k	Stewart	1	Grnk	57	n/k	n/k	n/k
Glencairn of Glasgow	s	850	Allan	5	Glasgow	651	1850	Québec	A1
Gleniffer	bg	318	Stevenson	6	Grnk	458	1826	Saint John N. B.	E1
Glenswilly of Glasgow	s	565	Henderson, T.	1	Glasgow	43	1838	New Brunswick	AE1
Glentanner of Aberdeen	bg	160	Murray	1	Tobermory	18	1811	Aberdeen	A1
Globe	n/k	n/k	Lindsay	1	Montrose	15	n/k	n/k	n/k
Grace	n/k	n/k	n/k	1	Whitehaven	132	n/k	n/k	n/k
Gratitude of Dundee	bg	170	Gellatly, J.	1	Fort William	55	1823	Sunderland	A1
Greenfield	bg	114	Holmes, J.	1	Grnk	28	1815	Irvine	A1
Hamilton of Glasgow	s	589	Dick, J.	1	Grnk	283	1842	Restigouche	A1
Hants of Greenock	bk	275	Neill, W.	1	Glasgow	71	1838	Nova Scotia	A1
Harlequin of Glasgow	bk	702	Craig, G.	4	Glasgow	835	1851	Québec	A1
Harmony (1)	n/k	n/k	Abrams	2	Grnk	369	n/k	n/k	n/k
Harmony (2)	bk	n/k	Young	1	Leith	79	n/k	n/k	n/k
Harmony of Whitehaven	bg	244	Young	1	Stornoway	36	1812	Whitehaven	A1
Harper	n/k	n/k	Murphy	1	Glasgow	235	n/k	n/k	n/k

Vessel	Type	Tons	Capt.	No. of Voyages	Depart	Psgr Nos	Year built	Place built	Lloyd's Code
Harringer	bk	n/k	Morrison	1	Aberdeen	170	n/k	n/k	n/k
Harrison Chilton of Liverpool	bk	398	n/k	1	Glasgow	130	1839	Whitby	AE1
Hector	n/k	n/k	Davison	3	Various	199	n/k	n/k	n/k
Hector of Dundee	sw	192	Anderson, W.	1	Glasgow	92	1801	n/k	A1
Hedleys of Newcastle	bk	279	n/k	2	Cromarty	347	1823	Newcastle	E1
Helen	n/k	n/k	Johnson	1	Montrose	18	n/k	n/k	n/k
Helen of Aberdeen	bk	366	Anderson	2	Aberdeen	121	1826	n/k	E1
Helen of Dundee	bg	203	Erskine, T.	2	Dundee	75	1821	n/k	n/k
Helen of Irvine	sw	157	Service, G.	1	Fort William	166	1775	Leith	A1
Helen of Montrose	bk	346	Johnston	3	Montrose	349	1846	N. B.	AE1
Helen Thompson	n/k	n/k	n/k	1	Troon	145	n/k	n/k	n/k
Henry	n/k	n/k	Anderson	2	Glasgow	214	n/k	n/k	n/k
Henry Kneeland	n/k	n/k	n/k	1	Glasgow	19	n/k	n/k	n/k
Henry of Montrose	bk	315	Ross	1	Dundee	30	1827	Newcastle	AE1
Herald of Greenock	s	801	Coubro	1	Grnk	319	1840	N. B.	AE1
Hercules of Aberdeen	bk	250	Walker, D.	6	Aberdeen	520	1781	Stockton	E1
Hercules of Liverpool	s	757	Postill, F.	1	Lochmaddy	59	1836	Richibucto	AE1
Heroine of Aberdeen	s	387	Walker, D.	4	Aberdeen	331	1831	Dundee	AE1
Hibernia of Aberdeen	bg	113	Lamb, R.	1	Stornoway	42	1816	Aberdeen	A1
Highland Lad	s	343	Vickerman	1	Tobermory	16	1816	Québec	E1
Highlander of Aberdeen	bg	174	Fluckhart	1	Cromarty	150	1817	Aberdeen	E1
Home	n/k	n/k	Grey	4	Glasgow	117	n/k	n/k	n/k
Hope (1)	bg	186	Duncan	1	Grnk	44	1802	Nova Scotia	E1
Hope (2)	bg	180	Henry, M.	1	Port Glasgow	47	1803	Nova Scotia	A1
Hope (3)	n/k	n/k	McFarlane	1	Leith	25	n/k	n/k	n/k
Hope (4)	n/k	n/k	Middleton	1	Maryport	73	n/k	n/k	n/k
Hope of Glasgow	bk	513	Kidston	1	Glasgow	28	1839	N. B.	AE1
Hope of Greenock	bk	231	Marden	1	Oban	184	n/k	n/k	n/k
Huntley	s	n/k	Wilson	1	Grnk	176	n/k	n/k	n/k
Hyndeford	bk	n/k	Carmichael	1	Glasgow	148	n/k	n/k	n/k
Ianthe	n/k	n/k	Hunter	1	Glasgow	37	n/k	n/k	n/k
Independence of Belfast	s	584	n/k	1	Liverpool	245	1839	Québec	A1
Indian	n/k	n/k	Matthias	1	Grnk	69	n/k	n/k	n/k
Industry	bk	291	Carr	2	Dundee	187	n/k	Prize, 1808	n/k
Iris	bk	n/k	Frank	2	Grnk	404	n/k	n/k	n/k
Isabella and Euphemia	n/k	n/k	Middleton, J.	1	Stornoway	32	n/k	n/k	n/k
Isabella of Dundee	bg	304	Donaldson, J.	2	Dundee	65	1825	Dundee	E1
Isabella of Irvine	bg	281	Miller	2	Grnk	135	1830	Québec	AE1

Vessel	Type	Tons	Capt.	No. of Voyages	Depart	Psgr Nos	Year built	Place built	Lloyd's Code
Islay	n/k	n/k	n/k	1	Stornoway	68	n/k	n/k	n/k
Jamaica of Glasgow	s	334	Martin	5	Grnk	579	1796	Greenock	AE1
James	bg	226	Jack, W.	1	Grnk	24	1812	Québec	A1
James Campbell of Glasgow	bk	305	Miller, J.	1	Glasgow	27	1842	Dumbarton	A1
James Dean of Greenock	bk	370	Wilson	1	Glasgow	29	1840	Québec	A1
James Redden of Dumfries	sw	244	n/k	1	Dumfries	31	1841	PEI	AE1
Jane (1)	bg	193	Wilson	1	Leith	65	1830	Québec	AE1
Jane (2)	sw	208	Allen, W.	2	Grnk	97	1819	Sunderland	A1
Jane (3)	n/k	n/k	Murdoch	1	Grnk	18	n/k	n/k	n/k
Jane Boyd of Aberdeen	bk	387	Ganson, H.	3	Aberdeen	379	1843	Aberdeen	n/k
Jane Brown of Glasgow	bk	282	Wylie, J.	3	Glasgow	94	1834	Greenock	A1
Jane Christie	n/k	n/k	Scott	1	Leith	34	n/k	n/k	n/k
Jane Kay	sw	235	Toft, D.	1	Cromarty	66	1831	Sunderland	A1
Jane of Sunderland	s	340	Rogers, J.	1	Grnk	16	1805	Sunderland	E1
Jane Wright	n/k	n/k	n/k	1	Grnk	50	n/k	n/k	n/k
Janet Izat of Alloa	bk	229	n/k	1	Tobermory	100	1828	Kinnear	A1
Janet of Glasgow	bk	444	McIntosh	1	Glasgow	190	1830	Québec	AE1
Jean	bg	n/k	Allan	1	Grnk	28	n/k	n/k	n/k
Jean Baptiste of Glasgow	bk	259	n/k	1	Glasgow	15	1836	Québec	AE1
Jean Hastie of Grangemouth	s	280	Robertson, J.	1	Thurso	44	1829	N. B.	E1
Jean of Ayr	n/k	n/k	Allan	1	Grnk	16	n/k	n/k	n/k
Jean of Irvine	s	167	MacDonald, J.	2	Fort William	274	1799	Saltcoats	A1
Jeanie Deans	n/k	n/k	Miller, D.	2	Glasgow	111	n/k	n/k	n/k
Jessie of Aberdeen	bg	154	Thomson, J.	1	Aberdeen	21	1814	Spey	A1
Jessie Stephens of Irvine	bk	440	Miller, D.	1	Glasgow	131	1847	Québec	A1
Jessy Logan	n/k	855	n/k	1	Grnk	27	n/k	n/k	n/k
John	n/k	n/k	Mann	1	Cromarty	120	n/k	n/k	n/k
Johns	n/k	n/k	Cochran, John	1	Grnk	47	n/k	n/k	n/k
John and Samuel of Liverpool	bg	188	Cook, F.	1	Stornoway	82	n/k	Levant	E1
John Cumming	n/k	n/k	n/k	1	Glasgow	83	n/k	n/k	n/k
John Hamilton of Greenock	s	809	Sillers	1	Grnk	326	1849	N. B.	A1
John Howard	bk	n/k	Smith	1	London	100	n/k	n/k	n/k
John Hutchison	n/k	n/k	Harrison	1	Thurso	76	n/k	n/k	n/k
John & Mary	n/k	n/k	Nicholson	1	Leith	79	n/k	n/k	n/k
John McKenzie of Greenock	s	791	Tilley	2	Grnk	659	1846	N. S.	A1
John of Bo'ness	n/k	252	Mitchell, J.	1	Leith	118	n/k	n/k	n/k
John Walker of Liverpool	bk	523	n/k	1	Skye	49	1832	N. B.	AE1
Joseph Green of Peterhead	s	353	Volum, J.	1	Cromarty	239	1819	Sunderland	AE1

Vessel	Type	Tons	Capt.	No. of Voyages	Depart	Psgr Nos	Year built	Place built	Lloyd's Code
Juliet	n/k	n/k	Teulon, J.	1	Glasgow	101	n/k	n/k	n/k
Juno of Aberdeen	bg	150	Henderson, J.	1	Dundee	20	1814	Newburgh	A1
Jupiter	n/k	n/k	n/k	1	Glasgow	18	n/k	n/k	n/k
Justyn of Leith	bk	803	Thomson, R.	1	Grnk	313	1849	Québec	A1
Kate of Newcastle	bk	478	Taylor, T.	1	Cromarty	43	1846	Sunderland	A1
Kent	bg	n/k	Stirling	2	Grnk	104	n/k	n/k	n/k
Kilmuir	n/k	n/k	Blair	1	Grnk	18	n/k	n/k	n/k
Kincardineshire of Aberdeen	bg	193	Goven	1	Aberdeen	55	1838	Cape Breton	AE 1
Lady Emily of Sunderland	sw	285	Smith, J.	1	Loch Laxford	64	1840	Sunderland	A1
Lady Falkland	n/k	n/k	Parker	1	Glasgow	361	1846	N. S.	AE1
Lady Grey of North Shields	sw	285	Grey, W.	1	Cromarty	105	1841	Sunderland	A1
Lady Hood of Stornoway	bg	107	n/k	1	Stornoway	78	1816	Aberdeen	AE1
Lady Kinnaird of Dundee	bk	321	n/k	1	Dundee	65	1839	Dundee	A1
Lady of the Lake	bg	118	Primrose, D.	1	Grnk	27	1815	Québec	A1
Lanarkshire of Glasgow	bk	629	Turner	1	Glasgow	80	1840	Québec	AE1
Lancaster	bk	220	Creighton	1	Dumfries	137	1787	Lancaster	E1
Lawther	n/k	n/k	Pewley	1	Workington	121	n/k	n/k	n/k
Lerwick	bg	n/k	Giffney	1	Dundee	83	n/k	n/k	n/k
Leven Lass of Glasgow	bg	199	Wright	2	Glasgow	98	1839	Dumbarton	A1
Lord Byron	bk	380	Robinson	1	Grnk	26	1825	Québec	A1
Lord Metcalfe of Aberdeen	bk	510	Bain	2	Aberdeen	82	1845	Québec	AE1
Lord Middleton of North Shields	sw	341	Kerr, G.	1	Leith	163	n/k	Carolina	E1
Lord Panmure of Dundee	bg	263	McNeill, J.	2	Dundee	138	1838	Dundee	A1
Lord Seaton of Aberdeen	s	440	Talbot, W.	3	Aberdeen	105	1840	Québec	A1
Lord Sidmouth of Glasgow	bk	595	McIntosh	1	Glasgow	306	1835	Québec	AE1
Lother	bk	n/k	Murphy	1	Annan	29	n/k	n/k	n/k
Magnet	sw	229	Goulder	1	Whitehaven	146	1812	Whitby	E1
Mahaica of Greenock	bk	256	Jump, W.	2	Glasgow	184	1837	Greenock	A1
Majestic	bg	n/k	Black	1	Leith	60	n/k	n/k	n/k
Malay	bg	215	Coverdale	1	Tobermory	50	1818	Greenock	E1
Margaret (1)	bg	125	Boyd	2	Grnk	42	1815	Irvine	A1
Margaret (2)	bg	218	Oliphant	1	Grnk	110	1820	Kirkaldy	A1
Margaret (3)	n/k	n/k	Wallace	1	Leith	160	n/k	n/k	n/k
Margaret Balfour of Dundee	bg	248	Gellatly, J.	3	Dundee	151	1828	Québec	A1
Margaret Bogle of Leith	s	324	Boyd	6	Glasgow	492	1804	Ayr	E1
Margaret Boyle	bk	n/k	Scott	1	Leith	20	n/k	n/k	n/k
Margaret of Greenock	bk	566	McBride, A.	1	Glasgow	238	1839	Miramichi N. B.	AE1
Margaret of Peterhead	sw	201	Shand, J.	1	Leith	16	1811	Peterhead	A1

Vessel	Type	Tons	Capt.	No. of Voyages	Depart	Psgr Nos	Year built	Place built	Lloyd's Code
Margaret Pointer	n/k	n/k	Miller, J.	1	Glasgow	51	n/k	n/k	n/k
Margaret Thompson	bk	272	Ogilvy, J.	1	Leith	125	1832	Kincardine	A1
Margaret Wilkie of Greenock	bk	240	Miller, J.	1	Grnk	111	1832	n/k	A1
Maria (1)	sw	200	Hewitt	1	Maryport	136	1819	Québec	E1
Maria (2)	n/k	n/k	Davieson	1	Cromarty	111	n/k	n/k	n/k
Mariner of Sunderland	n/k	255	Collins	1	Loch Eriboll	145	n/k	n/k	n/k
Marion of Glasgow	s	670	Reid	2	Glasgow	297	1848	Québec	A1
Marjory	bg	500	Stocks, J.	1	Thurso	24	n/k	n/k	n/k
Marquis of Stafford	n/k	n/k	n/k	1	Stornoway	500	n/k	n/k	n/k
Mars	sw	208	Blin	1	Mull	253	1806	Sunderland	A1
Martha	n/k	n/k	Denwood	1	Dumfries	43	n/k	n/k	n/k
Mary (1)	bg	n/k	Dunlop	2	Grnk	367	n/k	n/k	n/k
Mary (2)	s	308	Munro	1	Leith	32	1780	Hull	E1
Mary of Aberdeen	sw	139	Clayton, J.	1	Aberdeen	21	1810	Aberdeen	n/k
Mary of Glasgow	bk	343	Shearer	2	Glasgow	58	1844	Nova Scotia	AE1
Mary of Greenock (1)	s	290	Moore	1	Grnk	26	1818	Whitby	A1
Mary of Greenock (2)	bg	218	Shotton, J.	6	Glasgow	153	1832	Greenock	A1
Mary of Newcastle	bg	n/k	Jacobson	1	Loch Snizort, Skye	64	n/k	n/k	n/k
Mary Sharp	n/k	n/k	Woolf	1	Glasgow	17	n/k	n/k	n/k
Mayflower	s	n/k	Nichol	1	Glasgow	242	n/k	n/k	n/k
Melissa	s	652	Reid	1	Lewis Loch	330	1843	Québec	AE1
Melissa of Greenock	n/k	n/k	n/k	1	Glasgow	350	n/k	n/k	n/k
Menapia	n/k	n/k	Queen, J.	1	Glasgow	183	n/k	n/k	n/k
Merlin	n/k	n/k	Thompson, D.	1	Grnk	185	n/k	n/k	n/k
Messenger	n/k	n/k	Mather, W.	3	Glasgow	108	n/k	n/k	n/k
Minerva (1)	bg	166	Williamson	1	Grnk	60	1819	Anstruther	A1
Minerva (2)	bg	n/k	Adamson	1	Leith	59	n/k	n/k	n/k
Minerva of Aberdeen	sw	202	Strachan, W.	1	Fort William	26	1813	Aberdeen	A1
Minerva of Greenock	bk	349	Stewart	1	Glasgow	41	1813	Whitby	AE1
Mohawk of Greenock	s	426	n/k	4	Glasgow	161	1840	Greenock	A1
Molson of Dundee	sw	214	Elliot, J.	3	Dundee	300	1830	Dundee	AE1
Monarch	n/k	n/k	Crawford	1	Tobermory	259	n/k	n/k	n/k
Monarch of Glasgow	bk	316	Welsh	3	Grnk	74	1835	Greenock	A1
Montréal	s	306	Allen	1	Grnk	18	1814	Irvine	A1
Monument	n/k	n/k		1	Glasgow	87	n/k	n/k	n/k
Morningfield of Aberdeen	bg	141	Perie, J.	1	Stornoway	63	1816	Aberdeen	A1
Nailer	s	313	McColl	4	Grnk	379	1828	Québec	A1
Nancy of South Shields	s	330	Allan, R.	1	Leith	34	1772	Scarborough	E1

Vessel	Type	Tons	Capt.	No. of Voyages	Depart	Psgr Nos	Year built	Place built	Lloyd's Code
Navarino	n/k	n/k	n/k	1	Glasgow	27	n/k	n/k	n/k
Nelson	bg	n/k	Barrick	1	Leith	19	n/k	n/k	n/k
Neptune (1)	n/k	n/k	Clark	1	Glasgow	34	n/k	n/k	n/k
Neptune (2)	bg	n/k	Bell	2	Leith	207	n/k	n/k	n/k
Neptune of Ayr	bg	167	Neil	1	Grnk	22	1799	Ayr	E1
Neptune of Greenock	s	308	Boyd	1	Loch Nevis	600	1802	N. B.	A1
Neried	n/k	n/k	Whitehead	1	Dumfries	49	n/k	n/k	n/k
New York Packet	bk	n/k	Hossack	2	Glasgow	188	n/k	n/k	n/k
Nicholson	n/k	n/k	Craig	1	Maryport	183	n/k	n/k	n/k
Norfolk	s	n/k	Harrison	1	Berwick	41	n/k	n/k	n/k
Norway	n/k	n/k	Hughes	1	Glasgow	22	n/k	n/k	n/k
Ocean	n/k	n/k	n/k	1	Grnk	17	n/k	n/k	n/k
Octovara	n/k	n/k	n/k	1	Glasgow	59	n/k	n/k	n/k
Onyx of Grangemouth	bk	389	Hogg	1	Glasgow	120	1823	Stockton	AE1
Osprey of Leith	s	382	Kirk	1	Cromarty	90	1819	Greenock	AE1
Ossian of Leith	bg	194	Block	1	Fort William	127	1813	Leith	A1
Ottawa of Glasgow	s	480	McArthur, J.	4	Glasgow	125	1851	Dumbarton	A1
Oxford	s	401	Davidson	1	Leith	300	1804	Whitby	E1
Pacific of Aberdeen	bk	386	Morrison, J.	6	Aberdeen	495	1826	Aberdeen	AE1
Pactolus	n/k	n/k	Lloyd, T.	1	Glasgow	182	n/k	n/k	n/k
Palmona	s	n/k	Morison	1	Grnk	15	n/k	n/k	n/k
Panmore	n/k	n/k	n/k	1	Ayr	24	n/k	n/k	n/k
Papineau	bg	n/k	Morland	1	Glasgow	28	n/k	n/k	n/k
Paragon	bg	n/k	Mitchell	2	Leith	112	n/k	n/k	n/k
Patriot	n/k	n/k	n/k	1	Leith	19	n/k	n/k	n/k
Peace	n/k	n/k	Seator	1	Grnk	85	n/k	n/k	n/k
Pekin of Irvine	n/k	n/k	Crawford	1	Glasgow	44	n/k	n/k	A1
Percival of Leith	bg	269	Scott	2	Leith	132	1811	Sunderland	A1
Perdonnet	n/k	n/k	n/k	1	Glasgow	37	n/k	n/k	n/k
Perseverence of Aberdeen	bg	116	Philip, J.	1	Stornoway	52	n/k	Foreign	n/k
Peruvian of Glasgow	n/k	n/k	Boyd, J.	1	Glasgow	35	n/k	n/k	n/k
Pilgrim	n/k	n/k	Smith	2	Tobermory	139	n/k	n/k	n/k
Pilgrim of Aberdeen	bg	170	Allan, G.	2	Aberdeen	130	1828	Aberdeen	A1
Pitt	s	308	Hamilton	1	Grnk	37	1800	Ulverston, Cumbria	E1
Polly of Glasgow	bk	629	Wilson	3	Glasgow	409	1845	Québec	AE1
Portaferry	bg	283	Pollock, J.	2	Grnk	319	1819	Workington	E1
Portia	bk	n/k	Hirst	1	Grnk	171	n/k	n/k	n/k
Prescott of Leith	bg	163	Young	1	Leith	26	1799	Leith	E1
Prince Albert of Arbroath	sw	257	Rodger, A.	1	Thurso	125	1842	Arbroath	AE1
Prince George of Alloa	bg	312	Morison	3	Alloa	267	1789	London	AE1
Prompt of Bo'ness	s	333	Nairn	1	Grnk	133	1816	Montréal	A1
Psyche of Dundee	bg	147	Erskine, T.	1	Dundee	38	1815	Montrose	A1

Vessel	Type	Tons	Capt.	No. of Voyages	Depart	Psgr Nos	Year built	Place built	Lloyd's Code
Québec Packet of Aberdeen	bg	196	Anderson, A.	4	Cromarty	130	1822	Aberdeen	A1
Queen of the Isles of Stromness	bk	261	Leask	1	Glasgow	105	1842	Aberdeen	A1
Rebecca of Greenock	s	305	Laurie	11	Grnk	364	1816	Greenock	E1
Regent	bg	n/k	Steel	1	Leith	16	n/k	n/k	n/k
Renown of Aberdeen	bk	289	Walker, W.	3	Aberdeen	228	1842	Aberdeen	AE1
Renown of Kirkaldy	bg	159	Watts, J.	2	Leith	57	1795	Ely	E1
Retreat	n/k	n/k	Hamilton	1	Grnk	92	n/k	n/k	n/k
Retreat of Alloa	bg	356	Hudlass	1	Alloa	32	1805	Newcastle	AE1
Retrench of Greenock	bg	314	Cooper	1	Grnk	299	1826	N. B.	AE1
Richibucto of Aberdeen	bk	401	Ganson, H.	1	Grnk	45	1835	Richibucto	A2
Rival	bg	335	Wallace	1	Grnk	333	1825	New Brunswick	E1
Robert	n/k	n/k	Neil	1	Grnk	44	n/k	n/k	n/k
Robert & Margaret	s	420	n/k	1	Cromarty	66	n/k	n/k	n/k
Robert McWilliam of Aberdeen	sw	298	Williamson	1	Aberdeen	25	1825	N. B.	AE1
Robert Morrow of Kirkaldy	bg	273	n/k	1	Leith	60	1841	PEI	A1
Robert Murrow	n/k	n/k	n/k	1	Leith	41	n/k	n/k	n/k
Robertson	s	n/k	Neil	4	Grnk	111	n/k	n/k	n/k
Roger Stewart	s	300	Kerr	2	Grnk	179	1811	Massa	E1
Romulus	bk	n/k	Sangster	1	Glasgow	86	n/k	n/k	n/k
Romulus of Greenock	bk	467	Coll, T.	1	Grnk	58	1831	Miramichi	AE1
Roscius	n/k	n/k	McClaren	1	Grnk	47	n/k	n/k	n/k
Rose	bg	n/k	Johnson	1	Leith	45	n/k	n/k	n/k
Rose of Aberdeen	bk	253	n/k	1	Aberdeen	94	1843	Aberdeen	A1
Rosebud	n/k	n/k	Roy	1	Glasgow	80	n/k	n/k	n/k
Rosina of Campbeltown	bk	614	n/k	2	Grnk	622	1845	Québec	A1
Rothiemurchus of Leith	n/k	322	Watson, G.	2	Leith	133	1812	Speymouth	A1
Royal Adelaide of Greenock	bk	417	Dewar	1	Grnk	152	1830	Miramichi	AE1
Royal Bride of Dundee	sw	196	Welsh, G.	1	Dundee	78	1840	Dundee	A1
Royalist of Alloa	n/k	n/k	Beveridge	1	Grnk	15	n/k	n/k	n/k
Sally	n/k	n/k	Cumming	2	Grnk	73	n/k	n/k	n/k
Salmes	bg	287	Royal, H.	1	Inverness	250	1826	Québec	A1
Saphiras of Whitby	sw	277	Brown, R.	1	Loch Laxford	202	1838	Sunderland	A1
Sappho of Sunderland	n/k	n/k	MacDonald	1	Glasgow	78	n/k	n/k	n/k
Sarah (1)	n/k	n/k	Marianne	1	Maryport	165	n/k	n/k	n/k
Sarah (2)	n/k	n/k	McLean, W.	1	Glasgow	58	n/k	n/k	n/k
Sarah Botsford of Glasgow	bk	306	Wallace, M.	1	Glasgow	219	1840	New Brunswick	A1
Sarah Mariana	sw	194	Archibald	1	Maryport	164	1816	Chester	E1

Vessel	Type	Tons	Capt.	No. of Voyages	Depart	Psgr Nos	Year built	Place built	Lloyd's Code
Sarah of Aberdeen	bg	232	Allan, G	7	Aberdeen	303	1839	Aberdeen	n/k
Scotia	bk	n/k	Simpson	1	Grnk	33	n/k	n/k	n/k
Scotia of Belfast	s	624	Carrey	1	Grnk	194	1844	Richibucto	AE1
Sesostris of Glasgow	s	632	Logan	1	Glasgow	302	1840	New Glasgow N. S.	AE1
Shakespeare of Aberdeen	sw	179	Rosie	1	Aberdeen	84	1825	Aberdeen	AE1
Shandon	s	n/k	Greig	2	Glasgow	85	n/k	n/k	n/k
Sharp	sw	240	Almond	1	Cromarty	206	1831	Sunderland	A1
Sir J H Craig	s	250	Dease, J.	1	Leith	100	1811	Québec	E1
Sir William Wallace of Aberdeen (1)	bg	232	Anderson, D.	1	Aberdeen	28	1821	Aberdeen	n/k
Sir William Wallace of Aberdeen (2)	bg	183	Anderson, D.	6	Aberdeen	325	1835	Aberdeen	n/k
Sisters of Aberdeen	bg	177	Hull	1	Aberdeen	41	1833	Aberdeen	n/k
Skeen of Leith (1)	bg	250	Mason	2	Leith	59	1815	Leith	A2
Skeen of Leith (2)	n/k	212	Bennett	1	Leith	118	1827	Perth	n/k
Sophia	n/k	n/k	Neil	2	Grnk	55	n/k	n/k	n/k
Sophia of Greenock	bg	266	Neil	1	Grnk	43	1825	Greenock	A1
Sovereign (1)	n/k	n/k	Pearson	1	Leith	49	n/k	n/k	n/k
Sovereign (2)	n/k	n/k		1	Grnk	44	n/k	n/k	n/k
Spartan of Greenock	s	681	Morrison	1	Glasgow	244	1845	N. B.	AE1
Speculation	s	205	Douglass	2	Grnk	207	n/k	America	E1
Sprightly	n/k	n/k	n/k	1	Dundee	60	n/k	n/k	n/k
Springfield	n/k	n/k	n/k	1	Glasgow	42	n/k	n/k	n/k
Springhill of Irvine	bk	348	Auld	5	Grnk	ⁿ⁻2	1826	N. B.	E1
St. Andrew of New Brunswick	s	553	Leith, J.	1	Lochmaddy	133	1835	N. S.	n/k
St. George	n/k	n/k	Thomson	1	Maryport	26	n/k	n/k	n/k
St. Lawrence of Aberdeen	bk	352	Tulloch, J.	22	Aberdeen	1896	1841	Aberdeen	A1
St. Nicholas	bg	n/k	Morgan	1	Inverness	29	n/k	n/k	n/k
Stillman	n/k	216	Williamson, C.	1	Glasgow	60	n/k	n/k	n/k
Stirling Castle of Greenock	bg	351	Fraser	2	Grnk	582	1829	Miramichi	AE1
Stranraer	n/k	n/k	n/k	2	Stranraer	147	n/k	n/k	n/k
Sunbeam	s	810	Dow	1	Grnk	367	1850	Québec	A1
Superb of Greenock	bk	599	Shannon	2	Grnk	211	1837	Miramichi N. B.	A1
Superior of Peterhead	bk	306	Manson	1	Cromarty	191	1813	Shields	AE1
Susan of Glasgow	bk	321	Taylor	4	Glasgow	477	1847	PEI	A1
Swift of Sunderland	sw	280	Beveridge	1	Cromarty	215	1837	Sunderland	A1
Sylvanus of North Shields	sw	263	Lawson	1	Cromarty	41	1826	Sunderland	A1
Symmetry	n/k	n/k	n/k	1	Thurso	110	n/k	n/k	n/k

Vessel	Type	Tons	Capt.	No. of Voyages	Depart	Psgr Nos	Year built	Place built	Lloyd's Code
Tadmor	bk	638	Bovie	1	Glasgow	387	1848	N. B.	A1
Tamerlane of Greenock	s	390	Martin	5	Grnk	950	1824	N. B.	A1
Taurus of Aberdeen	sr	184	n/k	1	Aberdeen	134	1841	Aberdeen	A1
Tay of Glasgow	bk	512	Langwell	4	Grnk	853	1832	N. B.	AE1
Thistle of Aberdeen	sw	133	Allen, R.	1	Tobermory	43	1818	Aberdeen	A1
Thomas Worthington	s	n/k	Morrison	1	Grnk	96	n/k	n/k	n/k
Thompsons Packet of Dumfries	bg	201	Lookup	1	Dumfries	40	1817	n/k	A1
Thornhill	s	n/k	Bogart	1	Glasgow	253	n/k	n/k	n/k
Three Bells of Glasgow	s	730	n/k	4	Glasgow	381	1850	Dumbarton	A1
Tods of Perth	bg	109	McPherson, W.	1	Dundee	42	1816	Perth	A1
Trafalgar of London	bg	175	Mitchell, J.	1	Leith	100	1805	Hull	E1
Traveller of Aberdeen	bg	195	Goldie, J.	2	Tobermory	163	1819	Aberdeen	n/k
Traveller of Dundee	bg	195	Wighton	1	Dundee	42	1819	n/k	n/k
Triton	s	405	McClean	3	Cromarty	168	1815	Whitby	E1
Troubadour of Irvine	bk	298	McDowell, J.	1	Glasgow	224	1840	Nova Scotia	A1
True Briton	sw	216	Reid, J.	3	Grnk	125	1818	Blythe	A1
Tweed	bk	n/k	Slocombe	1	Cromarty	245	n/k	n/k	n/k
Union	s	231	Henry	2	Grnk	70	1807	America	E1
Universe of Aberdeen	n/k	n/k	n/k	1	Thurso	19	n/k	n/k	AE1
Urgent of Belfast	s	592	n/k	1	Stornoway	370	1839	Québec	AE1
Victoria of Dundee	sw	252	Berrie, J.	4	Dundee	200	1832	Dundee	AE1
Viewforth of Kirkaldy	bk	289	Elden	1	Cromarty	150	1830	Shields	A1
Wallace (1)	s	n/k	Wilkie	1	Glasgow	111	n/k	n/k	n/k
Wallace (2)	bg	n/k	Sim	1	Fraserburgh	117	n/k	n/k	n/k
Wanderer	bg	280	Cowan, F.	1	Glasgow	141	1839	N. B.	A1
Wandsworth of Glasgow	s	767	n/k	1	Grnk	377	1839	Québec	A1
Warner	bg	161	Crawford	1	Grnk	43	1817	Saltcoats	A1
Warsaw	n/k	n/k	n/k	1	Glasgow	31	n/k	n/k	n/k
Waterloo of Fort William	n/k	n/k	Kendal, J.	1	Fort William	108	n/k	n/k	n/k
Watermillock	bg	n/k	Conner	1	Glasgow	34	n/k	n/k	n/k
Welcome	n/k	n/k	McColl	1	Grnk	15	n/k	n/k	n/k
Westmorland	n/k	n/k	Duncan	1	Leith	76	n/k	n/k	n/k
Wexford of Wexford	s	254	Slatterly, J.	1	Grnk	200	1829	Québec	AE1
William & Ann	n/k	n/k	n/k	1	Glasgow	24	n/k	n/k	n/k
William Glen Anderson of Glasgow	bk	389	Gillespie	1	Aberdeen	152	1827	Richibucto N. B.	AE1
William Hutt	s	n/k	Rankin	1	Glasgow	138	n/k	n/k	n/k
William Shand	n/k	n/k	Hunter	1	Berwick	299	n/k	n/k	n/k
Wilson	n/k	n/k	n/k	1	Grnk	21	n/k	n/k	n/k

Vessel	Type	Tons	Capt.	No. of Voyages	Depart	Psgr Nos	Year built	Place built	Lloyd's Code
Wolfville of Ardrossan	bk	415	McMillan, J.	2	Loch Roag	328	1841	Nova Scotia	AE1
Woodfield	n/k	n/k	n/k	1	Glasgow	69	n/k	n/k	n/k
Young Norval	s	n/k	Luck	1	Grnk	37	n/k	n/k	n/k
Ythan	n/k	n/k	Cairns	1	Grnk	20	n/k	n/k	n/k
Zealous	n/k	n/k	Reed	1	Leith	182	n/k	n/k	n/k
Zephyr	n/k	650	Tucker	1	Cromarty	99	n/k	n/k	n/k

Notes

ONE—THE PROBLEMS OF CONQUEST

1 *Scots Magazine*, Vol. XXVII (1766) 606.
2 These French-speaking Roman Catholics were the descendents of the 3,000 or so French immigrants who had settled in New France by the middle of the seventeenth century.
3 Lower Canada was by far the largest of the British colonies, having a population of 250,000 by 1806. For population figures see Joseph Bouchette, *The British Dominions in North America: A Topographical and Statistical Description of the Provinces of Lower and Upper Canada, New Brunswick, Nova Scotia, the Islands of Newfoundland, Prince Edward Island and Cape Breton*, Vol. II (London: 1832) 235.
4 J.M. Bumsted, *The Peoples of Canada: A Pre-Confederation History*, Vol. 1 (Toronto: Oxford University Press, 1992) 65–79, 91–3.
5 W.S. Wallace, "Some notes on the Fraser Highlanders" in *Canadian Historical Review*, Vol. XVIII, No. 2 (1937) 133.
6 Dating back to 1295, the "auld alliance" was built on France and Scotland's shared interest in controlling English aggression against either country.
7 The business community's hostility to French culture is discussed in D.G. Creighton, *The Commercial Empire of the Saint Lawrence, 1760–1850* (Toronto: The Ryerson Press, 1937) 126–7, 153–62, 208–9, 227–30.
8 The Quebec Act also defined the boundaries of the colony and the political and legal systems which would be adopted. John A. Dickinson and Brian Young, *A Short History of Quebec*, 2nd edition (Montreal: McGill-Queen's University Press, 2000) 54–9.
9 Hilda Marion Neatby, *Québec, The Revolutionary Age, 1760–1791* (Toronto: McClelland & Stewart, 1966) 133–41.
10 Sir Henry Cavendish, *Government of Canada Debates of the House of Commons in 1774 on the Bill for making more effective provision for the government of the province of Quebec* (London: Ridgeway, 1839) 57.
11 The government investigated the factors behind the exodus of 1774–75. Detailed passenger lists were produced at the time and these have been reprinted in Viola Root Cameron, *Emigrants from Scotland to America 1774–1775: Compiled from a loose bundle of Treasury Papers in the Public Record Office, London England* (Baltimore: Genealogical Publishing Co., 1965). First published in 1930.

12 NLS MS 3431 f. 180 (Lee Papers): "Observations or remarks upon land and islands which compose the barony called Harris"—a prospectus of 1772 apparently drawn up for the projected sale of Harris by Norman MacLeod of MacLeod.

13 *EA* Sept. 28, 1773.

14 *AJ* Sept. 27, 1773. *SM* (1773) 557. The Lewis emigrants sailed to New York.

15 Kenneth MacKenzie, who had the title of Viscount Fortrose, was made Earl of Seaforth in 1771. He left no male heirs.

16 *AJ* Sept. 27, 1773.

17 Kelp, made from burnt seaweed, was exported and used in various chemical processes. The kelp industry declined in the 1820s due to cheap foreign imports of similar products. For details of the profitability of kelp production in the Highlands and Islands see J.M. Bumsted, *The People's Clearance: Highland Emigration to British North America, 1770–1815* (Edinburgh: Edinburgh University Press, 1982) 42, 86.

18 NLS MS 10787: Letter book of John Davidson of Stewartfield, ff. 1–2, Letter to George Gillanders, factor to Earl Seaforth, May 16, 1774. Also see letter to John Mackenzie, May 16, 1774.

19 Ibid, letter to John Mackenzie, Aug. 20, 1774.

20 Ibid, letter to George Gillanders, May 16, 1774.

21 The economic, social and political development of Lower Canada is discussed in R. Cole Harris and John Warkentin, *Canada Before Confederation: A Study in Historical Geography* (Ottawa: Carleton University Press, 1995) 65–109.

22 Geographical data for Lower Canada is taken from maps, published in 1972–74 by the Ministry of Lands and Forests, Québec Province, which show boundaries of the early seigneuries: 21L (Québec) 31G (Hull) 31H (Montréal).

23 The seigneurial system remained in use until 1856.

24 By 1791, some 32 per cent of the seigneuries were totally or partially owned by British residents. Dickinson and Young, *A Short History of Quebec*, 81, 170–3.

25 For background on Alexander Fraser, see *Dictionary of Canadia Biography* (Hereafter *DCB*) Vol. IV, 276.

26 In addition to Berthier, Cuthbert went on to purchase the seigneury of Nouvelle-York, part of Lanoraie, Dautré and Maskinongé, by 1781. He purchased Dorvilliers sometime after 1790 and seven years later bought properties in Montréal. *DCB*, Vol. IV, 190–1.

27 Cuthbert had married his first wife Margaret Mackenzie in 1749.

28 Kittson, Arthur, *"Berthier," hier et aujourd'hui* = *"Berthier," Yesterday and To-day* (French translation by Florence F. Martel) (Berthierville, QC: Imprimerie Bernard, 1953) 16–23.

29 For a description of the Glengarry settlements (1784 to 1818) see Lucille H. Campey, *The Scottish Pioneers of Upper Canada, 1784–1855: Glengarry and Beyond* (Toronto: Natural Heritage, 2005) 16–51.

30 The Highlanders were discontented because their new landlord intended to clear them from their land to create sheep farms. PRO CO 42/12 ff. 382–3: Lord Dorchester's Memorandum, Dec. 17, 1791.

31 Ibid.

32 The expected influx of Highlanders in 1792 did not occur because of the outbreak of war. PRO CO 42/94: Land Committee Report, Nov. 19, 1792.

33 The Colonial Office regularly received requests from Inverness-shire people for land grants near to the Glengarry settlements. For example see PRO CO 384/19 f. 107: William Fraser to Colonial Office, Sept. 11, 1828.

34 For details of the Upper Canada military settlements see Campey, *Scottish Pioneers of Upper Canada*, 35–68, 80–90.

35 Between 1815 and 1851 almost 800,000 British and Irish immigrants arrived at the Port of Québec, of whom only 50,000 settled in Lower Canada, the majority having settled in Upper Canada and the United States. Dickinson and Young, *A Short History of Quebec*, 112–3.

36 Bouchette, *The British Dominions in North America*, Vol. I, Appendix XVIII, 483–488.

37 LAC MG24 I178 ff. 2, 40: Daniel Drummond fonds.

38 In spite of widespread and repeated complaints within Britain over the high cost of timber, the protective tariffs remained in place until 1860. Ralph Davis, *The Industrial Revolution and British Overseas Trade* (Leicester: Leicester University Press, 1979) 48–49. Duties increased from 25s. per load in 1804 to 54s. 6d. per load in 1811.

39 Potash was the main product of the virgin forest, being the ashes left behind after trees were burned. A simple process turned the ashes into potash.

40 In spite of the higher transport costs in moving goods to the Port of Québec, Upper Canada supplied most of the wheat for export. With its harsher climate, poorer soil and less advanced agricultural techniques Lower Canada's wheat production lagged behind. Lower Canada was barely self-sufficient in wheat and in some years wheat had to be imported. Robert Montgomery Martin, *History, Statistics and Geography of Upper and Lower Canada* (London: 1838) 260–1. The factors behind Lower Canada's less productive agriculture have been analyzed in John McCallum, *Unequal Beginnings: Agriculture and Economic Development in Québec and Ontario Until 1870* (Toronto: University of Toronto Press, 1980) 25–44, 121–2.

41 Patrick Cecil Telford White (ed.), *Lord Selkirk's Diary 1803–04: A Journal of His Travels Through British North America and the Northeastern United States* (Toronto: The Champlain Society, 1958) 228. Hereafter referred to as *Lord Selkirk's Diary*.

42 MM P110 B08/001: Thomas Torrance to John Torrance, Oct. 22, 1804.

43 Lieutenant J.C. Morgan, *The Emigrants Notebook and Guide with Recollections of Upper and Lower Canada During the Late War* (London: 1824) 110.

44 Marjorie Whitelaw (ed.), *The Dalhousie Journals*, Vols. 1–3 (Ottawa: Oberon 1978–82) Vol. 3, 64.

45 Louis-Joseph Papineau was leader of the Parti Canadien (later the Patriotes). Governor Dalhousie regarded his and the British Crown's authority to be under threat from Papineau and the elected Assembly, which was seeking greater powers for itself. Dalhousie was replaced by Sir James Kempt in 1828. Fernand Ouellet, *Le Bas-Canada, 1791–1840: Changements structuraux et crise* (Ottawa: Éditions de l'Université d'Ottawa, 1976). Translated and adapted: Patricia Claxton, *Lower Canada, 1791–1840: Social Change and Nationalism* (Toronto: McClelland & Stewart, 1980) 387–420.

46 After Papineau had organized numerous petitions calling for Dalhousie's scalp, Dalhousie's supporters fought back and organized petitions which were favourable to Dalhousie.

47   The petitions are to be found in the Dalhousie Papers. For example see NAS
     GD 45/3/534/8; 534/12.

48   The British American Land Company was founded by a group of Montréal
     and London businessmen. Its role in promoting settlement in the Eastern Town-
     ships is discussed more fully in Chapter 5.

49   The Canada Company, which was founded in 1826 by the Scottish novelist John
     Galt, promoted the colonization of over two million acres of land in Upper
     Canada. It advertised Upper Canada with great gusto and attracted large num-
     bers of emigrants to the province.

50   For the later movement of Irish settlers into Pontiac County see Bruce S. Elliott,
     Irish Migrants in the Canadas: A New Approach (Kingston, ON: McGill-Queen's
     University Press, 1988) 161–70.

51   People of British ancestry had accounted for 35 per cent of Lower Canada's pop-
     ulation in 1836. Harris and Warkentin, *Canada Before Confederation*, 66–7.
     Martin, *History, Statistics and Geography of Upper and Lower Canada*, 207–11.

52   Taken from the 1861 Census. Scottish Presbyterian religious affiliations have
     been used to identify people with Scottish ancestry. Concentrations of Scottish-
     born people were greatest in the following townships: Chatham, Grenville, Saint
     Jerusalem and St. Andrews (Argenteuil County); St. Louis de Gonsaque
     (Beauharnois County); New Richmond (Bonaventure) Saint Jean Chrysostôme
     and Saint Malachie (Chateauguay County); Lingwick, Winslow and Whitton
     (Compton County); Hemmingford, Hinchinbrooke, Huntingdon and God-
     manchester, St. Anicet and St. Regis and Dundee (Huntingdon County);
     Inverness and Leeds (Megantic County); Lochaber (Ottawa County); Bristol,
     Clarendon and Litchfield (Pontiac County); Brompton and Gore, Cleveland, Mel-
     bourne and Shipton (Richmond County).

53   For instance, Huntingdon County's population was predominately British by
     the middle of the nineteenth century and yet it is almost entirely French today.
     H. Harry Lewis, "The Population of Quebec Province, Its distribution and
     national origins," *Economic Geography*, Vol. 16 (1940) 59–68.

54   Laurel Doucette (ed.), "Cultural Retention and Economic Change: Studies of the
     Hebridean Scots in the Eastern Townships of Quebec" in *Canadian Centre for Folk
     Culture Studies*, No. 34 (Ottawa: National Museums of Canada, 1980) 22–41.

55   Ouellet, *Le Bas-Canada*, 421–8. Bumsted, *Peoples of Canada*, 249–57.

56   LAC MG55/24#368: letter dated July 20, 1850.

57   Robert Sellar, *The Tragedy of Quebec: The Expulsion of its Protestant Farmers*
     (Toronto: Ontario Press, 1908) 13–20, 123–8, 196–205. [This title was reprinted
     by University of Toronto Press in 1974 (contains introduction by Robert Hill)].

58   "An important letter of a resident of Quebec as to the disabilities of protestants
     in Province of Ontario, 1890) typified the grievances being raised by Protestant
     farmers the Province of Quebec: the parish system" (Toronto: Equal Rights Asso-
     ciation for the over the growing powers of the Catholic Church. Colonization
     societies were formed at this time to encourage French Canadians back from
     the United States to the Eastern Townships.

59   John Irvine Little, *Crofters and Habitants: Settler Society, Economy, and Culture in a
     Quebec township, 1848–81* (Montreal: McGill-Queen's University Press, 1991) 183–9.

TWO—EARLY ARRIVALS

1 John Nairne writing to a friend in Scotland in 1798, quoted in George Mackinnon Wrong, *A Canadian Manor and Its Seigneuries: The Story of a Hundred Years, 1761–1861* (Toronto: Macmillan, 1926) 42.

2 *DCB*, Vol. V, 620–1.

3 Named after Abraham Martin, who was Champlain's St. Lawrence River pilot.

4 In addition to the Fraser's Highlanders (78th), the Royal Highland Regiment (42nd), better known as the Black Watch, and the Montgomery Highlanders (77th) also served in the Seven Years War. Michael Brander, *The Scottish Highlanders and their Regiments* (Haddington: The Gleneil Press, 1996) 161–3.

5 LAC MG23 GIII23 Vol. 5 45: James Murray's grant to John Nairne of the Murray Bay estate. The estate's boundaries ran along the St. Lawrence from Cape aux Oies to the south side of the Rivière Malbaie and extended back from this for three leagues (or roughly nine miles. Fraser's estate ran from the south side of the Rivière Malbaie to the mouth of the Rivière Noire.

6 J.R. Harper, *The Fraser Highlanders* (Montréal: Society of the Montréal Military & Maritime Museum, 1979) 122–7. Captains were allowed 3,000 acres, lower-ranked officers 2,000 acres and ordinary soldiers 50 acres. Helen Cowan, *British Emigration to British North America: The First Hundred Years* (Toronto: University of Toronto Press, 1961) 3–8.

7 Those clans who continued to support James VII and his son as legitimate kings of England were known as Jacobites. They were defeated by Cumberland's Hanoverian army on Culloden Moor and suffered heavy losses. This was the last pitched battle to be fought on British soil.

8 Members of the Fraser's Highlanders who are known to have remained in Québec include: David Cameron, Alex Ferguson, Sergeant Alexander Ferguson, Alexander Fraser, Jr., Donald Fraser, Hugh Fraser, John Fraser, William Fraser, Alexander Lawson, Lieutenant Archibald McAllister, John Mackenzie, Lieutenant Lauchlan McPherson, Thomas Reid, Alexander Shaw, Lauchlan Smith, Alexander Sutherland, Donald Sutherland, William Watson, Donald Blackburn and John Ross. Harper, *Fraser Highlanders*, 122–3.

9 Gordon Donaldson, *The Scots Overseas* (London: Robert Hale, 1966) 57–80. Bumsted, *The People's Clearance*, 1–26. Customs records for 1774–75 show that most Scots were leaving for North Carolina and New York. See Cameron, *Emigrants from Scotland to America 1774–1775.*

10 *SM*, Vol. XXX (1768) 446.

11 Some men "were preparing to embark for the Island of Saint John where they all have government land" *SM*, Ibid. The petition for land was submitted by Col. Simon Fraser on behalf of himself and 10 other members of the former Fraser's Highlanders Regiment: Major James Abercrombie, Major John Campbell, Capt. John MacDonell, Capt. Alexander Macleod, Capt. Hugh Cameron, Capt. Ronald MacDonell, Capt. John Fraser, Capt. Arch. Campbell, Capt. John Nairne. Harper, *Fraser Highlanders*, 127.

12 F.W.P. Bolger (ed.) *Canada's Smallest Province: A History of P.E.I.* (Charlottetown: Prince Edward Island 1973 Centennial Commission, 1973; reprinted, Halifax: Nimbus, 1991) 40. Colonel Fraser's group were allocated lots 38, 39, 41 and 42 in Kings County. See also Lucille H. Campey, *"A Very Fine Class of Immigrants": Prince Edward Island's Scottish Pioneers, 1770–1850* (Toronto: Natural Heritage, 2001) 16–31.

13   Wallace, "Some notes on the Fraser Highlanders," 131–40.

14   Wrong, *A Canadian Manor,* 47–50.

15   Ibid, 49.

16   However, Duncan McNicol appears in Malcolm Fraser's Account Book (1773–84) as one of Nairne's tenants (LAC MG 23 K1 Vol. XIII: 49). McNicol had fought in the Seven Years War as a member of the Fraser's Highlanders. Carl Beaulieu, *L'Alliance Écossaise au Québec* (Chicoutimi, QC: Éditions du patrimoine, 2001) 343–5.

17   Jean Des Gagniers, *Charlevoix, Pays Enchanté* (Sainte-Foy, QC: Presses de l'Université Laval, 1994) 164–73. John Nairne's estate was considerable. A plan produced in 1787 reveals "le Grand Parc" adjoining the house. LAC MG23 GIII23 Vol. 5, 8: Plan for cultivating the farm at Murray Bay.

18   Wrong, *A Canadian Manor,* 42–6, 105–6. *DCB,* Vol. V, 620–1. John Nairne's income from his estate was modest. A statement in 1798 shows that he earned only £120 from his farms, mills and whale oil business. However, he probably made additional income that year from his fur and timber exports. He had huge expenses in maintaining his estate and almost certainly relied on his army pay and other assets to sustain his country gentleman lifestyle.

19   The regiment was under the command of Lieutenant-Colonel Allan MacLean. Nairne rose to the rank of major by 1783. A 2nd battalion of Highlanders was raised in Nova Scotia.

20   Lord Dalhousie's comments in 1828, recorded in Whitelaw, *Dalhousie Journals,* Vol. 3, 160–1.

21   LAC MG23 GIII23 Vol. 5, 112: To the Memory of Colonel John Nairne.

22   *DCB,* Vol. IV, 330–1.

23   Private communication, with Evelyn M. Scullion of Ottawa. Malcolm Fraser's eldest son, Alexander, became one of the early partners of the North West Company. Malcolm Fraser was said to have fathered a number of illegitimate children. It would seem that he was the father of the "bastard child" of Mary Gagne, agreeing in 1802 to "indemnify the parish of Murray Bay for the child's birth, education and maintenance" (LAC MG23 GIII23 Vol. 5, 147–8).

24   Malcolm Fraser acquired John McCord's' house on Rue de la Fabrique in around 1790.

25   LAC MG23 K1 Vol. XII: Malcolm Fraser's Account Books (1768–70) 32, 50. Malcolm Fraser is reported to have spoken English, French and Gaelic. See W.S. Wallace, "Notes on the family of Malcolm Fraser of Murray Bay" in *Bulletin des Reserches Historique*, Vol. 39 (1993) 267–71.

26   LAC MG23 K1 Vol. XIII: Malcolm Fraser's Account Book (1773–84) 77, 100, 115. Col. Henry Caldwell, who was Irish-born, had fought in the Seven Years War. He became receiver-general of the Province of Québec.

27   LAC MG23 K1 Vol. XIII, 100. The Rivière-du-Loup seigneury was later known as Fraserville.

28   *DCB,* Vol. V, 330–31.

29   Joseph Bouchette, *A Topographical Description of the Province of Lower Canada, with remarks upon Upper Canada* (London: W. Faden, 1815) 563.

30   Joseph Bouchette, *A Topographical Dictionary of the Province of Lower Canada* (London: Longman & Co, 1832).

31 LAC MG23 K1 Vol. XII, 13.
32 Ibid, 35. John Fraser had been a member of the Fraser's Highlanders.
33 LAC MG23 K1, Vol. XIII, 104. John McLoughlin, who was of Irish descent, married Angelique, Fraser's eldest daughter. Private communication, Evelyn M. Scullion of Ottawa. He later became known as the "Father of Oregon" (see Wallace, "Notes of the family of Malcolm Fraser," 267).
34 LAC MG23 GIII23, Vol. 5, 50. Bond dated 1787. Hugh Blackburn, who was born in Edinburgh, served in the Royal Highland Emigrants Regiment.
35 Beaulieu, L'Alliance Écossaise, 33–5.
36 However, a visiting Presbyterian missionary, who visited Lower Canada in the mid-1830s, claimed there were people at Rivière-du-Loup who "urgently require a minister of our church." Rev. R.F. Binnington, "The Glasgow Colonial Society and its work in the development of the Presbyterian Church in British North America 1825–1840" (University of Toronto: unpublished Th.D. 1960) 139.
37 Ouellet, Le Bas-Canada, 22–36. Dickinson and Young, A Short History of Quebec, 70–2.
38 For example, in Nova Scotia the Native Peoples were systematically marginalized and thousands of Acadians were evicted from their lands.
39 Documents constitutionnels (1759–91) quoted in Ouellet, Le Bas-Canada, 23.
40 Ibid.
41 Des Gagniers, Charlevoix, Pays Enchanté, 167–70; Wrong, A Canadian Manor, 64–5.
42 Dickinson and Young, A Short History of Quebec, 54–9.
43 Haldimand to Lord North quoted in Ouellet, Le Bas-Canada, 24.
44 Robert Harvey, A Few Bloody Noses: The American War of Independence (London: John Murray, 2001) 179–82.
45 Some Loyalists were also stationed at St-Jean in Bleury seigneury. Wilbur Henry Siebert, "American Loyalists in the Eastern seigneuries and townships of the province of Québec" in Transactions of the Royal Society of Canada, 3rd series (1913) Vol. VII 3–41; Ouellet, Le Bas-Canada, 24.
46 Siebert, "American Loyalists in the Eastern seigneuries and townships," 27–30.
47 William Kingdom, America and the British Colonies (London: 1820) 99.
48 Binnington, "The Glasgow Colonial Society, " 138–39.
49 Norman MacDonald, Canada, 1763–1841: Immigration and Settlement (London: Longmans & Co., 1939) 481–2. Large numbers of troops were stationed at Chambly Fort during the War of 1812–14 (see Bouchette, A Topographical Dictionary of Lower Canada).
50 For details of the Loyalists who established the Glengarry settlements in Upper Canada, see Campey, Scottish Pioneers of Upper Canada, 16–34.
51 Cape Breton and Prince Edward Island also acquired a few Loyalists at this time.
52 There were 129 men, 52 women and 132 children in the first group, who were followed by a second group of 56 people. Wilbur Henry Siebert, "Loyalist settlements in the Gaspé Peninsula" in Transactions of the Royal Society of Canada, 3rd Series (1914) Vol. VIII, 399–405. Eleanor Blois Hall, The Loyalists of the Eastern Townships of Quebec (Stanbridge East, QC: United Empire Loyalists Association of Canada, Sir John Johnson Centennial Branch, 1984) 178–80.
53 Siebert, "Loyalist settlements in the Gaspé," 401.

54 Joseph Bouchette, *The British Dominions in North America*, Vol. I, 323–33. Siebert, "Loyalist settlements in the Gaspé," "Register of Inhabitants in 1786," 403.
55 Lilian F. Gates, *Land Policies of Upper Canada* (Toronto: University of Toronto Press, 1968) 12–3.
56 Following later boundary changes, Foucault (renamed Caldwell Manor) became incorporated into the State of Vermont.
57 Robert S. Allen, *The Loyal Americans: The Military Role of the Loyalist Provincial Corps and their Settlement in British North America, 1775–1784* (Ottawa: National Museum of Canada, 1983) 92–5. While Missisquoi County later became largely Francophone, the region still retains examples of Loyalist architecture.
58 Siebert, "American Loyalists in the Eastern seigneuries and townships," 38–41.
59 Raoul Blanchard, *L'est du canada français, "province de Québec"* (Paris: Masson & Cie, 1935) Vol. II, 345–7.
60 C.C. DuBerger, *Murray Bay Atlas and Maps of its Environs* (Murray Bay, QC: Arthur Cimon & Co., 1895). For example, the 1895 Atlas, which lists Murray Bay landowners, reveals few Scottish surnames. Where they appear they are associated with French-Christian names (e.g. Augustin McNichol).
61 Bouchette, *The British Dominions in North America*, 321–2.
62 The Montagnais homeland covered a vast territory running east of the St. Maurice River and extending along the north side of the St. Lawrence to the east coast of Labrador. Peter McLeod's father, Peter McLeod senior, had a total of twelve children by Marie-Magdelaine.
63 Beaulieu, *L'Alliance Écossaise*, 177–92.
64 Before establishing his 817 acre farm, Ross had worked for the North West Company, being in charge of fur trading in various parts of the Saguenay and Lac Saint-Jean regions. Ibid, 281–9.
65 A tribute written, 10 years after McLeod's death, by Samuel Kelso, a Scottish-born innkeeper living at Bagotville on Baie Ha! Ha! (Ibid, 190).
66 *DCB*, Vol. IX, 638–43. Blanchard, *L'est du Canada français*, Vol. II, 67–70.
67 Ibid, Vol. II, 71–3. In addition, their timber exports to the United States were worth £4,000.

THREE—NORTH OF THE OTTAWA RIVER

1 LAC MG24 I183: Archibald McMillan's letter-book, A. McMillan to John Munro, Dec. 15, 1806.
2 Tacksmen were an elite class in the Scottish feudal system who acted as factors or farm managers under a laird. They usually sub-let much of their own land to sub-tenants who did most of the work on the great Highland estates. With the introduction of improved farming methods in the 1770s the tacksmens' role became increasingly obsolete and many reacted to the sweeping changes by promoting emigration within their local population and were highly influential in encouraging large numbers to emigrate.
3 His business was based at Rue Saint-Paul, Montréal. *DCB* Vol. VI, 475–9.
4 See Campey, *Scottish Pioneers of Upper Canada*, 216–17 for the list of ship crossings. For full details of each emigrant group see Marianne McLean, *People of Glengarry, 1745–1820: Highlanders in Transition* (Montreal: McGill-Queen's University Press, 1991) 78–127.

5   Robert Brown, *Strictures and remarks on the Earl of Selkirk's observations on the present state of the Highlands* (Edinburgh: Abemethy & Walker, 1806) 36–38, Appendix (State of Emigrations 1801, 1802 and 1803); NLS MS 9646 ff. 19, 21, 23.

6   From 1790 to 1793 the Highlands and Islands lost around 900 people to Prince Edward Island and 650 people to Nova Scotia. See Campey, *"A Very Fine Class of Immigrants,"* 138–9 and Lucille H. Campey, *After the Hector: The Scottish Pioneers of Nova Scotia and Cape Breton, 1773–1852* (Toronto: Natural Heritage, 2004) 57–8, 236.

7   Sir John Sinclair, *First Statistical Account of Scotland*, 21 vols. (Edinburgh, 1791–99) Vol. XVII, 135–6. McLean, *Glengarry,* 128–35.

8   NLS MS 35.6.18: State of emigration from the Highlands of Scotland its extent, causes and proposed remedy (March 21, 1803) f. 19.

9   Campey, *After the Hector,* 63–78, 236–8.

10 NAS RH 4/188/2: Prize essays and Transactions of the Highland Society of Scotland, Vol. iii, 1802–03, 531–4. Second Report of the Committee on Emigration, June 1802.

11 LAC MG24 I183 ff. 7–9, 11. The passenger lists for the *Helen, Jean* and *Friends* crossings appear in Appendix 1. They are described in detail in Rae Fleming (ed.), *The Lochaber Emigrants to Glengarry* (Toronto: Natural Heritage, 1994) 5–16. Also see Somerled MacMillan, *Bygone Lochaber: Historical and Traditional* (Glasgow: K. & R. Davidson, 1971) 239, for a list of the additional passengers who boarded ship at Saltcoats, near Irvine, in the Firth of Clyde.

12 Archibald McMillan was assisted by his first cousin, Allan McMillan of Glenpean (Lochiel), whose brother had led the 1792 emigration to Upper Canada. McLean, *Glengarry,* 139–44.

13 *Lloyd's Shipping Register*, 1802; LAC MG24 I183 ff. 35, 73.

14 LAC RG1 L3 f. 66478: McMillan's petition for land Aug. 8, 1804.

15 As only adults paid full fares, children were computed as being a fraction of an adult. Using such a formula, the *Neptune's* 600 passengers were converted to 400 "full passengers." In addition to the *Helen, Jean, Friends* and *Neptune,* Québec arrivals in September 1802 also included the *Eagle* from Greenock "with 21 men, women and children" and the *Albion* from Fort William with 167 passengers (*QG* 11, Sept. 15, 1802).

16 *QG* Sept. 16, 1802. The group from the *Neptune* had three spokesmen: Norman Morrison, Duncan McDonald and Murdoch McLennan.

17 Around 25 to 30 families settled initially at Sir John Johnson's seigneury at Chambly, but most had returned to Glengarry by 1815. See Chapter 4.

18 McLean, *Glengarry,* 136–39.

19 LAC MG24 I183 (File 3) f. 40: Case heard in Montréal, Sept. 23, 1802. The J.P.s were James McGill and John M. Kindlay.

20 LAC MG24 I183 File 8, ff. 549–51: Lochaber, Templeton & Grenville townships, settlement projects; McLean, *Glengarry,* 190–5. For example McMillan's lists revealed that John McDonald, Hugh McDonell, Donald McDonell, Peter and two Malcolm McCuaigs lived in Côte St George.

21 Binnington, "The Glasgow Colonial Society," 138. LAC reel M-1355: Alexander McNaughty to Rev. Burns, Aug. 26, 1839.

22 *Lord Selkirk's Diary,* 200. An endowment system was introduced in 1792 for Protestant clergy and the Crown, thus creating reserves which could only be acquired by settlers through renting.

23 LAC MG24 I183 ff. 66477–9: McMillan's petition; for the list of names see ff. 66562-7.

24 Ibid, ff. 66691–2.

25 Bouchette, *Topographical Description of the Province of Lower Canada* (1815) 248–9.

26 Papineau later became Ottawa County.

27 LAC MG24 I183 ff. 238–9: Munro to McMillan, Sept. 15, 1806. Also see LAC RG1 L1, Vol. 14, f. 60: Report of the Committee of Council, Oct. 31, 1806.

28 LAC MG24 I183: McMillan to Duncan Cameron, Sept. 30, 1803, and to Ewan Cameron, Oct. 20, 1805.

29 Miles Macdonell, who had organized the 1790 crossing, petitioned the Québec governor, on their behalf, asking for provisions to see them through the winter. Many of the *British Queen*'s passengers originated from the Island of Eigg. The *British Queen* passenger list appears in Campey, *Scottish Pioneers of Upper Canada*, 183.

30 PRO CO 42/82, ff. 2–21: Council Minutes, Jan. 11, 1791.

31 The emigrants also received food supplies from Montréal merchants. They mainly settled together in Lochiel Township (then part of Lancaster), just north of present-day Alexandria. McLean, *Glengarry,* 116–21, 182–3.

32 PRO CO 42/82, ff. 6–7.

33 LAC RG1 L3 ff. 66605-10: List of emigrants presented by Archibald McMillan, May 6, 1806. Eighty-seven per cent of the Upper Canada contingent originated from Glengarry County and the rest came from Stormont County.

34 LAC MG24 I183: McMillan to John Munro, July 21, 1806.

35 *DCB,* Vol. VI, 478; MacMillan, *Bygone Lochaber*, 6–8.

36 McMillan was also the first postmaster of Grenville, holding the position from 1819–29 and a justice of the peace.

37 LAC MG24 I183: McMillan to John Munro, July 21, 1806.

38 LAC RG1 L1 Vol. 14, ff. 59–60: Report of the Committee of Council, Oct. 21, 1806.

39 LAC MG24 I183: McMillan to Ewan Cameron, Oct. 20, 1805.

40 LAC RG5 A1 ff. 44934–5: petition of John Corbet and others, March 10, 1827.

41 LAC MG24 I183 ff. 549–51: List of those who resigned their rights to land (1804–07).

42 LAC RG5 A1 ff. 44934-5. The 41 petitioners were Alexander McDonell (2), John McDougald, Widow Mary McDonell, Ronald McDonell, Angus McGillis, Hugh Kennedy, Dougald Macdonald, Angus Kennedy, Donald Kennedy, Allan Kennedy, John McDonald, Keneth McDonell, Donald McDonald (2), John Kennedy (2), Alexander Kennedy, Collin Campbell, Angus MacDonald, Duncan Macdonell, John Corbet, Duncan MacLean, John MacGill, Donald McDonell (2), Hugh Mcdonell, Archibald MacDonald, John MacCormick, Hector Mac-Cormick, Donald MacDonald, William McKinnon, Angus McCormick, Roderick McDonell, Angus McPhee, Alexander McMillan, John McGillis, Alexander Macphee, Alexander Corbet, Donald McGillis.

43 LAC MG24 I183: McMillan to John Munro, Sept. 10, 1807.

44   DCA Dundee and District Shipping Local Collection, D3113. The *Quebec Gazette,* July 6, 1809, recorded the arrival of the *Albion* (Master, R. Kidd) from Dundee with 60 passengers.

45   LAC MG24 I183: McMillan to Ewan Cameron, Oct. 20, 1805.

46   Bouchette, *Topographical Dictionary, Lower Canada* (entry for Lochaber). Also see entry for Grenville.

47   *DCB*, Vol. VI, 477.

48   LAC RG1 L3 f. 66475.

49   MacDonald, *Canada, 1763–1841: Immigration and Settlement*, 479–1.

50   LAC MG24 I183: McMillan to Col. Taylor, April 3, 1822.

51   Bouchette, *Topographical Description of Lower Canada* (1815), 249.

52   It was located at the mid-point of the township, where the Rivière Blanche joins the Ottawa River.

53   LAC reel M-1352: Donald Henderson, Alexander Cameron and William Grant to Rev. Burns, March 25, 1833. The Society, in connection with the Established Church of Scotland, for Promoting the Religious Interests of Scottish Settlers in British North America was founded. in 1825. Having been established by Glaswegians, it later came to be known by its condensed name—the Glasgow Colonial Society.

54   BAnQ, Ministère des terres et forêts du Québec, Map 31G (Hull) published in 1973, showing township and seigneury boundaries.

55   Large numbers from the Logie Almond district of Perthshire emigrated in the early 1830s. Although most went to Upper Canada, some may have been the founders of Glen Almond.

56   Binnington, *The Glasgow Colonial Society*, 138.

57   Ibid.

58   NAS GD 45/3/534/10: Petition submitted in 1827.

59   Bouchette, *Topographical Dictionary, Lower Canada*; Raoul Blanchard, *Les Pays de l'Ottawa*, Étude Canadienne troisième série (Grenoble, France: Allier, 1949) III, 53–8.

60   Philemon Wright originated from Woburn, Massachusetts. Elliott, *Irish Migrants in the Canadas*, 119–20.

61   Blanchard, *Les Pays de l'Ottawa*, 57. The 1861 Census shows that around 20 per cent of the population of both Masham and Wakefield were Church of Scotland worshippers. Many Irish settlers also settled along the Gatineau River beyond Wakefield and Masham (see Elliott, *Irish Migrants in the Canadas*, 161–70).

62   John L. Gourlay, *History of the Ottawa Valley* (Ottawa: 1896) 197. Eardley, Hull, Masham and Wakefield townships were later incorporated in Gatineau County.

63   NLS MS 3952 ff. 23–5: Ronald Rankin to William Robertson MacDonald of Kinloch, Moidart, Oct. 16, 1850.

64   Rankin referred to the "township of Saw" in his 1850 letter, indicating that even the name was unclear to him.

65   NLS MS 3952 ff. 23–5.

66   For the Upper Canada Highland influx during the Potato Famine years (1846–1855), see Campey, *Scottish Pioneers of Upper Canada*, 75–80, 134, 137, 147–50.

67   NLS MS 3952 ff. 23–5.

68 Benjamin Wales, *Memories of old St. Andrews and historical sketches of the Seigneury of Argenteuil* (Lachute, QC: Watchman Press, 1934) 58.
69 Bouchette, *Topographical Dictionary, Lower Canada.*
70 BAnQ, Ministère des terres et forêts du Québec, Map 31G (Hull).
71 Blanchard, *Les Pays de l'Ottawa*, 51.
72 1831 Lower Canada Census. Grenville's population was 1,262, while Lochaber's population was 236.
73 NAS RHP 35156: 1838–39 maps of Upper and Lower Canada.
74 Blanchard, *Les Pays de l'Ottawa*, 51; Bouchette, *Topographical Dictionary, Lower Canada.*
75 Binnington, "Glasgow Colonial Society," 129.
76 LAC (M-1354): Rev. Roach to Rev. Burns, April 30, 1837.
77 *DCB*, Vol. VI, 478.
78 Blanchard, *Les Pays de l'Ottawa*, 51.
79 C. Thomas, *History of the counties of Argenteuil, Québec and Prescott, Ontario, from the earliest settlement to the present* (Montréal: John Lovell, 1896) 63–5.
80 Blanchard, *Les Pays de l'Ottawa*, 51.
81 For details of the influx of weavers to Upper Canada, see Campey, *Scottish Pioneers of Upper Canada*, 35–68.
82 Wales, *Memories of Old St. Andrews*, 45, 58–9, 77.
83 LAC MG25-G276: McOuat and Bilsland family fonds.
84 Thomas, *History of the Counties of Argenteuil and Prescott*, 64.
85 Ibid, 104–7, 238–9.
86 Ibid, 106.
87 Bouchette, *Topographical Dictionary, Lower Canada.* The village of St. Andrews occupied both banks of the Rivière du Nord.
88 LAC MG29-C3: Reminiscences of a Scottish settler at Lakefield, Argenteuil County. The settler's name is not known and his notebook is undated. It was rescued from an ashcan in 1945 by Mr. Y.M. Begg of Sherbrooke Street West, Montréal.
89 Ibid.
90 Ibid.
91 Hugh Allan Halliday, *Terrebonne: From Seigneury to Suburb* (Welland, ON: Niagara College of Applied Arts and Technology, 1971) 12–5.
92 *DCB*, Vol. V, 560–7. The specially baked dried biscuits were consumed by the voyageurs on their long canoe journeys west.
93 Roderick Mackenzie had considerable literary interests. He established a library for North West Company workers in the Athabaska region and devoted much time to collecting documentary material on the fur trade which was later published. *DCB*, Vol. VII, 565–7.
94 Private communication with Evelyn M. Scullion of Ottawa. One son of Roderick Mackenzie's took up law, another went into the army while his three daughters married prominent businessmen or lawyers.
95 Roderick Mackenzie received a number of public appointments. He was made a lieutenant-colonel in the Terrebonne militia in 1812 and acted as a justice of the peace for a number of localities; but his most significant appointment was to the Legislative Council of Lower Canada, a position he occupied from 1817 to 1838.
96 Bouchette, *Topographical Description Lower Canada*, 108–11.
97 Ibid.

98 However, other former weavers declined this offer and moved instead to Huntingdon County (see Chapter 4).
99 MacDonald, *Canada, 1763–1841: Immigration and Settlement*, 482–3.
100 *Montreal Gazette*, Nov. 10, 1824.
101 Bouchette, *Topographical Dictionary, Lower Canada* (entry for Terrebonne).
102 BAnQ, Ministère des terres et forêts du Québec, Map 31H (Montréal).
103 NAS GD 45/3/534/12: Petition from the inhabitants of New Glasgow submitted, Dec. 11, 1827.
104 A. Shortt and A.G. Doughty (eds.), *Canada and Its Provinces: A History of the Canadian People and Their Institutions* (Toronto: Publishers' Association of Canada, 1913–17) Vol. XV, 159.
105 1861 Lower Canada Census.
106 MacMillan, *Bygone Lochaber*, 11–2. *DCB*, Vol. VI, 478–9. The 1852 Census shows that 545 MacMillans lived in Glengarry County.

FOUR—SOUTH AND WEST OF MONTRÉAL

1 Sellar, *The Tragedy of Quebec*, 16.
2 Bouchette, *Topographical Dictionary, Lower Canada* (entry for Beauharnois).
3 Raoul Blanchard, *L'ouest du Canada français: "Montréal et sa région"* (Montréal: Beauchemin, 1953) 69.
4 Blanchard, *L'ouest du Canada français*, 68–9; Bouchette, *Topographical Dictionary, Lower Canada* (entry for Beauharnois).
5 Blanchard, *L'ouest du Canada français*, 66–8.
6 The southwest corner of Hemmingford became Havelock Township in 1863. G.A. Rogers, "The Settlement of the Chateauguay Valley," in *Connections*, Vol. 14, No. 3 (1992) 2–6.
7 Siebert, "American Loyalists in the Eastern seigneuries and townships," 39–40. Some of these men may have been American Loyalists.
8 *AJ*, May 18, 1801.
9 Ibid.
10 MacDonald, *Canada, 1763–1841: Immigration and Settlement*, 481–2.
11 Dickinson and Young, *A Short History of Quebec*, 60–2. For example a militia of 260 men was raised at Baie-Saint-Paul (see Beaulieu, *L'Alliance Écossaise*, 258).
12 This regiment was formed in 1804 from the veterans of the Glengarry Fencibles Regiment which had been raised in 1794. McLean, *Glengarry*, 198–200.
13 Donald E. Graves, *Field of Glory: The Battle of Crysler's Farm, 1813* (Toronto: Robin Brass Studio, 1999) 97–8. Ouellet, *Le Bas-Canada*, 151–72.
14 Another factor in Britain's success was the British Navy's achievement in winning control of the Upper Great Lakes.
15 *DCB*, Vol. IX, 484–5.
16 Extract from *Cours d'Histoire du Canada* (8 Vols, 1919–34) quoted in Ouellet, *Le Bas-Canada*, 172.
17 Campey, *Scottish Pioneers of Upper Canada*, 35–68.
18 They sailed to Québec on the *John and Samuel* of Liverpool and were given financial help by the government to survive their first winter. Most settled in Glengarry (see Campey, *Scottish Pioneers of Upper Canada*, 48, 219, 295). Lord MacLeod's Skye estate comprised the parishes of Bracadale and Duirinish on the west side of Skye.

19 LAC RG1 L3 ff. 64296–8.

20 The St. Regis Natives were Iroquois who had formed Catholic settlements at St. Regis.

21 LAC RG1 L3 ff. 64296–8. The petitioners sought confirmation that the St. Regis lands they hoped to lease were part of the Indian reservation.

22 Robert Sellar, *History of the county of Huntingdon & of the Seigneuries of Chateau-guay and Beauharnois from their first settlement to the year 1838* (Huntingdon QC: Canadian Gleaner, 1888) 172–3. The terms of the lease were very liberal. Settlers paid $5 a year for 100 acres, the leases running for 99 years. Kintail, in Wester Ross, lies on the mainland close to Skye.

23 Ibid, 67.

24 Ibid, 169–73. Neil McDonell and Peter McKinnon had also signed the 1818 petition. Tolmie had not originated from Skye.

25 It was known initially as New Skye.

26 See grave lists compiled by Mr. Gerald A. Rogers in 1978 (available from QFHS). Modern-day Pointe-Fraser, near the now deserted Isle of Skye settlement, which was named after James Fraser who arrived in 1818, is a lasting reminder of the area's early Scottish connections. See also Robert J. Fraser, *As Others See Us: Scots of the Seaway Valley* (Beamsville, ON: Beamsville Express, 1959) 85–92.

27 Sellar, *History of Huntingdon*, 170.

28 Aubrey's Corners was located at the junction of the Dundee Centre Road and the Ridge Road. Named after Edward Aubrey who arrived in 1817. Sellar, Ibid, 184.

29 The kelp industry declined in the 1820s due to cheap foreign imports of similar products.

30 PRO CO 384/15, f. 494. *IJ*, Dec. 10, 1830; *QM*, Sept. 4, 1830. The *Malay* also carried over 200 Skye emigrants that same year. While most sailed to Cape Breton, 50 people arrived at Québec (see *QM*, Sept. 11, 1830).

31 PRO CO 384/23 f. 484.

32 Ibid, Bernisdale appears as Burnastill in the petition.

33 It was also known as the Broken Front Cemetery.

34 In addition to the exodus from the Macleod estate, large numbers also emigrated at this time from Lord MacDonald's estate on the east side of Skye. Most of Lord MacDonald's former tenants settled in Prince Edward Island (see Campey, *"A Very Fine Class of Immigrants,"* 80–9, 146–7) and Cape Breton (see Campey, *After the Hector*, 121–2, 258–59).

35 Before Rev. Moody's arrival the settlers had attended services at the Presbyterian church at Williamstown, Glengarry County.

36 Sellar, *History of Huntingdon*, 184.

37 LAC (M-1354) Rev. Roach to Rev. Burns, April 30, 1837.

38 Sellar, Ibid, 185.

39 Ibid, 184.

40 Ibid.

41 For details of some of the Scottish settlers of La Guerre, see Fraser, *Scots of the Seaway Valley*, 93–104. La Guerre, also known as Godmanchester village (now St-Anicet), lies at the junction of the east and west branches of the La Guerre River. The village had a Calvin Presbyterian Church which is now in ruins, see Burton Lang, *Place Names of South Western Quebec* (Howick, QC: self-published, 2001).

42 Sellar, Ibid, 184.

43 Robert McGee, *A Companion to Robert Sellar's History of the County of Hunting-don* and the Seigniories of Chateaugay and Beauharnois: Including Index, Maps, List of Settlers, Introduction and Sellar's Original "Postscript" (Huntingdon, QC: The Innismacsaint Press, 1987) 57.

44 Lang, *Place Names of South Western Québec*, 117.

45 Sellar, Ibid, 185.

46 Campey, *Scottish Pioneers of Upper Canada*, 52–68, 82–90.

47 Weavers also established communities in the Maritimes. A small group from Renfrewshire founded New Glasgow in Prince Edward Island in 1818 (see Campey, *"A Very Fine Class of Immigrants,"* 62) while a larger group of Dumfriesshire settlers founded the Dalhousie settlement in Nova Scotia by the 1820s (see Campey, *After the Hector,* 90).

48 They sailed on the *Alexander* from Greenock (*QM*, June 5, 1820). The *Alexander* carried ninety-six passengers in all. The group of twenty-one, who settled at Godmanchester Township, were later identified by Robert Sellar: Robert Allan; Robert Barrie, mason, New Monklands; James Brown, mason, Glasgow; Thomas Brown, weaver, Campsie; Thomas Brown and James Brown, brothers, grocers, Glasgow; Archibald Fleming, carpenter, Paisley; John Gillies, laborer, Ayrshire; John Harper, Paisley; William Hamilton, baker,(sic) and James Hamilton, farm helper,(sic) brothers, Motherwell; Robert Higgins, carpenter, Paisley; Peter Horn, weaver, Campsie; Thomas Marshall, weaver, Wishaw; James McArthur and William McArthur, weavers, brothers, Paisley; James Paul, mason, New Monklands; _____ Rorison, merchant, Glasgow; James Tannahill, mason, Tinnock; Hugh Wiley and John Wiley, masons, brothers, Paisley (Sellar, *History of Huntingdon*, 166).

49 Sellar, Ibid, 149.

50 MacDonald, *Canada, 1763–1841: Immigration and Settlement,* 486, 506. Lord Dalhousie donated books to a library founded by former weavers in Dalhousie Township, Upper Canada (Campey, *Scottish Pioneers of Upper Canada,* 87).

51 I am grateful to Ken Hamilton, of Halifax, for the information he supplied to me about his ancestor, James Hamilton.

52 Sellar, *History of Huntingdon*, 413–5.

53 Sellar, Ibid, 413.

54 *DCB*, Vol. IX 233–9. Edward Ellice, the son of Scottish-born Alexander Ellice, was nicknamed "the Bear" probably for his financial acumen. His father and four uncles established themselves in the fur trade and amassed a large fortune, although the family business was conducted principally under the name of Robert Ellice and Company. Edward Ellice was a founding director and deputy governor of the Canada Company and he also played a key role in the merger of the North West Company and the Hudson's Bay Company in 1821. But he was far more than a mere entrepreneur. Being concerned with wide-ranging social and political issues, he had a major impact on Canada's early development. For more information on Edward Ellice, particularly his contribution to the work of the Canada Company, see Robert C. Lee, *The Canada Company and the Huron Tract, 1826–1853: Personalities, Profits and Politics* (Toronto: Natural Heritage Books, 2004) 34, 38, 85–87, 92, 229–30.

55 Sellar, Ibid, 158.
56 Ibid, 159. Elgin Township was created from Hinchinbrook Township in 1855.
57 An early cemetery was located on an island near the Dalhousie settlement, east of Port Lewis. Following the construction of the Old Beauharnois Canal, the level of St. Francis Lake was raised and the island became submerged (see Lang, *Place Names*, 31).
58 Sellar, Ibid, 163.
59 NAS RHP 35156: 1838–39 maps of Upper and Lower Canada.
60 Sellar, Ibid, 392–3.
61 Lang, *Place Names*, 8, 26, 63. Clyde's Corners lies at the junction of Ridge Road and Smellie Sideroad, just to the north of Elgin.
62 Sellar, Ibid, 413–5.
63 *DWJ*, April 8, 1823.
64 Ibid.
65 NAS GD 1/92/9: James Aitchison to his father in Edinburgh, Aug. 12, 1834. His father hoped that his son would mend his spendthrift ways and sent him off to Hinchinbrook with £200. He was due to lodge with Peter Walker, a local farmer.
66 NAS GD 1/92/12A: James Aitchison to his father, Nov. 23, 1834.
67 LAC (M-1354) Rev. Roach to Rev. Burns, April 30, 1837. Rev. Walker was installed as minister in 1834.
68 St. Andrew's Presbyterian Cemetery was located at the back of the present Grove Hall in Huntingdon. No trace remains today (see Lang, *Place Names*, 103). The Muir and McNaughton settlement in the middle of Boyd settlement, just to the east of Huntingdon village, was founded by Scots (Ibid, 79).
69 Athelstan, to the south of Huntingdon village, was named after Athelstaneford in East Lothian (near Headdington). A Presbyterian cemetery lies on the Ridge Road, 0.4 miles east of the village. "Munro settlement" was established on the north side of the village (see Lang, Ibid, 79).
70 LAC (M-1354), Memorial of the Presbytery of Québec, Aug. 7, 1835.
71 NAS GD 45/3/534/8.
72 The County of Beauharnois, created in 1855, included only the northern part of the seigneury. The southwest corner of Beauharnois seigneury became part of Franklin Township in 1857. Also included in Franklin Township were parts of Hinchinbrook and Hemingford townships.
73 The Ellice family owned the seigneury until 1840 when it was sold to the London Land Company.
74 Sellar, Ibid, 252.
75 *DCB*, Vol. IX, 233–9. G.A. Rogers, "Pioneer Mill Sites in the Chateauguay Valley," in *Connections*, Vol. 15, No. 1 (Sept. 1992) 7–15.
76 LAC (M-1354), Rev. Roach, to Rev. James Henderson, October 24, 1834.
77 LAC (M-1354) Rev. Anderson to Rev. Burns, Feb. 20, 1837.
78 MacDonald, *Canada, 1763–1841: Immigration and Settlement*, 481–2.
79 Jamestown was named after Alexander Ellice's son James.
80 Georgetown was named after Alexander Ellice's son George.
81 The northeast end of the Scotch Concession, in present-day St-Urbain, is called "La Carcasse" by Francophones (see Lang, *Place Names,* 117).
82 Sellar, Ibid, 259–62.

83 Ibid, 235. Archibald Cameron later moved to Tullochgorum, east of Ormstown. This is a Gaelic place name, meaning grassy meadow. Lang, *Place Names*, 128.
84 Bouchette, *Topographical Dictionary, Lower Canada* (entry for Beauharnois). For example in 1828 South Georgetown was almost entirely Scottish as was Beechridge.
85 Rev. Walter Roach's report published in the *Eighth Annual Report of the Glasgow Colonial Society for promoting the religious interests of the Scottish settlers in British North America* (Glasgow: 1835).
86 LAC (M-1354), Memorial of the Presbytery of Québec, Aug. 7, 1835.
87 St. Paul's Presbyterian Cemetery in Ormstown was located behind the present-day McDougall Hall at the corner of Bridge and Lambton Streets (see Lang, Ibid, 112).
88 LAC (M-1354) Rev. Roach to Rev. Burns, May 26, 1836.
89 Ibid, April 30, 1837.
90 *Lord Selkirk's Diary*, 220.
91 Sellar, Ibid, 48–50. Beechridge is now in the municipality of Ste-Clotilde.
92 Burton Lang, *Beechridge Presbyterian Cemetery, Monument Inscription List* (Howick, QC: self-published, 2002). The Beechridge Presbyterian Church was built in the 1830s.
93 However, by 1819, Highlanders in Monnoir were seeking to acquire their own land in the Eastern Townships (see Chapter 5).
94 LAC RG1 L3 ff. 67158-61. The Scots were John McRae (3), Malcolm McCuaig, Duncan MacLelland, Duncan McLennan, Samuel Morrison, Finley McCuaig, Angus MacIntosh, Neil Morrison, Duncan McCuaig, Alexander McRae, Roderick McRae, John McLennan, Murdo McGillivray, William McPherson, Duncan McRae, John Donaldson, Abraham Brown, Thomas Brown, Farquchar McLennan.
95 Sellar, Ibid, 50.
96 NAS GD 202/70/12, Dunstaffnage Papers: James & John Rankin to Ewan Cameron, Aug. 2, 1804.
97 Ibid, John Cameron to Ewan Cameron, Oct. 12, 1805.
98 Ibid.
99 *8th Annual Report, Glasgow Colonial Society*, 1835.
100 Blanchard, *L'ouest du Canada français*, 70.
101 Côte St. Henry later became identified with the name of the area's largest town— Hudson. John Thompson, *Hudson: The Early Years Up to 1867* (Hudson, QC: Hudson Historical Society, 1999) 79–95.
102 Orcadians had become the Hudson's Bay Company principal overseas workforce by the late eighteenth century (see Lucille H. Campey, *The Silver Chief: Lord Selkirk and the Scottish Pioneers of Belfast, Baldoon and Red River* (Toronto: Natural Heritage, 2003) 120–42.
103 Bouchette, *Topographical Description of Lower Canada* (1815), 100.
104 OLA Y1: James Sutherland, in Montréal, to his brother John Sutherland in South Ronaldshay, Orkney, June 29, 1814.
105 The Orcadians were Euphemia Douglas and Robert Gray. Euphemia came with her English-born husband, Stephen Clark, who had previously worked as a shepherd on the Duke of Sutherland's estate in Golspie. This information, supplied by David M. Johnson of Toronto, is gratefully acknowledged. The other setters were Paul and Catherine Cameron, from Inverness-shire; George Grieve from Croick (Ross-shire) and William Manson from Caithness.

FIVE—THE EASTERN TOWNSHIPS

1   Duncan L. McLeod, *The Milan Story* (Milan, QC: self-published, 1976) 108.
2   Contrary to their name, the Eastern Townships occupy the southwest region of Québec province. The region derived its name from being to the east of Montréal.
3   NLS Acc 9479: William Hendry to his mother in Arran, Oct. 15, 1834.
4   Robert McLellan, *The Isle of Arran* (Newton Abbot, UK: David & Charles, 1970) 163–7.
5   Eric Richards, *The Highland Clearances: People, Landlords and Rural Turmoil* (Edinburgh: Birlinn Ltd., 2000) 61.
6   See Chapter 6.
7   PRO CO 384/20 ff. 127–30: John Richardson to Sir George Murray, Sec. of State, Dec. 3, 1828.
8   Ibid.
9   There were six additional families from Hamilton (family size is in parentheses): John McLehose (9) Samuel Legget (9) James Scott (10) William Brownlee (10) Andrew Russell (7).
10 PRO CO 384/22 ff 2-9: John Richardson to George Murray, April 8, 1829.
11 Donald McKenzie McKillop, *Annals of Megantic County, Québec* (Lynn, MA: self-published, 1962) 10–2, 21–2.
12 PRO CO 384/22 ff 3-5. The official report of their arrivals records 15 heads of household: Archibald McKillop (2) William Hen[d]ry, Alexander, Robert and William Kelso, Widow Margaret McMillan, Angus Brodie, Donald and Neil McKillop, Dugald McKenzie, Neil McMillan, John McKinnon, Donald Stewart, John Cook. Two names, Robert Stewart and Peter Sillers, were missing from the list.
13 PRO CO 42/389 ff. 61-5: Sir John Colborne to George Murray, Aug. 19, 1829.
14 PRO CO 42/224 ff. 90-3: James Kempt to George Murray, July 10, 1829.
15 *QG*, June 18, *IJ*, July 31, 1829.
16 Ibid. One of the "good roads" referred to was Craig's Road which was the major approach road from Québec City.
17 Annual Report of the Immigration Agent at Quebec, PP w/e June 6, 1835.
18 Ibid.
19 Albert Gravel, *La Pousse Gaelique Écossaise dans les Cantons de l'Est: translated into English in 1974 by (Mrs. Rose) Ida MacDonald, Scotstown, Que.* (Sherbrooke, QC: self-published, 1967) 1.
20 LAC RG1 L3 ff. 66255-62.
21 PRO CO 42/224 ff. 90-3: James Kempt to George Murray, July 10, 1829.
22 McKillop, *Megantic County*, 166.
23 Ibid, 23–6.
24 Ibid, 27.
25 Ibid, 31.
26 PRO CO 384/23 ff. 573-4: John Richardson to George Murray, 1830.
27 MacDonald, *Canada, 1763–1841: Immigration and Settlement*, 327–8.
28 Margaret Bennett, *Oatmeal and the Catechism: Scottish Gaelic Settlers in Quebec* (Montreal: McGill-Queen's University Press; Edinburgh: John Donald, 1998) 12–3.
29 PRO CO 43/75 f. 26: R.W. Hay to John Richardson, July 29, 1831.
30 PRO CO 43/29 f. 29: Viscount Howick to Lord Aylmer, Nov. 2, 1832.

31 PRO CO 42/241 ff. 218-21: Lord Aylmer to Lord Goderich, Feb. 8, 1833.

32 The Gosford Road became a major north/south thoroughfare linking the Chaudière Valley with Sherbrooke.

33 Donald E. Meek, "Evangelicalism and Emigration: Aspects of the Role of Dissenting Evangelicalism in Highland Emigration to Canada" in Gordon MacLennan (ed.), *Proceedings of the First North American Congress of Celtic Studies: Held at Ottawa from 26th–30th March, 1986* (Ottawa: Chair of Celtic Studies, University of Ottawa, 1988) 23, 28. The Congregational Chapel was demolished in 1949.

34 George H. Cook, *Memorial to the Arran Clearances* (Saint John, NB: self-published, 1977) 6; Peter Aitchison and Andrew Cassell, *The Lowland Clearances: Scotland's Silent Revolution, 1760–1830* (East Linton, UK: Tuckwell Press, 2003) 108–12.

35 McKillop, *Megantic County*, 109.

36 LAC (M-1355) Rev. Clugston to Rev. Burns, Nov. 6, 1839. Rev. Clugston was based at St. John's Church in Québec City.

37 LAC (M-1355) Rev. Clugston to Rev. Burns, March 10, 1840.

38 LAC (M-1356) Rev. Clugston to Rev. Burns, June 28, 1841.

39 McKillop, *Megantic County*, 109.

40 Ibid, 167.

41 John Mathison, *Counsel for Emigrants, and Interesting Information from Numerous Sources concerning British America, the United States and New South Wales, (Third edition with a supp.)* (Aberdeen: 1838) 108–11 (letter dated June 29, 1830).

42 Annual Report of the Immigration Agent at Québec, PP w/e June 6, 1835. The group had sailed on the *Amity* of Aberdeen.

43 LAC (M-1353) Rev. John Clugston, to Rev. Burns, July 11, 1833.

44 Ibid.

45 LAC (M-1356) Rev. Clugston to Rev. Burns, June 28, 1841.

46 LAC (M-1354) Memorial of the Presbytery of Québec, Aug. 7, 1833; Binnington, "The Glasgow Colonial Society," 129.

47 LAC (M-1353) Rev. John Clugston to Rev. Burns, July 11, 1833.

48 LAC (M-1353) Rev. Duncan Macaulay to Rev. Burns, October 26, 1833.

49 For details of weavers and their libraries, see Campey, *Scottish Pioneers of Upper Canada*, 86–8, 173–5.

50 See Chapters 3 and 4.

51 PP 1831–32 (724) XXXII.

52 For details of the Rideau Valley military settlements see Campey, *Scottish Pioneers of Upper Canada*, 35–68, 80–90.

53 This settlement was named after General Sir Gordon Drummond, who was then administering the government of Upper Canada.

54 *DCB*, Vol. VII, "Frederick George Heriot," 397–403.

55 For example, see the advertisement in the *Dundee, Perth and Cupar Advertiser* for the departure of the *Pilot*, for Québec in May 1817. It described the land grants and other special benefits, which it claimed were available to people who settled in the Rideau Valley and Drummondville settlements.

56 *DPC*, May 23, 1817. For details of the provisioning of the ship see PRO CO 384/1 ff. 12–5: Robert Auld to Henry Goulburn, June 1817.

57 A.R.M. Lower, "Immigration and Settlement in Canada 1812–1820," in *Canadian Historical Review*, Vol. iii (1922) 37–47.

58 I am grateful to David M. Johnson of Toronto, for the information he supplied to me about his great-grandfather, Joseph Findlay.
59 J.C. St-Amant, *L'Avenir, Townships de Durham et de Wickham* (Arthabaskaville: Imprimerie de "L'Echo des Bois-Francs," 1896) 113. In addition to Joseph Findlay, these people included George Sutherland, Hugh Bogie, Leonard Smith, John Husk, Robert Cross, John Hughes, William Montgomery, Joseph Atkinson, C. Connor, John McManus, John Whitaker, William Mountain, Abner Mills and Jacob Harrison.
60 MacDonald, *Canada, 1763–1841: Immigration and Settlement*, 485.
61 MM P589 ff. 65–6: Diary of James Murdock.
62 Ibid, f. 280.
63 Ibid, f. 004.
64 MM P021, Brodie family papers: Andrew Glen to Hugh Brodie, Oct. 6, 1824.
65 PP w/e 21 May, SRA TCN-21(2). They had sailed on the *Favourite* of Greenock.
66 LAC RG1 L3 ff. 66355-60.
67 MacDonald, *Canada, 1763–1841: Immigration and Settlement*, 485.
68 LAC RG1 L3 ff. 66361-4. Some of the names on this list are also to be found in the Upton petition (see above).
69 Ibid.
70 Ibid.
71 Ibid.
72 See Chapter 4.
73 For an analysis of the British American Land Company's role as a settlement promoter see John Irvine Little, *Nationalism, Capitalism and Colonization in Nineteenth–Century Québec: The Upper St. Francis District* (Kingston, ON: McGill-Queen's University Press, 1989) 36–61. For information on the formation of the Canada Company, see Lee, *The Canada Company, 15–44*.
74 Martin, *History, Statistics and Geography of Upper and Lower Canada,* 345–52. The dollar was worth about 4 shillings.
75 Cowan, *British Emigration*, 132–40. Many pamphlets were published at the time. See, for example, British American land Company, *Information Respecting the Eastern Townships of Lower Canada* (London: W.J. Ruffy, 1833).
76 Ague was a malarial fever.
77 W.G. Mack, *A Letter from the Eastern Townships of Lower Canada: Containing hints to intending emigrants as to choice of situation accompanied with a map* (Glasgow: 1837) 1–20.
78 Ibid, 19.
79 A1861. Also see W.T. Easterbrook and Hugh G.J. Aitken, *Canadian Economic History* (Toronto: University of Toronto Press, 1988) 276–7.
80 J.I. Little, "From the Isle of Lewis to the Eastern Townships: The origins of a highland settlement community in Québec 1838–81" in Catherine Kerrigan (ed.), *The Immigrant Experience: Proceedings of a Conference Held at the University of Guelph, 8–11 June 1989* (Guelph, ON: University of Guelph, 1992) 32–3.
81 1841 Emigration Select Committee, Appendix No. 2, Henry P. Bruyers, Sec. British American Land Company, to the Duke of Argyll, April 13, 1839.
82 MacKenzie acquired his Highland estates by marrying the late Lord Seaforth's daughter and heir. See James Hunter, *The Making of the Crofting Community* (Edinburgh: John Donald, 1976) 43.

NOTES 255

83 Richards, *Highland Clearances*, 189–91.
84 NAS GD 46/13/197: the Lord Advocate to Stewart Mackenzie [Earl of Seaforth], Nov. 29, 1836; GD 46/9/6/26: Stewart Mackenzie to Hugh Innis Cameron, Aug. 11, 1838.
85 Initially these six townships were in Sherbrooke County. Following later boundary changes, they fell into Compton and Frontenac counties. However, the boundaries changed again and, by 1861, all six townships were in Compton County.
86 1841 Emigration Select Committee A2176, A2177.
87 L.S. Channell, *History of Compton County and Sketches of the Eastern Townships of St. Francis and Sherbrooke County* (Belleville, ON: Mika Publishing, 1975) 256–8. Nine of the first arrivals from Lewis have been identified: Donald McKay, Murdo MacLean, Donald MacDonald, John MacLeod, Malcolem MacLeod, Donald MacLeod, Donald Matheson, Angus MacLeod and John MacLeod. Also see Leodhas MacLeod, *Township of Lingwick, last of the Québec Hebridean Crofters: Galson, Fisher Hill, Red Mountain, North Hill, Victoria Road, Lingwick* (London, ON: Mac-Media Publications, 2002) 15.
88 PP w/e 29 Sept; *QM*, Sept. 24, 1838.
89 NAS GD 403/63/31: Murdo McLeod to Mrs. Tolmie of Uiginish, June 26, 1838.
90 1841 Emigration Select Committee A519, A1369.
91 PP w/e September 29, 1838.
92 PRO CO 42/258 f. 71.
93 1841 Emigration Select Committee A1370.
94 For a detailed analysis of Scottish settlement in Winslow Township, see Little, *Crofters and Habitants*, 45–75.
95 PP 1842 (301) xxxi.
96 The Parish of Barvas lost 104 of its people in 1841–42 to the Eastern Townships, "all being persons with families." Report from the Commissioners appointed for inquiring into the Administration and Practical Operation of the Poor Laws in Scotland (HMSO, 1844) ; Answers to Questions 30 to 32 in the Appendices, 426.
97 Bill Lawson, *A Register of Emigrant Families from the Western Isles of Scotland to the Eastern Townships of Quebec* (Eaton Corner, QC: Compton County Historical Museum Society, 1988). Lawson records arrival years and geographical origins of each family.
98 PP w/e Sept. 4, 1842.
99 The company was left with 85,000 acres in Bury, Lingwick and Weedon townships. With its other acreages its land holdings still totalled over half a million acres.
100 Little, "From the Isle of Lewis to the Eastern Townships," 36–8.
101 Thomas Rolph, *Emigration and Colonization: Embodying the Results of a Mission to Great Britain and Ireland during the years, 1839, 1840, 1841 and 1842* (London: 1894) 205, 229.
102 PP w/e August 6, 1842, *IJ*, Aug. 19, 1842.
103 Gould became known as "Scot's Road." Lewis emigrants also settled at North Hill, Fisher Hill and Red Mountain near Gould. Laurel Doucette (ed.), "Cultural Retention and Economic Change, Studies of the Hebridean Scots in the Eastern Townships of Quebec" in *Canadian Centre for Folk Culture Studies No. 34* (Ottawa: National Museums of Canada, 1980) 14–6.

104   Mrs. Catherine M. Day, *Pioneers of the Eastern Townships* (Montréal: John Lovell, 1869) 406.
105   Six McIver families settled in Winslow Township and seven in Lingwick Township (see Lawson, *Register of Emigrant Families, Eastern Townships*).
106   The potash and pearl ash were transported to Montréal in wagons. James Ross, became Compton County's first representative in the Québec Legislative Assembly and is credited with being the founder of Gould (see ETRC P045, Vol. III) Also see Gravel, *La Pousse Gaélique Écossaise*, 14.
107   The Gould church became the Chalmer's Presbyterian Church in 1892, which was demolished and replaced by a smaller brick church in the early 1900s. Jean-Pierre, Kesteman, *Les Écossais de langue gaélique des Cantons de l'Est: Ross, Oscar Dhu, Morrison et les autres* (Sherbrooke, QC: GGC, 2000) 19. Channell, *History of Compton County,* 258.
108   The Edinburgh Ladies Association was founded by Mrs. Isabella Gordon MacKay in 1831. See Laurie Stanley, *The Well-Watered Garden: The Presbyterian Church in Cape Breton 1798–1860* (Sydney, NS: University College of Cape Breton Press, 1983) 64–84. The Association provided funds for Rev. John Fraser, Rev. Daniel Clark and Rev. McLauchlan to visit Lingwick Township in 1846. See Little, *Crofters and Habitants,* 184–6.
109   For example, see LAC (M-1354) Rev. John Clugston, Québec, L.C., to Rev. Robert Burns, November 14, 1836.
110   The 1861 Census would show that 93 per cent of the Presbyterians in the later Compton County (containing Bury, Lingwick, Winslow, Marston, Whitton and Hampden townships) were Free Church followers.
111   Poster entitled "Emigration to Canada," March 16, 1844, issued by James Soot, 27 Cowgate, Dundee.
112   British American Land Company advertisement in the *Inverness Journal*, April 5, 1844.
113   Between 1851 and 1855 Matheson funded the emigration costs of 2,337 people. They all went to Canada and the cost to him was £10,000. Richards, *Highland Clearances*, 246.
114   For details of the number of families who emigrated from the various Lewis districts in 1851 and their funding arrangements see John Munro MacKenzie, *Diary, 1851, John Munro MacKenzie, Chamberlain of the Lews* (Inverness: Acair Ltd., 1994). The diary was published by MacKenzie's great-grandson.
115   PP 1852 (1474) xxxiii; Richards, *Highland Clearances,* 219–24.
116   T.M. Devine, *The Great Highland Famine: Hunger, Emigration and the Scottish Highlands in the Nineteenth Century* (Edinburgh: John Donald, 1988) 212–23. Little, "From the Isle of Lewis to the Eastern Townships," 41. Matheson probably took advantage of the Emigration Advances Act of 1851 which provided loans to landlords, at reasonable rates, to help them finance the relocation costs of their tenants.
117   PP 1852 (1474) xxxiii. Devine, *Highland Famine*, 219–20, 325. The *Wolfville* carried a total of 149 passengers, of whom 69 were Matheson's former tenants. Fifty-seven people are unaccounted for and presumably sailed on one or more of the ships that sailed to Québec in 1851 (see Appendix IV).
118   *IJ*, July 3, 1851.
119   Campey, *Scottish Pioneers of Upper Canada*, 147–8.

120 Little, "From the Isle of Lewis to the Eastern Townships," 41, 54.

121 In his *Register of Emigrant Families, Eastern Townships,* Bill Lawson identifies eleven Barvas families who emigrated to Lingwick: three MacKays, two MacIvers, one MacRitchie and one Murray family, arrived in the early 1840, two more MacIver families, one MacAskill family and one Mackenzie family, arrived in 1851.

122 *IA,* Sept. 1, 1851, quoted in Devine, *Highland Famine,* 220.

123 Doucette, *Studies of the Hebridean Scots,* 16.

124 Guy Lalumière et al, *Stornoway 1858–1983* (Sherbrooke, QC: Albums souvenirs québécois, 1983) 8.

125 M.C. MacLeod, *Settlement of the Lake Megantic District in the Province of Québec, Canada* (New York: self-published, 1931). Not paginated.

126 Ibid.

127 Ibid.

128 Census data recorded in Doucette, *Studies of the Hebridean Scots,* 24.

129 Lambton Road, built during the 1840s, linked the upper St. Francis district with the Chaudière Valley and Québec (see Little, *Crofters and Habitants,* 46–56).

130 Doucette, *Studies of the Hebridean Scots,* 16–21.

131 The general store was opened in 1849 by a Mr. McClintock of Bury. Kesteman, *Les Écossais de langue gaélique,* 26.

132 Gravel, *La Pousse Gaélique Écossaise,* 7. Little, *Crofters and Habitants,* 190–91. Rev. McLean was replaced by Rev. John McDonald in 1864.

133 St. James Church was located about a mile and half southeast of Stornoway on the road to Springhill (later Nantes). ETRC PC004/003/005.

134 Eighteen families who arrived at Québec in 1852 were on their way to Hamilton, Upper Canada (see PP 1852–53 (1650) lxviii). One hundred and eighteen of the emigrants who arrived at Québec in 1855 were on their way to Upper Canada (see PP 1856 (325) xxiv).

135 Doucette, *Studies of the Hebridean Scots,* 16–7.

136 Lawson, *Register of Emigrant Families, Eastern Townships,* and Little, "From the Isle of Lewis to the Eastern Townships," 41–6.

137 At least three Lewis families from Galson had settled in Lingwick and Winslow townships between 1841 and 1845. Lawson, Ibid.

138 Ibid.

139 Kesteman, *Les Écossais de langue gaélique,* 30.

140 Article entitled "The Scottish Highlands of Quebec," in *The Clansman News* of 1970, which is quoted in Bennett, *Oatmeal and the Catechism,* xi.

141 Ibid.

142 Lake Megantic had its first Presbyterian church by 1874; this was replaced in 1889 by Knox Presbyterian Church. It became a United Church in 1925.

143 This church was replaced in 1920 by Bethany Church, also built in Milan. English services were conducted here until 1980.

144 ETRC P045, Dossier Transcriptions, L2.

145 Sir John Alexander Macdonald was Prime Minister of the Dominion of Canada from 1867–73 and 1878–91. Gravel, *La Pousse Gaélique Écossaise,* 3.

146 By 1891 saw and pulp mills were also located at Milan, Springhill, Weedon, Gould, Stornoway, Bury and Lake Megantic (see ETRC P045, Vol. II).

147 NLS Acc.9460: Diary of Rev. R. Macleod, 1901.

148 Ramsay assisted his Islay tenants to emigrate to western Upper Canada in 1862–63 and visited them in their new locations in 1870. Campey, *Scottish Pioneers of Upper Canada*, 103–4.

149 Freda Ramsay, *John Ramsay of Kildalton: Being an Account of His Life in Islay and Including the Diary of His Trip to Canada in 1870* (Toronto: P. Martin Associates, 1977) 64.

150 Bill Lawson, *A Register of Emigrants from the Western Isles of Scotland, 1750–1900*, Vol. 1, Isle of Harris (Northton, Isle of Harris: self-published, 1992) 63–4.

151 Lawson, *Register of Emigrant Families, Eastern Township*, 53, 82. Like the Cape Breton Highlanders, who moved to western Upper Canada in substantial numbers during the 1850s, they were attracted by the prospect of better land (see Campey, *Scottish Pioneers of Upper Canada*, 147–8).

152 ETRC P045, Dossier Transcriptions, L.1.

153 ETRC P045, Vol. III, "Gaelic in the Home and in the Community," 15.

154 Ramsay, *John Ramsay of Kildalton*, 90.

155 For example, a further large contingent arrived from Lewis in 1923, having sailed on the *Metagama* (see *Stornoway Gazette*, May 3, 1923). With the passing of the Crofters' Holdings (Scotland) Act of 1886, clearances were now outlawed. However, the legislation failed to stem the exodus from the Highlands and Islands since it offered no solutions to the region's deep-seated economic problems.

156 Of the 150 Lewis families studied by Bill Lawson, 60 settled in Winslow and 50 in Lingwick.

157 1881 Census. See Doucette, Ibid, 24.

158 Doucette, *Hebridean Scots*, 22–24.

159 1881 Census data for Compton County (containing Bury, Lingwick, Winslow, Marston, Whitton and Hampden townships). See Doucette, Ibid, 25.

160 Sellar, *Tragedy of Quebec*, 196–205.

161 Doucette, *Hebridean Scots*, 30.

SIX—THE GASPÉ SCOTS

1 Binnington, "The Glasgow Colonial Society," 139.

2 The Mi'kmaw village at Restigouche had previously been located near to present-day Campbellton in New Brunswick. The inhabitants had been removed in 1759 to their present location in the Gaspé, possibly to bring them to a Roman Catholic region of the country. See W.F. Ganong, "Monograph of the Origins of Settlements in the Province of New Brunswick," *Transactions of the Royal Society of Canada* 2nd series (10), sections 1–2 (1904) 162.

3 See Chapter 2.

4 Tracadièche derives from the Mi'kmaw word *tracadigash*, meaning "the place where there are many herons." It was later renamed in honour of Governor General Guy Carleton.

5 Cynthia Dow, "The Gaspé Peninsula" in *Connections*, Québec Family History Society (March 1981) 6–7.

6 Some Acadians had also settled in Restigouche but they had been forced to move out during the Battle of Restigouche, which was fought in 1760. They later re-established themselves between Carleton and Bonaventure.

7   Blanchard, *L'est du Canada français*, Vol. I, 56–65.

8   G. Wynn, "A Region of Scattered Settlements and Bounded Possibilities: North eastern America, 1775–1800," *Canadian Geographer*, Vol. 31 (1987) 319–38.

9   When New Brunswick was divided from Nova Scotia in 1784, it received 15,000 Loyalists while around 19,000 Loyalists settled in peninsular Nova Scotia.

10   Phillip Buckner, and John G. Reid (eds.), *The Atlantic Region to Confederation: A History* (Toronto: University of Toronto Press, 1993) 184–209.

11   Bouchette, *British Dominions in North America*, Vol. 1, 330–1.

12   NAS GD 45/3/153: Population in Baie-des-Chaleurs c. 1825. The Mi'kmaw First Nation community at Restigouche had 269 people and Cascapédia (Maria) had a population of 112.

13   Select Committee on Lower Canada (1828): A 405, A872.

14   Lucille H. Campey, *"Fast Sailing and Copper-Bottomed": Aberdeen Sailing Ships and the Emigrant Scots They Carried to Canada, 1774–1855* (Toronto: Natural Heritage, 2002) 114–20.

15   Bouchette, *British Dominions in North America*, Vol. 1, 331.

16   Of the 2,606 people living in this area, some 1,226 were Church of Scotland worshippers.

17   Census of Lower Canada, 1831; Blanchard, *L'est du Canada français*, Vol. I, 73.

18   LAC (M-1352) John Deans to Archibald McColl, March 26, 1830.

19   Ibid.

20   The Edinburgh Christian Instructor and Colonial Religious Register (Jan. 1839) quoted in Stanley, *The Well-Watered Garden*, 175.

21   Whitelaw, *Dalhousie Journals*, Vol. 3, 72.

22   *Ibid*, 67.

23   LAC (M-1354) Rev. Sheppard to Rev. Clugston, June 6, 1835.

24   Ibid.

25   NAS GD 45/3/139: letter from James Crawford in New Richmond, Feb. 28, 1825; LAC (M-1352) John Deans to Archibald McColl, March 26, 1830. *DCB*, Robert Ferguson, Vol. VIII, 292–3.

26   See Chapter 5.

27   PRO CO 384/22 ff. 2-5: John Richardson to George Murray, April 8, 1829.

28   Ganong, "Settlements New Brunswick," 81.

29   Ibid, 76.

30   LAC (M-1355) Rev. William Fleming to Rev. Angus McMillan, Nov. 10, 1839.

31   MacDonald, *Canada, 1763–1841: Immigration and Settlement*, 482.

32   NAS GD 45/3/88.

33   Whitelaw, *Dalhousie Journals*, Vol. 3, 73.

34   NAS GD 45/3/88: Col. Cockburn's letter, Sept. 20, 1822.

35   McPherson purchased the seigneury in 1801. Crane Island is situated in the Lower St. Lawrence opposite Cap-St-Ignace. MacDonald, *Canada, 1763–1841: Immigration and Settlement*, 482.

36   He noted that both islands were connected to each other by a marsh. Bouchette, *Topographical Description Lower Canada*, 547.

37   Alice Sharples, Baldwin, *Métis: Wee Scotland of the Gaspé* (Montréal: self-published, 1960) 12–15. The *Rebecca* arrived at Québec from Greenock in early September with 17 settlers (*QM*, Sept. 13, 1818).

38   Ken Annett, "Historical Gaspé of Yesterday: The Seigneury of Métis, 1675–1854," in *SPEC, Gaspésian Newspaper*, Vol. 1, July 10, 1980, 22–5.
39   Bouchette, *Topographical Description, Lower Canada*, 254–5.
40   Having first been married to David Ross of Québec, Angelique married McNider following Ross's death.
41   For instance, Captain Charles Brand came to Métis at this time.
42   Baldwin, *Métis*, 12–5.
43   LAC (M-1355) Rev. Clugston to Rev. Burns, Aug. 16, 1839.
44   LAC MG24 H9: Diary of Mrs. John McNider, 1822, 2.
45   Ibid, 5.
46   Ibid.
47   Ibid, 4.
48   Whitelaw, *Dalhousie Journals*, Vol. 3, 161–2.
49   Ibid.
50   NAS GD 45/3/614: Notebook, Feb. 28, 1821.
51   Bouchette, *Topographical Dictionary, Lower Canada* (see entry for Métis).
52   Ibid.
53   Ibid.
54   *Transcription of Tombstones in Métis Beach United Church Cemetery* (Pointe-Claire, QC: Québec Family History Society, 1986) no. 106.
55   LAC MG24 H9, 7.
56   The bishop who visited in 1822 was probably Very Rev. Bernard-Claude Panet.
57   Baldwin, *Métis*, 36. Bishop Mountain had been instrumental in founding Lennoxville College (now a university).
58   Ibid.
59   LAC (M-1355) Rev. Clugston to Rev. Burns, Aug. 16, 1839.
60   Blanchard, *L'est du Canada français*, Vol. 1, 145.
61   Ibid, 201–2.
62   Kempt was the Québec Governor from 1828 to 1830.
63   Rev. James Cairns, their first resident Presbyterian minister, had taken up his post by 1844.
64   Baldwin, Ibid, 36.
65   Father Blanchette's 1857 report to the Bishop of Québec recorded in Baldwin, *Métis*, 27.
66   Bouchette, *The British Dominions in North America*, 327. Blanchard, Ibid, Vol. I, 202.
67   The McNiders had no children, but Angelique had three daughters from a previous marriage.
68   *DCB*, Vol. VII, 575–6. Adam Lymburner McNider became a director of the Montreal Savings Bank in 1819 and three years later became a director of the Bank of Canada.
69   Baldwin, *Métis*, 24.
70   The Grand-Métis estate was later transformed into the magnificent Métis gardens which now attract many visitors.
71   Baldwin, *Métis*, 24–7.
72   LAC (M-1355) Rev. Clugston to Rev. Burns, Aug. 16, 1839.
73   Blanchard, *L'est du Canada français*, Vol. I, 58–63.

74 Ibid, 143–5.
75 Blanchard, Ibid, Vol. II, 275–7.
76 Blanchard, Ibid, Vol. I, 144–5.
77 Ibid, 61–2.

SEVEN—THE ATLANTIC CROSSING

1 Charles R. Peterkin (1841–1932) "Some recollections, incidents and adventures in the life of a boy born in Scotland in 1841 written by himself now in his eighty-fifth year" (Toronto, 1925). This unpublished memoir is the property of Mary F. Williamson, recently retired Fine Arts Bibliographer from York University, Toronto. Charles Peterkin was Mary's great-grandfather. Her permission to use this document is gratefully acknowledged.
2 The *Berbice* had been built in 1847 and had an "AE1" insurance rating from Lloyd's of London (see *Lloyd's Shipping Register*).
3 *QM*, June 14, 1853. The *Berbice*'s dimensions were: 107'8" x 23'4" x 17'2" (see ACA CE87/11/8).
4 Elliot regularly captained William Duthie's *Brilliant* of Aberdeen from 1836 to 1845 (see Campey, *"Fast Sailing and Copper-Bottomed,"* 30–8). He had also captained the *Molson* of Dundee when she sailed to Québec from Dundee with passengers in 1832–33 (*QM*, May 16, 1832, Aug. 1, 1833).
5 Peterkin, "Some recollections in the life of a boy born in Scotland."
6 Ibid.
7 The island was on the south shore, opposite Saint-Fabien.
8 Peterkin, "Some recollections in the life of a boy born in Scotland."
9 Ibid.
10 Ibid.
11 David S. MacMillan, "Scottish Enterprise and Influences in Canada, 1620–1900," in R.A. Cage (ed.), *The Scots Abroad: Labour, Capital, Enterprise, 1750–1914* (London: Croom Helm, 1985) 46–79.
12 For instance, Alexander Allan of Saltcoats, together with his sons, founded the Allan Line. Alexander rose from humble beginnings in 1809, when he became a part owner of one sailing ship. For further details of this Clyde-based shipping company, which came to dominate shipping in the St. Lawrence, see Campey, *Scottish Pioneers of Upper Canada*, 157–68.
13 NAS CS 96/1238 f. 59: Letter Book McKnight and McIlwraith, Haberdashers, Ayr (1802–03).
14 For example the *Eagle* carried 21 people to Québec in the summer of 1802 and returned with a cargo in December (see *QG*, September 11 and *Lloyd's List*). For other examples see the *Glasgow Courier* shipping advertisements, *Québec Gazette* passenger figures and *Lloyd's List* throughout the early 1800s.
15 The *Eagle*'s dimensions were: 78'3" x 24'6" x 15'4".
16 NAS CS 96/1238 ff. 31–2: letter to Mr. James William, Kirkcudbright, January 15, 1803.
17 A pilotage service was provided by expert pilots who used their local knowledge to navigate vessels in and out of harbour.
18 NAS CS 96/1238 ff. 31–2

19   The caboose or "cab-house" was the kitchen on the deck.

20   NAS CS 96/1238 ff. 31–2

21   For details of the Oughton's crossing to Prince Edward Island, see Campey, "A Very Fine Class of Immigrants," 36–9.

22   McKnight and McIlwarith's claim that "she carries 280 tons cargo" (in NAS CS 96/1238 ff. 31–2) was disingenuous since the figure was based on an out-of-date formula for calculating tonnage. Using the standard of measurement in force from 1773 the Eagle's tonnage was closer to 179 tons, the figure recorded for the ship in Lloyd's Shipping Register, 1802.

23   NAS CS 96/1238 ff. 31–2.

24   Lloyd's Shipping Register. See Appendix V for an explanation of the Lloyd's codes.

25   NAS CS 96/1238 ff. 31-2.

26   NAS CS 96/1238, ff. 54-5: letter dated April 1, 1803.

27   Ibid.

28   NAS CS 96/1238, f. 26: letter to Messrs Heron & Hope, Liverpool, Jan. 4, 1803. Also see f. 60: letter to John McDonald & Co., June 28, 1803.

29   Arthur R.M. Lower, Great Britain's Woodyard: British America and the Timber Trade, 1763–1867 (Montreal: McGill-Queen's University Press, 1973) 50–75.

30   Archibald Buchanan, the Quebec Immigration Agent, told the 1826 Emigration Select Committee that wheat and lumber were Québec's main exports (see A1823). In that year grain represented 23% of the goods imported from Québec to Scotland. Potash represented 39% while lumber and timber accounted for most of the remainder (see NAS RH2/4: Accounts of the exports and imports of the Provinces of North America, 1800–27).

31   Edwin C. Guillet, The Great Migration: The Atlantic Crossing by Sailing Ships Since 1770 (Toronto: University of Toronto Press, 1963) 13–19.

32   See Glasgow Herald shipping advertisements and J.M. Cameron, "A Study of the factors that assisted and directed Scottish Emigration to Upper Canada 1815–55" (unpublished Ph.D. thesis, University of Glasgow, 1970) 516–7. Steerage rates for the 1830s are to be found in NAS GD 46/13/184: Information published by His Majesty's Commissioners for Emigration respecting the British colonies in North America (1832). For the 1840s, when steerage rates from the Clyde rose once again to an average of £3. 10s. (passengers supplying their own food), see Anon., Information for Emigrants to British North America (1842) 7–8.

33   For example, Donald MacCrummer, an emigration agent based in Skye, told the Colonial Office that the "kilted heroes of Waterloo" could not afford his fares at £6 or £7, but if the tonnage restrictions were reduced from 2 tons per passenger to 1 ton per passenger, he could reduce his fares to what they can afford—£4 or £5. PRO CO 42/170, f. 362.

34   The physical characteristics of a vessel greatly affected sailing performance as well as passenger comfort and safety. For an analysis of the different types of Aberdeen-registered vessels which were used to take emigrants to British North America, see Campey, "Fast Sailing and Copper-Bottomed," 80–98.

35   With the passing of the Passenger Act of 1842, the space limit was increased to the more comfortable limit of six feet.

36 There was no legal limit on the space between decks until the passing of the Passenger Act of 1828 which stipulated five-and-one-half-feet between decks. In his evidence to the 1826 Emigration Select Committee, the Quebec Immigration Agent stated that most ships involved in the Atlantic trade had been giving their passengers at least five and a half feet between decks so the legislation did not offer an improvement on previous practice (see A843).

37 McKillop, *Megantic County*, 9.

38 *QG*, Oct. 23, 1820.

39 PRO CO 384/4, f. 29: Special Meeting of the Quebec Emigration Society, Oct. 11, 1819.

40 The proceeds of the immigrant tax were divided into fourths between the Quebec Emigrant Hospital, the Montreal General Hospital, the Quebec Emigrant Society and the Montreal Emigrant Society. Cowan, *British Emigration*, 56–7, 152–3.

41 For example, Archibald MacNiven, the emigration agent who arranged Atlantic shipping for Western isle emigrants, complained that the tax would stop emigration entirely. PRO CO 217/154 ff. 877.

42 Dickinson and Young, *A Short History of Quebec*, 113–4.

43 Ouellet, *Le Bas-Canada*, 215.

44 L. Winter (a French Canadian despite his name) quoted in in Ouellet, *Le Bas-Canada*, 217–8. The wealthy were generally less vulnerable to infectious diseases since they had more privacy and ate better food.

45 Article in *La Minerve*, June 18, 1832, quoted in Ouellet, *Le Bas-Canada*, 216.

46 PP 1836 (76) XL: Report on Emigration, 1834.

47 Around 18% of the 98,649 emigrants, mainly from Ireland, who boarded ship for Québec in 1847 died before reaching their destination. André Charbonneau and André Sévigny, *1847, Grosse Île: A Record of Daily Events* (Ottawa: Parks Canada, 1997) 1–32.

48 Irish immigrants predominated from at least 1825, when official figures first became available (see N.H. Carrier and J.R. Jeffrey, *External Migration: A Study of the Available Statistics, 1815–1950* (London: H.M. Stationery Off., 1953) 95–6).

49 It was this reliance of the emigrant trade on the timber vessel that helped to justify the continuation of the preferential tariff arrangements which so favoured North American timber. PP 1835(519)XIX. Evidence of Mr. Bliss, a shipowner to the *Select Committee on Timber Duties* A 2310–11.

50 By 1836 St. Lawrence timber exports were roughly the size of New Brunswick timber exports. PP 1829 (350) XVII, 1840 (317) XLIV.

51 However, only 1,152 out of 86,598 passengers known to have travelled to Québec from Scotland between 1831 and 1855 travelled in cabins.

52 Ships making regular voyages between the same ports were also known as packets. For further details of the cabin space available on such ships see David R. MacGregor, *Merchant Sailing Ships: Supremacy of Sail, 1815–1850* (London: Conway Maritime Press, 1984) 163–70.

53 Ouellet, *Le Bas-Canada*, 218–9.

54 The government often came under pressure from the British business community to reduce the timber tariffs. It therefore monitored the effectiveness of the tariffs in stimulating increased trade with British North America to help justify its policy of favouring North America timber.

55 PP 1840 (75) XLIV: "Return of vessels cleared at the British Northern Colonies, 1836, 1837, 1838." This source records the date of clearance, tonnage and crew numbers for each vessel which sailed from ports in British North America to ports in Britain. It also records the age of each vessel, the place where it was built and its dimensions.

56 With the Upper Canada Rebellion of 1837–38, emigrant arrivals plummeted but then they increased again by the early 1840s.

57 For vessel dimensions see Table 10 and for the long service of many of the captains see the listing of individual crossings in Appendix IV.

58 For further details of Cromarty's role as an embarkation port and the agents who managed the shipping services, see Campey, *Scottish Pioneers of Upper Canada,* 160–6.

59 The *Lloyd's Shipping Register* is available as a regular series from 1775 apart from the years 1785, 1788 and 1817.

60 However, the emigrant ships, which arrived at Québec from Scotland, were not unique in being of a consistently good quality. This was a general trend for most ships used by emigrant Scots who crossed the Atlantic.

61 Still in use today and run by a Classification Society with a world-wide network of offices and administrative staff, the *Lloyd's Register* continues to provide standard classifications of quality for ship building and maintenance.

62 The number of years that a ship could hold the highest code varied according to where it was built. In time rivalries developed between shipowners and underwriters and this led to the publication of two Registers between 1800 and 1833—the Ship Owners' Register (Red Book) and the Underwriters Register (Green Book). Their coverage was similar but not identical. By 1834 with bankruptcies facing both sides, the two Registers joined forces to become the *Lloyd's Register of British and Foreign Shipping.*

63 To locate a ship's code from the *Register* it is usually necessary to have the vessel name, the tonnage and/or captain's name   ı data is not always available and is highly problematic to locate. Some vessels may not have been offered for inspection, particularly in cases where a shipowner could rely on his personal contacts for business. The lack of a survey might arouse our suspicions but is not necessarily conclusive proof of a poor quality ship.

64 A—first class condition, kept in the highest state of repair and efficiency and within a prescribed age limit at the time of sailing; AE—"the second description of the first class," fit, no defects but may be over a prescribed age limit; E—second class, although unfit for carrying dry cargoes were suitable for long distance sea voyages; I—third class, only suitable for short voyages (i.e. not out of Europe). These letters were followed by the number 1 or 2 which signified the condition of the vessel's equipment (anchors, cables and stores). Where satisfactory, the number 1 was used, and where not, 2 was used. George Blake, *Lloyd's Register of Shipping 1760–1960* (London: Lloyd's, 1960) 12–13, 26–27.

65 Bennett, *Oatmeal and the Catechism*, 10.

EIGHT—QUÉBEC'S SCOTTISH HERITAGE

1 Bill Young quoted in Bennett, *Oatmeal and the Catechism*, 290–91.

2 Bennett, Ibid, 295–6.

3 Through his epic poem, *Donald Morrison, The Canadian Outlaw: A Tale of the Scottish Pioneers,* first published in 1892 when Morrison was in jail, Angus MacKay (Oscar Dhu) helped to win public support for Morrison. John Irvine Little, "The Bard in a Community in Transition & Decline: Oscar Dhu & the Hebridean Scots in the Upper St. Francis District" in Donald H. Akenson (ed.), *Canadian Papers in Rural History*, Vol. X (Gananoque, ON: Langdale Press, 1995) 46–7.

4 Bennett, *Oatmeal and the Catechism*, 297–8.

5 LAC MG23-GII9: Hugh Finlay fonds. Finlay's survey in 1787 of the postal route between Québec and Halifax gives details of land fertility and recommended sites for settlements.

6 *Lord Selkirk's Diary*, 220.

7 Pierre Berton, *The National Dream: The Great Railway, 1871–1881* (Toronto: McClelland & Stewart, 1971) 319.

8 Unlike the Irish influx, which was extremely large during the period from 1820 to 1870, the Scottish influx was a much smaller and more sustained migration dating back to the 1760s.

9 J.M. Bumsted, *The Scots in Canada*, Canada's Ethnic Group Booklet No. 1 (Ottawa: Canadian Historical Association, 1982) 17.

10 *DCB*, Simon McTavish, Vol. V, 560–7. John Cooper, *James McGill of Montréal: Citizen of the Atlantic World* (Ottawa: Borealis Press, 2003) xiii–xv, 159–69.

11 NAS GD 1/151: Letters of James Dunlop, 1773–1815. *DCB* James Dunlop, Vol. V, 284–7. MacMillan, "Scottish Enterprise and Influences in Canada, 1620–1900," in R.A. Cage *The Scots Abroad*, 46–79.

12 Richard Feltoe, *A Gentleman of Substance: The Life and Legacy of John Redpath (1796–1869)* (Toronto: Natural Heritage, 2004) 99–115. John Redpath's son, Peter, who took over the refinery, made substantial endowments to McGill University.

13 Sir William C. Macdonald was the grandson of Captain John MacDonald of Glenaladale, who, in 1772, founded the Scotchfort colony in Prince Edward Island. Its first settlers were Roman Catholic Highlanders who mainly originated from west Inverness-shire and the Western Isles.

14 Peter McGill was actually Peter McCutcheon. He changed his name to McGill in 1821 two years after he inherited an estate from his uncle, John McGill of York. Having been an officer with the Loyalists forces during the American Rebellion, John McGill moved to Upper Canada and took up a number of public appointments. When his wife died childless in 1819, he bequeathed a substantial estate to his nephew Peter McCutcheon, on the condition that he changed his name to McGill. Although McCutcheon changed his name soon afterwards, he did not inherit the bulk of the estate until his uncle's death in 1834. Peter McGill's career prospered and in later life he became chairman of the St. Lawrence and Champlain Railway, the first railway company in Canada.

15 Berton, *The National Dream*, 66.

16   Gerald J.J. Tulchinsky, *The River Barons: Montreal Businessmen and the Growth of Industry and Transportation, 1837–53* (Toronto/Buffalo: University of Toronto Press, 1977) 19–22. Also see Heather McNabb, "Montréal's Scottish Community, 1835–1865," Concordia University, Montreal, unpublished MA, 1999) 11–67.

17   John Bell also built the 291-ton *Betsey* of Dundee in 1828, which carried emigrants from Leith to Québec in 1833. It had a height between decks of just over six feet. (NAS CE/57/11: Register of Ships, Leith).

18   NLS MS7198 ff 71-2: John Bell to his brother-in-law James Greig in Kirkcaldy, June 2, 1832.

19   LAC MG25 G321: Porteous family collection, File 2.

20   *DCB*, John Mure, Vol. VI, 531–4.

21   AU MS 2814: Thomas Reid papers. See especially 2814/3/1/8, 2814/2/3/59, 2814/3/2/14.

22   Arthur Richard Preston (ed.), *For Friends at Home: A Scottish Emigrant's Letters from Canada, California and the Cariboo, 1844–64* (Montreal: McGill-Queen's University Press, 1974) 63.

23   Ibid, 45, 52, 66.

24   MM P021, Brodie family papers: Obituary in the *Montreal Witness* (Hugh Brodie died in 1852). Brodie worked initially as a farm manager for John Lilly in Chambly and later acquired 200 acres of his own land at Côte-St.-Pierre near the City of Montréal.

25   Ibid, Archibald Cameron to Hugh Brodie, April 22, 1816.

26   Ibid, obituary in the *Montreal Witness.*

27   LAC MG24 I3: McGillivray of Glengarry family papers. See Vol. 4 for the list of "Subscribers for life." Also see *DCB* Vol. VI, 454–7.

28   Thanks largely to efforts of the Highland Society of London, the wearing of the kilt, which had been banned following the Jacobite uprising of 1745–46, became the accepted national dress of Scotland.

29   LAC MG24 I3: McGillivary of Glengarry family papers, Vol. 6: Report of the inaugural meeting held November 10, 1818.

30   Although Montréal's fur traders were mainly Scottish they conducted their business through London, not Scotland.

31   LAC MG24 I3 Vol. 6, 3, 15

32   *Prince Edward Island Register*, Nov. 29, 1825.

33   *IJ*, September 9, 1825.

34   The Montréal Caledonian Society, founded in 1855, sponsored the first ever Highland Games which were held that year. The games were revived in the late 1970s and are now held annually, attracting forty to fifty pipe bands. For further details of the Caledonian Society, see Gerald Redmond, *The Sporting Scots of Nineteenth Century Canada* (London and Toronto: Associated University Presses, 1982) 162.

35   Ted Cowan, "The Myth of Scotch Canada," in Marjory Harper and Michael E. Vance (eds.), *Myth, Migration and the Making of Memory: Scotia and Nova Scotia, c. 1700–1990* (Halifax, NS: Published for the Gorsewood Research Institute for Atlantic Canada Studies by Fernwood Publishing & John Donald Publishers, 1999) 49–72.

36   Bill Young's reminiscences in Bennett, *Oatmeal and the Catechism*, 16–7.

37   Bennett, Ibid, 267.

38 Ibid.

39 McKillop, *Megantic County*, 31.

40 The poem was written in 1894. Little, "The Bard in a Community in Transition" 45–80.

41 This verse was included in the collection of poems in Angus MacKay's *By Trench and Trail in Song and Story* (Seattle & Vancouver: MacKay Printing and Publishing Co., 1918) 116–9.

42 Bennett, *Oatmeal and the Catechism*, 153.

43 Reminiscences of John L. Mullowney, who lived in Springhill from the 1880s, quoted in Bennett, *Oatmeal and the Catechism*, 145–6.

44 Ibid, 83.

45 Redmond, *The Sporting Scots*, 106–7.

46 *Montréal Star,* Jan. 1934, quoted in Redmond, Ibid, 108.

47 Ibid, 112.

48 Shinty is a Gaelic word. Originating in pre-Christian times, it is western Europe's oldest team game. Played with a ball and stick, it continues to be played today, as an amateur sport, mainly in the Highlands. For the connection between shinty and ice hockey, see Redmond, Ibid, 265–8.

49 Ibid, 265. Also see Henry Roxborough, *One Hundred Not Out: Story of Nineteenth-Century Canadian Sport* (Toronto: Ryerson Press, 1966) 164.

50 Ibid, 266.

Bibliography

A. Primary Sources (Manuscript)

Aberdeen City Archives (ACA)
CE 87/11: Aberdeen Shipping Registers

Aberdeen University (AU)
AU MS 2814: Thomas Reid Papers

Bibliothèque et Archives nationales du Québec (BAnQ)
Ministère des terres et forêts du Québec, Maps 21L (Quebec), 31G (Hull), 31H (Montréal)

Dundee City Archives (DCA)
CE 70/11: Register of Ships
D3113: Dundee and District Shipping Local Collection
Poster entitled "Emigration to Canada," 16 March, 1844, issued by James Soot of Dundee

Eastern Townships Resource Centre (ETRC)
P004/003/005: St. John's Church Winslow
P045: Celtic Research Group fonds—dossier transcriptions, 1982–85

Library and Archives Canada (LAC)
M-1352, M-1353, M-1354, M-1355: Glasgow Colonial Society Correspondence, 1829–43 (microfilm reels)
MG23 GII9: Hugh Finlay fonds, 1787
MG23 GIII23: John & Thomas Nairne fonds, 1762–1802
MG23 J5: John Hay fonds, 1788
MG23 K1: Malcolm Fraser & family fonds, 1768–70, 1773–84
MG24 I183 (H-1099): Archibald McMillan's letter book, 1802–32
MG 24 H9: Diary of Mrs. John McNider, 1822
MG24 I178: Daniel Drummond fonds

MG24 I183 ff. 2, 7–9, 11: Passenger lists, *Helen* of Irvine, *Jean* of Irvine and *Friends of John Saltcoats*, 1802
MG24 I3: McGillivray of Glengarry family papers Vol. 4, Highland Society Papers
MG25 G276: McQuat & Bisland family papers, 1818
MG25 G321: Porteous family collection, 1830
MG29 C3: Reminiscences of a Scottish Settler, Lakefield, Argenteuil County
MG55/24#368: Thomas Brown to his brother William, 1850
RG1 L1 ff.46, 58-60 (C-96): Archibald McMillan's lists of settlers, 1806
RG1 L3 ff.66477-9 (C-2545): Archibald McMillan's petition for land, 1804
RG1 L3 ff.66558-67 (C-2545): Distribution of holdings in Templeton Township, 1804
RG1 L3 ff.66605-10, 66691-2 (C-2545): Archibald McMillan's settler list, 1806
RG1 L3 ff.67158-61 (C-2545): Highlander petition from Monnoir, 1804
RG1 L3 ff.66361-4 (C-2545): Highlander petition for land in Dudswell and Bury townships, 1819
RG1 L3 ff. 66255-62 (C-2545): Petition of Scottish emigrants for land in Leeds Township, 1811
RG1 L3 (C-2545): Highland families claiming land in Upton Township, 1819
RG1 L3 ff.66475-6 (C-2545): Alexander McMillan's petition for land in Lochaber and Petite Nation, 1823
RG1 L3 LCLP Vol.1 ff.64296-7 (C-2543): Skye petitioners, 1818
RG5 A1 ff.44934-5 (C-6863): Petition of John Corbet, 1827

McCord Museum (MM)
P021: Brodie family papers
P110: Walker family papers
P309: Letter-book of John Schank
P589: Diary of James Murdoch

National Archives of Scotland (NAS)
CE 57/11: Register of Ships, Leith
CS 96/106-118: J. & A. Todd business papers, 1809–20
CS 96/1238: Letter Book McKnight and McIlwraith, Haberdashers, Ayr (1802–03)
CS 96/1534-1538: John McDonald & Co., 1799–1804
CS 96/2581-9, 2624-44: Alexander & John Burnside; Burnside & Waddell business papers, 1759–1833
CS 96/431: Sederunt books, Messrs Tod & Glass, 1811–15
E.504: Customs records, collectors quarterly accounts, 1776–1830:
    /1 Aberdeen, /2 Alloa, /5 Banff, /7 Thurso, /9 Dumfries, /11 Dundee,
    /12 Fort William, /15 Greenock, /17 Inverness, /22 Leith, /25 Oban,
    /27 Perth, /33 Stornoway, /35 Tobermory.
GD 1/92: Letters of James Aitchison, 1834–38
GD 1/151: Letters of James Dunlop, 1773–1815
GD 45: Dalhousie papers.
GD 46: Seaforth muniments
GD 46/13/184: Information published by His Majesty's Commissioners for Emigration respecting the British Colonies in North America (London, Feb. 1832)

GD 110/1215: Printed maps, Upper and Lower Canada, 1835–36
GD 202: Campbell of Dunstaffinage papers
GD 403: Mackenzie papers
RH2/4: Accounts of the exports and imports of the Provinces of North America, 1800–27
RH 4/188/2: Prize essays and Transactions of the Highland Society of Scotland, Vol.
    III, 1802–03
RHP 35156/1-2: Plans of Upper and Lower Canada, 1838–39

National Library of Scotland (NLS)
Acc. 7290: Letter from Mrs. Wilhelmina Black to Mrs. Richardson in Wigtownshire,
    1838
Acc. 9460: Diary of Reverend D. McLeod, 1901
Acc. 9479: William Hendry to his mother in Arran, 1834
Adv MS 35.6.18: Melville Papers, State of Emigration from the Highlands of Scotland,
    its extent, causes and proposed remedy, London, March 21, 1803
Adv MS 46: Murray papers, 1828–30 maps
GD 46/13/184: *Information published by His Majesty's Commissioners for Emigration
    respecting the British Colonies in North America* (London, Feb. 1832)
MS 3431 f. 180 (Lee Papers): "Observations or remarks upon land and islands which
    compose the barony called Harris"
MS 3952: Robertson-MacDonald papers
MS 7198: John Bell's letters to his brother-in-law James Greig in Kirkaldy, Fife, 1830–32
MS 9646: "On Emigration from the Scottish Highlands and Islands attributed to
    Edward S. Fraser of Inverness-shire (1801–04)"
MS 10787: Letter book of John Davidson of Stewartfield, 1774

Orkney Library and Archives (OLA)
Y1: Letter from James Sutherland, in Montréal, to his brother John Sutherland in South
    Ronaldshay, Orkney, June 29, 1814

Public Record Office (PRO)
CO 42: Correspondence, Canada
CO 43: Entry Books, Canada
CO 217: Nova Scotia and Cape Breton Original Correspondence
CO 226: Prince Edward Island Correspondence
CO 384: Colonial Office Papers on emigration containing original correspondence con-
    cerning North American settlers
CO 385: Colonial Office Papers on emigration, Entry Books of correspondence

Strathclyde Regional Archives (SRA)
CE 59/11: Register of Ships, Glasgow
CE 60/11: Register of Ships, Greenock
T/CN 21: Report Books, Glasgow
T/CN 26: Clyde Bills of Entry

Private Collections
Clan Donald Centre, Skye, "Ships to Megantic County"
Peterkin, Charles R., (1841–1932) "Some recollections, incidents and adventures in the life of a boy born in Scotland in 1841 written by himself now in his eighty-fifth year" (Toronto, 1925)

B. Printed Primary Sources and Contemporary Publications

Anon, "An important letter of a resident of Quebec as to the disabilities of protestants in the province of Quebec: the parish system" (Toronto: Equal Rights Association for the Province of Ontario, 1890).
Anon., *Information for Emigrants to British North America* (1842).
Bouchette, Joseph, *A Topographical Description of the Province of Lower Canada, with remarks upon Upper Canada* (London: W. Faden, 1815).
_____, *A Topographical Dictionary of the Province of Lower Canada* (London: Longman & Co, 1832).
_____, *The British Dominions in North America: A Topographical and Statistical Description of the Provinces of Lower and Upper Canada, New Brunswick, Nova Scotia, the Islands of Newfoundland, Prince Edward Island and Cape Breton,* Vols. I, II (London: 1832).
British American Land Company, *Information respecting the Eastern Townships of Lower Canada* (London: W.J. Ruffy, 1833).
Brown, Robert, *Strictures and Remarks on the Earl of Selkirk's observations on the present state of the Highlands* (Edinburgh: Abemethy & Walker, 1806).
Cavendish, Henry, Sir, *Government of Canada Debates of the House of Commons in 1774 on the Bill for making more effective provision for the government of the province of Quebec* (London: Ridgeway, 1839).
Census of Lower Canada, 1831, 1861, 1881.
Day, Mrs. Catherine M., *Pioneers of the Eastern Townships* (Montréal: John Lovell, 1869).
Du Berger, C.C., *Murray Bay Atlas and Maps of its Environs* (Murray Bay, QC: Arthur Cimon & Co., 1895).
Fowler, Thomas, *Journal of a Tour through British North America to the Falls of Niagara containing an account of the cities, towns and villages along the route in 1831* (Aberdeen: 1832).
Glasgow Colonial Society, *Seventh Annual Report of the Glasgow Colonial Society for promoting the religious interests of the Scottish settlers in British North America* (Glasgow: 1833).
Glasgow Colonial Society, *Eighth Annual Report of the Glasgow Colonial Society for promoting the religious interests of the Scottish settlers in British North America* (Glasgow: 1835).
Gourlay, John L., *History of the Ottawa Valley* (Ottawa, ON: 1896).
Head, Sir Francis Bond, *The Emigrant* (London: John Murray, 1846).
Kingdom, William, *America and the British Colonies* (London: 1820).
Lloyd's Shipping Register 1775–1855.
Lovell J. and Son, *Gazetteer of British North America containing the latest and most authentic descriptions of over 8,900 cities, towns, villages and places in the provinces of Ontario, Quebec, Nova Scotia, New Brunswick, Prince Edward Island, Manitoba, British Columbia, North West Territories and Newfoundland* (Montréal: 1895).

Mack, W.G., *A letter from the Eastern Townships of Lower Canada, containing hints to intending emigrants as to choice of situation accompanied with a map* (Glasgow: Robertson, 1837).

Lovell's Gazetteer of British North America (Montréal: John Lovell, 1873).

Mackay, Angus (Oscar Dhu), *By Trench and Trail in Song and Story* (Seattle & Vancouver: Mackay Printing & Publishing Co., 1918).

MacTaggart, John, *Three Years in Canada: An account of the actual state of the country in 1826–7–8 comprehending its resources, productions, improvements and capabilities and including sketches of the state of society, advice to emigrants, etc.* Two Volumes (London: 1829).

Martin, Robert Montgomery, *History, Statistics and Geography of Upper and Lower Canada* (London: 1838).

Mathison, John, *Counsel for emigrants and interesting information from numerous sources & original letters from Canada and the United States* (Aberdeen: 1834).

Mathison, John, *Counsel for emigrants, and interesting information from numerous sources concerning British America, the United States & New South Wales (Third edition with a supp.)* (Aberdeen: 1838).

Morgan, Lieutenant J.C., *The Emigrants Notebook and Guide with Recollections of Upper and Lower Canada during the Late War* (London: 1824).

Oliver, Andrew, [late of Montréal] *A View of Lower Canada interspersed with Canadian tales and anecdotes and interesting information to intending emigrants* (Edinburgh: Menzies, 1821).

Rattray, William J., *The Scot in British North America*, 4 vols. (Toronto: 1880–83).

Rolph, Thomas, *Emigration and Colonization: Embodying the Results of a Mission to Great Britain and Ireland during the years, 1839, 1840, 1841 and 1842* (London: 1894).

Smith, W.H., *Smith's Canadian Gazetteer: Statistical and general information respecting all parts of the Upper Province or Canada West* (Toronto: 1846).

St. Amant, J.C., *L'Avenir, Townships de Durham et de Wickham* (Arthabaskaville: Imprimerie de "L'Echo des Bois-Francs," 1896).

St. Andrew's Society of Montréal, *44th Annual Report Nov. 1878–Nov. 1879* (Montréal: St. Andrew's Society, 1880).

Sellar, Robert, *History of the County of Huntingdon & of the Seigneuries of Chateauguay and Beauharnois from their first settlement to the year 1838* (Huntingdon, QC: Canadian Gleaner, 1888).

Sellar, Robert, *Hemlock: A Tale of the War of 1812* (Montréal: F.E. Grafton, 1890).

Sinclair, Sir John, *First Statistical Account of Scotland,* 21 vols. (Edinburgh: 1791–99).

Stewart, Charles James, *A short view of the present state of the eastern townships in the province of Lower Canada* (Montréal: Mower, 1815).

Thomas, C, *History of the counties of Argenteuil, Quebec and Prescott, Ontario, from the earliest settlement to the present* (Montréal: John Lovell, 1896).

Telford, Thomas, *A Survey and Report of the Coasts and Central Highlands of Scotland* (London: 1803).

C. Parliamentary Papers

Annual Reports of the Immigration Agent at Quebec (1831–55)
Colonial Land and Emigration Commissioners, Annual Reports (1841–55)
Emigration Returns for British North America 1830–40
Report from the Commissioners appointed for inquiring into the Administration and Practical Operation of the Poor Laws in Scotland, 1844; Answers to Questions 30–32 in the Appendices
Report from the Select Committee appointed to enquire into the condition of the population of the Highlands and Islands of Scotland, and into the practicability of affording the People relief by means of Emigration, 1841, VI
Reports from the Select Committee appointed to inquire into the expediency of encouraging emigration from the United Kingdom, 1826, IV; 1826–27, V
Report from the Select Committee on Timber Duties, 1835, XIX

D. Contemporary Newspapers

Aberdeen Herald
Aberdeen Journal
Dumfries and Galloway Courier
Dundee Courier
Dundee Perth and Cupar Advertiser
Dumfries Times
Dumfries Weekly Journal
Edinburgh Advertiser
Elgin Courant
Glasgow Chronicle
Glasgow Courier
Glasgow Herald
Greenock Advertiser
Inverness Advertiser

Inverness Courier
Inverness Journal
John O'Groat Journal
Kelso Mail
La Minerve
Montreal Gazette
Montréal Telegraph
Perthshire Courier and General Advertiser
Prince Edward Island Register
Quebec Gazette
Quebec Mercury
Scots Magazine
Scotsman
Stornoway Gazette

E. Contemporary Material of Later Printing

Anon., *Illustrated Atlas of the Eastern Townships and south western Quebec* (Owen Sound, ON: Richardson, Bond & Wright, 1972 [original printed in 1881]).
Cameron, Viola Root, *Emigrants from Scotland to America 1774–1775: Compiled from a loose bundle of Treasury Papers in the Public Record Office, London England* (Baltimore: Genealogical Publishing Co., 1965).
Douglas, Thomas, Fifth Earl of Selkirk, *Observations on the Present State of the Highlands of Scotland, with a view of the causes and probable consequences of emigration,* 1805, in Bumsted, J.M. (ed.), *The Collected Writings of Lord Selkirk,* Vol. I (Winnipeg: The Manitoba Record Society, 1984).
McDougall, Elizabeth Ann Kerr and John S. Moir (eds.), *Selected Correspondence of the Glasgow Colonial Society 1825–1840* (Toronto: Champlain Society, 1994).
MacDougall, Robert, *The Emigrant's Guide to North America,* edited by Elizabeth Thompson (Toronto: Natural Heritage, 1998) (first published 1841).

MacKenzie, George A., *From Aberdeen to Ottawa in 1845: The Diary of Alexander Muir* (Aberdeen: Aberdeen University Press, 1990).

MacKenzie, John Munro, *Diary, 1851, John Munro MacKenzie, Chamberlain of the Lews* (Inverness: Acair Ltd., 1994).

Preston, Arthur Richard (ed.), *For Friends at Home: A Scottish Emigrant's Letters from Canada, California and the Cariboo 1844–64* (Montreal: McGill-Queen's University Press, 1974).

Reid, Richard (ed.), *The Upper Ottawa Valley to 1855: A collection of documents edited with an introduction by Richard Reid* (Toronto: Champlain Society, 1990).

White, Patrick Cecil Telford, (ed.) *Lord Selkirk's Diary 1803–04: A Journal of his Travels through British North America and the Northeastern United States* (Toronto: The Champlain Society, 1958).

Whitelaw, Marjorie, (ed.) *The Dalhousie Journals* Vols. 1-3 (Ottawa: Oberon 1978–82).

F. Secondary Sources

Adam, Margaret I., "The Highland Emigration of 1770," *Scottish Historical Review*, Vol. XVI, 1919.

Adams, Ian and Somerville, Meredyth, *Cargoes of Despair and Hope: Scottish Emigration to North America, 1603–1803* (Edinburgh: John Donald, 1993).

Aitchison, Peter and Andrew Cassell, *The Lowland Clearances: Scotland's Silent Revolution, 1760–1830* (East Linton, UK: Tuckwell Press, 2003).

Allen, Robert S., *The Loyal Americans: The Military Role of the Loyalist Provincial Corps and their Settlement in British North America, 1775–1784* (Ottawa: National Museum of Canada, 1983).

Annett, Ken, "Historical Gaspé of Yesterday: The Seigneury of Métis, 1675–1854" in *SPEC, Gaspésian Newspaper*, Vol. 1, July 10, 1980, 22–5.

Appleton, Thomas E., *Ravenscrag: The Allan Royal Mail Line* (Toronto: McClelland & Stewart, 1974).

Archambault, Lison, *Inverness Quebec/Canada* (translated by Richard Stephani) (Inverness, QC: Corporation touristique d'Inverness, 1987).

Baldwin, Alice Sharples, *Métis: Wee Scotland of the Gaspé* (Montréal: self-published, 1960).

Barrett, Clark, "The Glengarry Indian Lands," in *Ontario Genealogical Society Bulletin*, Vol. 8, 1969.

Beaulieu, Carl, *L'Alliance Écossaise au Québec* (Chicoutimi, QC: Éditions de patrimoine, 2001).

Bennett, Margaret, *Oatmeal and the Catechism: Scottish Gaelic Settlers in Quebec* (Montreal: McGill-Queen's University Press; Edinburgh: John Donald, 1998).

Berton, Pierre, *The Invasion of Canada, 1812–1813* (Toronto: McClelland & Stewart, 1980).

_____, *The National Dream: The Great Railway, 1871–1881* (Toronto: McClelland & Stewart, 1971).

Binnington, Reverend R.F., "The Glasgow Colonial Society and its Work in the Development of the Presbyterian Church in British North America 1825–1840" (unpublished Th.D. thesis, University of Toronto, 1960).

Blake, George, *Lloyd's Register of Shipping, 1760–1960* (London: Lloyd's, 1960).

Blanchard, Raoul, *L'est du Canada français, "province de Québec"* (Series: Publications de l'Institut scientifique franco-canadien) (Paris: Masson & Cie, 1935).

_____, *L'ouest du Canada français: "Montréal et sa region"* (Series: Publications de l'Institut scientifique franco-canadien) (Montréal: Beauchemin, 1953).

_____, "Les Pays de l'Ottawa," in *Étude Canadienne troisième séries*, Vol. 3 (Grenoble, France: Allier, 1949).

Bolger, F.W.P. (ed.) *Canada's Smallest Province: A History of P.E.I.* (Charlottetown: Prince Edward Island 1973 Centennial Commission, 1973; reprinted, Halifax: Nimbus, 1991).

Brander, Michael, *The Scottish Highlanders and their Regiments* (Haddington: The Gleneil Press, 1996).

Brock, William R., *Scotus Americanus: A Survey of the Sources for Links Between Scotland and America in the Eighteenth Century* (Edinburgh: Edinburgh University Press, 1982).

Buckner, Philip *English Canada, the Founding Generations: British Migration to British North America, 1815–1865*, Canada House Lecture Series 0265–4253, No. 54 (London: Canadian High Commission, Canada House, 1993).

Buckner, Phillip and John G. Reid (eds.), *The Atlantic Region to Confederation: A History* (Toronto: University of Toronto Press, 1993).

Bumsted, J.M., *Interpreting Canda's Past*, Vol. I (Toronto: Oxford University Press Canada, 1993).

_____, *The Peoples of Canada: A Pre-Confederation History*, Vol. I (Toronto: Oxford University Press, 1992).

_____, *The People's Clearance: Highland Emigration to British North America, 1770–1815* (Edinburgh: Edinburgh University Press, 1982).

_____, *The Scots in Canada*, Canada's Ethnic Group Booklet No. 1 (Ottawa: Canadian Historical Association, 1982).

Cage, R.A. (ed.) *The Scots Abroad: Labour, Capital, Enterprise, 1750–1914* (London: Croom Helm, 1985).

Caldwell, Gary and Eric Waddell, *The English of Quebec: From Majority to Minority Status* aQuébec: Institut québécois de recherche sur la culture, 1982).

Calvin, Delano Dexter, *A Saga of the St. Lawrence: Timber and Shipping Through Three Generations* (Toronto: Ryerson Press, 1945).

Cameron, J.M., "A Study of the Factors That Assisted and Directed Scottish Emigration to Upper Canada 1815–1855" (unpublished Ph.D. thesis, University of Glasgow, 1970).

Campbell, R.H., *Scotland Since 1707: The Rise of an Industrial Society* (Edinburgh: Donald, 1985).

Campbell, Wilfrid, *The Scotsman in Canada*, Vols. I & II (London: Sampson Low & Co., 1911).

Campey, Lucille H., *"A Very Fine Class of Immigrants": Prince Edward Island's Scottish Pioneers, 1770–1850* (Toronto: Natural Heritage, 2001).

_____, *After the Hector: The Scottish Pioneers of Nova Scotia and Cape Breton, 1773–1852* (Toronto: Natural Heritage, 2004).

_____, *"Fast Sailing and Copper-Bottomed": Aberdeen Sailing Ships and the Emigrant Scots They Carried to Canada, 1774–1855* (Toronto: Natural Heritage, 2002).

_____, *The Scottish Pioneers of Upper Canada, 1784–1855: Glengarry and Beyond* (Toronto: Natural Heritage, 2005).

_____, *The Silver Chief: Lord Selkirk and the Scottish Pioneers of Belfast, Baldoon and Red River* (Toronto: Natural Heritage, 2003).

Carrier, N.H., and J.R. Jeffrey, *External Migration: A Study of the Available Statistics, 1815–1950* (London: H.M. Stationery Off., 1953).

Channell, L.S., *History of Compton County and Sketches of the Eastern Townships of St. Francis and Sherbrooke County* (Belleville, ON: Mika Publishing, 1975).

Charbonneau, André and André Sévigny, *1847, Grosse Île: A Record of Daily Events* (Ottawa: Parks Canada, 1997).

Cook, George H., *Memorial to the Arran Clearances* (Saint John, NB: self-published, 1977).

Cooper, John, *James McGill of Montréal: Citizen of the Atlantic World* (Ottawa: Borealis Press, 2003).

Cowan, Helen, *British Emigration to British North America: The First Hundred Years* (Toronto: University of Toronto Press, 1961).

Cowan, Ted, "The Myth of Scotch Canada," in Marjory Harper and Michael E. Vance (eds.), *Myth, Migration and the Making of Memory: Scotia and Nova Scotia, c. 1700–1990* (Halifax, NS: Published for the Gorsewood Research Institute for Atlantic Canada Studies by Fernwood Publishing & John Donald Publishers, 1999) 49–72.

Craig, Gerald M., *Upper Canada: The Formative Years, 1784–1841* (Toronto: McClelland & Stewart, 1993 (originally published 1963).

Creighton, D.G., *The Commercial Empire of the Saint Lawrence, 1760–1850* (Toronto: The Ryerson Press, 1937).

Davis, Ralph, *The Industrial Revolution and British Overseas Trade* (Leicester: Leicester University Press, 1979).

Des Gagniers, Jean, *Charlevoix, Pays Enchanté* (Sainte-Foy, QC: Presses de l'Université Laval, 1994).

Devine, T.M., and Rosalind Mitchison (eds.), *People and Society in Scotland, 1760–1830*, Vol. I (Edinburgh: John Donald, 1988).

Devine, T.M., "Highland Migration to Lowland Scotland 1760–1860," in *Scottish Historical Review*, Vol. LXII, 1983.

_____ (ed.), *Scottish Emigration and Scottish Society* (Edinburgh: John Donald, 1992).

_____, "Temporary Migration and the Scottish Highlands in the Nineteenth Century," in *Economic History Review*, Vol. 32 (1979).

_____, *The Great Highland Famine: Hunger, Emigration and the Scottish Highlands in the Nineteenth Century* (Edinburgh: John Donald, 1988).

_____, *The Scottish Nation, 1700–2000* (London: Allen Lane, 1999).

Dickinson, John A. and Brian Young, *A Short History of Quebec*, 2nd edition (Montreal: McGill-Queen's University Press, 2000).

Dictionary of Canadian Biography, Vols. V–XIII (Toronto: University of Toronto Press, 1979–85).

Donaldson, Gordon, *The Scots Overseas* (London: Robert Hale, 1966).

Doucette Laurel (ed.), "Cultural Retention and Economic Change: Studies of the Hebridean Scots in the Eastern Townships of Quebec" in *Canadian Centre for Folk Culture Studies*, No. 34 (Ottawa: National Museums of Canada, 1980).

Dow, Cynthia, "The Gaspé Peninsula" in *Connections,* Quebec Family History Society, March 1981.

Duncan, K.J., "Patterns of Settlement in the East" in Stanford W. Reid (ed.), *The Scottish Tradition in Canada* (Toronto: McClelland & Stewart, 1976) 49–75.

Easterbrook, W.T. and Hugh G.J. Aitken, *Canadian Economic History* (Toronto: University of Toronto Press, 1988).

Elliott, Bruce S., *Irish Migrants in the Canadas: A New Approach* (Kingston, ON: McGill-Queen's University Press, 1988).

Emmerson, George S., "The Gaelic Tradition in Gaelic Culture," in Stanford W. Reid (ed.), *The Scottish Tradition in Canada* (Toronto: McClelland & Stewart, 1976) 232–47.

Epstein, Clarence, "Early Protestant Church Architecture in Montréal" in *British Journal of Canadian Studies* Vol. 10 (2), 1995, 258–70.

Feltoe, Richard, *A Gentleman of Substance: The Life and Legacy of John Redpath (1796–1869)* (Toronto: Natural Heritage, 2004).

Fleming, Rae (ed.), *The Lochaber Emigrants to Glengarry* (Toronto: Natural Heritage, 1994).

Fraser, Robert J., *As Others See Us: Scots of the Seaway Valley* (Beamsville, ON: Beamsville Express, 1959).

Gagnon, Alain-G & Luc Turgeon, "Managing Diversity in 18th & 19th Century Canada: Quebec's Constitutional Development in Light of the Scottish Experience" in *Commonwealth & Comparative Politics*, Vol. 41, No. 1, 2003, 1–23.

Ganong, W.F., "Monograph of the Origins of Settlements in the Province of New Brunswick," in *Transactions of the Royal Society of Canada*, 2nd series (10), sections 1–2, 1904.

Gates, Lilian F., *Land Policies of Upper Canada* (Toronto: University of Toronto Press, 1968).

Glazebrook, G.P. de T., *A History of Transportation in Canada*, Vol. 1 (Toronto: McClelland & Stewart, 1964).

Gough, Barry, *Fighting Sail on Lake Huron and Georgian Bay: The War of 1812 and Its Aftermath* (St. Catharines, ON: Vanwell, 2002).

Graham, Gerald S., *Sea Power and British North America, 1785–1820: A Study in British Colonial Policy* (Cambridge, MA: Harvard University Press, 1941).

Graham, Ian Charles Cargill, *Colonists from Scotland: Emigration to North America, 1707–83* (Ithaca, NY: Published for the American Historical Association by Cornell University Press, 1956).

Gravel, Albert, *La Pousse Gaelique Écossaise dans les Cantons de l'Est: translated into English in 1974 by (Mrs. Rose) Ida MacDonald, Scotstown, Que.* (Sherbrooke, QC: self-published, 1967).

Graves, Donald E., *Field of Glory: The Battle of Crysler's Farm, 1813* (Toronto: Robin Brass Studio, 1999).

Gray, Malcolm, *The Highland Economy, 1750–1850* (Edinburgh: Oliver & Boyd, 1957).

Guillet, Edwin C., *The Great Migration: The Atlantic Crossing By Sailing Ships Since 1770* (Toronto: University of Toronto Press, 1963).

Hall, Eleanor Blois, *The Loyalists of the Eastern Townships of Quebec* (Stanbridge East, QC: United Empire Loyalists Association of Canada, Sir John Johnson Centennial Branch, 1984).

Halliday, Hugh Alan, *Terrebonne: From Seigneury to Suburb* (Welland, ON: Niagara College of Applied Arts and Technology, 1971).

Hamilton, Henry, *The Industrial Revolution in Scotland* (Oxford: Clarendon Press, 1932).

Harlow, Vincent Todd, *The Founding of the Second British Empire, 1763–1793* (London: Longmans Green & Co., 1952).

Harper, J.R., *The Fraser Highlanders* (Montréal: Society of the Montréal Military & Maritime Museum, 1979).

Harper, Marjory, *Adventurers & Exiles: The Great Scottish Exodus* (London: Profile Books, 2003).

_____, *Emigration from North-East Scotland*, Vol. 1, *Willing Exiles* (Aberdeen: Aberdeen University Press, 1988).

_____, "Image and Reality in Early Emigrant Literature," in *British Journal of Canadian Studies*, Vol. 7 (1992).

_____ and Michael E. Vance (eds.), *Myth, Migration and the Making of Memory: Scotia and Nova Scotia, c. 1700–1990* (Halifax, NS: Published for the Gorsewood Research Institute for Atlantic Canada Studies by Fernwood Publishing & John Donald Publishers, 1999).

Harris, R. Cole, and John Warkentin, *Canada Before Confederation: A Study in Historical Geography* (Ottawa: Carleton University Press, 1995).

Harris, Richard Colebrook, *The Seigneurial System in Early Canada: A Geographical Study* (Québec: Presses de l'Université Laval, 1966).

Harvey, Robert, *A Few Bloody Noses: The American War of Independence* (London: John Murray, 2001).

Herman, Arthur, *The Scottish Enlightenment: The Scots' Invention of the Modern World* (London: Fourth Estate, 2001).

Hill, Robert, *Voice of the Vanishing Minority: Robert Sellar and the Huntingdon Gleaner, 1863–1919* (Montreal: McGill-Queen's University Press, 1998).

Hirsch, R. Forbes, "The Upper Ottawa Valley Timber Trade: A Sketch" in *The Historical Society of Ottawa*, Bytown Pamphlet Series, No. 14, April 1985.

Hunter, James, *The Making of the Crofting Community* (Edinburgh: John Donald, 1976).

Hutchison, P.P., "The Early Scots in Montréal" in *Scottish Genealogist*, Vol. XXIX, No. 4, 1982.

Igartua, José, "A Change in Climate: The Conquest and the Marchands of Montréal" in *Canadian Historical Association, Historical Papers*, 1974, 115–34.

Johnson, Stanley Currie, *A History of Emigration from the United Kingdom to North America, 1763–1912* (London: Frank Cass & Co., 1966).

Johnston, H.J.M., *British Emigration Policy 1815–1830: Shovelling Out Paupers* (Oxford: Clarendon Press, 1972).

Kerrigan, Catherine (ed.), *The Immigrant Experience: Proceedings of a Conference Held at the University of Guelph, 8–11 June 1989* (Guelph, ON: University of Guelph, 1992).

Kesteman, Jean-Pierre, *Les Écossais de langue gaélique des Cantons de l'Est: Ross, Oscar Dhu, Morrison et les autres* (Sherbrooke, QC: GGC, 2000).

Kittson, Arthur, *"Berthier," hier et aujourd'hui = "Berthier," Yesterday and To-day* (French translation by Florence F. Martel) (Berthierville, QC: Imprimerie Bernard, 1953).

Lalumière, Guy, et al., *Stornoway, 1858–1983* (Sherbrooke, QC.: Albums souvenirs québécois, 1983).

Lang, Burton, *Beechridge Presbyterian Cemetery: Monument Inscription List* (Howick, QC: self-published, 2002).

_____, *Place Names of South Western Quebec* (Howick, QC: self-published, 2001).

Lawson, Bill, *A Register of Emigrants from the Western Isles of Scotland, 1750–1900*, 2 vols. (Northton Isle of Harris: self-published, 1992).

_____, *A Register of Emigrant Families from the Western Isles of Scotland to the Eastern Townships of Quebec* (Eaton Corner, QC: Compton County Historical Museum Society, 1988).

Lawson, James, *The Emigrant Scots* (Aberdeen: Aberdeen & North East Scotland FHS, 1988).

Lee, Robert C., *The Canada Company and the Huron Tract, 1826–1853: Personalities, Profits and Politics* (Toronto: Natural Heritage, 2004)

Lenman, Bruce, *An Economic History of Modern Scotland, 1600–1976* (London: Batsford, 1977).

Levitt, Ian and Christopher Smout, *The State of the Scottish Working Class in 1843: A Statistical and Spatial Enquiry Based on Data from the Poor Law Commission Report of 1844* (Edinburgh: Scottish Academic Press, 1979).

Lewis, Harry H., "Population of Quebec Province: Its Distribution and National Origins" in *Economic Geography*, Vol. 16, 1940, 59–68.

Lindsay, Jean, *The Canals of Scotland* (Newton Abbot: David & Charles, 1968).

Little, J.I., "From the Isle of Lewis to the Eastern Townships: The Origins of a Highland Settlement Community in Quebec, 1838–81" in Catherine Kerrigan (ed.), *The Immigrant Experience: Proceedings of a Conference Held at the University of Guelph, 8–11 June 1989* (Guelph, ON: University of Guelph, 1992).

Little, John Irvine, *Borderland Religion: The Emergence of an English-Canadian Identity, 1792–1852* (Toronto: University of Toronto Press, 2004).

_____, "Canadian Pastoral" in *Journal of Historical Geography*, Vol. 29, No. 2 (2003), 189–211.

_____, *Crofters and Habitants: Settler Society, Economy, and Culture in a Quebec Township, 1848–81* (Montreal: McGill-Queen's University Press, 1991).

_____, *Nationalism, Capitalism and Colonization in Nineteenth-Century Quebec: The Upper St. Francis District* (Kingston, ON: McGill-Queen's University Press, 1989).

_____, "The Bard in a Community in Transition & Decline: Oscar Dhu & the Hebridean Scots in the Upper St. Francis District" in Donald H. Akenson (ed.), *Canadian Papers in Rural History*, Vol. X (Gananoque, ON: Langdale Press, 1995).

Lower, Arthur R.M., *Great Britain's Woodyard: British America and the Timber Trade, 1763–1867* (Montreal: McGill-Queen's University Press, 1973).

_____, "Immigration and Settlement in Canada, 1812–1820," in *Canadian Historical Review*, Vol. III, 1922.

_____, *Settlement and the Forest Frontier in Eastern Canada* (Toronto: Macmillan, 1936).

Macdonagh, Oliver, *A Pattern of Government Growth, 1800–1860: The Passenger Acts and Their Enforcement* (London: Macgibbon & Kee, 1961).

MacDonald, Norman, *Canada, 1763–1841: Immigration and Settlement* (London: Longmans & Co., 1939).

MacGillivray, Royce and Ewan Ross, *A History of Glengarry* (Belleville, ON: Mika, 1979).

MacGregor, David R., *Merchant Sailing Ships: Supremacy of Sail, 1815–1850* (London: Conway Maritime Press, 1984).

MacKay, Donald, *The Lumberjacks* (Toronto: Natural Heritage, 1998).

MacKintosh, W.A. and W.L.G. Jaergs (eds.) *Canadian Frontiers of Settlement*, Vol. IX (Toronto: Macmillan, 1936).

MacLeod, Leodhas, *Township of Lingwick, Last of the Quebec Hebridean Crofters: Galson, Fisher Hill, Red Mountain, North Hill, Victoria Road, Lingwick* (London, ON: Mac-Media Publications, 2002).

MacLeod, M.C., *Settlement of the Lake Megantic District in the Province of Quebec Canada* (New York: self-published, 1931).

MacMillan, Somerled, *Bygone Lochaber: Historical and Traditional* (Glasgow: K. & R. Davidson, 1971).

Marrelli, Nancy & Simon Dardick (eds.), *The Scots of Montreal: A Pictorial Album* (Montréal: Véhicule Press, 2004).

Martell, J.S., *Immigration to and Emigration from Nova Scotia, 1815–1838* (Halifax, NS: PANS, 1942).

McCallum, John, *Unequal Beginnings: Agriculture and Economic Development in Quebec and Ontario Until 1870* (Toronto: University of Toronto Press, 1980).

McGee, Robert, *A Companion to Robert Sellar's History of the County of Huntingdon and the Seigniories of Chateaugay and Beauharnois: Including Index, Maps, List of Settlers, Introduction and Sellar's Original "Postscript"* (Huntingdon, QC: The Innismacsaint Press, 1987).

McKillop, Dugald McKenzie, *Annals of Megantic County, Quebec* (Lynn, MA: self-published, 1962).

McLean, Marianne, *People of Glengarry 1745–1820: Highlanders in Transition, 1745–1820* (Montreal: McGill-Queen's University Press, 1991).

McLellan, Robert, *The Isle of Arran* (Newton Abbot, UK: David & Charles, 1970).

McLeod Duncan L., *The Milan Story* (Milan, QC: self-published, 1977).

McNabb, Heather, "Montreal's Scottish Community, 1835–1865" (Unpublished MA thesis, Concordia University, Montreal, 1999).

Meek, Donald E., "Evangelicalism and Emigration: Aspects of the Role of Dissenting Evangelicalism in Highland Emigration to Canada" in Gordon MacLennan (ed.), *Proceedings of the First North American Congress of Celtic Studies: Held at Ottawa from 26th–30th March, 1986* (Ottawa: Chair of Celtic Studies, University of Ottawa, 1988).

Messamore Barbara J., *Canadian Migration Patterns* (Toronto: University of Toronto Press, 2004).

Meyer, D. Vane, *The Highland Scots of North Carolina* (Durham, NC: University of North Carolina Press, 1961).

Moir, John S., *Enduring Witness: A History of the Presbyterian Church in Canada* (Toronto: Presbyterian Publications, 1975).

_____, *The Church in the British Era: From the British Conquest to Confederation*, Volume Two of *History of the Christian Church in Canada*, John Webster Grant (gen. ed.) (Toronto: McGraw-Hill Ryerson Ltd., 1972).

Munro, William Bennett, *The Seigniorial System in Canada: A Study in French Colonial Policy* (New York: Longmans, Green, 1907).

Neatby, Hilda Marion, *Quebec, The Revolutionary Age, 1760–1791* (Toronto: McClelland & Stewart, 1966).

Ouellet, Fernand, *Le Bas-Canada, 1791–1840: Changements structuraux et crise* (Ottawa: Éditions de l'Université d'Ottawa, 1976). Translated and adapted: Patricia Claxton, *Lower Canada, 1791–1840: Social Change and Nationalism* (Toronto: McClelland & Stewart, 1980).

Prebble, John, *The Highland Clearances* (London: Penguin, 1969).

Puche, Victor, "Immigration, Diversity & Ethnic Relations in Quebec" in *Canadian Ethnic Studies* Vol. 34, No. 3 (2002) 5–28.

Quebec Family History Society, *Transcription of Tombstones in Métis Beach United Church Cemetery* (Pointe-Claire, QC: Quebec Family History Society, 1986).

Ramsay, Freda, *John Ramsay of Kildalton: Being an Account of His Life in Islay and Including the Diary of His Trip to Canada in 1870* (Toronto: P. Martin Associates, 1977).

Raudzens, George K., "The Military Impact on Canadian Canals, 1815–25," in *Canadian Historical Review,* Vol. LIV, 1973.

Read, Colin, *The Rising in Western Upper Canada 1837–38: The Duncombe Revolt and After* (Toronto: University of Toronto Press, 1982).

Redmond, Gerald, *The Sporting Scots of Nineteenth Century Canada* (London and Toronto: Associated University Presses, 1982) 162.

Reid, W. Stanford (ed.), *The Scottish Tradition in Canada* (Toronto: McClelland & Stewart, 1976).

Richards, Eric, *The Highland Clearances: People, Landlords and Rural Turmoil* (Edinburgh: Birlinn, 2000).

Rogers, G.A., "Pioneer Mill Sites in the Chateauguay Valley," in *Connections*, Vol. 15, No. 1 (Sept. 1992).

_____, G.A., "The Settlement of the Chateauguay Valley" in *Connections,* Vol. 14, No. 3 (1992) 2–6.

Roxborough, Henry, *One Hundred Not Out: Story of Nineteenth-Century Canadian Sport* (Toronto: Ryerson Press, 1966).

Rudin, Ronald, *The Forgotten Quebecers: A History of English-Speaking Quebec, 1759–1980* (Québec: Institut québécois de recherche sur la culture, 1985).

Sellar, Robert, *A Scotsman in Upper Canada: The Narrative of Gordon Sellar* (Toronto: Clarke, Irwin, 1969).

_____, Robert, *The Tragedy of Quebec: The Expulsion of its Protestant Farmers* (Toronto: Ontario Press, 1908). (This title was reprinted by University of Toronto Press in 1974 and contains an introduction by Robert Hill.)

_____, Robert, *The U.S. Campaign of 1813 to Capture Montreal: Crysler, the Decisive Battle of the War of 1812* (Huntingdon, QC: Gleaner Press, 1913).

Senior, Elinor Kyte, *Redcoats and Patriotes: The Rebellions in Lower Canada, 1837–38* (Stittsville, ON: Canada's Wings, 1985).

Shortt, A. and Doughty, A.G. (eds.), *Canada and Its Provinces: A History of the Canadian People and Their Institutions* (Toronto: Publishers' Association of Canada, 1913–17).

Siebert, Wilbur Henry, "Loyalist Settlements in the Gaspé Peninsula" in *Transactions of the Royal Society of Canada* 3rd series, Vol. VIII (1914) 399–405.

_____, Wilbur Henry, "American Loyalists in the Eastern Seigneuries and Townships of the Province of Quebec" in *Transactions of the Royal Society of Canada* 3rd series, Vol. VII (1913) 3–41.

Stanley, Laurie, *The Well-Watered Garden: The Presbyterian Church in Cape Breton 1798–1860* (Sydney, NS: University College of Cape Breton Press, 1983).

Thompson, John, *Hudson: The Early Years up to 1867* (Hudson, QC: Hudson Historical Society, 1999).

Tulchinsky, Gerald J.J., *The River Barons: Montreal Businessmen and the Growth of Industry and Transportation, 1837–53* (Toronto/Buffalo: University of Toronto Press, 1977).

Wales, Benjamin, *Memories of Old St. Andrews and Historical Sketches of the Seigniory of Argenteuil* (Lachute, QC: Watchman Press, 1934).

Walker, M.G., "Sir John Johnson, Loyalist" in *Mississippi Valley Historical Review* Vol. III, No. 3 (1916) 318–46.

Wallace, W.S., "Some Notes on the Fraser Highlanders" in *Canadian Historical Review* Vol. XVIII, No. 2 (1937) 131–40.

_____, "Notes on the family of Malcolm Fraser of Murray Bay" in *Bulletin des Reserches Historique* Vol. 39 (1993), 267–71.

Willson, Beckles, *The Life and Letters of James Wolfe* (London: Heinemann, 1909).

Wrong, George Mackinnon, *A Canadian Manor and Its Seigneuries: The Story of a Hundred Years, 1761–1861* (Toronto: Macmillan, 1926).

Wynn, G., "A Region of Scattered Settlements and Bounded Possibilities: North Eastern America, 1775–1800," in *Canadian Geographer*, Vol. 31, 1987.

Young, Brian and Geoffrey James, *Respectable Burial: Montreal's Mount Royal Cemetery* (Montreal: McGill-Queen's University Press, 2003).

Index

About the Author

Dr. Lucille Campey is a Canadian, living in Britain, with over thirty years experience as a researcher and author. It was her father's Scottish roots and love of history which first stimulated her interest in the early exodus of people from Scotland to Canada. She is the great-great-grand-daughter of William Thomson, who left Morayshire, on the northeast coast of Scotland in the early 1800s to begin a new life with his family, first near Digby then in Antigonish, Nova Scotia. He is described in D. Whidden's *History of the Town of Antigonish* simply as "William, Pio-neer" and is commemorated in the St. James Church and cemetery at Antigonish. Lucille's mother, Cécile Morency, who was born in Ste-Marie-de-Beauce, is a descendant of Guillaume Baucher dit Morency who settled in Île d'Orléans in 1659.

Lucille was awarded a Ph.D. by Aberdeen University in 1998 for her research of Scottish emigration to Canada in the period 1770–1850. *Les Écossais* is the sixth in a series which she has written about the Scottish exodus to Canada. In a review of two of Lucille's recent books, Dr. James Cranstoun, Chairman of the Council of the Scottish Genealogy Society, stated that they "continue the same high standards of meticulous schol-arship and lucid presentation apparent in the earlier books." Lucille is currently working on her seventh book which will deal with emigra-tion from Scotland to New Brunswick.

A Chemistry graduate of Ottawa University, Lucille worked initially in the fields of science and computing. After marrying her English husband, she moved to the north of England where she studied medieval settlement patterns in the north of England and acquired a Master of Philosophy Degree from Leeds University. Having lived for five years in Easter Ross in Scotland while she completed her doctoral thesis, Lucille and Geoff returned to England, and now live near Salisbury in Wiltshire.